Vision Accomplished?

VISION ACCOMPLISHED?

The Enigma of Ho Chi Minh

☆   ☆   ☆   ☆

N. Khac Huyen

The Macmillan Company, New York, New York

Collier-Macmillan Limited, London

The Macmillan Company
866 Third Avenue, New York, N.Y. 10022
Collier-Macmillan Canada Ltd., Toronto, Ontario

Library of Congress Catalog Card Number: 78-147929

First Printing

Printed in the United States of America

To My
Long-suffering
Countrymen

Contents

Preface   xi

Introduction   xiii

1 THE YOUNG REVOLUTIONARY   1

EARLY CHILDHOOD   1
BEGINNINGS OF A REVOLUTIONARY   8
WHY DID HO JOIN THE SOCIALIST AND THE COMMUNIST PARTIES?   13

2 THE AGENT OF INTERNATIONAL COMMUNISM   16

ACTIVITIES IN FRANCE   16
ACTIVITIES IN SOVIET RUSSIA AND ASIA   23
JOURNEY TO CHINA   24
FOUNDER OF THE INDOCHINESE COMMUNIST PARTY   31

3 THE ARCHITECT OF A COMMUNIST REVOLUTION   49

RETURN TO VIETNAM   50
FOUNDER OF THE VIET MINH LEAGUE   52
RELATIONS WITH THE ALLIES   57
HO, THE LIBERATOR   68

4 PRESIDENT OF THE NASCENT REPUBLIC 86

ANGLO-FRENCH COLLUSION 86
THE CHINESE PROBLEM 97
THE FOREIGN FRONT 112
THE FRENCH PROBLEM 116
ACCORD OF MARCH 6, 1946 118
THE DALAT CONFERENCE 139

5 THE DIPLOMAT 144

THE CHARMING VISITOR 144
THE FONTAINEBLEAU CONFERENCE 149
THE MODUS VIVENDI OF SEPTEMBER 14, 1946 155
TRIUMPHANT RETURN 159
BEGINNING OF A CONFLICT 164

6 PRESIDENT HO AGAINST FRANCE 176

THE PERSISTENT CONCILIATOR 176
HO AND THE "BAO DAI SOLUTION" 195
GUERILLA LEADER 214
THE VICTOR 232

7 CHAIRMAN HO AGAINST THE UNITED STATES 244

THE GENEVA AGREEMENTS OF 1954 245
HO AND THE U.S. IMPERIALISTS 250
THE "LIBERATION" OF SOUTH VIETNAM 260
THE IRRECONCILABLE CHAIRMAN 265

8 COMRADE HO BETWEEN PEKING AND MOSCOW 274

1949–1956, PERIOD OF CHINESE INFLUENCE 275
SOVIET INFLUENCE, 1957–MID-1962 282
MID-1962–1964, RETURN OF PEKING 287
RETURN OF MOSCOW, 1965–1969 297

9 DEATH OF A REVOLUTIONARY 312

NO LONGER A RUMOR 312
HO'S WILL 315
LAST RITES 317

Contents

Conclusion 319

Appendix A: *Declaration of Independence of the*
Democratic Republic of Viet-Nam 321
Appendix B: *Geneva Agreements* 323
Appendix C: *On the Use of Vietnamese Names* 341
Appendix D: *Political Parties 1945–1946* 342
Appendix E: *Important Dates* 343

Notes 349

Selected Bibliographies 365

Index 373

MAPS

Pre-Partition Indochina 231
Post-Partition Indochina 242

Preface

WHILE A GREAT deal has been said of the Vietnam war, very little has been written about Ho Chi Minh, the guiding soul of the Democratic Republic of Vietnam for a quarter of a century. Although Ho is gone, his policies will continue to affect the course of events in Indochina and Southeast Asia for many years to come.

After perusing numerous documents and materials, both Communist and non-Communist, I have reached the conclusion that Ho had consistently followed a plan which he had formulated in 1911, when he left Vietnam for France to embark upon a revolutionary career, and which he kept basically unchanged throughout his life. He was a determined man with a well-conceived plan, a nationalist revolutionary dedicated to the expansion of Communism in Indochina. Ho successfully exploited the impatience of the West and its ignorance of his motives and goals. While Ho's understanding of the West was more than adequate, the West's evaluation of Ho has been tragically defective. Many Western diplomats, politicians, scholars, and, notably, reporters often attributed ideas and policies to Ho, ideas and policies that had not even entered his mind. These assumptions, ironically, often became self-fulfilling prophecies. Ho reacted to the West the way the West saw him, and he usually emerged as the winner.

The result of three years of research, this book is a sincere attempt to present as much as possible of what was significant about

Ho's revolutionary career, his role in the Communist revolution in Vietnam, and his skillful exploitation of the Vietnamese independence movement by focusing on the complex events in Indochina since the Second World War and on the various policies that have led to the present tragedy.

To the College of St. Catherine I owe a debt of gratitude. Its administration accommodatingly allowed me a great deal of freedom to arrange my classes in such a way that I could pursue my research.

To my colleague and friend, Professor Harold W. Chase of the University of Minnesota, I express my sincere appreciation for his helpfulness. He read portions of the manuscript and gave me great encouragement.

I wish to thank Mr. Alick Bartholomew, Senior Editor at Macmillan, for providing me with expert editorial advice. He has been especially helpful and generous with his time.

I am particularly indebted to my wife, Kathleen, not only for her patience and understanding, but also for her consistent encouragement and helpful suggestions. She has shared with me the problems encountered in my research and cheerfully served as a sounding board. Her constructive criticisms and, above all, her understanding are affectionately acknowledged.

Finally, I wish to express my loving appreciation to my three sons, Remi, Michael, and Roland, who patiently suffered a lack of fatherly attention during my seemingly endless years of research and writing.

N. KHAC HUYEN

St. Paul, Minnesota
December, 1970

Introduction

A QUARTER OF a century has passed since Ho Chi Minh made his debut on the international political stage. Ever since September 2, 1945, when he appeared in public for the first time as Ho Chi Minh and President of the Democratic Republic of Vietnam (DRV), to proclaim to his people and to the nations of the world that "all men are born equal; they are endowed by their Creator with certain unalienable Rights; among them are Life, Liberty, and the pursuit of Happiness," and that "Vietnam has the right to be a free and independent country—and in fact it is so already," this frail, gentle, and shy-looking man with a thin goatee played the game of politics with such skill that his adversaries were held in awe. For twenty-five years prior to his coming to power, Ho had patiently labored for the international Communist movement, undergone severe privations, risked imprisonment, fought against great odds, learned and mastered the technique of survival. Successively a member of the French Communist party, the Russian Communist party, the founder of the Indochinese Communist party (ICP), the Viet Minh League, and the Lao Dong party, the architect of a successful Communist revolution, the head of a Communist state, the obstinate Asian leader who held at bay two leading Western powers, Ho was indeed an unusual revolutionary whose achievements were second to none. This fragile man has left an indelible impact on the international political scene, the effect of which will be felt for a long time to come.

While he was a well-known political figure, his past up to 1945 was shrouded in mystery. Soon after his first public appearance, the rumor began to circulate that Ho Chi Minh or "Ho Who Enlightens" was none other than Nguyen Ai Quoc or "Nguyen Who Loves His Country," the Comintern agent who had founded the Indochinese Communist party fifteen years earlier in Hong Kong. Thereupon, the French police feverishly searched their files, studied them for more positive clues, and compared Ho Chi Minh's picture with that of Nguyen Ai Quoc, who had been reported dead in China in 1933. French photography experts unanimously confirmed that Nguyen and Ho were the same person. Besides other unmistakably identical traits, the right ear in both pictures was pointed, while the left was regular in shape. Thus the DRV President was the same man whose innumerable aliases and adroit disguises had deceived many, including the well-organized French Sûreté, which, according to Bernard Fall, was "beyond doubt one of the best secret police organizations outside the Soviet orbit."[1] While Communist sources finally testified to his identity, Ho Chi Minh, in the early days of his rule, had persistently denied that he was Nguyen Ai Quoc. In 1946, Raoul Salan, the French general in charge of truce negotiations with the Viet Minh, asked Ho if he was Nguyen. The DRV President firmly denied it.[2] To the few Vietnamese who dared to raise the same question, Ho simply gave an evasive answer. Not until after 1958, when a group of Communist diplomats stationed in Hanoi paid an official visit to the house in which Ho had spent his childhood, did publications of the DRV confirm Ho's real identity.[3]

A shrewd calculator, a consummate actor, a patient revolutionary, and a ruthless agitator, Ho was a man of many personalities. An American OSS (Office of Strategic Services) officer, who worked with Ho at his jungle headquarters in Northern Tonkin during World War II, speaks of him as "an awfully sweet guy." Jean Sainteny, the French official who carried out nonproductive negotiations with him during the crucial 1945–47 period, describes him as "an ascetic man whose face revealed at the same time intelligence, energy, cunning and shrewdness."[4] M. N. Roy, the Indian ex-Communist who underwent extensive Marxist indoctrination with Ho at Moscow's University of the Toilers of the East in 1924, remembers

him as "an unimpressive personality" and a poor student. Whatever
opinion a person may have of Ho, he cannot escape the conclusion
that the late North Vietnamese President was a remarkably successful leader. And in the revolutionary lexicon, it is success that counts.
Ho was not the genius that his admirers claimed him to be; neither
was he the monster that his opponents pictured. He certainly
thought of himself as a dedicated man in the service of a good
cause. He never hesitated to resort to any means to achieve his
political objectives. He was the man who pretended to be an uncle
to his people, the man whose popularity was greatly exaggerated by
his supporters: "In the remotest villages of Vietnam, North and
South, every little child, as soon as he can speak, babbles to his
mother 'I will be good, Uncle Ho will be pleased.'"[5] He was also
the good old Uncle Ho who ruled with an iron fist and who, for
reasons of state, silenced forever half a million of his stubborn
"nephews" and "nieces" during the infamous period of land reform
in North Vietnam (1953–56).

Yet, in spite of his success and ruthlessness, Ho was basically a
humble man. His appearance denoted the simplicity of a man devoted to the service of his people and a total disregard for unneces-
sary comforts. Shortly before he was to read the Declaration of
Independence on September 2, 1945, his associates suddenly discovered that Ho was not properly attired for the historic occasion.
He wore a wrinkled long-sleeved white shirt, faded khaki shorts,
and a pair of old sandals made of discarded automobile tires! After
a frantic shopping expedition, his aides brought back a clean khaki
suit and a pair of manufactured sandals. For "reasons of state," the
old revolutionary obligingly gave in.[6] The favorite attire of President
Ho Chi Minh was not much different from that of the revolutionary
Nguyen Ai Quoc. Whether he attended a cabinet meeting, presided
over a banquet honoring visiting dignitaries, or talked to a group of
children, Ho invariably wore his white high-buttoned linen jacket
and trousers and slippers. "They call me 'Excellency.' Funny, eh?"
he casually remarked to a foreign visitor.

Before delving into the past of this unusual man, one should
recall the conditions that gave rise to the nationalist movement in
Vietnam and paved the way for Ho's revolution. While it is true
that favorable circumstances make heroes out of ordinary men, it is
also true that outstanding men create favorable circumstances for

themselves. Ho Chi Minh, undoubtedly, was such an outstanding man.

Ever since the French completed their conquest of Vietnam in 1884, armed and nonarmed revolts of Vietnamese against their alien rulers took place intermittently. The first armed rebellion, the *Can Vuong* or Monarchist Movement (1885–1913), which involved kings, court officials, and scholars, was just the beginning phase in the continuous struggle against French occupation.

The realization that modern Western technology and philosophy were superior to Confucianism motivated the Vietnamese elite to request the colonial administration to build more schools to train native children in the modern sciences. Confronted with a French refusal to comply with their legitimate wish, progressive Vietnamese scholars launched the *Dong Kinh Nghia Thuc,* generally known as the Scholars' Movement (1907–08), to propagate Western ideas through a nationwide network of private schools. The French retaliated by suppressing these schools and incarcerating their organizers. This autocratic measure led other scholars to organize peasants' demonstrations asking for tax reduction and educational reforms. These futile manifestations resulted in nothing but bloodshed, deportation, and execution of scholars.

The *Dong Du* or Exodus to the East Movement (1905–39) deserved special attention as it was started by Vietnamese leaders who firmly believed that only an acquisition and assimilation of Western knowledge would save Asia from colonialist exploitation. Underlying this belief was the admiration for Japan, which, after three decades of adoption of Western techniques, had emerged as a strong nation, independent and free from foreign domination and influence, powerful enough to defeat China in 1895 and Russia a decade later. Thus Japan, an Asian country, had acquired sufficient industrial and military might in a relatively short period of time to humiliate a European power. The *Dong Du* movement, organized by the great nationalist Phan Boi Chau, recruited young men for scientific, military, and political training in Japan. A number of Vietnamese were also sent to the Whampoa Political and Military Academy in China. The movement had gained considerable momentum when it was dealt a fatal blow in 1925 by an act of Communist treachery, which will be discussed in the second chapter of this book.

The arrest, trial, and subsequent conviction of the widely revered Phan Boi Chau aroused intensive nationalist fervor in the country and led to the formation of the Viet Nam Quoc Dan Dang (VNQDD) or Vietnam National Party (1927–33, 1945–46) by a group of intellectuals endowed with a more Westernized outlook. In 1927, a number of teachers, writers, and journalists set up a publishing house in Hanoi and put out political literature with a twofold purpose: (*a*) to popularize the main currents of modern political thought, and (*b*) to acquire financial resources to support their nationalist movement. Very quickly, the French Sûreté lowered its ax by closing down the enterprise. Its premises, however, continued to serve as a meeting place for the group that founded the VNQDD late that year. Patterned after the Chinese Kuomintang, the VNQDD also adopted Sun Yat-sen's three principles (nationalism, democracy, livelihood) in its program. Although dedicated and well-intentioned, the new party's members could offer nothing more than a vague political and social platform. Assembled around Nguyen Thai Hoc, a teacher and the acknowledged leader of the movement, were members of the teaching profession, civil service, private industry, and junior officers in the Indochinese Guard. A little over a year after its founding the party's prestige soared to its highest mark. There were 120 cells with a membership of 1,500 of whom 120 were military personnel. With a view to overthrowing the colonial regime, Nguyen Thai Hoc and his lieutenants intensified their clandestine activities, recruited adherents, stored supplies, and made preparations for a general insurrection that would take place in a few years.

The opportune time the VNQDD had waited for never came. The assassination of René Bazin, a French agent in charge of recruiting coolies for the rubber plantations in the South, by an unknown Vietnamese provoked a swift reaction from the French police which upset Nguyen Thai Hoc's timetable. Any murder of Frenchmen was automatically viewed as part of a nationalist plot to undermine French sovereignty in Indochina. Well-known VNQDD leaders were arrested and sent to prison while Hoc remained free but was closely watched. The tightening surveillance of the French Sûreté cast a threatening shadow on the nationalist leader who feared that if he did not act, it might be too late. Under these unfavorable circumstances, the hard-pressed Nguyen Thai Hoc made the fateful decision of carrying out his attack sooner than planned. Orders for a general uprising were hastily given. Because of poor communication and a lack of coordination, the premature revolt failed miserably. The French repression was both severe and savage. The village that hid the conspirators was pitilessly bombed and reduced to ashes. Scores of leaders and supporters of the movement were arrested. Many, including Nguyen Thai Hoc, were sent to the guillotine on July 17, 1930. By the summer of 1933, the VNQDD had ceased to exist. Twelve years later, it reappeared on the political scene to be swallowed up by the Viet Minh organization.

Thus all the movements of resistance against French rule had ended in frustration. This failure might be attributed to the prevailing international conditions, which did not lend themselves to the emancipation of colonial people. Prior to World War II, the imperialist West was not ready to give up its territorial possessions in Asia and Africa. And France, one of the most influential imperialist powers, never entertained the thought of forsaking her *mission civilisatrice*. The war, however, brought about drastic changes. France had been ignominiously defeated by Germany and became a second-rate power. In spite of her humiliating experience, France still desperately tried to hang on to her overseas possessions. This was going to be France's most dramatic postwar blunder. The spirit of independence had captured the imagination of the oppressed people and shaken the foundation of imperialism. One after another, the colonies rose up against their mother countries. Hiding under a nationalist façade, the Communists exploited the independence movement in Vietnam and consolidated their position throughout the country. Most Vietnamese did not realize that their nationalist revolution was Communist-led. Even if they had, it would not have mattered. Their main concern was independence from foreign rule. If the Communists contributed their share and participated in the national effort, they should deserve everyone's support. France, on her part, gave a helping hand to Ho Chi Minh. By refusing to recognize the legitimate wish of the Vietnamese for independence, she unjustifiably sacrificed the cream of her army in a futile war, provided Ho with an excellent pretext to rally his people behind him, and unwittingly contributed toward the building of a Communist regime in Vietnam.

1 ☆ The Young Revolutionary

Early Childhood

In Northern Annam[1] lies a region famous for its rebellious spirit, the outstanding contributions it has made to the fatherland, and the great leaders it has produced who have magnificently enriched the history of their country. From this region came Mai Thuc Loan, the inspiring rebel who led a successful revolt against the Tang rulers early in the eighth century (722), established his capital in Ve Son, now Nam Dan District, and reigned under the name of Mai Hac De or Black Emperor. It was here that Le Loi, the peasant founder of the Le Dynasty (1428–1788), took refuge during his arduous ten-year campaign against the Ming overlords in the fifteenth century. Thanks largely to the generous supplies and volunteers provided by the people of Nghe An and Ha Tinh or Nghe-Tinh, as the region has been called, Le Loi's army eventually drove out the alien rulers. Three centuries later, when the Chinese reinvaded Vietnam, Nghe-Tinh again was called upon to play its usual role. With abundant contributions from these two provinces, Nguyen Hue (1752–92), the future Emperor Quang Trung, recaptured the fallen capital, expelled the Ch'ing conquerors, and restored peace and unity to the country.

The establishment of French rule in Vietnam caused constant unrest throughout the country, especially in Nghe-Tinh where a

succession of nationalist leaders again emerged. Leading the pro-
cession was Phan Dinh Phung (1846–95), the great scholar and revered leader of an armed uprising which bravely challenged an
immensely better equipped colonial army for ten years, and which
the French tried to suppress by resorting to the most barbarian and
sacrilegious methods.[2] The most famous Nghe An rebel was Phan
Boi Chau (1867–1941), the grand old man of Vietnamese nationalism, who fought the French with an unequalled fervor for a quarter
of a century until his arrest in 1925. Sometimes cajoling, sometimes
threatening, the French unsuccessfully employed all available tricks
to stop his activities, offered him the highest position at the Court of
Annam and in the colonial administration in addition to huge sums
of money, condemned him to death in absentia, granted him amnesty, and used diplomatic pressure to have him imprisoned abroad,
first by the British in Hong Kong, then by the Chinese in Canton. A
very brilliant and farsighted scholar, Chau was the first prominent
nationalist who became painfully aware of the superiority of Western science and technology and convinced that if his country wished
to regain its independence, it must assimilate Western learning and
know-how.

The Nghe-Tinh rebellious spirit, which has permeated through
the centuries, remains as alive today as it had been under alien rule.
Vinh, the capital of the region and the scene of many a peasant
demonstration against the French administration, has also witnessed other popular outbursts against the Hanoi regime. While
Nghe-Tinh can justifiably boast of its great men, its majestic green
mountains and sky-blue waters, and its savorous, juicy Xa Doai
oranges, the best in Vietnam or, as the local people claim with a
slight touch of modesty, the best in the world, it is not blessed with
a fertile soil or a mild climate. Its rice fields are often dried by torrid
winds or flooded by devastating rains which frequently visit the
region. Out of this difficult land the peasants, who compose the
overwhelming majority of the local population, have to eke an un-
describably meager living. The men in the coastal area engage in
fishing, constantly fighting the fury of the sea. If you cannot overcome natural calamities, learn to live with them; such is the attitude
of these people who accept their fate with admirable resignation.
This stoicism of a people hardened by natural conditions over

which they have no control does not imply, however, a readiness to suffer any kind of injustice, especially the sort imposed by men. Independent, proud, rebellious, the Nghe-Tinh people have often revolted against autocratic rule. If one is asked to depict their temperament, the following traits will emerge: independence, austerity, strong will, perseverance, and total dedication. These moral attributes, these qualities required of a successful leader, have been remarkably developed by the revolutionaries from Nghe-Tinh.

The poverty and pride of these people may be best illustrated by an amusing story that has found widespread circulation, not only in the two provinces, but also throughout the country. Whenever a man from Nghe-Tinh travelled, he always took along a small wooden fish, made in such a way that it looked like a fried one. In view of his poverty, he could not afford to order in the village inn anything more than some rice and a bowl of *nuoc mam*, the national sauce.[3] He would furtively slip the fish into the *nuoc mam* and thus convey the impression that he was eating well and avoid the embarrassing feeling of appearing poor in public. For this reason the Nghe-Tinh people are teasingly but admiringly referred to as *dân cá go*, or wooden fish folks.

Such is the country of the Nguyen Sinh; such is the temperament of its people. Sometime in the nineteenth century, in the village of Kim Lien, district of Nam Dan, province of Nghe An, lived a scholar who enjoyed his forced retirement by attending to a garden. He had been dismissed from his post of district prefect for insubordination. A man of integrity who had earned the title of *Cu Nhan* (Master of Arts) and a small landlord, he was fondly admired and respected by the rice peasants in the area. Between tending his garden and composing patriotic poems, the retired mandarin discussed philosophy with his son Nguyen Sinh Sac (or Huy). Ever since his fifth birthday, Sac had studied the Chinese characters, dreaming of becoming a man of letters and a mandarin like his father. Endowed with a strong will and a propensity for learning, Sac rapidly mastered the Chinese ideograms and devoured the classical works of Chinese literature. Soon the boy became a serious young man, and qualified himself for the triennial examinations that were held in the capital with the express purpose of recruiting mandarins. At last, Nguyen Sinh Sac realized his dream. After successfully undergoing a series of rigorous tests, he was conferred the title of *Pho Bang*, or Doctor of Classical Humanities, and saw a promising future ahead of him. After a brief celebration in his village, the young *Pho Bang* went to the capital to accept an appointment in the Ministry of Rites, which he was to leave shortly for the post of vice-prefect in the district of Binh Khe.

The peasants were overburdened with all kinds of taxes imposed by the French administration. This mandarin from Nghe An, himself the son of a peasant, openly opposed this policy of exploitation. Fully aware of their miserable lot, Nguyen Sinh Sac refused to pressure them to meet their tax quota. For this contempt for the duties he was expected to fulfill and for his political activities in favor of Phan Boi Chau, Nguyen Sinh Sac, like his father, was relieved of his post. Thereupon, the rebellious mandarin returned to his birthplace where the villagers gave him a hero's welcome. It was in the peaceful and loving atmosphere of Kim Lien that Sac's youngest child, Nguyen Sinh Cung, the future Ho Chi Minh, was born on May 19, 1890. Unlike his brother and sister, who had received the traditional education based on the study of the classical works of Chinese literature, Ho was sent to a public school to study the *quoc ngu*[4] and French in addition to Chinese ideograms. At the age of nine, Ho and his mother, who had been charged with stealing French weapons for the rebels, fled to Hue, the imperial city. His father, persecuted by the French Sûreté, had left for Saigon, where he earned a meager living by practicing Oriental medicine.

Remaining in the village were Ho's brother Khiem and sister Thanh. Khiem, though a hard-working student, consistently failed in the regional examinations and became a teacher of Chinese characters in his village. In 1946, after learning that the President of the Republic was none other than his brother Cung, Khiem hurriedly left for Hanoi to see him. Upon his arrival in the capital, Khiem was directed to a relative's home in the Thai Ha suburb, where Ho secretly visited him one night. The two brothers talked for an hour, after which Khiem returned to Kim Lien where he died two years later.[5] The secrecy of the meeting can be easily understood. At that time, Ho took great care to conceal his real identity and background.

Ho's sister Thanh was well known both for her learning and for her revolutionary ideas. Endowed with a remarkable wit and intelligence, she too practiced Oriental medicine in her village. A spinster all her life, she died in 1953 without ever again seeing her illustrious brother.

Ho's stay in Hue was a short one. After his mother's sudden death, the young boy found himself back at Kim Lien. It was the time when the Department of Public Works of the colonial administration built the Laos route from Vinh, the provincial capital of Nghe An, to the Song Lam Valley. All men from eighteen to fifty years of age were liable to impressment for construction work. Conscripted coolies were sent to work in mountainous areas infested with anopheline mosquitoes, poisonous snakes, and undrinkable water. Many left their homes, but few returned. Once taken away, a man was considered dead. With a burning torch in one hand and a gun in the other, government soldiers brutally invaded villages at night, searching houses, and snatching men from the arms of their screaming children and despairing wives. From his house windows, young Ho watched this seemingly endless scene, which profoundly disturbed him. In view of their social position, the Nguyen Sinh family were exempted from forced labor.

Upon reaching his tenth birthday, Ho, according to the prevailing practice of the time, was given another name, Nguyen Tat Thanh, or Nguyen Who Will Succeed. And succeed he did, for in 1907 Ho received his *certificat d'études primaires*.[6] The young man journeyed to southern Annam and received an appointment as an elementary school teacher in Phan Thiet, the town famous for its *nuóc mám*. Ho taught *quoc ngu* and French in a school adjacent to a *nuóc mám* factory. The smell of fermented fish gave the school a peculiarly "heavy" atmosphere, one in which Ho meditated about his future. While the young teacher seemed to approach his task with dedication, his mind was wandering elsewhere. He had read and memorized the "Advice to Young Men to Go Abroad to Study," composed by the famous revolutionary from Nghe An, Phan Boi Chau. In this poem, Chau exhorted Vietnamese to follow the examples of men who had travelled throughout the world, discovered America, explored Africa, visited the poles, and even dreamed of reaching the moon. Only through contact with and assimilation of Western techniques could Vietnamese broaden their vistas and build a prosperous nation for themselves. This wise counsel greatly impressed the young teacher. One day in the autumn of 1911, the punctual Ho failed to show up for classes.

On October 11, 1911, the first Chinese Revolution broke out in Wuchang, opposite Hankow on the Yangtze river. As Sun Yat-sen left the United States for China, Ho went to Saigon to discuss the situation with his father. After extensive discussions and consultation with their friends, they decided that Ho should go to France to absorb Western science and survey conditions in Europe, especially in the mother country, before embarking upon a revolutionary career. But how to finance a trip abroad, one which required much more money than both Ho and his father could ever save? An acceptable solution soon presented itself. Ho registered at a merchant marine school which trained people for various duties on board ship. Upon completing his courses three months later, Ho was hired by the liner *Latouche-Tréville* as a kitchen helper. In order not to embarrass his family and to conceal his identity, he assumed the name of Ba. Thus began the adventurous life of the future leader of the Viet Minh revolution. It was a long voyage which took Ho to the major ports of Europe, Africa, and America. On one of his trips to the New World, the young Vietnamese seaman debarked in New York and visited Harlem. It was then that he observed, or, more correctly, read about the conditions of American Negroes and lynching, "a little-known aspect of American civilization," which he later depicted in an indignant article printed in *La Correspondance Internationale*:

It is well known that the black race is the most oppressed and most exploited of the human family. It is well known that the spread of capitalism and the discovery of the New World had as an immediate result the rebirth of slavery which was, for centuries, a scourge for the Negroes and a bitter disgrace for mankind. What everyone does not perhaps know, is that after sixty-five years of so-called emancipation, American Negroes still endure atrocious moral and material sufferings, of which the most cruel and horrible is the custom of lynching. . . .

Imagine a furious horde. Fists clenched, eyes bloodshot, mouths foaming, yells, insults, curses. . . . This horde is transported with the wild delight of a crime to be committed without risk. They are armed with sticks, torches, revolvers, ropes, knives, scissors, vitriol, daggers; in a word, with all that can be used to kill or wound.

Imagine in this human sea a flotsam of black flesh pushed about, beaten, trampled underfoot, torn, slashed, insulted, tossed hither and thither, bloodstained, dead.

The horde are the lynchers. The human rag is the Black, the victim.

In a wave of hatred and bestiality, the lynchers drag the Black to a wood or a public place. They tie him to a tree, pour kerosene over him, cover him with inflammable material. While waiting for the fire to be kindled, they smash his teeth, one by one. Then they gouge his eyes. Little tufts of crinky hair are torn from his head, carrying away with them bits of skin, baring a bloody skull. Little pieces of flesh come off his body, already contused from the blows.

The Black can no longer shout: his tongue has been swollen by a red hot iron. His whole body ripples, trembling, like a half-crushed snake. A slash with a knife: one of his ears falls to the ground. . . . Oh! How black he is! How awful! And the ladies tear at his face. . . .

The Black is roasted, browned, burned. But he deserves to die twice instead of once. He is therefore hanged, or more exactly, what is left of his corpse is hanged. And all those who were not able to help with the cooking applaud now. . . .

When everybody has had enough, the corpse is brought down. The rope is cut into small pieces which will be sold for three or five dollars each. Souvenirs and lucky charms quarrelled over by ladies.

"Popular justice," as they say over there, has been done. Calmed down, the crowd congratulate the "organizers," then stream away slowly and cheerfully, as if after a feast, make appointments with one another for the next time.

While on the ground, stinking of fat and smoke, a black head, mutilated, roasted, deformed, grins horribly and seems to ask the setting sun, "Is this civilization?"[7]

This vivid description of lynching undoubtedly conveyed the impression that Ho had been an eyewitness to the scene. Did he actually see what he described? There is little doubt that his brief stopover in New York did not provide Ho with either the time or the opportunity to have such an experience. Most of what he learned about the American Negroes and their plight had come from his reading. A good story-teller with a rich imagination, Ho had the tendency to present second-hand information as if it were part of his own experience. This was characteristic of his early writings.

Ironically, the lynching scene in America contained many of the features that were to characterize the execution of uncooperative "nephews" and "nieces" of Uncle Ho during the brutal land reform years (1953–56) in North Vietnam.

Beginnings of a Revolutionary

Once in France, Ho, at his father's request, called upon Phan Chau Trinh, the leader of the Private Schools Movement, who had been saved from prison by the influential League of Human Rights and brought to Paris in 1911. Ho's father, who had known Phan Chau Trinh when both men served their sentence in the Poulo Condore jail, hoped that his son would rely on the exiled nationalist leader for guidance and advice. After a short stay with Phan, Ho decided that he could not accept the old revolutionary's political ideas. While Phan believed that Vietnam's independence and modernization could be achieved through peaceful cooperation with the colonial administration, Ho maintained that peaceful cooperation had been tried and found wanting and that national independence could not be obtained without a revolution.

Ho thus left Phan and tried to find his own solution to the Vietnam problem. On one of his tours of duty aboard the French liner, Ho, finding himself back in Saigon, paid a visit to his father. The old man, who had been in contact with Phan Chau Trinh and consequently aware of Ho's decision, could not tolerate his impertinence, which conflicted with the time-honored Confucian tradition of filial piety and obedience. In a fit of anger, he seized his cane and threatened to attack his son. Ho fled in a hurry. Greatly disturbed by his father's lack of understanding, the young man withdrew to his ship. It was the last meeting between Ho and his father, two revolutionaries belonging to two different generations. Perhaps it was this unhappy incident, in addition to his devotion to the cause of revolution, that led Ho to renounce his family. Although officially known as a bachelor all his life, Ho reportedly had lived for many years in China with a Chinese woman who bore him a daughter. As a result of his revolutionary activities, which caused him to often flee from place to place, Ho eventually lost contact with them. This report seemed to be corroborated by the DRV President himself late in

1945. During one of his visits to the home of a Vietnamese professor in Hanoi with Harold Isaacs, then a *Newsweek* correspondent in the Far East, he was surrounded by the professor's children.

Old Ho Chi-minh was awkwardly embarrassed when the six-year-old brought him a packet of his drawings, covered by an elaborately designed dedicatory page addressed to him. "I am all alone," he said afterward. "No family, nothing. . . . I did have a wife once . . ." but he left it at that.[8]

In 1949, after the Communists had taken over in China, Ho asked the Chinese authorities to help locate his Chinese "wife" and daughter. The inquiries, however, were unsuccessful.

At the outset of World War I, the young Vietnamese seaman bade farewell to the sea and landed in Great Britain where he lived until 1917. Ho took on odd jobs, shovelling snow in the winter for the London school system, gardening in the summer, and working as a kitchen helper at the Carlton Hotel, which had the famous Frenchman Escoffier as its chef. Ho was so good at making pastries that the French chef took him under his tutelage and wanted to train him to be a cook. The Vietnamese, however, had other plans. It was in the British capital that the future chairman of the Lao Dong Party established contact with the Overseas Workers' Association, an anticolonialist and antiimperialist organization of Chinese and Indian seamen. Ho devoted a great deal of his time and energy to this group, and soon revealed himself to be an inexhaustible firebrand. England, however, was not his appropriate sphere of action. There were too few Vietnamese in the British Isles. Besides, London was not the place where decisions affecting the fate of Indochina were made.

The Russian Revolution of November, 1917, caused serious repercussions in the Western world. Ho had been reading extensively about the social, political, and economic conditions of Russia, whose history had been marked by sporadic peasant revolts and whose autocratic Tsars and Tsarinas had opposed all reforms. The success of the Russian Revolution captured the intense interest of the young Vietnamese, who dreamed of leading one in his country some day. Given competent leadership and favorable conditions, a revolution would succeed in Vietnam. While leadership could be learned, favorable conditions could be created. With this conviction, Ho left England, where he had learned a great deal from the agitators for Ireland's independence.

By the end of 1917, Ho arrived in France, where 80,000 of his fellow countrymen were either serving in the French army or working in factories. He settled down in Paris, earning his living at various jobs, working as a cook, a laundry boy, a gardener, and finally as a photo finisher under the name of Nguyen Ai Quoc. The following advertisement appeared in many issues of the socialist newspaper, *La Vie Ouvrière*, in 1918:

You who wish to have a living remembrance of your parents, have your photos retouched at Nguyen Ai Quoc's, 9 Impasse Compoint, Paris 17th District.

Habitually, Ho devoted half of his time to retouching photographs and the remainder to other activities, such as reading, writing, and visiting with friends. Dressed in his eternal black flannel suit, this frail young man with fulgurant brown eyes was one of the most faithful patrons of the library on the Quai de Jemmapes. It was here that Ho, the avid reader, devoured books on French literature and philosophy, the works of Marx and Shakespeare, wrote articles for newspapers or letters to deputies in the National Assembly, and engaged in frequent discussions with members of the French Socialist party such as Léon Blum, Marcel Cachin, Marius Moutet, the future Minister of Colonies, Jean Longuet, a nephew of Karl Marx and leader of the orthodox wing of the party, to mention just a few. Ho thus pursued his political education, adhering to the Human Rights League, and joining the Socialist Party.

The publication of President Woodrow Wilson's Fourteen Points at the end of World War I raised false hopes among the colonial people who believed that a new day had dawned for them. In a rented suit, Ho, then twenty-eight years old, appeared every day in the corridors of the Versailles Palace, hoping to see the American President and other leaders of the victorious Allied powers to plead for Vietnam's autonomy. Unfortunately, the great Western leaders had no time for a lowly Annamese. However modest the aspirations of the Vietnamese might be, the big powers were not interested in the fate of a little Asian country. This disappointing experience impressed on the young nationalist that the ideal of equality, justice, and self-rule did not apply to the "colored" people of the world. Ho's moderate eight-point program, prepared in collaboration with Nguyen The Truyen, a Vietnamese chemical engineer and patriot whom Ho had met upon his arrival in France, did not even suggest Vietnam's independence from France. It simply proposed general amnesty for political prisoners, reform of the Indochinese judicial system by recognizing equality between Europeans and natives, basic democratic freedoms, abolition of forced labor, the salt tax and rice alcohol monopoly, substitution of government by decree with government by law, and appointment of a permanent Vietnamese Committee to advise the French government in matters related to Vietnam. The Western leaders, unwittingly, chose to ignore the frail young man in the dark, rented suit. Was it the turning point in Ho's life? Perhaps it was. Ho began to drift toward the East, and never changed direction.

In postwar France, the Socialists were submerged in a bitter debate, which was to cause a serious split within their party. Domestically, the right wing sought to achieve its objective within the existing framework, while the left wing advocated a revolution in the Russian style. On the colonial issue, the traditionalist elements, while supporting the colonies' claim to independence, were deadset against opposing the national policy. The progressive faction, on the contrary, favored immediate emancipation for the colonies in accordance with Lenin's "Thesis on National and Colonial Questions." Ho, naturally, sided with the latter group.

It was also a period during which the proletariat and young intelligentsia turned to Bolshevik Russia for inspiration. The new Soviet leaders were then preoccupied with their war against imperialism on all fronts. One of their basic objectives was the liberation of the colonies, which they considered as a source of wealth and power for capitalism. From its founding in March, 1919, the Third International had emphasized the need to organize both the people in the colonies and the workers in the metropolis. At its second Congress in July, 1920, it again underlined the importance of revolutionary organizations in the colonies and convoked to this effect the Congress of the Oriental People to be held in Baku in September of that year, when, as Ho was to write in 1924:

For the first time, the proletariat of the conquering Western States and that of the subject Eastern countries fraternally joined hands and deliberated in common on the best means to defeat their common enemy, imperialism.

Following this historic congress, despite internal and external difficulties, revolutionary Russia has never hesitated to come to the help of peoples awakened by its historic and victorious revolution. One of its first important acts was the founding of the University of the East.[9]

Three months after the Baku Congress, the French United Socialist Party convoked its Eighteenth National Congress at Tours from December 25 to 30. Inspired by a strong faith in the solidarity of the proletariat throughout the world, Ho, as the first Indochinese delegate, attended the deliberations of his party. In his first speech delivered to a political assembly, the young Vietnamese impressed on his audience the need to emancipate the oppressed masses in the colonies. Deploring the abuses of French imperialism in Indochina, he made an impassioned appeal to his fellow party members to help put an end to this exploitation of men by men:

Today, instead of contributing, together with you, to world revolution, I come here with deep sadness to speak as a member of the Socialist Party, against the imperalists who have committed abhorrent crimes on my native land. You all have known that French imperialism entered Indochina half a century ago. In its selfish interests, it conquered our country with bayonets. Since then we have not only been oppressed and exploited shamelessly, but also tortured and poisoned pitilessly. Plainly speaking, we have been poisoned with opium, alcohol, etc. I cannot, in some minutes, reveal all the atrocities that the predatory capitalists have inflicted on Indochina. Prisons outnumber schools and are always overcrowded with detainees. Any natives having socialist ideas are arrested and sometimes murdered without trial. Such is the so-called justice in Indochina. In that country, the Vietnamese are discriminated against, they do not enjoy safety like Europeans or those having European citizenship. We have neither freedom of press nor freedom of speech. Even freedom of assembly and freedom of association do not exist. We have no right to live in other countries or to go abroad as tourists. We are forced to live in utter ignorance and obscurity because we have no right to study. In Indochina the colonialists find all ways and means to force us to smoke opium and drink alcohol to poison and beset us. Thousands of Vietnamese have been led to a slow death or massacred to protect other people's interests.

Comrades, such is the treatment inflicted upon more than 20 million Vietnamese, that is more than half the population of France. And they are said to be under French protection! The Socialist Party must act practically to support the oppressed natives. . . .

Right from the beginning of my speech I have already asked everyone to keep absolute silence. The Party must make propaganda for socialism in all colonial countries. We have realized that the Socialist Party's joining the Third International means that it has practically promised that from now on it will correctly assess the importance of the colonial question. We are very glad to learn that a Standing Delegation has been appointed to study the North Africa question, and, in the near future, we will be very glad if the Party sends one of its members to Indochina to study on-the-spot the questions relating to this country, and the activities which should be carried out there. . . .

On behalf of the whole of mankind, on behalf of all the Socialist Party's members, both left and right wings, we call upon you! Comrades, save us![10]

At this congress, the two wings of the French Socialist Party parted company. The right wing opted for the Second International while the left wing voted to join the Third International. Unlike the First and the Second Internationals, which lacked a practical program, the Third had a well-defined policy. Ho, as expected, chose the Third International, accepted Moscow's "Twenty-one Conditions," and thus became a founding member of the French Communist party. Though a member of the Communist Federation of Seine, Ho, being a Vietnamese, not a French citizen, could not run for the Chamber of Deputies.[11]

Why Did Ho Join the Socialist and the Communist Parties?

When Ho left Vietnam, his main desire was to see his country free from foreign domination. His ideology was patriotism, if one could consider it an ideology. The eight-point program, which Ho subsequently tried to present to the Allied representatives who met in Paris, was simply a list of demands of a people who wanted to be free and independent. Even Ho's membership in the French Socialist party was not an indication of his penchant for socialism. Neither did his admiration for Lenin and enthusiasm for the Russian Revolution have any ideological connotations.

As Ho was to admit candidly later,[12] at the beginning he did not understand what was a party, a trade union, and what was socialism or Communism. He joined the French Socialist party because its members had shown sympathy toward him and toward the struggle of the oppressed people. He "supported the October Revolution only instinctively, not yet grasping all its historic importance," and "loved and admired Lenin because he was a great patriot who liberated his compatriots." When heated discussions took place within the Socialist party on the question whether the French organization should remain in the Second International or join Lenin's Third International, Ho became thoroughly puzzled. Convinced that a revolution could be waged with either International, he was, however, primarily interested in finding out which one sided with the colonial people. At one of the party meetings, Ho decided to raise the important question, to which an answer was promptly given: "The Third International." He was also given Lenin's "Thesis on the National and Colonial Questions," which he found very difficult to read:

There were political terms difficult to understand in this thesis. But by dint of reading it again and again, finally I could grasp the main part of it. What emotion, enthusiasm, clear-sightedness, and confidence it instilled to me! I was overjoyed to tears. Though sitting alone in my room, I shouted aloud as if addressing large crowds: "Dead martyrs, compatriots! This is what we need, this is the path to our liberation!"[13]

From then on, Ho had complete confidence in Lenin and the Third International. Prior to this sudden "revelation," Ho had usually sat quietly through many a meeting, listening attentively, and refraining from expressing support for any position as all arguments sounded logical to him. Now, inspired by Lenin's thesis, the young socialist from Indochina participated in all debates with unexpected fervor, refuting all allegations attacking Lenin and the Third International with the familiar question: "If you do not condemn colonialism, if you do not side with the colonial people, what kind of revolution are you waging?" In an attempt to expound and win support for his position, the impassioned debater attended not only the meetings of the left wing but also those of the right wing and other factions of the Socialist party. Ho was greatly influenced by his comrades and teachers Marcel Cachin, Vaillant Couturier, and

Gaston Monmousseau with whom he was to vote for joining the Third International.

At the beginning, as Ho revealed later, it was patriotism, not Communism, that attracted him to Lenin and the Third International. His increasing understanding of Marxism-Leninism and participation in practical activities, however, gradually led him to believe that only Socialism and Communism could liberate the oppressed nations and working people throughout the world. To this young man from Nghe An, "Leninism is not only a miraculous 'book of the wise,' a compass for . . . Vietnamese revolutionaries and people: it is also the radiant sun illuminating our path to final victory, to Socialism and Communism."[14] Lenin himself was a source of inspiration.

It is not only his genius, but his disdain of luxury, his love of labor, the purity of his private life, his simplicity, in a word, it is the grandeur and beauty of this master which exert an enormous influence upon the Asian peoples and irresistibly draw their hearts toward him.

Accustomed to being treated as backward and inferior people, they consider Lenin as the embodiment of universal brotherhood. Not only are they grateful to him, but they love him tenderly. To him, they show a veneration which is almost filial devotion.[15]

These words reveal his deep admiration for the Bolshevik leader. It was circumstance that transformed Nguyen the Patriot (Nguyen Ai Quoc) into Nguyen the agent of international Communism.

2 ☆ The Agent of International Communism

~~~~~~~~~~~~~~~~~~~~~~~~~~~~~~~~~~

FOR A QUARTER OF A CENTURY, from 1920 when he joined the French Communist party to 1945 when he emerged as the President of the Democratic Republic of Vietnam, Ho devoted all his energy to the cause of international Communism, working tirelessly among Vietnamese in France, China, and Siam, receiving Marxist indoctrination in Moscow, founding the Indochinese Communist party (ICP) in Hong Kong and the Viet Minh League in southern China. To his task Ho brought a fanatic zeal, which generated trust from his Soviet masters and obedience from his Vietnamese followers.

Activities in France

Having cast his lot with Lenin, Ho stepped up his agitation among the subject people from the French colonies then living in France. In 1921, in collaboration with Nguyen The Truyen, he organized the *Union Inter-coloniale* (Intercolonial Union), a group composed of exiled patriots from French overseas possessions. While the apparent objective of the Union was the emancipation of the colonies, its real purpose was the propagation of Communism. Its Manifesto, written by Ho himself, emphasized class struggle and appealed to the proletariat throughout the world to participate in the common fight against capitalism and imperialism:

Brothers of the colonies! In 1914, the powers at grips with a frightful cataclysm, turned to you and asked you then to agree to contribute your share of sacrifice to safeguard a country said to be yours and of which you had until then known only the spirit of domination.

To induce you to do so, the advantages your cooperation would bring you were unfailingly dangled before your eyes. But once the storm was over, as before, you remain subjected to the system of denizenship, exceptional jurisdiction, and deprived of the rights which make the dignity of a human being: freedom of association and to hold meetings; freedom of the press; the right to circulate freely, even in your own country. So much for the political side.

From the economic point of view, you remain subjected to the heavy and unpopular head tax and porterage tax; to the salt tax; to poisoning by and enforced consumption of spirits and opium, as in Indochina; to night watching as in Algeria to guard the property of the colonial sharks.

For equal work, your efforts remain less remunerative than those of your European comrades.

In a word, you were promised wonders.

You have now realized that they were only lies.

What is to be done to achieve your emancipation?

Applying the formula of Karl Marx, we say to you that your deliverance can only come through your own efforts.

It is to help you in this task that the Intercolonial Union has been founded.

It includes, with the cooperation of metropolitan comrades sympathetic to our cause, all those originating from the colonies now residing in France.

Means of action: In order to accomplish this work of justice, the IU intends to set the problem before public opinion with the help of the press and the spoken word (conferences, meetings, use of the tribunes of deliberating assemblies by those of our friends who hold effective mandates), and finally, by every means in our power.

Oppressed brothers of the metropolitan country! The dupes of your bourgeoisie, you have been the instruments of our conquest: carrying out this same Machiavellian policy, *your bourgeoisie today intends to use us to repress any desire on your part for independence.*

In the face of Capitalism and Imperialism our interests are the same: Remember, the words of Karl Marx:
"Workers of all lands, unite!"

The Union published a monthly review, *Le Paria*, which was devoted primarily to colonial affairs. Besides Ho, who wrote many emotional articles denouncing the abuses of colonialism, the contributors included Marcel Cachin, the senior French Communist, and other Algerian, Syrian, Senegalese, and West Indian Communists. Coming out every month at the beginning, *Le Paria* was published at less and less regular intervals later on, especially after Ho's departure from France early in 1924. There were in total thirty-eight issues, the first appearing in April, 1922, and the last one in April, 1926. While colonialism in general was under attack, French colonialism was Ho's main target. With a view to emphasizing the Communist nature of the paper, the original masthead of *Le Paria*, "Tribune of the Colonial People," was changed to "Tribune of the Colonial Proletariat" from January, 1924, on.

To reach their countrymen in both France and Vietnam, Ho and his faithful friend Nguyen The Truyen also edited a paper in Vietnamese called *Viet Nam Hon*, or the "soul of Vietnam." Numerous copies of this short-lived publication were smuggled into Vietnam by Vietnamese seamen employed on French liners. Ho travelled extensively throughout France, trying to organize his countrymen into a cohesive front, addressing large groups of Vietnamese workers and soldiers awaiting repatriation in the southeastern port of Marseilles. Seizing every opportunity to contact his compatriots in France, especially those who had just arrived from Vietnam or who had travelled to different parts of the world, Ho bombarded them with questions, listened quietly, learned a great deal, but always refrained from talking about himself or his plans. Into everyone's hand, Ho discreetly slipped a copy of *Le Paria* or the *Viet Nam Hon*.

In 1922, Khai Dinh, Emperor of Annam, arrived in France to attend a colonial exhibition. Ho seized this opportunity to ridicule the puppet monarch and the customs of his court by publishing a play called *Le dragon de bambou* (The Bamboo Dragon). As it has not been heard since, one is inclined to believe that the play was not something Uncle Ho would brag about.

It was also during this period that Ho wrote *Le Procès de la Colonisation française* (French Colonization on Trial), a series of pamphlets in which he severely indicted the French colonial system in Asia, Africa, and the Middle East. Besides working on *Le Procès*, editing *Le Paria* and *Viet Nam Hon*, and writing articles for *La Vie Ouvrière* and *l'Humanité*, French Socialist and Communist papers, Ho also chose to earn a living as a photo retoucher. Such a hectic life did not leave him much time for anything else. His stay in France did not convert the determined Marxist to the French ways of living. Always preoccupied with serious matters, he had no time for women or drink. His main weakness was American cigarettes, which he smoked regularly, to the end of his life, between his tirades against American imperialism.

Ho's writings during this period were also designed to promote solidarity among the working people of the world, particularly the unity between the French workers and the oppressed people in the colonies. Constantly referring to Lenin's statement that "the workers of colonizing countries are bound to give the most active assistance to the liberation movements in subject countries," Ho deplored the indifferent attitude of the French proletariat toward the colonial people. In order to fraternize with the oppressed people and support their struggle for freedom, Ho argued, the workers in the mother country must know what a colony was and what kinds of injustice were inflicted upon its inhabitants.

Unfortunately, there are many militants who still think that a colony is nothing but a country with plenty of sand underfoot and of sun overhead, a few green coconut palms and colored folk, that is all. And they take not the slightest interest in the matter.[2]

Ho's writings and his activities in the midst of the Vietnamese community in France did not ingratiate him and his close friends with the French Sûreté, which began to keep a close watch on them. Annoyed, the defiant agitator wrote an open letter to the then Minister of Colonies, Albert Sarraut, ridiculing the French official with a humor seldom found in his writings:

Your Excellency,
We know very well that your affection for the natives of the colonies in general, and the Annamese in particular, is great.
Under your proconsulate the Annamese people have known true pros-

perity and real happiness, the happiness of seeing their country dotted all over with an increasing number of spirit and opium shops which, together with firing squads, prisons, "democracy," and all the improved apparatus of modern civilization, are combining to make the Annamese the most advanced of the Asians and the happiest of mortals.

These acts of benevolence save us the trouble of recalling all the others, such as enforced recruitment and loans, bloody repressions, the dethronement and exile of kings, profanation of sacred places, etc.

As a Chinese poem says, "The wind of kindness follows the movement of your fan, and the rain of virtue precedes the tracks of your carriage." As you are now the supreme head of all the colonies, your special care for the Indochinese has but increased with your elevation. You have created in Paris itself a service having the special task—with special regard to Indochina, according to a colonial publication—of keeping-watch on the natives, especially the Annamese, living in France.

But "keeping watch" alone seemed to Your Excellency's fatherly solicitude insufficient, and you wanted to do better. That is why for some time now, you have granted each Annamese—dear Annamese, as Your Excellency says—private *aides-de-camp*. Though still novices in the art of Sherlock Holmes, these good people are very devoted and particularly sympathetic. We have only praise to bestow on them and compliments to pay to their boss, Your Excellency.

We are sincerely moved by the honor Your Excellency has the extreme kindness to grant us and we would have accepted it with all gratitude if it did not seem a little superfluous and if it did not excite envy and jealousy.

At a time when Parliament is trying to save money and cut down administrative personnel, when there is a large budget deficit, when agriculture and industry lack labor, when attempts are being made to levy taxes on workers' wages, and at a time when repopulation demands the use of all productive energies, it would seem to us antipatriotic at such a time to accept personal favors which necessarily cause loss of the powers of the citizens condemned—as *aides-de-camp*—to idleness and the spending of money that the proletariat has sweated hard for.

In consequence, while remaining obliged to you, we respectfully decline this distinction flattering to us but too expensive to the country.

If Your Excellency insists on knowing what we do every day, nothing is easier: We shall publish every morning a bulletin of our movements, and Your Excellency will have but the trouble of reading.

Besides, our timetable is quite simple and almost unchanging.

Morning: from 8 to 12 at the workshop.

Afternoon: in newspaper offices (leftist, of course) or at the library.
Evening: at home or attending educational talks.
Sundays and holidays: visiting museums or other places of interest.
There you are!
Hoping that this convenient and rational method will give satisfaction to Your Excellency, we beg to remain. . . .

Nguyen Ai Quoc[3]

Having witnessed and suffered himself humiliations inflicted by the colons, Ho easily lost patience with anyone who thought fit to defend colonial rule. To him colonialism was not an abstract theory; it was a reality in the conquered and oppressed nations; it was personified by specific Frenchmen, those sadists who tortured and killed the subject people with impunity. In an open letter to Léon Archimbaud, a Parliament member from Drome, who had written an article refuting the charges brought by certain Communist deputies against the colonial regime as exaggerated and false, the Vietnamese revolutionary angrily said:

First, the Minister of Colonies himself was obliged to recognize that a "contemptuous state of mind toward native life" exists. And that he "denied no act of brutality" denounced by Deputy Boisneuf. And then can you deny, M. Archimbaud, that during the last few years, that is to say, following the war for "the rule of law" for which 800,000 natives came to work "voluntarily" or to be killed in France, that your civilizers —with impunity—have robbed, swindled, murdered, or burnt alive Annamese, Tunisians, and Senegalese?
. . . Either you are harebrained and have forgotten the Baudoins, the Darles, the Lucases, and so many others making up the galaxy which is the honor and pride of your Colonial Administration, and who, after having committed heinous crimes, receive as punishment only promotions and decorations. Or else you are treating your readers as complete fools.[4]

Ever since he chose the Bolshevik ways, Ho had been longing for a pilgrimage to the land of Lenin, his idol. Much remained to be done in France, however, and the nationalist-turned-Communist patiently waited for the opportune moment to come. Meanwhile, he recruited promising young Vietnamese and sent to Moscow for information on Marxist indoctrination and revolutionary training.

Ho's opportunity to make his first visit to the Soviet Union finally came. As a native of a colony who had personally experienced colonial rule and written extensively on the subject, Ho rapidly gained recognition as the French Communist party's specialist on colonial affairs. In this capacity he was sent to Moscow to attend the Fourth Comintern Congress, which lasted from November to December, 1922. During his first sojourn in the Soviet capital, the future architect of the Viet Minh Revolution managed to meet Lenin and other Communist luminaries such as Trotsky, Bukharin, and Stalin, an event whose significance has been carefully underlined by his associates. Until his death Ho was thus the only non-Russian Communist who knew the leading figures who had ruled the Soviet Union since the Revolution of 1917. One of the most important decisions reached by the Comintern at this Congress was the creation of the Southeast Asian Bureau of which Ho was to become a very active member. Shortly after the close of the Congress, Ho left the Soviet Union. He returned to Moscow in June, 1923, to attend the Peasants' International Congress (Krestintern) and remained there until November. On October 16, Ho was elected to the ten-man Executive Committee of the Krestintern, an event that filled him with enthusiasm and gratitude for the international Communist movement. His new duties clearly defined, Ho journeyed back to Paris early in November to make arrangements for his final departure from the "mother" country. During his last days in France, an exuberant Ho excitedly contacted his friends and followers from the French African colonies, urging them to "go back to their countries, penetrate the masses to awaken, organize, unite and train them and lead them to fight for freedom and independence."[5] With the excitement of a man who had discovered a remedy to the world's problems, Ho invited Kyo Komatsu, a Japanese writer whom he had befriended in Paris, to go to Moscow with him to witness the beginning of a new era. Disappointed by the latter's refusal to acquiesce in his proposal, the Vietnamese asked: "What kind of art can you practice in this rotten society? We will make the revolution and then you can write for free men in a classless society!"

As the year drew to a close, the frail Vietnamese revolutionary quietly left France. He did not return until 1946, and this time as President of the Democratic Republic of Vietnam.

Activities in Soviet Russia and Asia

Ho arrived in Moscow shortly after Lenin's death, in time to pay his last respects to the deceased Bolshevik leader and to witness the ferocious struggle for power that had begun to take shape between Stalin and Trotsky. Refraining from discussing controversial issues and from taking sides, a trait that was to become his trademark, the shrewd Vietnamese thoughtfully observed everything that went on and learned a great deal about political competition and the art of survival. A period of intensive study and formal education began for Ho. As Linov, he registered at the University of the Toilers of the East and, as Lin, he attended the Institute of National and Colonial Affairs. Eager to familiarize himself with Communist ideology, Ho devoured books and periodicals on Bolshevik tactics and underwent a thorough training in Marxism-Leninism. Not only did he acquire new names which confounded the French police, he also added Russian to the list of languages he had mastered with remarkable ease: French, English, German, Chinese (several dialects), and, of course, Vietnamese.

Ho's fanatic devotion, tireless drive, and simple manners left a very favorable impression upon the Russian leaders. For a man who, a few years earlier, had not understood the difference between a party and a trade union, socialism and Communism, Ho's rapid rise in the Communist movement was remarkable. As the Colonial Representative and a member of the French Communist party, he was invited to address the Fifth Congress of the Comintern held in Moscow from June 17 to July 8, 1924. In his Report on the National and Colonial Questions, which was loaded with facts and figures, Ho unequivocally and intrepidly condemned the Communist parties of France, Great Britain, Holland, Belgium, and other countries:

What have they done to cope with the colonial invasions perpetrated by the bourgeois class of their countries? What have they done from the day they accepted Lenin's political program to educate the working class of their countries in the spirit of just internationalism, and that of close contact with the working masses in the colonies? What our Parties have done in this domain is almost worthless. As for me, I was born in a French colony, and am a member of the French Communist Party, and I am very sorry to say that our Communist Party has done hardly anything for the colonies.[6]

Ho then went on to complain that the Communist newspaper had failed to introduce the colonial questions to the militants, to awaken the workers in the colonies, and to win them over to the cause of Communism. The papers had also refrained from criticizing the oppressive policies pursued by the Ministry of Colonies, conveying the impression that the Party had no concern for the colonial people. As an example, Ho mentioned *l'Humanité*, the French Communist paper, which had not even published the International Peasants' Appeal to the colonies issued by the Comintern. In an attempt to correct these shortcomings, Ho proposed the following measures:

1. To publish in *l'Humanité* a new feature of at least two columns weekly devoted to regular coverage of colonial questions.
2. To increase propaganda and choose Party members among the natives of the colonial countries in which there are already branches of the Communist International. ·
3. To send comrades from the colonial countries to study at the Eastern Communist University in Moscow.
4. To come to an agreement with the United General Confederation of Labor on the organization of working people from colonial countries working in France.
5. To set Party members the task of paying more attention to colonial questions.[7]

That he addressed the Fifth Congress of the Comintern and suggested a new course for the French Communist party to follow was a significant indication of Ho's growing influence. Shortly afterward, he was entrusted with more delicate missions for which he had to leave the land of Lenin.

Journey to China

China was in the midst of a revolution. Humiliated by the Western powers which, both at the Versailles Conference following World War I and at the Washington Conference of 1921–22, had refused to give serious consideration to her request for the abrogation of unilateral treaties which had reduced her to the status of a quasicolony, the Middle Kingdom, under Sun Yat-sen's leadership, was waging a war against imperialism. Rejected by the West, Sun approached the Soviet Union whose objective in the Far East happened to coincide with China's, i.e., the eradication of Western influence. Moscow eagerly seized this opportunity to offer aid, which the Chinese promptly accepted. Ironically, the Kuomintang, which was to be driven off mainland China by Mao Tse-tung's forces in 1949, owed a great deal to the Comintern for its reorganization and methods of operation. Entertaining no thought of cooperation with the Soviet Union, it nevertheless accepted a Russian loan of three million rubles to establish the Whampoa Military Academy. A mission headed by Alexander Joffe went to China and, on January 26, 1923, a joint statement was issued by the Soviet emissary and Sun Yat-sen, under which Moscow promised to help China achieve unity and independence. Subsequently, another Russian mission under the leadership of Michael Borodin, an expert propagandist, and General Vassily Bluecher, popularly known as General Gallen, an able military instructor, arrived in Canton to assist in the reorganization of both the Kuomintang and the Chinese army. This was the heyday of Soviet-Kuomintang cooperation. As the Supreme Political Adviser of both the Chinese Government and the Nationalist Party, Borodin enjoyed enormous influence in China, a factor that was to benefit Ho considerably.

Since 1905, Canton had been a meeting center for Vietnamese nationalists. Answering the appeal of Phan Boi Chau, the leader of the *Dong Du* (Exodus to the East) Movement, many young men had arrived from Indochina to acquire the new knowledge (Western science) and to engage in revolutionary activities. The unsuccessful attempt on the life of Merlin, the Governor General of Indochina, by the émigré Pham Hong Thai on June 19, 1924, during the former's visit to Shamian in Canton, bespoke the fervor of the Vietnamese exiles. With a view to providing these political agitators with leadership and promoting Communism in the Asian colonies, the Comintern dispatched one of its seasoned agents to China late in 1924.

One day in December, a frail but determined-looking young man arrived at the Soviet mission in Canton. He was introduced by Borodin as Ly Thuy or Lee Suei, the new secretary, translator, and interpreter of the mission. While no one knew his real identity, many assumed that he was a Soviet citizen of Chinese descent. Soon after his arrival, Ly Thuy established contact with the Vietnamese nationalists in Canton, and impressed them with his command of their language. They should not have been surprised, however, for Ly Thuy was none other than Nguyen Ai Quoc, the man whose anti-French writings they had avidly read. In an attempt to delude both the police and his non-Marxist compatriots, Ho again assumed another alias. To the Vietnamese colony in Canton, he was known as Vuong Son Nhi. As Borodin's interpreter and confidant, Ho moved freely in both Kuomintang and Communist circles, and had ample opportunity to observe the first phase of the Nationalist-Communist collaboration. Under such favorable circumstances, the astute Vietnamese revolutionary began his propaganda activities among his exiled compatriots. As Truong Chinh was to point out later, Ho

drawing experience from the attempt on the life of Merlin, which had failed, . . . arrived at the following conclusion: the assassination of this or that governor could not overthrow the colonial regime or lead the revolution to victory. To this end, a strong political party was needed, which would organize the masses, and give them the leadership needed for carrying out an insurrection and winning power.[8]

As most of the Vietnamese refugees in Canton belonged to one or another patriotic group, Ho pretended to share their aims and passed himself off as a fervent nationalist. He established contact with the *Tam Tam Xa* (Heart-to-Heart Association), a revolutionary society organized in 1923 by Le Hong Phong, the future Secretary General of the Indochinese Communist Party (ICP) from 1935 to 1939. Very rapidly, with the assistance of its leaders, Ho reorganized the *Tam Tam Xa* and rechristened it the *Viet Nam Thanh Nien Cach Menh Dong Chi Hoi*, or "Vietnamese Revolutionary Youth Organization," known briefly as the *Thanh Nien*. In addition to Ho and Le Hong Phong, its members included Ho Tung Mau, Hong Son, and others, men who were to play prominent roles in the Viet Minh Revolution. According to Truong Chinh,

The Vietnam Revolutionary Youth League was but a transitional stage leading to the founding of a Communist Party, the Communists within the League being organized into "Communist groups" which would prepare for the setting up of a Communist Party in Vietnam.[9]

With its headquarters established in Canton, the Central Committee of the party published a weekly paper, the *Thanh Nien*, and translated Communist works into Vietnamese. Unlike *Le Paria*, the *Thanh Nien* came out regularly from June, 1925 to April, 1927. There were in total eighty-eight issues, in which Ho elaborately discussed colonial issues and developed Lenin's thesis on the revolution in the colonies. In spite of its small circulation (about 100), the paper was a great success as it reached numerous readers both in China and in Vietnam.

Ho also organized training courses for his young fellow countrymen, taught them dialectical materialism, the Marxist concept of class struggle, and the revolutionary techniques which he had learned at the University of the Toilers of the East. As a manual of instruction, he used *The Road of the Revolution*, which he had written himself. Among the young newcomers from Indochina, there was a man who rapidly gained Ho's trust and remained his confidant. His name was Pham Van Dong, Prime Minister of the DRV. The accelerated training courses lasted only three months, after which the graduates were sent either to Moscow for further political indoctrination, to the Whampoa Military Academy for combat training, or back to Vietnam to organize secret cells and recruit young men for the Canton school. Upon his cadres Ho inculcated a strong sense of dedication to the party and its cause. Disloyal members, i.e., those who refused to obey the party's directives, were severely punished. One of Ho's favorite methods was to forward their names to the French Sûreté, which was always eager to put them behind bars. This turned out to be one of the most effective disciplinary measures. Ho's cadres had no choice but to remain loyal and trustworthy regardless of the many dangers they might incur in Indochina.

Ho's ruthless methods of operation and his readiness to sacrifice any man to achieve his objectives could be illustrated by another shocking incident, which took place in June, 1925. To finance his revolution in Vietnam, Ho needed funds which had to be raised in a hurry. One day, he came up with a perfidious idea which he promptly put to test. As the French had been so eager to capture the celebrated nationalist leader Phan Boi Chau, who had been living in exile in China, arrangements could be made for his delivery to the French authorities in exchange for a large ransom.

Thereupon, Ho sent a letter inviting Phan to come to Canton to discuss matters of common interest and to attend the founding of the Vietnamese branch of the World Federation of Small and Weak Nations. Full of hope and enthusiasm, Phan accepted the invitation. As he arrived at the Shanghai railway station en route to Canton, French agents, who had been informed by Ho of his whereabouts, immediately seized and took him to the French concession in Shanghai. Phan was subsequently shipped back to Vietnam, tried, convicted, and given a life sentence at hard labor. Although pardoned later, he was confined to his house and forbidden to receive visitors. For this betrayal of the grand old man of Vietnamese nationalism, a man from his native province of Nghe An who had been a source of inspiration to him, Ho allegedly received 150,000 Indochinese piasters. The callous Communist later justified his action on the following grounds:

   a. Phan Boi Chau, as an influential nationalist leader, would be a dangerous rival to the Communists in their scheme to control the anti-French movement;
   b. The ransom money would be used for a just cause, i.e., the promotion of Communism;
   c. The arrest, trial, and execution of Phan Boi Chau would arouse the Vietnamese people against French rule and intensify the spirit of resistance.[10]

This reasoning should dissipate any doubt one may entertain about Ho's ruthlessness. Sacrificing Phan Boi Chau to the Communist cause, Ho also expected the French to execute his fellow Nghe Anese.

In spite of his preoccupation with the *Thanh Nien* organization, Ho, the Comintern agent, did not neglect his other responsibilities. With the assistance of the Indian M. N. Roy and several Koreans, who had received their political training in Moscow, he set up the League of Oppressed Peoples of Asia whose members came from the various Western-ruled colonies in the East. The League, which was to become the South Seas Communist party, was just another Comintern front organization in the Far East.

Ho's operations had been proceeding smoothly when the Kuomintang-Communist cooperation suddenly came to an end. Increasingly alarmed by the progress of the Communist propaganda,

Chiang Kai-shek occupied Shanghai and waged a war against Mao Tse-tung, declaring that the Kuomintang would not admit a "super-government under Borodin," and that "if the Communists wish to dominate us, and the Russians to ill-treat us, that means the end of their activity." Confronted with such an unpleasant situation, the Borodin mission, including Ho, hurriedly left for Hankow, where they contacted Wang Ch'ing-wei, the leader of the radical wing in the Kuomintang and Chiang Kai-shek's main opponent. Borodin offered to support Wang against Chiang in their struggle for the leadership of their party on condition that Wang carry out a policy of land reform. In spite of the Russian promises and Ho's persistent argument, Wang chose to make peace with Chiang. Greatly disappointed, the Soviet delegation left for Moscow.

Before his departure from China, Ho had made arrangements for Ho Tung Mau, who together with Hong Son had joined the Chinese Communist party, to assume the leadership of the *Thanh Nien*. Mau prevailed upon the Cantonese authorities to permit his group to continue its activities with the understanding that they should be directed exclusively against French colonialism. In December, 1928, however, Mau and other members of the *Thanh Nien* were arrested by the Chinese police. Hong Son, consequently, became the head of the party. Faced with an increasing repression by the Kuomintang, the *Thanh Nien* subsequently moved its headquarters first to Kuang si, then to Hong Kong in May, 1929.

Following his return to Moscow, Ho received a brief assignment to the Anti-Imperialist League in Berlin. Whatever he did in Germany has been a state secret, but his sojourn in that country was long enough for him to learn its language. Early in 1928, after attending the Congress against Imperialism in Brussels. Ho journeyed to Switzerland and Italy, then left for Asia.

There were from 30,000 to 40,000 Vietnamese settlers in Siam. It was in their midst that appeared, in the autumn of 1928, a frail, gentle-looking Buddhist monk, who was also a fascinating story-teller. He travelled from village to village, encouraging people to form associations for self-improvement. With the permission of the local authorities, the bonze encouraged the Vietnamese émigrés to build schools. To set up an example, the slender man of Buddha himself carried bricks in waived bamboo baskets, mixed mortar, actively and enthusiastically particpated in construction work. As soon as a school was erected, each village, at the monk's suggestion, provided for the maintenance of a teacher, who would teach *quoc ngu* and other elementary subjects to children in the daytime and to adults in the evening. The school also served as a meeting place for the villagers. Their daily chores finished, people gathered here to study, read newspapers and magazines, discuss their affairs, and, most importantly, to listen to the kindly monk who was so well versed in politics. He used historical themes to put his ideas across, constantly reminding his listeners of their country's glorious past and humiliating present, its indomitable spirit, and its heroic resistance to foreign rule. The abuses and crimes of the colonial regime, so vividly described by the persuasive monk, aroused a slumbering indignation in the Vietnamese exiles, rekindled their patriotic feelings, and rendered them more receptive to his ideas.

While emphasizing the need to restore Vietnam to its rightful place, the holy man also talked about a wonderful Western country, whose enlightened and selfless leaders and people were deeply interested in helping Vietnamese recover their independence. He seemed to know it so well, explaining in the most minute details its perfect classless system, a society in which all men were equal, and in which no one would think of exploiting his fellow men for selfish motives for everyone contributed according to his ability and everyone received everything he needed. It was the country of the Soviets; it was the USSR. This man in the saffron robe also circulated songs and stories which he had composed himself and put in the *luc-bat* (six-eight) form, poems in which hexameters and octometers are alternated and which are very easy for Vietnamese to memorize. The people he influenced and trained in this fashion, in their turn, went from village to village to continue his work and spread his words. Many even crossed the border into Vietnam, carrying with them newspapers and other materials which the bonze had produced.

Who was this man of Buddha who knew history and world events so well? This saintly monk was none other than Nguyen Ai Quoc, the dedicated Comintern agent, the future Ho Chi Minh. He organized the Vietnamese resistance and spread Communism wherever he went, in France, in China, in Siam, and in Indochina. Under the guise of patriotism, Ho sought to infiltrate and control all anti-French organizations in order to carry out the first phase of his Communist revolution. The cadres he formed in Siam were to become successively members of the *Thanh Nien*, the Indochinese Communist party, and the *Lao Dong* party. When the *Viet Nam Quoc Dan Dang* (Vietnam Nationalist Party) attempted to gain adherents in Siam, its advance was effectively checked by the *Thanh Nien*, which enjoyed widespread support among the Vietnamese émigrés in the Thai country. These settlers, whose allegiance goes to the DRV, have become a serious menace to the tranquillity and security of Thailand (formerly Siam).

Founder of the Indochinese Communist Party

The *Thanh Nien* cadres who had infiltrated into Vietnam set up the first Communist cell in Tonkin and took upon themselves the task of making preparations for the founding of a Communist party in Indochina. At the first National Congress of the *Thanh Nien*, held in Hong Kong from May 1 to 9, 1929, a serious conflict between the Central Committee and the Tonkinese delegation emerged. The North Vietnamese leaders, whose clandestine activities inside the country constantly put their lives in danger, proposed that an Indochinese Communist party should be founded to coordinate all operations both inside and outside Vietnam. The majority of the delegates, however, following Ho's advice to spread Communism under the cover of nationalism, defeated the proposal. Greatly disturbed, the Tonkinese delegation left Hong Kong. Upon their return to Vietnam, ignoring both the Comintern directives and the authority of the *Thanh Nien* Central Committee, they founded the *Dong Duong Cong San Dang*, or Indochinese Communist Party, in June, 1929, in North Vietnam. The new party included most of the cadres of the *Thanh Nien*, whose organizations in Tonkin were promptly dissolved, a large segment of the *Tan Viet Cach Mang Dang*, or Revolutionary Party of New Vietnam, which had been founded in 1925 in Northern Annam by a group of intellectuals upon their return from Poulo Condore where they had been deported for their participation in the 1908 movements,[11] and members of the land reform society secretly known as the *Cao Vong Thanh Nien Dang*, or Hope of Youth Party, which had been organized by Nguyen An Ninh in 1927 in Cochinchina.

Both the *Thanh Nien* and the newly formed Indochinese Communist Party (ICP) feverishly competed for Comintern recognition. Alarmed by the success of the dissident group and anxious to retain its cadres mostly in the South, the *Thanh Nien* Central Committee promptly transformed what remained of the organization into the *An Nam Cong San Dang*, or Annamese Communist Party (ACP). Under these circumstances and motivated by the same fear, the *Tan Viet* brought its members in Central and Southern Annam into a new party, the *Dong Duong Cong San Lien Doan*, or Indochinese Communist League (ICL). Thus, in 1929, three Communist parties existed simultaneously in Vietnam, the ICP in Tonkin and Northern Annam, the ACP in Cochinchina, and the ICL in Southern Annam, each claiming to be the only genuine, revolutionary party organized along Marxist-Leninist lines. Submerged in a ferocious struggle for influence, all three did not hesitate to resort to any means available, including leaking their opponents' names (Ho's favorite method) to the French police. At the same time, they tried to establish contact with the Communist International.

Paralyzed by the internecine strife and convinced that Ho, who had founded the *Thanh Nien*, trained, and inspired its members, would be the only person capable of bringing the rival factions together, the Hong Kong-based Central Committee of the ACP sent him an urgent appeal, which was immediately forwarded to the Comintern. An order from the Executive Committee of the Communist International commanding Ho to take appropriate action subsequently reached him in Siam, where he had been since August, 1928, organizing Vietnamese settlers and directing propaganda activities in Malaya and the Dutch East Indies. Thereupon, Ho dispatched an invitation to the Vietnamese Communist factions requesting them to send delegates to Hong Kong for a very important meeting.

One winter day in 1930, Nguyen Luong Bang, an adventurous seaman who had smuggled into Vietnam copies of Vuong Son Nhi's (Ho) *The Road of the Revolution* and who was destined to become one of the leaders of the Viet Minh Revolution, received in Shanghai an unsigned love letter which said: "Darling, I wait for you in Tien Thi's billiard room." Greatly excited, the young seaman hurried to the rendezvous place, which was the largest bazaar in that Chinese city, expecting to meet a sweet, beautiful lady. With a mixed feeling, Bang found, instead of his "darling," a slender man who, in spite of the biting cold in Shanghai, was scantily dressed in a cheap Sun Yat-sen suit. It was comrade Vuong (Ho), the zealous revolutionary who had founded the *Thanh Nien* five years earlier in Canton. During their conversation, Bang worriedly inquired about Nguyen Ai Quoc who had been reported dead in prison. Ho, or comrade Vuong, of course, did not know anything about it.[12]

Thus, Ho arrived in Hong Kong early in January, 1930. After a few hectic weeks of meeting and consultation, the determined Comintern agent convened the Unification Conference on February 3, at which he emphasized the need for solidarity and unity of action in the face of stubborn imperialism, reiterating the Third International position that "the most important and most urgent task for all Indochinese Communists consisted in founding a revolutionary party, i.e., a mass Communist Party. It should be a unified party and the only Indochinese Communist Party."[13] As expected, Ho prevailed upon the splinter groups to recognize the authority of the Hong Kong-based Central Committee. The three rival parties, the ICP, the ACP, and the ICL, were consequently amalgamated into the *Viet Nam Cong San Dang*, or Vietnamese Communist Party. Thus February 3, 1930, was a very important date for Vietnamese Communists; it was the day on which their party was officially created. With a view to illustrating the common cause of the peoples of Indochina, and as an early indication of its ambitions, the party, at its October congress held in Hong Kong, decided to change its name to *Dong Duong Cong San Dang*, or Indochinese Communist Party (ICP). In spite of serious misgivings, Ho, as a concession, acquiesced in the delegates' proposal to transfer the Central Committee to Haiphong. The cautious revolutionary had for good reasons feared that the presence of the ICP headquarters in Tonkin might subject the party to the pressure of hotheaded and impetuous cadres and thus expose it to the alert French Sûreté.

The Outline of the Party Platform, adopted by the Unification Conference, clearly reflected Ho's belief, acquired in Moscow, that the

proletarian dictatorship should be preceded by a bourgeois democratic revolution. To carry out the first phase of the revolution, the
ICP program included the following points:

1. Overthrow French imperialism, feudalism, and the reactionary
Vietnamese capitalist class.
2. Make Indochina completely independent.
3. Establish a worker-peasant and soldier government.
4. Confiscate the banks and other enterprises belonging to the imperialists and put them under the control of the worker-peasant and
soldier government.
5. Confiscate the whole of the plantations and property belonging to
the imperialists and the Vietnamese reactionary capitalist class and dis-
tribute them to poor peasants.
6. Implement the eight-hour working day.
7. Abolish public loans and poll tax. Waive unjust taxes hitting the
poor people.
8. Bring back all freedoms to the masses.
9. Carry out universal education.
10. Implement equality between man and woman.[14]

The Central Committee was no sooner installed in Haiphong
than the party decided to transfer it to Saigon. In addition to 1,500
hard-core members, the illegal party had almost 100,000 affiliates in
trade and peasant unions.[15] As Paul Isoart, the penetrating French
student of Vietnamese affairs, points out:

The party had to form rapidly a solid revolutionary framework, canaliz-
ing the discontent with mandarinal abuses, the rising cost of living,
insufficient wages or increased taxes, extolling the sentiment for independence, the social idealism of the students, exploiting typhoons, floods,
droughts and poverty. Little by little, it set up its political-administrative
framework. The Central Committee or Tong Bo, installed first in Haiphong then in Saigon, issued directives to the local committees in Tonkin
(Bac Bo), Annam (Trung Bo), and Cochinchina (Nam Bo). The
country was divided into provinces, sectors, communes, and villages and
placed under the jurisdiction of committees. The element at the base, the
chi bo or cell, was composed of the workers of the same enterprise or the
inhabitants of the same street. This territorial organization was paralleled
by a professional and social organization grouping the workers' associations (Cong San), the women (Phu Nu), the youth (Thanh Nien), the
military (Binh Si), the peasants, the students, and the old people. Even
then, the party already made attempt to control the population through

these parallel hierarchies which were to become the strength of the Viet Minh. Doctrinal unity was ensured by strict discipline and errors were punished by death. Every member had a cover name. Catering to the innate love of the Vietnamese for the mystery of secret societies, a number of cells still resorted to the blood oath.[16]

Although Tran Phu was the Party Secretary General, Ho alone was in charge of the relations between the ICP and the other organizations of the Third International: the Far Eastern Bureau in Shanghai, the Secretariat of the Pan-Pacific Syndicated Confederation, the Communist parties of Indonesia, Malaya, and Siam of which he assumed control from March, 1930, to June, 1931, the French Communist party, and the Anti-Imperialist League created in Berlin in 1925. At its Ninth Plenary Session in April, 1931, the Central Executive Committee of the Third International recognized the ICP as a national section of the Comintern, gave it a monthly allowance of approximately $1,250, and brought it under the nominal control of the French Communist party.

The year 1930 was one of revolutionary upsurge in Indochina. As discussed previously, the *Viet Nam Quoc Dan Dang* (VNQDD) leaders, victims of unfavorable circumstances, had to carry out their rebellious scheme earlier than planned. With the exception of the successful mutiny of the rifle battalion in Yen Bay on February 9, the movement was a tragic fiasco, due to poor organization, lack of coordination, a last-minute change of plan, and the alertness of the French police. As a result of these uprisings, the VNQDD leadership was effectively eliminated and the party disappeared from the Vietnamese political scene for fifteen years. In the midst of this turbulence, the Communists played it safe, refraining from taking part in the hopeless rebellion although they had incited the people to revolt against the colonial administration. Three possible explanations have been suggested for this Communist aloofness: (*a*) the ICP did not feel itself strong enough to take part in the mutiny; (*b*) a severe repression of the nationalist uprisings would intensify the anti-French feeling among Vietnamese; (*c*) the elimination of the VNQDD by the French regime would clear the field of nationalist competition with the Communists.

Of these theories, the last two seemed to be quite plausible as they were the very ones Ho had used to justify his betrayal of the great nationalist Phan Boi Chau in Hong Kong in 1925. At any rate,

the disappearance of the Viet Nam Nationalist Party offered the ICP
an unexpected opportunity to accelerate its "patriotic" propaganda
and gain support from the aroused anti-French population.

A succession of strikes broke out in the rubber plantations at Phu
Rieng, Dau Tieng, Xa Cut, etc., in Cochinchina in February-March,
1930, and at the Nam Dinh weaving mill the following month,
affecting thousands of workers. Similarly, mass demonstrations
against the deteriorating economic conditions and unabated taxes
took place in various parts of the country. In North Annam, the
hotbed of rebels, thousands of angry peasants marched on administrative centers to present their grievances and beg the government
to help alleviate their plight. In the process, however, they burned
tax rolls and sacked public buildings. Most famous of the demonstrations was the march of 6,000 destitute peasants on the town of
Vinh, the capital of Ho's native province. Against these unarmed
people who came to request a reduction of their unusually heavy
taxes, the French Resident Governor used planes and bombs.[17]

This brutal repression of the peasants did nothing but intensify
the anger of the people in North Annam, which had been seething
with revolution. While realizing that the Nghe An rebellion was
bound to fail, the ICP nevertheless decided to assume the leadership
of the movement with a twofold objective: (*a*) to save it, if possible, and (*b*) to enable the Communists to have some practical
revolutionary experience. With the ICP active participation, the
peasant insurrection was instantaneously transformed into a revolution. Inspired by the success of the Chinese soviets in Kiangsi, the
ICP leaders decided to set up peasant soviets in several districts in
the province of Nghe An, which they called *Xo-viet Nghe An*, and
proceeded to put into practice its first agrarian reforms. Land was
taken away from landlords and divided among peasants, people's
courts were established and committees organized to run the *xo-
viet*, which displaced the regular French-controlled administration.
For several months, they maintained themselves surprisingly well.
Meanwhile, similar *xo-viet* sprung up in other parts of Northern
Annam which lasted until the spring of 1931. Parallel with the Nghe
An movement were the insurrections in Central Annam, specifically
in Quang Ngai, Pham Van Dong's native province, and in Ben Tre,
Tra Vinh, Vinh Long, Sadec, and Long Xuyen in Cochinchina. The
Southern uprisings, however, did not set up a revolutionary regime

like the *Xo-viet Nghe An*. In the face of such an unpardonable challenge to its rule, the enraged colonial administration became obsessed with one thought: revenge. The retaliation was both vigorous and brutal. French troops and aircraft indiscriminately rained bullets and bombs upon the rebellious villages. What did the revolution cost the Vietnamese? 10,000 dead, 50,000 imprisoned, and uncounted sufferings. As historian Joseph Buttinger remarks,

There is indeed no darker year in the entire period of French rule in Vietnam than 1931. Shocked Frenchmen have collected enough evidence to show that people were killed not in the heat of battle—there were no battles—but rather in a wild and strange excitement of the chase—the chase of human beings, who were hunted down and killed as animals are hunted down and killed for sport, by soldiers as drunk from many murders as much as from too much alcohol.[18]

By the end of 1931, when order was restored throughout the country, scores of Communist cadres had been securely put behind bars. Among the victims figured Tran Phu, the first Secretary General of the ICP, Truong Chinh, who held the same post from 1941 to 1956, Pham Van Dong and Vo Nguyen Giap, the present DRV Prime Minister and Minister of Defense, respectively.

In the meantime, Ho remained in Hong Kong in his capacity as Comintern representative. While Tran Phu was the nominal head of the party, it was Ho who directed its activities from his safe haven in the British crown colony. In spite of his attempt to disassociate himself from the ICP disastrous experiment in the years of 1930–31, the blame for this discomfiture should lay squarely on Ho's shoulders. In order perhaps to absolve himself, the shrewd revolutionary dispatched a letter to the Central Committee on April 30, 1931, in which he criticized his party's lack of realism, failure to pay adequate attention to the concrete situation in each locality, sectarianism in mass organizations, and insufficient concern for the policies of the Anti-Imperialist League, and emphasized:

All Party members, all Party cells must discuss the Central Committee's directions and resolutions. . . . This aims at raising the level of the Party members, ensuring that all directions and resolutions will be carried into effect, and unifying the thoughts and actions of the Party membership.[19]

Meanwhile, increasing Communist activities in Southeast Asia had put both the British and the French police on the alert. Late in the spring of 1930, the British authorities arrested two French agents of the Comintern, Joseph Ducroux and Hilaire Noulens. Among the papers found in their possession were letters and messages that revealed that Ho was in charge of the Southern Section of the Comintern Far Eastern Bureau. On June 5, 1931, Ho was arrested in Hong Kong. The French authorities immediately requested his extradition. The British, however, decided to exercise their jurisdiction over him. In the ensuing trial, Ho was found guilty of subversive activities and sentenced to six months in prison. The judgment was subsequently voided on condition that he be returned to Indochina, where the French tribunal in Vinh had sentenced him to death *in absentia*. Thereupon, the International Red Relief Association hired a lawyer, Frank Loseby, to challenge the Hong Kong court's decision. An appeal was made to the Privy Council in London, which subsequently reversed the judgment on the ground that Ho was a political refugee and, consequently, not subject to extradition. Upon his release, Ho left for Singapore, where he was again arrested and returned to Hong Kong. As a result of tuberculosis, he was admitted to a hospital instead of a prison. Shortly afterward, Ho suddenly vanished. It was then rumored, and even believed by the French Sûreté, that the professional agitator had died of tuberculosis in a Hong Kong jail. This rumor was also corroborated by two leading European Communist papers, the French *l'Humanité* and the British *Daily Worker*, and the Soviet press. Did Ho escape, or was he given freedom? British authorities, curiously, remained silent on the circumstances surrounding his disappearance. It has been believed that the calculating Comintern agent obtained his release by agreeing to work for the British Intelligence Service. In view of his past dealings, notably his delivery of Phan Boi Chau in 1925 and his betrayal of the "uncooperative" *Thanh Nien* members in the late 1920s to the French police, and his intelligence activities in behalf of the Kuomintang and the American Office of Strategic Services during World War II, one should not reject this theory as pure imagination.

In any case, Ho's whereabouts and activities following his disappearance from Hong Kong were shrouded in mystery. It seemed that he temporarily fell out of favor with the Kremlin and was recalled to Moscow for more training and indoctrination. The disastrous failure of the *Xo-viet Nghe An*[20] and other ICP-led uprisings in Indochina, which resulted in the imprisonment of top Communist cadres, the arrest of Ho himself, and the seizure of incriminating Comintern documents by the British authorities must have disturbed the Third International leaders considerably. And Ho was held responsible for these shortcomings. According to a North Vietnamese source,[21] Ho, after regaining his freedom early in 1932, left Hong Kong for Shanghai where he resumed his contact with the Chinese Communist party. From Shanghai he departed for Moscow and, in 1933, the dedicated Comintern agent once again became a student. This time, he attended the Lenin School, which trained high-ranking cadres for the Soviet Communist party. In February, 1935, when the ICP held its First Congress in Macao, Ho, the founder of the party, was curiously absent. The same source mentioned above simply stated that Ho's busy work in Moscow prevented him from attending the Congress. A possible explanation is that the Comintern leaders, still perturbed by Ho's failure in the Far East, did not want him to make contact with his comrades and disciples before he had sufficiently reassessed the situation and learned more about revolutionary tactics. As Ho had been the only link between the ICP and other Comintern organizations, his removal from Asia had the immediate effect of isolating the former from other Communist parties, particularly the Soviet Communist party, when it needed guidance and advice. Stalin's disapproval of Mao's unorthodox interpretation of Marxism-Leninism had led him to write off the Chinese Communist party and to neglect the ICP, which he apparently considered as a branch of the Chinese organization.

While Ho was on his way back to Moscow, the badly dislocated ICP began a rebuilding program in 1932. Their isolation from the Comintern did not seem to hurt the Vietnamese Communists very much. Through a small group of Chinese Communists and the *Thanh Nien* cadres in Siam, and through Vietnamese seamen who frequently called at the ports of Shanghai, Nanking, and Hong Kong, the ICP managed to maintain contact with the outside movement, notably with the Chinese Communist party. With the exception of those who had been sent to the guillotine or died in prison, many Communists arrested at the height of the terror of 1930–31 were pardoned or released. Far from dampening their spirit, their stay in jail proved to be quite beneficial. A generous supply of propaganda materials had been smuggled into prisons and secretly circulated among the political detainees, who, upon their release, became more convinced of the correctness of their cause and more determined to spread revolutionary ideas among the oppressed masses. In spite of a new and elaborate police network erected to prevent a revival of the Communist movement, the ICP recovered considerably faster than its members had expected.

It was further given a new impetus by the return in October, 1932, of Tran Van Giau, a graduate of the Stalin School. Giau immediately proceeded to revitalize the regional committee in Saigon, publish the *Co Do* (Red Flag) and the *Tap Chi Cong San* (Communist Review), and reorganize the Indochinese section of the Anti-Imperialist League. He concentrated upon the workers who soon banded together in cells or clandestine trade unions. Unlike Tonkin and Annam, which were protectorates, Cochinchina, as a colony, enjoyed a relatively liberal regime, which accorded significant freedom to the French-language press. Cleverly exploiting this liberty, one of the rare democratic rights recognized in Indochina, the Communists used the press to propagate their views. As the Third International had condemned the use of terror, the Vietnamese Communists now resorted to the legal methods of opposition. Instead of assassination, they resorted to persuasion; instead of swords, they used pens; instead of dividing the people, they tried to unite them in a common cause. Consequently, instead of dissipating his strength, the Stalinist Giau entered into collaboration with Ta Thu Thau, a Trotskyist who had returned from France early in 1932. Shortly after his arrival in Cochinchina, Thau had organized a group of adherents to the Fourth International, which was promptly disbanded by the French Sûreté. Undaunted, the Trotskyist leader regrouped his men in a new association set up allegedly to educate the workers.

In January, 1933, the first joint Stalinist-Trotskyist enterprise came into existence. With a view to avoiding official censorship imposed on Vietnamese publications, Tran Van Giau and Ta Thu Thau put out a French-language paper, *La Lutte* (Struggle), which rapidly made its influence felt in the Cochinchinese capital. In the summer of that year, with the active support of *La Lutte*, two Communist candidates, one Stalinist and one Trotskyist, were elected to the Saigon Municipal Council in spite of strong official disapproval.

Thus, the revival of the ICP after 1932 took place primarily in the South. Not until 1934 did the party begin slowly to pick up its pieces in the North, organizing rural friendly societies in Annam, and reemerging as the Indochinese Democratic Front in Tonkin. Contact between the dispersed members and the regional committees was soon restored. It was then decided that a Congress should be convened to reassess both the domestic and the international situations and revamp the party program. Subsequently, in February, 1935, without Ho, the ICP held its First Congress in Macao, China, where it reiterated its allegiance to the Comintern. The reorganized party transferred its Central Committee to Saigon and, in August, received recognition from the Third International.

Meanwhile, world events took an unusual turn. In the face of the mounting pressure from imperialist Japan, the growing power of Nazi Germany, and the increasing strength of the anti-Comintern coalition, the Soviet Union decided on rapprochement with the Western democracies. Fascism had replaced capitalism as the archenemy of Soviet socialism. At its Seventh World Congress in August, 1935, the Comintern issued new directives ordering all Communist parties to join with the non-Communist governments in the common struggle against fascism. This sharp reversal of the Comintern policy was too bitter a pill for the ICP to swallow, and caused considerable objection and anguish within its ranks. Not only were Vietnamese Communists told to put aside their opposition to French rule and their campaign for democratic rights, they were also ordered to collaborate with the colonialists in the struggle against the Axis powers. Such a position would certainly be interpreted by the Vietnamese population as a betrayal on the part of the ICP, whose main appeal lay in its campaign for national independence. In its view, the rising power of Germany and Japan, instead of constituting a threat to Indochina, offered it an excellent opportunity to destroy French rule in Asia. After heated debates and considerable soul-searching, and under the pressure of other Communist organizations, notably the French Communist party headed by Maurice Thorez, who had been directed by Stalin to

keep a watchful eye on the Vietnamese Communist movement since
Ho's departure from Asia, the ICP grudgingly complied with the
Third International orders. At its meetings in May, 1936, the Central Committee proceeded with the establishment of a united front
for peace and against fascism, which embraced all the Indochinese
peoples, classes, and political parties.

In the meantime, in June, 1936, the Popular Front government,
based on an antifascist coalition of the Communist, Left, and Center parties, came to power in France. Announcing reforms for the
colonies, the new government promised to treat the peasants and
workers in the French overseas possessions on the same basis as
their counterparts in France, to "place them all on a plane of moral
equality, social justice and human brotherhood," to deny none of its
"republican or socialist convictions," and to take its "role of civilizer
and emancipator seriously."[22] As a gesture of good will, Paris replaced the hated Governor General René Robin with Jule Brevié, a
liberal and honest man. Upon assuming his office, the new governor
granted amnesty to political prisoners and extended certain liberties
of the press and assembly to the local people. Among the persons
released from the Poulo Condore and Son La prisons were Pham
Van Dong, Dang Xuan Khu, alias Truong Chinh, and Ha Ba Cang,
alias Hoang Quoc Viet, the future President of the trade unions in
the DRV. It was these top cadres who, profiting by the relatively
tolerant policy of the Brevié administration, rebuilt their illegal
organization in Annam and in Tonkin. With the severe repression of
1930–31 still vivid in its mind, the ICP took extreme measures to
protect its members. A number of able and experienced cadres were
smuggled out to China, while others camouflaged their illegal activities by cooperating with the moderate nationalist organizations
under the cover of the Indochinese Democratic Front, or working
in the Indochinese Sections of the French Socialist Party and the
League of Human Rights. The Front, which included both Vietnamese and progressive Frenchmen residing in the colony, was ably
led by two dedicated militants, Pham Van Dong and Vo Ngyen
Giap. In spite of the existing system of limited suffrage, it succeeded in having a number of its members elected to the Hanoi
Municipal Council and to the Chamber of Representatives in Hanoi
and Hue.

Meanwhile, fully aware of the foreign Communist disapproval of the Comintern reversed position vis-à-vis the imperialist powers and, particularly, of the smoldering opposition within the ICP ranks to such a *volte-face*, and apparently foreseeing new opportunities to open to the Communist movement in Asia, Moscow again dispatched its reliable and reeducated agent back to the Far East. In 1936, Ho, consequently, returned to China, where he closely followed the political development in his homeland, attempting to guide the movement he had launched. Unable to make the trip himself, Ho sent Le Hong Phong, an alternate member of the Executive Committee of the Communist International, back to Vietnam to give direct leadership to the ICP. From his safe haven in China, the experienced revolutionary regularly dispatched directives to the ICP Central Committee and sent articles to several papers published by the Communist party and the Democratic Front. As Ho pointed out in his report to the Communist International in July, 1939, the ICP, under his guidance, strictly adhered to the Moscow line, and even ceased to insist on national independence:

1. For the time being, the Party cannot put forth too high a demand (national independence, parliament, etc.). To do so is to enter the Japanese fascists' scheme. It should only claim for democratic rights, freedom of organization, freedom of assembly, freedom of press and freedom of speech, general amnesty for all political detainees, and struggle for the legalization of the Party.

2. To reach this goal, the Party must strive to organize a broad Democratic National Front. This Front does not embrace only Indochinese people but also progressive French residing in Indochina, not only toiling people but also the national bourgeoisie.

3. The Party must assume a wise, flexible attitude with the bourgeoisie, strive to draw it into the Front, win over the elements that can be won over and neutralize those which can be neutralized. We must by all means avoid leaving them outside the Front, lest they should fall into the hands of the enemy of the revolution and increase the strength of the reactionaries.

4. There cannot be any alliance with or any concession to the Trotskyite group.[23] We must do everything possible to lay bare their faces as henchmen of the fascists and annihilate them politically.

5. To increase and consolidate its forces, to widen its influence, and to work effectively, the Indochinese Democratic Front must keep close contact with the French Popular Front because the latter also struggles for freedom, democracy, and can give us great help.

6. The Party cannot demand that the Front recognize its leadership. It must instead show itself as the organ which makes the greatest sacrifices, the most active and loyal organ. It is only through daily struggle and work that the masses of the people acknowledge and correct policies and leading capacity of the Party and that it can win the leading position.

7. To be able to carry out this task, the Party must uncompromisingly fight sectarianism and narrow-mindedness and organize systematic study of Marxism-Leninism in order to raise the cultural and political level of the Party members and help the non-Party cadres raise their level. We must maintain close contact with the French Communist Party.[24]

It is interesting to note that the position taken by the ICP within the Democratic Front was the very same adopted by the Communists within the Viet Minh movement.

On September 20, 1936, a very important event took place in Vietnam. The Indochinese Congress, attended by over a thousand delegates from all political groupings, conservative, moderate, Communist, was convened in the imperial city of Hue. Among the committees selected on this occasion was one charged with the task of drawing up a bill of demands to be presented to the Commission of Inquiry, which had been dispatched by the Léon Blum government to study the situation in Indochina with a view to recommending improvements. Upon its arrival, the Commission, headed by Justin Godart, was welcomed with a succession of strikes in the Saigon-Cholon area in Cochinchina, in the Hongay and Dong Trieu coal mines, and in the Nam Dinh weaving mills in Tonkin. The strikers demanded wage increase, the abolition of corporal punishments, freedom to organize trade unions, etc. In January, 1937, these workers' activities eventually led to the passage of a labor law that, among other things, prohibited the employment of children under ten years of age and the assignment of women and children under eighteen to evening work, and provided for minimum wage, eight-hour day, and paid vacation. The new legislation, however, did not satisfy the workers, who were constantly aroused by the Communist agitators, who, in turn, had other motives in mind.

Meanwhile, both the French Socialist and Communist parties, then members of the coalition government, had abandoned their earlier antiimperialist position and shared the popular feeling that Indochina might fall into the Japanese hands. Thereupon, the Socialist Minister of Colonies, Marius Moutet, emphasizing the official policy of keeping Indochina French, directed the colonial administration to "maintain public order by all legitimate and legal means, even by prosecution of those who attempt to make trouble, if this should prove necessary," and see to it that "French order must reign in Indochina as elsewhere."[25] The French Communist party, on its part, sent a delegation to Vietnam to remind the ICP of the new Comintern decision regarding the necessity of joining forces with the capitalists to thwart the fascist scheme of world conquest, and to urge the Vietnamese comrades to suspend temporarily their illegal activities. Such was the liberalism of the French Popular Front government! The ICP acquiesced only halfway in the French Communist request. With a view to giving their movement a cloak of legitimacy, the Vietnamese organized themselves into two groups: an overt section engaged in legal operations, and a clandestine section entrusted with the task of erecting a network of secret cells. At the same time, the Stalinists cooperated with the Trotskyists and other revolutionary elements in various legal nationalist front organizations.

The Stalinist-Trotskyist collaboration, however, soon ran into difficulty. In opposition to the Stalinist shift in emphasis, the Trotskyists continued to underline the importance of the struggle against imperialism, condemning both the French and the Indochinese Fronts. Ta Thu Thau vehemently criticized the ICP program of democratic reforms, rejecting the contention that Japan should be considered as the main threat to Indochina, and labelling the Stalinists "allies of the bourgeoisie" and "defenders of democracy." Thau also accused the ICP of placing the interests of the French and Soviet Communist parties above those of the Indochinese people. Plagued by mutual distrust and tactical differences, and determined to outdo each other in illegal maneuvers, the Stalinist-Trotskyist coalition was precariously maintained until the Saigon municipal elections of 1937, in which Thau and the Stalinists Duong Bach Mai and Nguyen Van Tao were elected. After their last meeting on July 14, 1937, Tran Van Giau and Ta Thu Thau parted company.

With *La Lutte* remaining under his control, the Trotskyist leader continued his attack on the Popular Front. After publishing an article in which he accused the Paris government of betraying the socialist cause, Thau was given a two-year prison sentence, obvi-

ously with the approval of the Socialist Minister of Colonies, Marius
Moutet. The imprisonment of their leader did not soften the Trotskyists, who went on to emphasize class struggle and the fight against
Western capitalism. In view of their effective propaganda and the
prestige of their dedicated leader Ta Thu Thau, whose adamant
opposition to colonialism was widely known, the Trotskyists
wielded considerable influence among the workers and nationalist
elements in Cochinchina. Shortly after his release, Thau and two of
his lieutenants, Tran Van Thach and Pham Van Hum, won an impressive victory in the April 30, 1939, elections for the Colonial
Council in Saigon, winning 80 per cent of the votes, and thus handsomely defeating their Stalinist and moderate opponents. Following
this smarting defeat, the Stalinists split, with Duong Bach Mai remaining the leader of the official Communist party and Nguyen
Van Tao forming his own faction.

Meanwhile, war broke out in Europe in the autumn of 1939. And
the Stalin-Hitler pact, another Soviet diplomatic somersault which
dizzied all foreign Communists, drastically altered the situation in
both France and Indochina. In agreement with the pact, Moscow
issued new directives ordering the international Communist movement to oppose the West's anti-Hitler policy. Subsequently, on September 26, 1939, the Paris government outlawed the French Communist party, which had opposed the war against Germany. Similar
action was simultaneously taken by the colonial administration
against the Indochinese Communists. Some 800 Stalinists and Trotskyists were arrested and the rest driven underground. Among the
victims were Ta Thu Thau, Duong Bach Mai, Nguyen Van Tao,
and Le Hong Phong, who, together with his wife, was executed in
1942. While the repression virtually eliminated the Trotskyists, it
did not seriously affect the Stalinists, whose tightly knit clandestine
organization remained intact. As a precautionary measure, however,
the ICP transferred its Central Committee back to China. Many top
cadres, including Pham Van Dong, Vo Nguyen Giap, and Truong
Chinh, also hurriedly left the country and arrived in Kuangsi by the
end of the year. In a plenary session held from November 6 to 8,
1939, the ICP, adopting an "antiwar" position consonant with the
Comintern line, replaced the old Indochinese Democratic Front
with the United Front of Anti-Imperialist Indochinese Peoples. With
the support of the Soviet Union, "the fortress of world revolution,"

the new organization would "overthrow French imperialism and the indigenous feudalists."[26] Demonstrations were consequently organized to oppose the sending of Indochinese troops abroad, requisitions, tax increase, etc., all aiming at sapping the war effort.

Following France's humiliating defeat by Germany in June, 1940, the ICP intensified its subversive activities against the colonial regime, riding the nationalist wave that had swept the country. Ho was in Kunning when the Decoux regime[27] entered into alliance with the Japanese authorities in Indochina. It was this development that prompted the veteran Communist to issue a declaration denouncing the collusion of French colonialism with Japanese expansionism, and calling on Vietnamese to take arms against the new alliance. Copies of the declaration were smuggled into Vietnam where they found a very receptive and very agitated population. Impotent and helpless, the Decoux administration docilely governed Indochina on behalf of the Japanese, who, undisturbed by administrative problems, freely made use of the country's resources, military installations, and means of communication.

The Franco-German armistice of June, 1940, raised false hopes among Vietnamese nationalists and led the ICP cadres to think that their time had come. With a view to establishing a republican government which would rally to the cause of the Chinese Resistance, the Soviet Union, and World Revolution, Ho made preparations for an armed uprising. On September 24, as Japanese troops landed in the port city of Haiphong, a successful armed insurrection against the French occurred in Bac Son, where guerilla tactics were used. According to Truong Chinh, the Bac Son rebellion gave birth to the first guerilla unit led by the ICP.[28] This success, in addition to the pressure from the pro-Japanese government of Thailand and the Communists' inflated estimate of their own strength, caused the Committee of Cochinchina to undertake an armed uprising of its own on November 22, 1940. Originating in the Plaine des Joncs, the Communist-led movement rapidly spread to the Western provinces. A number of districts, such as My Tho and Bac Lieu, were virtually removed from French control. For the first time, the gold-starred red flag, which was to become the official flag of the DRV, appeared in Cao Lanh. The colonial administration struck back, swiftly, decisively, and ferociously. Troops and aircraft were used against the ill-equipped insurgents. Bombs and other explosives

erased entire towns. In two weeks, the rebellion was crushed. Six
thousand persons were arrested. All the prisons in Cochinchina
were filled. Once again, the Communists were put on the run. With
a view to absolving himself from the responsibility for misreading
the situation, which had resulted in such a catastrophic failure, Ho,
through the ICP Central Committee headquartered in southern
China, put the blame on the Cochinchinese Committee. It was explained that the prudent Ho had opposed armed insurrection at
that time. His order, however, allegedly came too late.[29]

3 ☆ The Architect of a Communist Revolution

~~~~~~~~~~~~~~~~~~~~~~~~~~~~~~~~~~~

DURING HIS LAST sojourn in China and prior to his return to Vietnam, the shrewd Comintern agent, fully aware of the feeling of the Vietnamese nationalists and, particularly, of the bourgeois whose sympathy he needed to cultivate, strictly adhered to the line he had prescribed for the *Thanh Nien* in Canton in 1925, i.e., to spread Marxist ideology under the cover of nationalism. Whether he lived among his wildest admirers or whether he worked in the midst of his alert persecutors, Ho always took great care to conceal his identity. Thus, in 1936, after reaching China, Ho journeyed to the border province of Yunnan where, as comrade Tran, he was lodged by the barber Hoang Quang Binh who had a shop in the little town of Tsungshan. Always dressed in a faded khaki outfit, this revolutionary comrade, looking as gentle as a peasant of ancient times, did not attract much attention from Binh, who had idolized the rebellious Nguyen Ai Quoc. But how could the barber suspect anything about this kindly old man who, besides conducting courses in politics and revolution, advised him to wash his smock frock more often and keep it clean in order to attract more customers, to do everything to perfection, to keep his little house neat, to be considerate toward his wife, and, particularly, to stop beating her?

In the beginning, no one paid much attention to the good old comrade who, after every meal, carefully checked the waist belt of the barber's gluttonous little boy to make sure that it had not be-

come too tight for him, and loosened it if necessary. Gradually,
however, his commonsense advice and attentive gestures inspired
trust, and comrade Tran became "Uncle"[1] Tran. Ho thus made good
use of his innate virtues and acting talent to generate trust and
mislead many people he came into contact with. How could any
one imagine that the simple and gentle exterior of Uncle Tran
concealed one of the most ruthless minds in the service of international Communism? Years later, when hearing Ho's voice on radio,
a voice distinguished by the heavy Nghe Anese accent which had
not changed in spite of the revolutionary's prolonged exile abroad,
the barber of Tsungshan suddenly realized who the old comrade he
had lodged was. Hoang Quang Binh, however, was not the only one
who was surprised by such a discovery.

Return to Vietnam

After the mass arrests of Vietnamese Communists by the brutally
zealous French Sûreté, Pham Van Dong and Vo Nguyen Giap fled
to China where, in May, 1940, they joined Ho. It was Giap's first
encounter with the man whose writings he had avidly read, and
whose exploits he had greatly admired. During their stay in China,
both Dong and Giap were introduced to Mao Tse-tung's Eighth
Route Army. The future victor of Dienbienphu also spent some
time in Yenan, then the capital of Communist China, where he
studied guerilla tactics.

Meanwhile, France collapsed before the might of Hitler's troops.
And in Indochina, Admiral Decoux signed a treaty of alliance with
Japan. From Kunming, Ho issued a tract denouncing the Franco-
Japanese collusion and calling on Vietnamese to rise up to liberate
their fatherland. It was Ho's first appeal to his people. With a view
to coordinating the ICP activities and discussing his impending return to Vietnam, Ho called a meeting of his party's members then
working in China. During one of the debates, the Communist
leader brought up the question of armed uprising. Foremost in
everyone's mind was the problem of military supplies. To his worried comrades Ho simply said: "Capture enemy arms to kill the
enemy." This advice was to be faithfully followed by the Viet Minh

troops, who defeated the French Expeditionary Corps with the latter's own arms.

Eluding both the Kuomintang and the Japanese police, which maintained a vigilant surveillance in the southern provinces of China, the Vietnamese partisans gradually moved closer to the Indochinese frontier. By the end of November, 1940, the first group arrived in Tsing Tsi, a small Chinese village in the border area of Kwangsi province, located some 60 miles north of Cao Bang. As the year drew to a close, the last group were finally united with their comrades. Among the newcomers who travelled on a crowded boat, there was a Chinese journalist who apparently spoke only French in addition to his native language. Every time he wanted to communicate with his Vietnamese companions, he had to rely on a certain Lam Boi Khiet, who served as interpreter. Only three persons on the boat knew the identity of the mysterious Chinese reporter who, perhaps because of the language barrier, did not seem to be interested in the conversation going on among the Vietnamese. Only when a young man inadvertently dropped a lit cigarette end on his clothes did the journalist betray himself. Suddenly forgetting who he was supposed to be, the goateed "Chinese," in flawless Vietnamese, warned his young companion to be more careful. Until then, the crowd on the boat had not been aware that their "Chinese" fellow traveller also spoke Vietnamese. But why should he not have known their language? He was none other than Nguyen Ai Quoc, the future Ho Chi Minh. And Lam Boi Khiet was none other than Pham Van Dong, the DRV Prime Minister-to-be.

The group, which included Ho, Dong, and Giap, arrived in Cao Bang in February, 1941. It was Ho's first visit to Vietnam in nearly three decades. Things had not changed much since he left. The country was still ruled over by foreigners. It still remained unsafe for revolutionaries. Ho finally found a secure hideout in the grottoes of Pac Bo, a remote jungle village in the border province of Cao Bang, from which he could vanish into China in case of pursuit by the Japanese police or the French Sûreté. It was here that the trio, Ho, Dong, and Giap, established their headquarters, while other cadres went to their assigned areas throughout the country to organize the resistance movement.

The first task Ho set up for his men was to organize a political army of propagandists and agitators, which would be enlarged as rapidly as possible. The veteran Communist firmly believed that when the masses were sufficiently aroused and became conscious of their power, they would voluntarily respond to a call to arms against the French colonialists and the Japanese expansionists. Ho thus put into practice one of the basic lessons he had learned in the Soviet Union and China: A revolutionary army could not operate successfully without mass participation and support; it needed the people for recruits, supplies, information, and protection. It was Mao Tse-tung who had taught Ho that "the people are the sea and the guerilla is the fish." The Vietnamese Communist remembered his lessons very well, indeed.

Founder of the Viet Minh League

After a thorough analysis of both the national and the international situations, Ho proceeded to call a meeting of Vietnamese Communist cadres. Thus, the Eighth Plenum of the ICP Central Committee, the most important meeting that outlined the course of the resistance war, was held in the Pac Bo grottoes[2] from May 10 to 19, 1941. Ho, "who then represented the Communist International, was in the chair."[3] Present at the meeting were members of the ICP Central Committee, and delegates from various mass organizations[4] and several nationalist groupings. The decisions adopted on the closing day of this historic session, May 19, which by coincidence or by design happened to be Ho's birthday, "were strictly implemented by the entire Party membership and led to the victory of the August 1945 Revolution."[5]

While convinced of the "inevitable" victory of the Soviet Union and her allies over the fascist aggressors, of the developing contradictions between the Japanese and the French in Indochina, and of the growing political consciousness of the local people then living under the double oppression of the foreigners, the party was nevertheless apprehensive that influential elements of the nationalist bourgeoisie would rally to the Japanese, who had encouraged the Vietnamese to oppose the French, and take the masses along with them. In order to forestall such an eventuality, to take advantage of the opportune situation, "one that would happen only once in a thousand years,"[6] and to eventually seize power, the ICP had to act in a hurry. Consequently, the class struggle theme was temporarily shelved in favor of that of national liberation. The mass organizations, which had been founded by the Communists, immediately assumed the new patriotic name of National Salvation Associations. This superficial metamorphosis of the ICP-controlled organizations achieved the desired effect of misleading the masses, whose desire for independence had been feverishly aroused. With a view to bringing all resistance elements under his control, winning power, then eliminating the nationalist competitors and creating a Communist state, Ho decided to form a united front whose announced program would be to coordinate all nationalist activities, drive out the French and Japanese fascists, regain national independence, and build a Democratic Republic of Vietnam. Thus was founded the Viet Nam Doc Lap Dong Minh Hoi, or Vietnam Independence League, popularly known thereafter as the Viet Minh.[7] While the League included many nationalist elements, the bulk of its membership consisted of ICP veterans. Among its leaders figured such seasoned Stalinist militants as Pham Van Dong, Vo Nguyen Giap, Truong Chinh, Ho Tung Mau, and Ha Ba Cang, in addition to Ho himself. The founding of the Viet Minh was the culmination of Ho's personal efforts. He had patiently approached the leaders of various non-Marxist groupings and convinced them of the need for a broad union against the French and the Japanese.

At the close of the Eighth Plenum of the ICP Central Committee, Ho drafted a proclamation to the Vietnamese people, which was practically an appeal to arms. In order not to reveal Ho's whereabouts and the location of the Viet Minh headquarters, the address was broadcast from the Chinese town of Liaochu eighteen days later, on June 6, 1941. In this highly emotional *Letter from Abroad*, Ho summoned his compatriots to action, appealing to all Vietnamese, elders, prominent personalities, intellectuals, peasants, workers, traders, and soldiers throughout the country to "rise up quickly to organize the Association for National Salvation to fight the French and the Japanese." Abundant reference was made to the glorious past of Vietnam, to the stubborn resistance spirit of "the sons and daughters of Lac Hong"[8] which had permeated through the centuries, to such national heroes as Tran Hung Dao, who, in the thirteenth century, had led a popular army that defeated the Mon-

golian invaders, to such recent revolutionary leaders as Phan Dinh
Phung, Hoang Hoa Tham, and Luong Ngoc Quyen, to the admirable
feats of other patriots in Thai Nguyen, Yen Bay, and Nghe-Tinh.
The uprisings in the South and at Do Luong, said Ho, had "testified
to the determination of our compatriots to shed their blood as their
glorious predecessors did, heroically to annihilate the enemy."
These independence movements failed, explained Ho, not because
the French invaders were strong, but because the situation was not
ripe and the Vietnamese were not united. The opportunity for national liberation, however, had come. France had been defeated by
Germany. The Japanese, bogged down in China and hamstrung by
the British and American forces, were not able to use all their troops
to contend with a united and single-minded people. Therefore, Ho
continued:

Rich people, soldiers, workers, peasants, intellectuals, employees,
traders, youth, and women who warmly love your country! At the
present time national liberation is the most important problem. Let us
unite together! As one in mind and strength we shall overthrow the
Japanese and French and their jackals in order to save people from the
situation between boiling water and burning heat.

Dear compatriots!

National salvation is the common cause to the whole of our people.
Every Vietnamese must take part in it. He who has money will contribute his money, he who has strength will contribute his strength, he
who has talent will contribute his talent. I pledge to use all my modest
abilities to follow you, and am ready for the last sacrifice.

Revolutionary fighters!

The hour has struck! Raise aloft the insurrectionary banner and guide
the people throughout the country to overthrow the Japanese and
French! The sacred call of the Fatherland is resounding in your ears; the
blood of our heroic predecessors who sacrificed their lives is stirring in
your hearts! The fighting spirit of the people is displayed everywhere
before you! Let us rise up quickly! Unite with each other, unify your
action to overthrow the Japanese and the French.

Victory to Vietnam's Revolution!

Victory to the World's Revolution![9]

This emotional and eloquent appeal, which reminded Vietnamese
of their present misery and glorious past, inevitably found a lasting
echo in their hearts.

Unlike other nationalist movements, whose only professed objective was national independence, the Viet Minh offered a particularly concrete program incorporating the following points:

1. Establishment of a democratic republic with universal suffrage
2. Extension of full citizenship rights to the ethnic minorities
3. Recognition of all basic liberties
4. Equality of man and woman
5. Abolition of all old taxes
6. Compulsory and free education
7. A social security system
8. Agrarian reforms
9. Respect of individual property.

In view of the soundness of this program, which reflected the basic wishes of all Vietnamese, many a nationalist found it difficult to oppose. Convinced, however, that the League was merely a Communist attempt to grasp power, scores of non-Marxist leaders refused to join the united front and fought it from the beginning. As historian Buttinger aptly points out, Ho, realizing that he could not deceive the leadership of other nationalist parties, did not attempt to attract them but their followers to the Viet Minh, and thus tried to maneuver them politically into cooperating with the ICP.[10]

Immediately after its founding, the League organized guerilla units and made preparations for a general armed insurrection. The first guerilla bands, however, as we have seen, were soon transformed into a political army of propagandists and agitators. While his associates carried on their activites in various parts of the country, Ho remained in Pac Bo, dividing his time between training cadres and pounding at his rusty typewriter. He translated into Vietnamese such Russian and Chinese works as the *History of the Communist Party of the Soviet Union* and Sun Tzu's *Art of War*, wrote *Guerilla Warfare, Experiences of Chinese Guerillas, Experiences of French Guerillas*, and edited a journal, *Viet Nam Doc Lap*, or Independent Vietnam.

The founding of the united front should not be considered as one of Ho's ingenious ideas. The Comintern had issued a new directive ordering all foreign Communist parties to attempt to take over the leadership of their respective national movement against fascism and to include in it as many nationalist and social organizations as possible. It was a revival of the Indochinese Democratic Front, an alliance of all parties under Communist control. The conditions in Vietnam following the fall of metropolitan France and the signing of the Franco-Japanese treaty regarding Indochina were particularly suited to this strategy. While a few non-Communist names figured on the list of Viet Minh leaders, Ho himself was the Secretary General and thus maintained firm control of the organization.

Ho's triumph derived partly from the extremely favorable circumstances under which he operated, partly from his personal qualities: patience, dedication, and ruthlessness. Like Ho, most nationalist leaders realized that independence could be won only by a united front embracing all anti-French elements. Unlike Ho, however, the nationalist leaders lacked his ruthlessness, his fanatic devotion to a cause, his revolutionary experience acquired abroad, and a well organized apparatus such as the ICP. In the ensuing struggle for power and influence, Ho naturally emerged as the winner.

The Viet Minh divided the country into three sections or *Bo*: Bac Bo (Tonkin), Trung Bo (Annam), and Nam Bo (Cochinchina), each controlled by a committee. At the top of the Viet Minh structure was a Central Committee, of which Ho was consistently elected Secretary General from May, 1941, to August, 1945. Very rapidly, in spite of a tight network erected by the French Sûreté, the Central Committee established contact with the secret cells throughout the country. A series of uprisings followed. On November 11, 1941, members of the Indochinese Guard revolted against their French commanders and seized the Do Luong (North Annam) garrison. Their leader, Sergeant Cung, however, was killed a few days later during his march on the provincial capital of Vinh. Other revolts broke out in Tourane (Central Annam) and in Saigon, all allegedly fomented by Ho's organization. Meanwhile, the Viet Minh concentrated most of their activities in the northern regions of Tonkin close to the Chinese border. Protected by thick and nearly impenetrable woods, and endowed with numerous grottoes, the province of Cao Bang offered the Viet Minh an ideal haven from which they could practically vanish into China. Its population consisted primarily of Tho, mountaineers whose rugged independence and rebellious spirit were widely known. Among these tribal people, the Viet Minh program, which advocated full citizenship rights for the ethnic minorities, found a very receptive ear. Since the fall of France in June, 1940, these highlanders, aroused by Vietnamese agitators, had been challenging the French authorities with impunity. Of the armed bands that exercised effective control over the area, the most important group was led by a very capable thirty-two-year-old Tho, Chu Van Tan, the man destined to become the Defense Minister in the first Ho Chi Minh cabinet. With his assistance, Vo Nguyen Giap, a former school teacher, trained the first units of his Liberation Army. For four years, the man who was to humiliate the French Expeditionary Corps at Dienbienphu infatigably worked among the Tho and other tribesmen whose confidence he rapidly won, trained guerilla units, and set up an effective intelligence network.

Relations with the Allies

While Ho took in hand the direct leadership of his party and of the Communist-controlled independence movement, his cadres in China engaged in a feverish propaganda among the Vietnamese émigrés in Kwangsi and Yunnan, attempting to rally them to the Viet Minh cause. Increasingly, however, the Marxist tone of their propaganda, which appealed to both Vietnamese and Chinese, worried the Kuomintang authorities who decided to clamp down on them.

Meanwhile, in the face of powerful Japanese forces and of still redoubtable French troops, the practical Ho became fully aware that his liberation movement needed considerable outside military aid. Since the Viet Minh had professed to fight both the French and the Japanese, since they alone could provide the Chinese with invaluable information on the Japanese troops' maneuvers in Indochina, and since Chungking was anxious to play a vital role in Vietnam after the war, Ho naturally expected that his request for military assistance from the Kuomintang would not be acted upon unfavorably. In view of the delicate nature of such a negotiation, which required a man with considerable experience, a man who knew China and her leaders reasonably well, Ho decided to undertake the responsibility himself. Besides enlisting the Kuomintang support, the Viet Minh leader also hoped to convince the Vietnamese nationalists still living in China of the need for a broad union. Thus, on a rainy day in August, 1942, Ho set out on another journey to China. As cautious as ever, the seasoned revolutionary did not want to take any chance with either the Japanese police or the French Sûreté. Disguised as a poor blind highlander of Nung nationality, Ho, groping his way with a stick, was guided toward the border by another Nung. Upon reaching the frontier, Ho was picked up by a Chinese comrade. Again he underwent another metamorphosis. The poor blind Nung was transformed into a Chinese journalist equipped with forged credentials. This time, however, in spite of his clever disguise, Ho did not get very far. While Ho's identification papers were judged to be in order, his Chinese comrade's were not. Consequently, both were detained by the local police. Shortly afterwards, Ho decided to reveal his true identity and admitted that he was the Viet Minh leader who had come to China with the express purpose of offering the Kuomintang his organization's intelligence service in exchange for Chinese military aid.

Contrary to Ho's expectation, the Kuomintang, which had broken with the Communists and looked with disfavor upon the Viet Minh activities in both China and Vietnam, coldly rejected his proposal. Worse still, on August 28, 1942, General Chiang Fa-ku'ei, the military governor of Kwangsi, ordered the ICP leader to be imprisoned on the charge that he was a French spy! Very rapidly, the Viet Minh cadres in Tonkin learned of their mentor's misfortune. No sooner had they heard of Ho's arrest and imprisonment than another paralyzing news reached them: Ho had died in a Kuomintang jail! For several months, Ho's presumed death had been accepted as a reality until one day his comrades received a newspaper mailed from China which contained, in its margin, a short but optimistic poem in the old revolutionary's own handwriting. A vigorous campaign launched by the ICP for the release of the "old anti-fascist militant" resulted in a more lenient treatment for him. Removed from the revoltingly primitive Chinese jail, Ho was temporarily kept under house arrest then moved to various prisons in Liuchow and Kweilin. "It was at Kweilin that my teeth began to fall out," said Ho jokingly later to an American reporter. "I looked at myself once and tried never to look again. I was skin on bones, and covered with rotten sores. I guess I was pretty sick."[11] During this year-long confinement, the revolutionary turned poet-philosopher, in elegant classical Chinese, put his ideas into short poems or, as he said, "using my tears for ink, I turn my thoughts into verses."

Looking at the leg irons which securely locked the prisoners to the floor at night, both the poet and the philosopher in Ho spoke out with feeling:

With hungry mouth open like a wicked monster,
Each night the irons devour the legs of people:
The jaws grip the right leg of every prisoner:
Only the left is free to bend and stretch.

And, alluding to himself who, as a professional agitator constantly pursued by the police, had not felt safe at any place except in jail:

Yet there is one thing stranger in this world:
People rush in to place their legs in irons.
Once they are shackled, they can sleep in peace.
Otherwise, they would have no place to lay their heads.[12]

As he meditated on his own fate, the old revolutionary, convinced of the correctness of his cause and confident of his abilities, could not help feeling optimistic about the future. Just as Marx maintained that the exploited masses in a capitalist society were not without hope for they were destined to replace the owning class in a new historical synthesis, Ho strongly believed that misfortune tested men and that the prisoners of today would be the rulers of tomorrow:

People who come out of prison can build up the country.
Misfortune is a test of people's fidelity.
Those who protest at injustice are people of true merit.
When the prison doors are opened, the real dragon will fly out.[13]

Never a dreamer, he nevertheless indulged occasionally in sentimental nostalgia:

My heart travels a thousand li toward my native land.
My dream intertwines with sadness like a skein of a thousand threads . . .
Using my tears for ink, I turn my thoughts into verses.[14]

or

The clouds embrace the peaks, the peaks embrace the clouds,
The river below shines like a mirror, spotless and clean.
On the crest of the Western Mountains, my heart stirs as I wonder
Looking toward the Southern sky and dreaming of old friends.[15]

He was primarily a revolutionary teacher. While indicting the ways of the world:

Having climbed over steep mountains and high peaks,
How could I expect on the plains to meet greater danger?
In the mountains, I met the tiger and came out unscathed.
On the plains, I encountered men, and was thrown into prison.[16]

the pragmatic militant nevertheless expressed sobering thoughts:

Coldness to one, and warmth toward the other:
That is the way of the world, as from time immemorial
The waters flow down to the sea.[17]

In his poems as in his other writings, Ho revealed himself to be a practical revolutionary, not a poet, although he sometimes versified with feeling. During his confinement, it was apparently safer for him to put down his thoughts in short, inoffensive poems than to write long political tracts.

In spite of his long stay in Chinese jails, Ho did not seem to have any bitter memories of the unhappy experience. With casual humor he compared the treatment given him as a prisoner with the honor accorded him as head of state. "How funny life is," said he. "When I was in prison in China, I was let out for fifteen minutes in the morning and fifteen minutes in the evening for exercise. And while I took my exercise in the yard, there were always two armed guards standing right over me with their guns. Now I'm president of the Viet Nam Republic, and whenever I leave this place there are two armed guards right over me, with their guns."[18]

While Ho was languishing in jail, China took measures to promote her own interest. Mindful of her traditional suzerainty over the neighboring states in general and over Vietnam in particular, China firmly believed that she had a very important role to play in Indochina. With Japan's defeat in sight and convinced of American support, Chungking had entertained no doubt about its ability to eliminate the French and set up an independent Vietnamese state, which would drift into China's sphere of influence. Certain developments, however, suddenly clouded the picture. On the one hand, the Communist-controlled Viet Minh became bolder and bolder and their propaganda more and more aggressive and successful. On the other, the Japanese authorities began to establish contact with Vietnamese nationalists and arouse the latter's traditional distrust of China. With a view to keeping a trump card in Indochinese affairs and setting up a counterweight to both the Communist-controlled and the pro-Japanese independence movements, General Chiang Fa-ku'ei, at the instigation of Nguyen Hai Than, an old VNQDD leader and protégé of the Kuomintang, proceeded to organize the Vietnamese nationalists in China. There were in Yunnan and Kwangsi, besides the Viet Minh elements, a considerable number of adherents of the pro-Kuomintang VNQDD, the pro-Japanese Phuc Quoc Hoi (National Restoration Party), and other nationalist associations. Chiang set up the Dai Kien Special Training Camp near Liuchow to train Vietnamese in military and political tactics and intelligence techniques.

In an attempt to unite the quarrelsome non-Communist leaders, the Kwangsi governor called a meeting to which all Vietnamese organizations in southern China were invited. The Liuchow Conference, held October 4 to 16, 1942, resulted in the formation of the *Viet Nam Cach Menh Dong Minh Hoi*, or Vietnam Revolutionary League. Although the ICP was barred from the new organization, the Viet Minh, which claimed to be an all-embracing front by itself, was permitted to join the ten-member league (membership was extended to groups, not to individuals). At the head of the *Dong Minh Hoi*, the Kuomintang understandably placed Nguyen Hai Than, the old pro-Chinese nationalist leader. With a monthly allowance of 100,000 Chinese dollars, the Revolutionary League was expected to organize an espionage apparatus in Indochina and stir up disorder in Tonkin. If Chungking attempted to bring the Vietnamese Communists under its surveillance and at the same time make use of the Viet Minh intelligence network, it was bound to fail. The Viet Minh, under Ho's order, remained aloof. While refusing to cooperate with the Chinese, it nevertheless circulated inside the country the claim that the creation of the *Dong Minh Hoi* had been one of its achievements, and pretended to be the organization's spokesman.

Meanwhile, in spite of all talks of cooperation, the nationalist groups within the League remained split by personal rivalries and, in view of their lack of contact and support inside Vietnam, failed miserably in their attempt to set up an espionage machinery. Within a few months, it became obvious that Nguyen Hai Than was incapable of inspiring or uniting the disparate members of the *Dong Minh Hoi* and that Chungking had not obtained what it needed most, i.e., reports on the Japanese troop movements in Indochina. Sensing the Chinese dilemma, Ho, who was still in prison, struck a bargain with Chiang Fa-ku'ei. He offered to place his intelligence organization at the general's disposal in return for his release. It is interesting to note that Chiang and Ho were no strangers to each other; the two men had met back in 1925, when Ho, as Ly Thuy, was the secretary and interpreter of the Borodine mission and Chiang a military leader in Canton. The warlord of Kwangsi, however, suspected of entertaining some sympathy for the pro-Japanese government in Nankin and faced with imperative demands for information from Chungking, decided to accept Ho's offer. One problem, however, arose. The reputation of Nguyen Ai Quoc, the shrewd agent of international Communism, would certainly make him a *persona non grata* to Chungking, which kept a copious dossier on him. To overcome this difficulty, the Vietnamese Communist once again changed his name. It is not clear whether this was done on his own initiative or at Chiang Fa-ku'ei's suggestion. In any case, Nguyen Ai Quoc became Ho Chi Minh, or Ho Who Enlightens. Thus, under this resounding name, the calculating man from Nghe An entered history.

Thereupon, the military governor of Kwangsi informed Chiang Kai-shek that he had found a Vietnamese revolutionary with a great capacity, Ho Chi Minh, who had offered to organize an intelligence network and stir up unrest in Indochina on behalf of the Allies. Ho Chi Minh? No one knew him in Chungking. The Chinese government, consequently, welcomed the offer.[19] On September 16, 1943,

Ho obtained his freedom. Upon his release, he was appointed chief of the Dong Minh Hoi, and thus became the recipient of the 100,000 Chinese dollar monthly allowance which had gone to Nguyen Hai Than. The Viet Minh derived immeasurable and unexpected benefits from this apparent cooperation with Chungking. By a stroke of fate, the helpless prisoner Nguyen Ai Quoc was transformed into the influential Ho Chi Minh, leader of the Revolutionary League. With the monthly subsidy paid him by the Chinese authorities and the facilities of the Dai Kien Special Training Camp, Ho freely engaged in propaganda and recruiting activities among the nationalist groups. In return for this Kuomintang support, the Viet Minh, with its well-oiled clandestine organization, soon provided Chungking with abundant information on the Japanese troops in Indochina. Although the Viet Minh reports were often inaccurate, their sheer number made a good impression on the Chinese.[20]

Meanwhile, Chinese financial and technical assistance also enabled the Viet Minh to intensify its antifascist propaganda in Indochina and led it to put forth the claim that it was the arm of the Allied powers inside the country.

In the spring of 1943, under Ho's directive, the Viet Minh propaganda exploited the popular resentment against the rice requisition undertaken by the French administration on behalf of the Japanese troops. At the same time, self-defense and guerilla units began to roam at will in the border provinces. From their base in Cao Bang, they spread into Bac Kan and Thai Nguyen, won the support of the population under their control, and thus openly challenged the French administration. Although poorly armed, these guerillas were ably led by Vietnamese who had received their military training at the Dai Kien School and by Man and Tho chiefs of whom the most capable was Chu Van Tan, the first Minister of Defense of the DRV. The success of these so-called self-defense groups was an eloquent testimony to the organizational skill and military acumen of Vo Nguyen Giap, the man whom Ho had chosen two years earlier to organize the Viet Minh propaganda and guerilla units in these provinces.

The Viet Minh activities on behalf of China soon alarmed both the Decoux regime and the French Military Mission, which repre-

sented the French government-in-exile then known as the Algiers
Committee, in Chungking. This Kuomintang-Viet Minh collusion
augured no good for the continued presence of France in Indochina, a presence which both the Gaullists and the Decoux men
agreed ought to be preserved at all cost. To these Frenchmen the
war against Japan was but a troublesome step toward the restoration of France's rule over her Southeast Asian colonies. With such a
frame of mind, they could not conceive or even tolerate the thought
of collaborating with the Viet Minh or any other nationalist elements to whom they contemptuously referred as "Annamese rebels."[21] Consequently, the Viet Minh propaganda, exhorting the
democratic elements of the French population in Indochina, the
antifascists, the Gaullists who disapproved of the puppet Decoux
government to rally behind the anti-Japanese front, fell on deaf
ears. Similarly, Ho's repeated appeals to the Algiers Liberation
Committee, with which the Viet Minh tried to associate itself, went
unheeded. Thus, the restoration of France's control over Indochina
remained the common objective of the Decoux regime and the Algiers Committee. General De Gaulle, in fact, made it abundantly
clear in his December 5, 1943, statement that Indochina would
remain French. While promising political and economic reforms,
the head of the Algiers Committee affirmed that the Indochinese
states would be simply given an autonomous status within the
French Union. This declaration was bitterly attacked by the Vietnamese Stalinists, who spoke, as adherents of the ICP, not as members of the Independence League:

So the French who struggle against German domination are now hoping
to maintain their own domination over other peoples! We, Indochinese
Communists, protest most vigorously against the inconsistency of the
Algiers Committee. By working for the formation of a broad anti-fascist
front in Indochina, we want to deliver ourselves as well as anti-fascist
foreigners from the oppression of the Nipponese militarist fascists. But to
think that we are thereby sacrificing our national independence in favor
of domination by Gaullists or any one else is pure sophistry.
      The Algiers Liberation Committee is mistaken in believing that the
Indochinese people will be satisfied with flatteries, assurances, and promises. We, ourselves, prepare for the future of our country. We want
complete liberty.

The Gaullists in Indochina . . . hope to get out of this situation with the intervention of the Allied forces. But the Allied powers who called themselves liberators at Teheran do not have the right to impose any kind of yoke on other people, even when this yoke is "humanized" and sweetened by the partisans of De Gaulle![22]

Once again, the two-faced Ho put his calculating mind to work. While the ICP accused the Gaullists of bad faith, the Viet Minh cautiously refrained from making any unfavorable comments in regard to Free France, but continued, instead, to emphasize publicly the need for unity among the antifascist elements in Indochina:

Republican France has arisen and calls on its children to strenuous combat for liberty and peace. The revolutionary peoples of Indochina are preparing for the overthrow of fascist domination. The Chinese Army is ready to cross the frontier of Tonkin in order to chase from Indochina the Nipponese invaders and their lackeys of every description. May all the forces of liberty and progress in Indochina unite together to parry in time an imminent political crisis![23]

Under this dual policy, Ho sought to eliminate his enemies by playing off one against the other, i.e., by compromising with the Gaullists, who would undoubtedly struggle against the French fascists, and with the Chinese, who would fight both the Japanese and the French as soon as they entered Indochina.[24]

Meanwhile, the colonial administration took vigorous measures to meet the Viet Minh challenge. French troops began to patrol deep into the frontier provinces of Tonkin, gradually forced the Viet Minh guerillas to withdraw, and eventually restored French authority over the area. At the same time, Decoux informed both the Gaullist Mission in Kunming and the Kuomintang authorities that Ho Chi Minh was none other than Nguyen Ai Quoc, the astute Comintern agent, and that the Viet Minh was using the Chinese to its own advantages. This information did not seem to upset the Chinese leaders, many of whom, besides General Chiang Fa-ku'ei, had undoubtedly been familiar with Ho's background but still entertained the illusion that they could control him.

As previously discussed, the Dong Minh Hoi had never operated as a harmonious, pro-Chinese revolutionary league, and the Viet Minh adherence to the organization had simply provided Ho with an excellent opportunity both to keep himself informed of the Chinese ambitions and to carry out his activities in its name. Ho's shrewd maneuver soon had an unsettling effect on the Kuomintang leaders, who had become painfully aware of the incompetence of their Vietnamese protégés, notably Nguyen Hai Than and his VNQDD. The imminence of Japan's defeat prompted Chungking to take measures to promote its interest in Indochina. With a view to transforming the Dong Minh Hoi into an instrument that could be used to install a pro-Chinese government in Hanoi, General Chiang Fa-ku'ei, under Chiang Kai-shek's order, convoked another nationalist Congress at Liuchow from March 25 to 28, 1944. After tumultuous debates, during which the Viet Minh independent activities had been severely condemned, all the delegates again stressed the need for unity, and reaffirmed their adherence to the Revolutionary League and their determination to work together for the liberation of Vietnam. As a result of the Congress' deliberation, the control of the Dong Minh Hoi was again placed in the hands of the ineffective VNQDD. A Provisional Republican Government was formed, headed by Truong Boi Cong, a relatively unknown member of the Vietnam Nationalist Party. Ho obtained a ministerial post in the government-in-exile, which promptly announced its intention to liberate Vietnam from French and Japanese fascism with Chinese assistance.

The second Liuchow Congress, however, did not change the nature of the Dong Minh Hoi. Nor did it bring Ho under Chiang Fa-ku'ei's control. A semblance of unity was restored which, ironically, worked for the benefit of the Viet Minh. The formation of the Provisional Republican Government, like the establishment of the Dong Minh Hoi, was just another Chinese illusion. Immediately following the close of the Congress, the nationalist delegates hurried back to Yunnan, waiting for the day when they would return under Chinese protection to Vietnam. Meanwhile, they wasted their time and energy in internecine disputes.

Ho Chi Minh, on his part, steadily and successfully worked his way into the controlling position in the Provisional Republican Government. Claiming to act in the name of the Revolutionary League and of the government-in-exile, the Viet Minh intensified its propaganda, firing the imagination of the masses who wanted nothing more than national freedom. As a result of Ho's growing boldness and independence, relations between the Viet Minh and the Kuomintang soon became strained, and Chinese aid ceased to flow to Ho's organization. To compensate for the loss of Chinese support, the Vietnamese Communist leader promptly looked to the Americans, establishing contact with the U.S. Office of Strategic Services (OSS). In the winter of 1944–45, Ho, on several occasions, approached Colonel Paul E. Helliwell, then head of the OSS intelligence in China, seeking arms and ammunition in return for cooperation in the war, i.e., intelligence, sabotage against the Japanese, and rescue of Allied pilots shot down in Indochina. According to Helliwell, Ho was given six .38 caliber revolvers and twenty thousand rounds of ammunition as a token of appreciation for the Viet Minh rescue of three American pilots.[25] Not satisfied with this insignificant aid, the persistent Vietnamese Communist subsequently made contact with Richard Heppner, the OSS intelligence officer who had replaced Helliwell late in the war. Ho's efforts were rewarded with additional assistance from the OSS and other Allied agencies in China. As an American intelligence chief in the Far East revealed, Ho even "offered to be our man, and we never grabbed his hand because we couldn't bankroll him."[26] Thus, in the pursuit of his objectives, this callous Communist who would not stop at anything, had successively collaborated or offered to collaborate with the French Sûreté, the British police, the Chinese Kuomintang, then the American intelligence service.

In November, 1944, after Ho had slipped back into Tonkin, the British helpfully dropped supplies to Free French and Viet Minh guerillas in the border provinces. While the amount of aid Ho received from the Allied forces in China was of limited value from the military point of view, it paid off handsomely in a propagandistic sense. It gave credence to the Viet Minh claim that the Provisional Republican Government, of which Ho was the self-appointed spokesman, enjoyed the support of the Allied powers. It was indeed a very significant gain for the Communist-led movement, especially when many Vietnamese began to feel that the course of the war had turned against the Axis states, and that an Allied-backed government would certainly be the one which would assume power in an independent Vietnam.

Ho, the Liberator

A keen student of politics, Ho closely followed the developments in Europe and in Asia. On August 6, 1944, he made a prophetic analysis of the situation in his homeland:

> Germany is almost beaten, and her defeat will lead to that of Japan who will not be able to withstand a general offensive. Then the Americans and the Chinese will enter Indochina while the Gaullists rise against the Japs. The latter will perhaps topple the French fascists prior to this and set up a military government.
> All puppet governments, incapable and weak, will fall. Indochina will plunge into anarchy. We shall not need to seize power, for there will be no power. We shall set up a government which will extend its rule wherever our enemies, the French and the Japanese, are absent, or incapable of maintaining their prestige due to their military weakness. . . .
> Our next uprising will thus be carried out under very favorable conditions, unique in the history of our country. In view of the propitious occasion and favorable factors, it would be unforgivable not to take advantage of them. It would be a crime against the history of our country.[27]

Thus, during the summer of 1944, the Viet Minh began to make preparations for such an undertaking. Against Vo Nguyen Giap's suggestion of a general armed insurrection in Tonkin at that time, however, Ho counseled prudence. Realizing both the Viet Minh limitations and the enemy's military capabilities, the cautious revolutionary bided his time. Instead of direct confrontation, he opted for a guerilla war of harassment. In October, Ho again crossed the frontier and went to Pac Bo. Escorted by Chu Van Tan's guerillas, the old leader immediately left the grottoes for Thai Nguyen where he established his headquarters to direct the struggle. Also returning with Ho were about two hundred volunteers who had received their military training in Kwangsi, and who travelled in small groups to avoid detection by the Japanese and French intelligence. Shortly, after Ho's return, the armed struggle began. On November 8, the Viet Minh launched an attack against a garrison in the provincial capital of Thai Nguyen. With the active assistance of the Vietnamese elements of the Indochinese Guard, who were supposed to defend the military post, the attackers easily overran it. Very rapidly, Viet Minh bands infiltrated into the northern mountain provinces, attacking isolated outposts with the express purpose of capturing arms and ammunition and impressing the population. At the same time, their propaganda exhorted the people to rally behind the Independence Movement to expel the Japanese and French fascists. Persuasion and threats were freely used to win popular support. Frequent assassinations of village notables and "reactionaries" also brought home to the people the Viet Minh message.

In December, 1944, Ho issued official instructions regarding the establishment of the Vietnam Propaganda Unit for National Liberation. This unit, composed of seasoned cadres from the small guerilla bands that had operated in the border provinces of Tonkin, was under the command of Vo Nguyen Giap. In his instructions explaining the purpose of "the embryo of the Liberation Army," Ho said:

1. The Vietnam Propaganda Unit for National Liberation shows by its name that greater importance should be attached to the political side than to the military side. It is a propaganda unit. To act successfully, in the military field, the main principle is concentration of forces. Therefore, in accordance with the new instruction of the Organization, the most resolute and energetic officers and men will be picked out of the ranks of the guerilla units in the provinces of Cao Bang, Bac Can, and Lang Son and a great amount of weapons will be concentrated to establish our main force.

Because ours is a national resistance by the whole people, we must mobilize and arm the whole people. Therefore, when concentrating our forces to set up the first unit, we must maintain the local armed forces, coordinate their operations and assist each other in all aspects. On its part, the main unit has the duty to guide the cadres of the local armed units, assist them in drilling, and supply them with weapons if possible, thus helping these units to grow unceasingly.

2. With regard to local armed units, we will gather their cadres for training, send trained cadres to various localities to exchange experience, maintain liaison, and coordinate military operations.

3. Concerning tactics, we will apply guerilla warfare, which consists in being secret, rapid, active, now in the East, now in the West, arriving unexpectedly and leaving unnoticed.

The Vietnam Propaganda Unit for National Liberation is the first-born unit. It is hoped that other units will soon come into being.

At first its size is small; however, its prospect is brilliant. It is the embryo of the Liberation Army and can move from North to South, throughout Vietnam.[28]

Meanwhile, confronted with an open Viet Minh challenge and fearful of a general insurrection, which would irreparably endanger French rule, the Decoux regime decided to act. Savage reprisals were inflicted upon individuals and villages that had cooperated with the rebels. Military operations were conducted against the guerillas who seemed determined to fight and engage French patrols. By the winter of 1944–45, the Viet Minh movement spread throughout Northern Tonkin, notably the provinces of Bac Kan, Tuyen Quang, Bac Giang, Lang Son, Cao Bang, and Ha Giang, which, together with Thai Nguyen, constituted what was called "the liberated zone," a region from which French control was eliminated. While claiming to fight both the French colonialists and the Japanese fascists, the Viet Minh vehemently condemned the rice requisitions made by the Decoux administration on behalf of the Nipponese authorities in spite of widespread famine. In view of the half-hearted Japanese effort to track down the Viet Minh, the latter's popularity went crescendo, notably among the peasantry. Profoundly disturbed, the French, late in the winter, decided to undertake mop-up operations to reconquer the "liberated zone" and liquidate the rebellion. The French plan, however, was never carried out. On March 9, 1945, the Japanese struck. For all practical purposes, France's rule over Indochina came to an end.

On March 11, Emperor Bao Dai proclaimed that the 1884 Franco-Annamese Treaty making Vietnam a French protectorate had been abrogated, and that Vietnam had become an independent state. At the same time, the monarch declared his country's determination to collaborate with Japan to promote a co-prosperity area in East Asia. After a series of consultations with various political figures, Bao Dai announced the formation of a government under Professor Tran Trong Kim, a nationalist of renown who, like many of his countrymen, believed that Vietnam's independence could be achieved through collaboration with the occupation authorities. The new government, however, soon ran into difficulty. While exerting their pressure on Tran Trong Kim, the Japanese nevertheless left the Viet

Minh undisturbed to intensify their activities, consolidate their bases, and undermine the central government. In spite of its achievements in the face of Japanese opposition and the Viet Minh disruptive propaganda, the Kim government suffered considerably from its apparent identification with Japan, as the Viet Minh had warned:

> In overthrowing the French yoke, the Japs plan to occupy our country and turn it into a Japanese colony where they will reserve for themselves the monopoly of plundering our people, abusing our women, slaying our patriots. They are here not to liberate our people. They are here to seize our rice stocks, our cotton, our oil; they will arrest all our young men and turn them into Japanese cannon-fodder.[29]

Thus, from the outset, the Kim government with a pro-Japanese label was doomed to fail. The political situation was further aggravated by the economic conditions. In addition to the intensifying American aerial attacks, which had destroyed railways, bridges, and means of transportation and, consequently, isolated food-deficient Tonkin from the rest of the country, and a flood which had wiped out its crop, the continued Japanese rice requisition plunged the North into the most dreadful despair. Nearly one million people starved to death. In the face of such a crisis, the Tran Trong Kim cabinet was not (nor would any other government be) able to find an answer. The Viet Minh eagerly exploited these exasperating conditions, encouraging the people to stop all deliveries to the Japanese, participate in large scale demonstrations and strikes, destroy Japanese ammunition depots, and plunder Japanese food stores.

In the meantime, Ho, sensing the impending Japanese defeat and the consequential arrival of Allied troops, was determined to make full political and military preparations for an eventual take-over. The Viet Minh propaganda went into full swing. With a view to welcoming the Allies and confronting the French with a *fait accompli*, Ho proceeded to form a government which, he hoped, would be well entrenched by the time the Allied representatives landed in Indochina. An independent Vietnam under Ho's control would be thus assured.

In retrospect, the Japanese coup brought forth four immediate consequences, which benefited the Viet Minh considerably:

1. It effectively eliminated the French Sûreté and, thus, greatly facilitated the Viet Minh clandestine activities.

2. It established a government which was stained with affiliation with Japan and doomed to fail because of Japanese obstruction.

3. It left the Communist-controlled "Provisional Republican Government" as the only anti-French, anti-Japanese organization.

4. It drove the French out of Tonkin and left it under Ho's control.

From the "liberated zone," Ho, on July 1, launched an appeal asking Vietnamese to support his regime instead of the "puppet government" of Tran Trong Kim because

Revolutionary administrative centers have been set up in different localities. The people's Revolutionary Committees, directly elected by different organizations of the population, are using revolutionary methods to bring back freedom and happiness to the whole people.

The properties of the population in the Liberated Zones are being effectively protected. Properties belonging to the invaders have been seized. They have become public property or have been distributed to the poor. Democratic rights and liberties are being translated into actual deeds. All citizens are equal in status. All men and women have equal rights before the law. The sick and the poor are given assistance, robbery and banditry are completely stamped out. All taxes and impositions have been abolished, and land taxes reduced. The working hours are shortened. Boys and girls are either pursuing their studies or fighting on the battlefields. Rich and poor, young and old, are working day and night to supply our armies. Over one million of our compatriots already enjoy revolutionary liberties and happiness. A "New Vietnam" has come into being.[30]

While condemning the Gaullist attempt to restore the old order in Indochina, Ho, at the same time, maintained contact with the French Mission in Kunming. In a July, 1945, memorandum transmitted through the good offices of the OSS to the Free French representatives in China, the Communist double-dealer even proposed temporary reestablishment of French rule until Vietnam's independence was assured, i.e., for a period of five to ten years. The document read:

We, the Viet Minh League, ask that the following points be announced by the French and observed in their future policy in Indochina:

1. A parliament shall be elected by universal suffrage. It shall legislate

for the country. A French governor shall exercise the functions of president until our independence is assured. This president shall choose a cabinet or group of advisers approved by the parliament. The precise powers of these organs will be delineated in the future.

2. Independence shall be given to this country in a minimum of five years and a maximum of ten.

3. The natural resources of this country shall be returned to its inhabitants after making just compensation to thier present holders. France shall be given economic concessions.

4. All liberties proclaimed by the United Nations shall be guaranteed to Indochinese.

5. The sale of opium shall be prohibited.

We hope that these conditions will be judged acceptable by the French government.[31]

Whether the memorandum in question was a trick or a sincere effort on Ho's part to reach an agreement with France was not the point. The Gaullist Mission in Kunming, after studying the Vietnamese proposal, gave only a noncommittal answer, on the ground that all decisions concerning the future of Indochina had to come from Paris. Thus, the first opportunity to reach a Franco-Viet Minh understanding was lost, an understanding which would have changed the course of events in Vietnam. There is reason to believe that the Viet Minh leader was anxious to reach an agreement with France. His duplicity is easy to comprehend. On the one hand, Ho tried to appear to his people as the only genuine anti-Japanese, anti-French leader by condemning both the Nipponese and the Gaullists; on the other, he wanted to reach an understanding with France who would recognize him as the legitimate head of an autonomous Vietnamese state. Once secure in his position, he would eliminate all nationalist competition and strike a more profitable bargain with France.

An attempt to bring together Ho Chi Minh and Jean Sainteny, the head of the French Mission in Kunming, was made by the end of the same month (July). The initiative came from Laurie Gordon, a former representative of the American oil company Texaco in Indochina. He had set up an intelligence network operating in Indochina until the Japanese coup, after which he departed for Yunnan where he continued to work as a free-lance intelligence agent. Thanks to his various connections in Vietnam, Gordon also maintained contact with the Viet Minh organization. Through his good offices, it seems, arrangements were made for the parachuting of a team of American and French military instructors near the Viet Minh jungle headquarters in July.

In any case, the Ho-Sainteny meeting never took place, due partly to the precipitating events, partly to the diluvian rains which fell on the region and made air travel extremely hazardous. According to the Allied officers assigned to Ho's headquarters during that period, the Viet Minh leaders, very anxious to meet the French representatives, made elaborate preparations, ordering tricolor flags and slogans to be made to welcome the Sainteny delegation.[32]

Meanwhile, Ho astutely played his cards, constantly seeking Allied support for his organization. The Japanese coup of March 9, 1945, had suddenly deprived the Allies in China of a source of information regarding the Japanese troops' movement in Indochina. The OSS, anxious to make use of the Viet Minh intelligence network, soon set up a liaison mission at Ho's headquarters. United States military supplies were parachuted into the "liberated zone." With American aid and advice, Viet Minh guerillas launched a few attacks against Japanese military convoys and isolated outposts, but carefully avoided engaging the still redoubtable Japanese in direct confrontation. Ho also had other reasons for not challenging the Nipponese troops, whose days in Indochina were already numbered. He wanted to keep his strength intact and ready for the final struggle against the French and, especially, other competing nationalist groups. In the meantime, Ho concentrated on propaganda. The Viet Minh "exploits" against the Japanese were grossly exaggerated and widely publicized. Everywhere, the Viet Minh repeatedly put forth the claim that they were allies of the Soviet Union, the United States, and China, announced that Japan's defeat was imminent, and threatened collaborators, i.e., those who had worked or were suspected of having worked for the French and the Japanese, with severe punishment.

In May, Ho arrived in Tan Trao, a small, remote jungle village in the province of Tuyen Quang, where he was to set up a liaison center to facilitate contact between the Viet Minh organizations in the delta, the highland, and abroad. Upon his arrival, the Communist leader, whose health had been eroded by the thirteen-month confinement in China, overwork, and the humid jungle climate, fell

seriously ill. His temperature ran high. He was in a deep coma. He
was dying. The revolution was about to lose its guiding spirit. To
his associates, Ho's death was no longer a matter of speculation or
rumor. It appeared to be a reality. There was no medicine, only
quinine and aspirin. In an agony of despair, his lieutenants sent for
an old medicine man from the nearest mountain. After examining
the weakening revolutionary, the man in whom the Viet Minh
cadres put all their hope, the medicine man prescribed a remedy:
burned plant roots mixed with very thin rice soup. The plant happened to be one that grew in abundance in the area. While the
prescription might sound strange to Westerners, it was quite familiar to Vietnamese who were used to taking Oriental medicine. The
burned roots were supposed to combat fever, and the rice soup to
restore the patient's strength. Excellent prescription! Three days
later, to everyone's relief, Ho recovered. Was it the plant roots and
the rice soup or his sheer stubbornness that kept Ho alive? Perhaps,
a combination of both.

Soon after his recovery, Ho suggested that, in view of the rapidly
changing conditions, the Viet Minh General Committee should convene a National Congress in July. Because of "difficulties of communication,"[33] however, the Congress was not held until the very
moment of Japan's surrender.

Meanwhile, the tide turned in Ho's favor. On August 6, 1945, an
atom bomb fell on Hiroshima. The Pacific war was reaching its conclusion. On August 10, Japan capitulated. In the evening of August
13, the National Congress of the ICP, convinced that the opportune
moment had come, decided to launch a general insurrection and to
found a "democratic republican" regime in Vietnam. The decision
was promptly approved by the Viet Minh General Committee, and
an Insurrection Committee was immediately set up.

Before seizing control of the nationalist movement, Ho wanted to
ascertain that his attempt would not fail. Aware that foreign, especially American, recognition of his organization would enhance the
Viet Minh prestige both at home and abroad and legitimatize the
government he was about to form, the veteran Communist sought
to contact the U.S. Mission in China through the good offices of a
young American Army officer, whom Robert Shaplen simply refers
to as Lt. John, and who had been parachuted into Ho's jungle
headquarters in May, 1945. The two men had lived and worked

together for several months. Ho had apparently developed some liking for the American officer, whom he easily impressed, and whom he intended to use for his own benefit. Equipped with a portable radio, John helped establish contact between Ho, on the one hand, and the French and American Missions in China, on the other. The old revolutionary and the young American often discussed world affairs, exchanged toasts, and shared such delicacies as stewed tiger livers! This "little old man sitting on his hill in the jungle" impressed John as a gentle, "awfully sweet guy," a non-Marxist patriot who knew a great deal about almost everything.[34]

Thus, shortly after Japan's surrender, Ho, playing on their mutual friendship and trying to oblige John with a bottle of wine, asked the American to use his portable radio to wire two Viet Minh messages to the U.S. headquarters in China. In one communication, Ho sought to ingratiate himself with the Americans and the French by claiming to have discovered a Dai Viet (an anti-Viet Minh nationalist party) terroristic plot against the French, a plot which Ho allegedly planned to foil. In the second message, Ho begged the United States to intervene on the Viet Minh behalf by prevailing upon the United Nations to recognize Vietnam's independence. Ho's letter to John, written in English, reads as follows:

Dear Lt. (John),

I feel weaker since you left. Maybe I'd have to follow your advice—moving to some other place where food is easy to get, to improve my health. . . .

I'm sending you a bottle of wine, hope you like it.

Be so kind as to give me foreign news you got.

. . . Please be good enuf to send to your H.Q. the following wires.

1. Daiviet [an anti-Viet Minh nationalist group] plans to exercise large terror against French and to push it upon shoulder of VML (Viet Minh League). VML ordered 2 million members and all its population be watchful and stop Daiviet criminal plan when & if possible. VML declares before the world its aim is national independence. It fights with political & if necessary military means. But never resorts to criminal & dishonest act.

Signed—National Liberation Committee of VML

2. National Liberation Committee of VML begs U.S. authorities to inform United Nations the following. We were fighting Japs on the side of the United Nations. Now Japs surrendered. We beg United Nations to

realize their solemn promise that all nationalities will be given democracy and independence. If United Nations forget their solemn promise & don't grant Indochina full independence, we will keep fighting until we get it.

Signed—Liberation Committee of VML

Thank you for all the troubles I give you. . . .

Best greetings!

Yours sincerely, Hoo [sic][35]

The Dai Viet terroristic campaign against the French existed only in Ho's imagination. The astute Communist apparently tried to arouse the French and, hopefully, the Americans against the Dai Viet, and use them to eliminate his nationalist competitors. He also attempted to place, in advance, all responsibility for future attacks against the French, attacks which the Viet Minh had in fact contemplated, on his rivals' shoulders.

At the same time, Ho reiterated the claim that the Viet Minh had fought on the side of the Allies and, therefore, should deserve the United Nations' support. In one stroke, Ho sought to get rid of his nationalist competitors and to gain international recognition for his movement. A very shrewd move, indeed!

Having taken all possible precautions, Ho proceeded with his plan. On August 16, a People's Congress, attended by more than "sixty delegates from big and small national minorities and of all political convictions,"[36] was held in Tan Trao. The Congress approved the Viet Minh order for a general insurrection, and appointed the National Committee for the Liberation of Vietnam, which was in fact the Provisional Government of the Democratic Republic of Vietnam. The latter was headed by Ho Chi Minh, then unknown to most Vietnamese. As Truong Chinh, then Secretary General of the ICP, was to point out later,

Because the people's Congress opened immediately after the general insurrection order had been launched, it had to hold a "lightning" session allowing the delegates to return quickly to their local regions and, together with the local militants, to lead the decisive struggle.[37]

The fact that the Congress was convened so hastily, that forty delegates who were on their way to the meeting had to turn back, and that the more than sixty who attended the "lightning" session had to hurry back to their posts indicated that the Viet Minh, in spite of their propaganda, had not expected Japan to surrender so suddenly. The Japanese capitulation thus found Ho unprepared for the occasion and significantly upset his timetable.

In reference to the Vietnamese Communist strategy, Truong Chinh added:

> During the historic Congress, the Indochinese Communist Party advocated an extremely clear policy: to lead the masses in insurrection in order to disarm the Japanese before the arrival of the Allied forces in Indochina; to wrest power from the Japanese and their puppet stooges and finally, as the people's power, to welcome the Allied forces coming to disarm the Japanese troops stationed in Indochina.[38]

In spite of this "extremely clear policy," there is sufficient ground to believe that Ho gave no serious thought to disarming the Japanese, a task which undoubtedly was beyond the power of his poorly-equipped guerillas to tackle. In fact, Ho had cautiously avoided provoking the Japanese, who, in turn, maintained a benevolent attitude toward the Viet Minh maneuvers.

After the closing of the Tan Trao Congress, at which he had appeared for the first time before the people's delegates, Ho officially issued an appeal for general insurrection:

Dear compatriots,

Four years ago, in one of my letters, I called on you to unite together. Because unity is strength, only strength enables us to win back independence and freedom.

At present, the Japanese army is crushed. The National Salvation movement has spread to the whole country. The Revolutionary Front for the Independence of Vietnam (Viet Minh) has millions of members from all social strata: intellectuals, peasants, workers, businessmen, soldiers, and from all nationalities in the country: Kinh, Tho, Nung, Muong, Man, etc. In the Front our compatriots march side by side without discrimination as to age, sex, religion, or fortune.

Recently, the Viet Minh Front convened the Vietnam People's Congress and appointed the National Liberation Committee to lead the entire people in the resolute struggle until national independence is won.

This is a great advance in the history of the struggle waged for nearly a century by our people for their liberation.

This is a fact that enraptures our compatriots and fills me with great joy.

However, we cannot consider this as good enough. Our struggle will be a long and hard one. Because the Japanese are defeated, we shall not be liberated overnight. We still have to make further efforts and carry on the struggle. Only a united struggle will bring us independence.

The Viet Minh Front is at present the basis of the struggle and solidarity of our people. Join the Viet Minh Front, support it, make it greater and stronger!

At present, the National Liberation Committee is, so to speak, in itself our provisional government. Unite around it and see to it that its policies and orders are carried out throughout the country!

In this way, our Fatherland will certainly win independence and our people will certainly win freedom soon.

The decisive hour in the destiny of our people has struck. Let us stand up with all our strength to free ourselves!

Many oppressed peoples the world over are vying with each other in the march to win back their independence. We cannot allow ourselves to lag behind.

Forward! Forward! Under the banner of the Viet Minh Front, move forward courageously![39]

Such a reasonable appeal, which emphasized unity in the struggle for independence, was enthusiastically received by the masses. Viet Minh propaganda leaflets, posters, and slogans appeared everywhere, claiming that the League was the united front of all nationalist elements and a trusted ally of the victorious powers. Very rapidly, the revolutionary fervor overcame the entire people, who realized that the war had ended and that national independence was within their grasp. A genuine popular revolution was on the move. Few were aware that the revolution was Communist-led. Fewer still knew who Ho Chi Minh was. Many, however, were impressed by such a meaningful name. And all were carried away by their ardent desire for freedom.

On August 18, Viet Minh adherents, followers, and admirers roamed the streets of Hanoi. Huge public meetings and demonstrations took place in the capital and in the provinces. The gold-starred red flag was seen flying everywhere. Viceroy Phan Ke Toai, the representative of Emperor Bao Dai in Tonkin, meekly resigned in favor of a Viet Minh Citizens' Committee. The Japanese authorities witnessed these developments with apparent detachment, looking indifferently at the Viet Minh military units who occupied all important public buildings. They also turned over to the insurgents the stocks of arms belonging to the Indochinese Guard. In contrast to the violent anti-Japanese propaganda before V-J Day, which had been undoubtedly intended for the Allies' consumption, the Viet Minh attitude toward the Nipponese authorities was one of deference. This cautious policy paid off handsomely. Unchallenged and unmolested, the Japanese benignly looked on while the revolution followed its course. Thus, without firing a shot, the Viet Minh entered and occupied Hanoi and took over the government. Within two weeks after V-J Day, it had triumphed over the entire country.

Meanwhile, in Hue, Emperor Bao Dai reportedly decided to call on the Viet Minh to form a new government. Had it not been for the unsettling development in the capital, Ho, who was obviously anxious to head a government most likely to be recognized by the Allied powers, would have welcomed the Emperor's overture. On August 21, a large meeting was convoked in Hanoi by the General Association of Students. A group of left-wing intellectuals, acting independently of the Viet Minh Central Committee, successfully pushed through a motion which

1. Called for the abdication of the Emperor of Annam, the installation of a republican regime, the grant of power to a provisional government formed by the Viet Minh;

2. Asked the Viet Minh League to open negotiations immediately with the other parties with a view to forming a provisional government;

3. Appealed to all parties, all strata of the population, and the largest masses of people to support the provisional government in order to begin the work of consolidating national independence.[40]

The motion was promptly transmitted via telegraph to Bao Dai. Subsequently, on the advice of his entourage, who apparently believed that the Viet Minh had enjoyed considerable Allied support, the Emperor abdicated, declaring that he would rather be a citizen of an independent state than a ruler of an enslaved nation. In his August 24 statement, the monarch said:

Happiness of the Vietnamese people!
Independence of the Vietnamese Nation!
For these We declare that We are ready to make any and every sacrifice.   For these We wish our sacrifice would be useful to our Fatherland. . . .
In the present crisis, Unity is Life, Division is Death.
Constating that the urge for Democracy of the people in the North has

risen too high, and that if We kept waiting until the opening session of the National Congress, friction between North and South would be unavoidable. Such a conflict would cause more suffering to our countrymen and afford exploitable opportunity to foreigners. . . .

We have decided to abdicate and to hand over the power to the Democratic Republican Government. . . .[41]

By calling on the new government to "treat kindly those parties and groups which had fought for the independence of the country, although they were not in line with the popular masses," and by exhorting "all parties and groups, all classes of society as well as the Royal Family to strengthen and support unreservedly the Democratic Republican Government in order to consolidate our national independence," the Emperor, unwittingly, helped legitimize the ICP-controlled movement and prepare the way for a Communist take-over in his country.

On August 29, exactly two weeks after the Japanese surrender, and five days after the abdication of the legitimate ruler, Ho announced the formation of a Provisional Government, which included most of the members of the National Liberation Committee. While assuming himself the presidency and the Ministry of Foreign Affairs, Ho made a token concession by offering three nonsensitive portfolios to non–Viet Minh members.[42] He also skillfully maneuvered ex-Emperor Bao Dai, now citizen Vinh Thuy, into accepting the position of Supreme Counsellor to his government.

All these events led to the climactic day of September 2, 1945. At the Ba Dinh Square in Hanoi, at a rally, attended by half a million people whom the Viet Minh organizers had brought in for the occasion, Ho Chi Minh presented the new government of the DRV and proclaimed the independence of Vietnam. Ho's Declaration of Independence opened with a paragraph borrowed from the American document:

All men were created equal; they are endowed by their Creator with certain unalienable Rights; among these are Life, Liberty, and the pursuit of Happiness.

This immortal statement was made in the Declaration of Independence of the United States of America in 1776. In a broader sense, this means: All the peoples on the earth are equal from birth, all the peoples have a right to live, to be happy and free.

To further explain the principles of government which he claimed to advocate, but was determined to flout, Ho added:

The Declaration of the French Revolution made in 1791 on the Rights of Man and the Citizen also states: "All men are born free and with equal rights, and must always remain free and have equal rights."
Those are undeniable truths.

After paying homage to these ideals of government, Ho launched a bitter attack on the French imperialists who

for more than eighty years, . . . abusing the standard of Liberty, Equality, and Fraternity, have violated our Fatherland and oppressed our fellow citizens. They have acted contrary to the ideals of humanity and justice.

In the field of politics, they have deprived our people of every democratic liberty.

They have enforced inhuman laws; they have set up three distinct political regimes in the North, the Center, and the South of Vietnam in order to wreck our national unity and prevent our people from being united.

They have built more prisons than schools. They have mercilessly slain our patriots; they had drowned our uprisings in rivers of blood.

They have fettered public opinion; they have practiced obscurantism against our people.

To weaken our race they have forced us to use opium and alcohol.

In the field of economics, they have fleeced us to the backbone, impoverished our people and devastated our land.

They have robbed us of our ricefields, our mines, our forests, and our raw materials. They have monopolized the issuing of bank notes and the export trade.

They have invented numerous unjustifiable taxes and reduced our people, especially our peasantry, to a state of extreme poverty.

They have hampered the prospering of our national bourgeoisie; they have mercilessly exploited our workers.

In the autumn of 1940, when the Japanese fascists violated Indochina's territory to establish new bases in their fight against the Allies, the French imperialists went down on their bended knees and handed over our country to them.

Thus, from that date, our people were subjected to the double yoke of the French and the Japanese. Their sufferings and miseries increased. The result was that, from the end of last year to the beginning of this

year, from Quang Tri Province to the North of Vietnam, more than two
million of our fellow citizens died from starvation. On March 9, the
French troops were disarmed by the Japanese. The French colonialists
either fled or surrendered, showing that not only were they incapable of
"protecting" us, but that, in the span of five years, they had twice sold
our country to the Japanese.

In spite of these grievances, Ho continued, the Viet Minh had,
on several occasions before the Japanese putsch of March, 1945,
urged the French to collaborate with it against the Japanese. Disregarding the French rebuff to its overtures, the League, after the
Japanese coup, "helped many Frenchmen to cross the frontier,
rescued some of them from Japanese jails, and protected French
lives and property." Since the autumn of 1940, however, Ho went
on, Vietnam had ceased to be a French colony and become a
Japanese possession, and the Vietnamese had wrested their independence from the Japanese and not from the French.

To conclude his harangue, Ho announced his government's decision to break off all relations of a colonial character with France,
to abrogate all treaties signed by France on Vietnam's behalf, and
to abolish all the special privileges the French had acquired in the
country, and emphasized:

A people who have courageously opposed French domination for
more than eighty years, a people who have fought side by side with the
Allies against the fascists during these last years, such a people must be
free and independent.

For these reasons, we, members of the Provisional Government of the
Democratic Republic of Vietnam, solemnly declare to the world that
Vietnam has the right to be a free and independent country—and in fact
it is so already. The entire Vietnamese people are determined to mobilize
all their physical and mental strength, to sacrifice their lives and property
in order to safeguard their independence and liberty.[43]

With a view to underlining Ho's remarks and to reminding the
victorious powers of their aims in the war, Minister of Interior Vo
Nguyen Giap, in his message to the Vietnamese people on the
same day, again reiterated:

From the Atlantic Charter to Teheran, Yalta and San Francisco,
everywhere the principle of self-determination has been defended and

proclaimed. The democratic powers have declared that they will fight for world peace, and there is no reason why they should allow imperialist France to send her troops here to wage a conquering war upon us. The democratic powers have declared that they will fight for equality among nations and there is no reason why they should help imperialist France to return here to oppress and plunder our people.

It is inconceivable to us, as well as to the whole world, that after we have fought the Japanese on the Allies' side, after we have shed our blood in the battle of the Pacific, we should be considered by our Allies as a people that deserves to be placed once more under the domination of those French imperialists who had assented to the Japanese occupation of Indochina, who offered Japan important bases to attack the Allies, who shamefully surrendered to the fascist Japanese and collaborated with them.[44]

It was not by sheer coincidence that the President of the nascent Democratic Republic of Vietnam borrowed a paragraph from the American Declaration of Independence. OSS members, on a mission at the Viet Minh jungle headquarters in the summer of 1945, recall the Communist leader's attempt to obtain a copy of the American document. "He kept asking me if I could remember the language of our Declaration," relates a former U.S. Army officer. "I was a normal American, I couldn't. I could have wired up to Kunming and had a copy dropped to me, of course, but all he really wanted was the flavor of the thing. The more we discussed it, the more he actually seemed to know about it than I did."[45]

As he had successfully led the few Americans who worked with him to believe that he was a genuine non-Marxist patriot, Ho similarly attempted to lead the United States government to think that he was a nationalist leader who seriously adhered to the principles of the American Declaration of Independence and, thus, should deserve American support. A penetrating observer of world politics, Ho fully realized that, of the Allied powers, the United States was the only country that could significantly influence French policy vis-à-vis Indochina. Consequently, the DRV President eagerly sought to cultivate American friendship and support for his government. On Independence Day, speaking through his Minister of Interior, Ho also paid a glowing tribute to the United States, "the Great American Republic":

As far as . . . the United States are concerned, we have had particularly intimate relations which it is for me a pleasant duty to dwell upon. . . .

The United States of America are a Republic which has no territorial interests in this country. They have paid the greatest contributions to the Vietnamese fight against fascist Japan, our enemy, and so the Great American Republic is a good friend of ours.[46]

4 ☆ *President of the Nascent Republic*

No SOONER had he "solemnly" declared to the world that "Vietnam has the right to be a free and independent country—and in fact is so already" than Ho Chi Minh was confronted with a multitude of intricate problems. He had proclaimed Vietnam's independence. Now he must protect it against the French who were not ready to give up what they had always considered as part of overseas France. A very unusual challenge for a very unusual man! Ho's task was twofold: (*a*) to set up an effective government in a war-torn country, inexperienced in self-rule, and (*b*) to deal with the British and the Chinese whom the Allies sent into Indochina to disarm and repatriate the defeated Japanese troops. Having at his disposition the well-organized and well-entrenched Indochinese Communist Party (ICP), Ho approached the domestic aspect of his task with relative ease. On the foreign front, however, the Viet Minh leader immediately ran into serious difficulties. His regime's survival depended on whether or not the British and the Chinese favored a French return to Indochina.

Anglo-French Collusion

In spite of the practical elimination of French rule in Indochina by the Japanese and the rising nationalist fervor that had swept across the colonies, Paris obdurately insisted on continuing its "civilizing mission" and restoring the old order in its former Southeast Asian possessions. To many Frenchmen

it was incredible that the Annamites should desire to reject French rule. With intolerable ingratitude, a handful of malefactors had conspired with the Japanese against the French. The insurgents, one heard endlessly from Frenchmen in high place and low, were nothing but a handful of agitators and paid terrorists, tools of the Japanese who stood momentarily between the benevolent French and the great mass of the people who yearned only to have the French return and desired only to till their lands in the peace assured by French rule. Some of the older French residents were bewildered, like the aging dentist's wife in Saigon who rocked back and forth on her chair and said: "The Annamites astounded me! What more could we have ever done for them than we did? Why, do you know we organized a municipal council here in which they were to have half the seats! What more could they want?" She was in dead earnest. . . . Others, usually officials, liked to refer to the *mission civilisatrice* of France overseas. It appeared that France had in reality conferred an immense cultural boon on the naked and ignorant Indochinese and had done so, what's more, at considerable sacrifice.[1]

Unfortunately, it was these anachronistic Frenchmen who influenced the policy-makers in Paris. Thus ignorant and disdainful of the Indochinese conditions, the French Provisional Government set forth its position in the Declaration of March 24, 1945, which, in fact, reiterated the policy statement made by the Algiers Liberation Committee on December 8, 1943.[2] Among other things, the Declaration provided for:

a. A Federation embracing all the five territories of Indochina, which were to form with France and her other colonies a French Union;

b. A Federal Government, presided over by a French Governor General, and composed of Ministers responsible to, and selected by, the Governor General from among Indochinese and French residents in Indochina;

c. An elected Federal Assembly, in which French and local interests were to be represented, and whose functions would be limited to voting taxes and the budget, deliberating on bills, and examining commercial and good-neighbor treaties;

d. Democratic rights for Indochinese;

e. Economic autonomy within the framework of the French Union;

f. French responsibility for foreign relations and defense.[3]

Such a policy, announced shortly after the Japanese coup of March 9, 1945, which to all intents and purposes had terminated French rule in Indochina, was both ill-timed and insulting to the Vietnamese who had enjoyed independence from a white power. The March 25 declaration, unfortunately, was neither the first nor the last expression of an anachronistic policy that has so tragically affected the fate of Indochina.

Following V-J Day, the British Royal Air Force parachuted a handful of officials from the Free French Mission in Calcutta, including Pierre Messmer and Jean Cedile, the French Commissioners designate for Tonkin and Cochinchina, respectively, to take over the administration from the Japanese. Upon their descent on Annam and Tonkin, the Frenchmen were immediately captured and detained by the Viet Minh. The Cedile team in Cochinchina was similarly seized and kept under house arrest by the Japanese but only for two days. Cedile was soon allowed to establish contact with Frenchmen and Vietnamese leaders in Saigon.

Meanwhile, Leclerc and his famous Armored Division were sent to Indochina to "peacefully" reoccupy the country. En route to Saigon, the French general stopped in Karachi where he received an invitation from British Admiral Mountbatten, Commander of the Allied forces in Southeast Asia, to visit him at his headquarters in Kandy, Ceylon. On August 22, when the two men met, Mountbatten informed Leclerc of the Postdam decision of which, surprisingly, the French general had not been aware: Indochina was to be divided into two zones along the 16th parallel with the Chinese occupying the North and the British the South. The British admiral also told his visitor that General de Gaulle, who was in Washington at that time, could probably prevail upon President Truman to revise the accord and put pressure on Chiang Kai-shek. "You have a slight chance to obtain satisfaction," said Mountbatten, "now that Roosevelt is gone. If Roosevelt were still living, you would not reenter Indochina."[4] Mountbatten also promised equipment, ammunition, and logistic support to Leclerc's forces. It was, however, estimated that it would take at least two months before French troops could be assembled and shipped to Indochina.

It was a matter of common knowledge that President Roosevelt had suggested trusteeship for Indochina while Prime Minister Churchill, apprehensive that such a policy would have serious repercussions in Burma, had strongly opposed any change in the status of the Western colonies in Asia. The Labour government, which took office after the elections of July, 1945, did not modify this position in any significant way. Its official declarations, on the contrary, clearly favored the French government. In his statement to the House of Commons regarding British policy in Indochina, Foreign Secretary Bevin said, on October 24, 1945:

His Majesty's Government do not desire to be unnecessarily involved in the administration or in the political affairs of non-British territories, and their object is to withdraw British troops as soon as circumstances permit. . . . The French Government, in a declaration of policy issued on 24th March last, promised a wide measure of autonomy to Indochina, and . . . this liberal attitude on the part of the French Government has been reflected in the very conciliatory manner in which the local French representatives have dealt with the Annamite leaders. There has also been close and friendly cooperation between the British and French Commanders. In the meanwhile every effort is being made to expedite the movement of French troops to Saigon in sufficient numbers to enable them to take over from the British forces.[5]

Thus praising the French, the British actively worked toward the restoration of French rule in Indochina. Unlike the Chinese in the North who opposed a French return, the British in Cochinchina zealously helped the French reestablish the old order. With such cooperation, the French rapidly occupied Saigon and gradually reconquered Cochinchina from which they launched military operations against Ho's Democratic Republic.

Ever since the Japanese putsch of March 9, 1945, a coalition of political groups had come into existence in Cochinchina. It included the politico-religious sects of Cao Dai and Hoa Hao, the pro-Japanese parties of Phuc Quoc (National Restoration) and Dai Viet (Great Vietnam), the Trotskyists, and several other minor parties. Not until August 14, on the eve of Japan's surrender, did the occupation authorities give their blessing to the so-called United National Front organized with a view to taking power after their departure. Two days later, an Executive Committee was formed to which the Japanese formally transferred power. These nationalists immediately entered into negotiation with the Japanese command to obtain arms for their militia. Aware that any Japanese-nationalist agreement to this effect would reduce their

chance of leading the revolution in Cochinchina, Ho's cadres met
with the leaders of the United National Front. Playing on the
weakness of the nationalist group, the Communists emphasized
that the Front, which had been formed with the consent of the
Japanese command, would be treated as a Nipponese creation and
thus unacceptable to the Allied powers. The Viet Minh, they
argued, who had fought on the Allied side and won their confidence, would be in a better position to deal with them and preserve Vietnam's independence. All other organizations should,
therefore, rally behind the Viet Minh. In the meantime, the Ho Chi
Minh-led revolution had triumphed in Hanoi and Hue. On August
23, realizing their vulnerable position and succumbing to the Viet
Minh pressure, the United National Front leaders gave in. On
August 25, one day following Emperor Bao Dai's abdication,
which helped legitimize Ho's regime, the Nam Bo Committee or
Provisional Executive Committee for the South was formed, which
claimed itself to be the Southern branch of the Hanoi government.
Of its nine members, seven were Communist, including President
Tran Van Giau. On the same day, a monstrous demonstration took
place in Saigon, attended by hundreds of thousands who, waving
the Viet Minh gold-starred red flags, marched in perfect order
from 9 A.M. to 6 P.M. The demonstration clearly bespoke the Viet
Minh prestige and organizational talent. In a swift move, the Nam
Bo Committee took over power in Saigon, installing itself in the
Government Palace and the City Hall, occupying public buildings,
and running the public services, including the police. With the
formation of the Nam Bo Committee and its control by the Viet
Minh, Ho's men dominated the independence movement throughout the country.

On August 27, Cedile, the French Commissioner designate for
Cochinchina, met with the Provisional Executive Committee,
notably its three Communist members, President Tran Van Giau,
Commissar for Foreign Affairs Pham Van Bach, and Commissar of
the Interior Nguyen Van Tao. Cedile had nothing to offer but the
French government's declaration of March 24, 1945. The Communists, understandably, rejected it as a basis for discussion, insisting
on French recognition of Vietnam's independence. This meeting,
like many ensuing Franco-Viet Minh negotiations, ended in frustration for both sides.

The leaders of the United National Front, in the meantime, became increasingly aware that the Viet Minh were exploiting the nationalist movement for their own ends. Their anger exploded when they learned that Giau had been in contact with Cedile. In an attempt to forestall any nationalist maneuver, the Nam Bo Committee, on Ho's order, organized on September 2 another huge demonstration with several purposes in mind: (*a*) to celebrate independence, (*b*) to show the Viet Minh strength, and (*c*) to impress the Allies with a big welcome. That afternoon, a crowd of several hundred thousand men and women marched in columns on the main streets of Saigon. Unlike a similar one which took place on the same day in Hanoi, however, the mass demonstration in Saigon was marked with disunity. The different groups, Cao Dai, Hoa Hao, Binh Xuyen, Phuc Quoc, Dai Viet, Trotskyist, Viet Minh, etc., paraded their own banners and shouted their own slogans. While they were apparently united in the thought of national independence, they were divided in their desire to be independent from each other. The march which had begun in peace and order ended in violence and chaos. Toward the end of the day, shots were fired. Several Frenchmen were killed. Many others were arrested and their houses ransacked. "The Viet Minh later charged," writes an American reporter, "that French provocateurs had used drunken liberated prisoners of war to provoke disorders. The French version was that Annamites, inflamed by the day's speeches, had begun attacking Europeans. The Annamites scornfully rejected this charge, pointing out in correspondence with the British headquarters that there had been Europeans in the watching crowd all afternoon without incident. The Annamites, moreover, had every interest in maintaining order. The French had every interest in fomenting disorder."[6]

While it was not clear who began the shooting, one thing was indeed obvious. The Viet Minh were not able to control the crowd. What had started out as a demonstration of Viet Minh strength ended as an indication of the Viet Minh inability to maintain order. The September 2 incident also intensified the distrust and resentment that Frenchmen and Vietnamese had of each other, and brought the British into the scene. Since the Viet Minh controlled the Nam Bo Committee, which was in fact the government in Saigon, they were responsible for the disorder of September 2.

Aware of the repercussions which such an explosive situation might cause, and of the ugly mood of the masses who wanted nothing short of independence and were unwilling to tolerate foreign interference, the Viet Minh appealed for moderation, denouncing the extremists and fomenters of trouble. In reply to the call for "arms to the people" by the International Communist League, a Trotskyist group that had not participated in the United National Front, Tran Van Giau issued the following statement on September 7, 1945:

A group of persons have organized a meeting demanding that the population be armed. The Japanese and Allied authorities, informed of this, fear that new and more bloody difficulties will ensue. . . . According to international agreement, the Japanese Army must assure order up to the arrival of the Allied army of occupation and everyone cannot but know that the Japanese forces here are still intact despite the surrender. Japanese General Headquarters has therefore decided to: (1) disarm the national troops, (2) confiscate machine guns or other arms, (3) ban all political movements which trouble order and security, (4) ban all demonstrations without prior authorization of Japanese General Headquarters, (5) disarm the population. In the interest of our country we call on all to have confidence in us and not let themselves be led by people who betray our country. It is only in this spirit that we can facilitate our relations with the Allied representatives.[7]

In an attempt to unburden themselves of the responsibility for the deteriorating conditions following the September 2 incident, the Viet Minh blamed the extremists for the Japanese intervention:

Who are those who have provoked these measures (by the Japanese)? In this situation can they oppose a superior military force? Have they means with which to make diplomatic protests? Democratic liberty which we, the Administrative Committee, have given to the People, these irresponsible individuals have used to harm the people, to harm the country. So, for the people's rights, for the nation's life, the Viet Minh Executive Committee appeals to the population to unmask the egoistic provocateurs. This alone will permit us to surmount the difficulties of the moment and get the people out of the trap which has been set by their enemies.[8]

The Viet Minh insistence on a friendly welcome for the Allies and their condemnation of the call for "arms to the people," in addition to their secret contact with the French, were criticized as treasonable by other nationalist and Trotskyist groups. The attitude of the Allied representatives strengthened the latter's position. Upon its arrival on September 6, the first British mission also demanded the disarming of all Vietnamese, including the police and militia. Rejecting the British request, the Cao Dai, Hoa Hao, and Trotskyists at the same time mounted a concerted attack against the Viet Minh. Faced with such pressure and a lack of popular support, Tran Van Giau gave in on September 10, agreeing to reshuffle the Nam Bo Committee by admitting more non-Viet Minh members, and to resign from its chairmanship in favor of the "independent" Pham Van Bach, who was actually a Communist sympathizer. The reconstituted Executive Committee of thirteen members, of whom only four were Communist, ceased to be a Viet Minh monopoly. This concession seemed to be a defeat for Ho who had hoped that his henchman Tran Van Giau would head a Communist government when the Allied troops arrived. In appearance, Ho was losing ground in Cochinchina. In reality, however, the old fox continued to outmaneuver his adversaries. In spite of the compromise, a struggle for power went on within the Executive Committee. The ruthless Giau methodically picked his targets, starting with his Trotskyist opponents. Among his famous victims was the popular Trotskyist leader Ta Thu Thau, a personal friend of Ho Chi Minh. Thau was killed in Quang Ngai on Giau's order and with Ho's approval while he was en route to Saigon, returning from a visit with the President of the Democratic Republic of Vietnam (DRV). Having taken care of the Trotskyists, Giau then launched military operations against the Cao Dai and Hoa Hao forces in various parts of Cochinchina.

Meanwhile, on September 12, the first battalion of British troops, composed entirely of Nepalese Gurkhas, landed in Saigon, accompanied by a company of French soldiers from Calcutta. A bad portent of the events to come! On the following day, General Douglas D. Gracey, Commander of the British occupation forces, arrived in the midst of growing tension between Vietnamese and Frenchmen. Before his departure from India for Cochinchina, Gracey had expressed the view that Indochina was exclusively a French affair and that it would be only a matter of weeks before the French took over the civil and military control of the country.[9] His mission, therefore, would be to disarm the Japanese and lay ground for the French return in Indochina. The British general's attitude greatly encouraged the French colons who were exceedingly eager to take reprisals against the Viet Minh "adventurers," "agitators," and "hoodlums." Commissioner Cedile, whose power was limited to negotiating with the Vietnamese on the basis of the March 24, 1945, declaration, gradually fell under the influence of the Saigon colons who counselled firmness and inflexibility instead of compromise. Such was the situation as Gracey found it upon his landing in Saigon.

Apparently ill-informed, the British commander was nonetheless well disposed toward the French. The Nam Bo Committee immediately sought to establish contact with him, offering to help the Allied mission in its task of disarming the Japanese. Gracey arrogantly refused to deal with them on the flimsy ground that the Viet Minh government was merely a Japanese creature. The British general's contempt for the Vietnamese was later corroborated by himself. "They came to see me and said welcome and all that sort of thing," Gracey remarked in his address to the Royal Central Asian Society in 1953. "It was an unpleasant situation and I promptly kicked them out."[10] Anxious to restore the French right to reoccupy Indochina, the British gave full support to Cedile's position. With the swiftness of an effective field commander and the determination of a man fully convinced of the superiority of the white race, Gracey repeated the earlier British order that all Vietnamese be disarmed. The general's high-handed action and his indiscreetly offensive pro-French attitude, instead of restoring order as he had claimed to do, disturbed the precarious peace that had prevailed in Saigon, gave encouragement to the French colons, and smashed the Viet Minh hope of enlisting Allied support for their cause.

On September 17, the Nam Bo Committee called a general strike in protest against the Anglo-French collusion and arrested a number of Frenchmen and Vietnamese collaborators. Cedile urged Gracey to take immediate action to save French lives and property, giving the British abundant reports of alleged mistreatment of French nationals and of a planned Viet Minh armed uprising in Saigon. Gracey hesitated. Then on September 19, at his press conference, French Commissioner Cedile provokingly stated that "the Viet Minh do not represent public opinion. They are incapable of maintaining order and preventing looting. First, there must be order. Then we shall constitute a government in accordance with the March 24 Declaration."[11] Such French intransigence precluded any meaningful negotiation with the Nam Bo Committee. The Vietnamese soon realized that Cedile would not have taken such an uncompromising stand without British approval. Gracey, in fact, made public his position by suppressing all Vietnamese newspapers and declaring martial law in Saigon on September 21. "He banned all demonstrations and public meetings and made illegal the carrying of arms of any description, including sticks, staves, and bamboo spears, except by Allied soldiers. Crimes against public order became military offenses and the penalty for sabotage and looting was death."[12] On the following day, the British commander took an even bolder step. After having taken control of the Saigon prison and released the French parachutists who had been incarcerated by the Japanese, Gracey's men went to the barracks where the French 11th Colonial Infantry Regiment had been confined since the Japanese coup of March 9, selected some 1,400 men, then armed them for action. Toward the evening, these French soldiers, anxious to show that they too knew how to fight, attacked any Vietnamese who happened to be on the street. They worked through the night, took over the Saigon police stations one by one, successively occupied the central post office, the treasury, and, just before dawn, the City Hall, the seat of the Viet Minh government. "Annamite sentries were shot down. Occupants of the building were either killed or taken prisoner. Records were seized and scattered. Scores of Annamites were trussed up and marched off. Foreign eyewitnesses that morning saw blood flow, saw men bound and beaten. They saw French colonial culture being restored to Saigon."[13]

While numerous Vietnamese were arrested, the members of the Nam Bo Committee escaped from the capital. September 23, 1945, was thus a day of victory for French colonialism. As the tricolor flag again flew over Saigon, the French population, who had lived in fear for three weeks, wildly celebrated their "comeback" by insulting and attacking their Vietnamese "enemies" while French and British soldiers looked on. Foreign correspondents, including French reporters, were shocked by the outrage.[14] Faced with such provocation, the Vietnamese fought back. Fighting broke out on the streets of Saigon. Thereupon, General Gracey offered his good offices, inviting the Viet Minh leaders to negotiate with the French.

"But why," Gracey's chief political spokesman was asked, "why would you not talk with the Viet Minh before the shooting started?"

"Because you cannot negotiate when a pistol is held at your head," the British official replied.

"You mean you can negotiate only when you hold a pistol at the other party's head?"

He shrugged.[15]

Very rapidly Saigon became a city without laws. Fighting spread throughout the capital, accompanied by kidnaps and massacres. Greatly embarrassed by world opinion which had been focused on the events in Cochinchina, and aware that the situation had gotten out of hand, Gracey thrusted the responsibility for restoring order on the Japanese command, warning that, unless they complied, they would be treated as war criminals! Thus, Japanese troops, who had been waiting to be disarmed and repatriated, were used against the Vietnamese whom the British and the French erroneously and monotonously labelled as Japanese agents. The Japanese were instructed to extend their patrols far outside their position, while Allied, i.e., British and French, soldiers took in thousands of Vietnamese prisoners and turned them over to the French authorities for trial. Gracey even had the temerity to declare that as soon as General Leclerc arrived and was ready to assume command, the responsibility for maintaining order would be put into French hands. In word and in deed, General Gracey convincingly proved that the British mission in Indochina was twofold: to restore French rule and to disarm the Japanese. He carried out the first part with astonishing zeal and the second with unusual nonchalance.

As Foreign Secretary Bevin remarked, every effort was made "to expedite the movement of French troops to Saigon in sufficient numbers to enable them to take over from the British forces."[16] Thousands of French soldiers landed in Saigon every week. By the end of the year, approximately, 50,000 French troops equipped with modern American weapons took over as the British prepared to withdraw. From Saigon they gradually spread into the countryside, taking control of the provincial capitals one after another.

The last Viet Minh stronghold in Camau, the southernmost point of Vietnam, fell to the French on February 6, 1946. Although the French claimed that the South had been "pacified," Ho's guerillas roamed the countryside, attacking French outposts and Vietnamese villages protected by French troops.

On January 28, after having transferred civil and military power to the French authorities and left huge quantities of weapons and ammunition to Leclerc's army, Gracey finally left Saigon. The British commander had fulfilled his mission. Now it was up to the French to complete their conquest. From Hanoi, Ho Chi Minh watched the events in Cochinchina with anger and frustration. In vain he lodged one protest after another to the British. In vain he sent repeated appeals to the Allied powers. In vain he tried to mobilize world opinion against the French.

The Chinese Problem

As the Allied representatives in the South worked against the Viet Minh interest, their counterparts in the North did not entertain much sympathy for the Hanoi government. Ho Chi Minh's only consolation lay in the fact that the Chinese, unlike the British, strongly opposed a French return to Indochina.

On August 12 and 13, 1945, Jean Sainteny, the head of the French intelligence mission in Kunming, China, apprehensively warned his government that the Chinese, with the support of important American leaders, were preparing to expel the French from their Southeast Asian colonies. A Chinese occupation of North Indochina would be the worst of all solutions, and he recommended that France should oppose such an injustice which would seriously damage her prestige in Asia.[17] This warning was followed eleven days later by Chiang Kai-shek's disavowal of any territorial ambitions in Indochina and a pledge of neutrality in regard to Indochinese affairs. On August 28, four Kuomintang armies, the 52nd, 60th, 62nd, and 93rd, totalling 180,000 men under the command of General Lu Han, crossed the Tonkinese frontier. This large figure was given by the Chungking government to the French who, under the terms of an agreement, had to bear the cost of the occupation. It included whole Chinese armies which, though moving across North Indochina in transit, were nevertheless counted as part of the permanent garrison which numbered approximately 50,000. "The Indochina deal was in every way a felicitous one for Chiang Kai-shek," writes Harold Isaacs, "even serving his domestic political purposes. As the occupying force he sent in the best units of the Yunnan provincial armies controlled by Governor Lung Yun, Lu Han's brother-in-law. Then Chiang Kai-shek knocked over Governor Lung in a swift coup at Kunming and acquired full control, for the first time, of Yunnan Province."[18]

It would be of interest to note that Governor Lung Yun had been the protector of Vietnamese nationalists, notably adherents of the Viet Nam Quoc Dan Dang (VNQDD), in Yunnan. Thus, the arrival of Lu Han spelled nothing but trouble for Ho Chi Minh. To further complicate the situation, General Chiang Fa-ku'ei, the Governor of Kwangsi and founder of the Dong Minh Hoi (DMH), appointed General Siao Wan Chief of the Political Secret Services in Indochina and entrusted him the difficult task of bringing the Vietnamese nationalist movement under Chinese control.

Into Indochina the Cantonese contingents of the occupation army brought members of the DMH and their leader Nguyen Hai Than, while the Yunnanese troops were accompanied by elements of the VNQDD and their chief Vu Hong Khanh. On their way to Hanoi, the Chinese disarmed and replaced all local Viet Minh militia and committees with their men from the DMH and the VNQDD. Much of the delta between Hanoi and Haiphong was thus placed in the hands of the Kuomintang protégés. Even the control of the capital was divided between the Viet Minh and the pro-Chinese nationalist elements. The VNQDD and the DMH, generously supplied with arms and money, openly fought the Viet Minh militia and engaged in feverish propaganda activities against Ho's government, publishing newspapers, distributing tracts denouncing the Communist exploitation of the independence movement. Other nationalist groups soon joined in the anti-Viet Minh struggle.

Soon after their arrival, the Chinese armies aroused widespread resentment. While some appeared well-trained, too many, including large numbers of destitute camp followers, were ragged and ill-disciplined. They rapidly revealed their intention to treat Indo-

china as a conquered territory and exploit it to the fullest extent.
General Lu Han comfortably installed himself in the Governor
General's palace, from which Jean Sainteny, the self-appointed
French representative, had been expelled on September 9, while
other Chinese officers occupied the best buildings available. The
presence in the North of large numbers of Chinese, of whom Vietnamese have had a historical distrust, was a disaster for the local
people and a grave crisis for the government. Unlike the small
British contingents in the South who had brought along their own
provisions, the huge Chinese armies lived off the land and, consequently, deprived the underfed and starving Vietnamese of their
scarce food. Lu Han also arbitrarily made the almost worthless
Chinese currency a legal tender at an advantageous rate of exchange, which was fixed at 1.5 Indochinese piaster for 1 Chinese
customs "gold" unit or 20 Chinese dollars. This inflated rate, nearly
ten times the value of the Chinese currency on the black market in
southern Chinese cities, permitted Lu Han and his cohort to make
enormous purchases in the local market. Very rapidly, the northern
market was flooded with Chinese "gold units." Displaying an utter
disregard for the deplorable conditions of the Vietnamese people,
the Chinese took from both the rich and the poor whatever they
needed or wanted. "Scarcely a door-knob, a light fixture, or a sash
weight remained in the city when the Chinese had left."[19] While
their soldiers plundered the country, the Kuomintang generals and
their civilian associates rapaciously acquired real estate and other
profitable enterprises (theaters, hotels, restraurants, residential and
rental properties, factories, mines, etc.), using persuasion or threat
of force, if necessary.

Lu Han also laid claim to all Japanese ammunition, weapons,
war material, stocks, and property. These looting techniques led to
numerous clashes between Chinese and Vietnamese who, in vain,
appealed to their government for help. Painfully aware of his own
limitations, Ho Chi Minh counselled patience. He could ill afford
antagonizing the Chinese whose forces he was not in a position to
challenge. A false step might mean the end of his government.
Thus, in spite of the Chinese predatory actions which exhausted his
country's economy, Ho often paid tribute to the Kuomintang. General Siao Wan was no stranger to Ho. As an aide to Governor
Chiang Fa-ku'ei and a former director of the Dai Kien Training

School, Siao had committed the Viet Minh leader to prison in 1942. Now, Chief of the Political Secret Services in North Indochina, the Chinese general could easily oust Ho and destroy him whenever the old revolutionary appeared insensitive to Chinese interest.

Familiar with the methods of operation of the Chinese warlords, Ho had decided to buy their cooperation. Upon Lu Han's arrival in Hanoi, Ho had welcomed him with a magnificent gift, a solid gold opium smoking set. The expensive present came from the proceeds of the "Gold Week,"[20] which the Viet Minh had organized for the express purpose of obtaining funds to pay for the weapons sold by the Chinese troops. The "Gold Week" brought in 400 kilograms or 800 pounds of gold and 20 million piasters, the bulk of which was used to bribe the Chinese occupants. With a view both to reminding the Kuomintang command of their mission and to distracting the Vietnamese from their unhappy conditions, official publications of the DRV repeatedly emphasized that the Chinese armies had been sent to Indochina specifically to disarm the Japanese, that they entertained no hostile designs regarding Vietnam's sovereignty, and that they had come as friends to help the nascent republic defend its independence.

Though officially the Chinese were responsible for the maintenance of law and order, the actual administration of the country was in the hands of the Ho government. The 3,500 French troops who had been disarmed and interned at the Hanoi citadel continued to live there under severe restrictions, while some 1,000 of their comrades in arms who had fled to China following the Japanese putsch in March were not allowed to reenter Tonkin. From the beginning Lu Han conveyed the clear impression that he would not permit a French return, and made no effort to conceal his intention to remove all vestiges of French authority. Consequently, Sainteny was expelled from the Governor General's Palace, and the tricolor flag was not even allowed to fly over the French mission's headquarters. During his visit to Hanoi early in October, General Ho Ying-chin, the Chinese Chief of Staff, also reaffirmed his government's intention to help Vietnam achieve independence from France, and emphatically stated that no French troops would enter Indochina, notably the area under Chinese control, without Allied permission. However encouraging the Kuomintang attitude might be, Ho remained distressed by the thought of dealing with his nationalist competitors who enjoyed strong Chinese support. The former Comintern agent adroitly played his cards. Instead of protesting against the Chinese exploitation of his country, Ho spent huge sums of money exacted from his impoverished people to bribe the rapacious Kuomintang warlords and thus bought their recognition of his regime. It was not Ho's shrewdness alone, however, that saved him. The unpreparedness of his nationalist opponents and the greed of the Chinese command were greatly responbile for his survival.

The DMH and the VNQDD felt themselves betrayed by the Viet Minh, who, in spite of the March, 1944, agreement[21] under which Ho had accepted a post in the Provisional Government, had set up an independent government of their own at the expense of the nationalist organizations. Following a warning by Nguyen Hai Than on his arrival in Hanoi that the Chinese would not tolerate a government led by Ho Chi Minh, the Viet Minh leader hurriedly called on his former jailer, General Siao Wan. In return for a very expensive gift, the Chinese intelligence chief agreed to give Ho additional time. Nguyen Hai Than, however, continued to insist that Ho include in his government representatives from all the oganizations that had taken part in the clandestine struggle for independence, threatening to use force, i.e., Chinese troops, if necessary. Both the DMH and the VNQDD persisted in their demand for a government of National Union to lead the fight against the returning French imperalists.

On their part, the Chinese command, for a moment, toyed with the idea of sacking Ho's government. Distressed, however, by the incompetence of their quarrelsome DMH and VNQDD protégés who could not compete with the Viet Minh without direct, active Chinese support, Lu Han and his entourage demurred. The replacement of Ho's regime with an inexperienced, inefficient pro-Chinese government would be a most unwise political move. It might push Ho, who had a well-run organization and a considerable following, to take up armed resistance and, consequently, plunge the North into chaos. To the greedy Chinese the most disastrous result of such an undertaking would be the end of their plunder. However, the Chinese command, notably Siao Wan, whose attempts to limit and control the Viet Minh activities in China had been frustrated by the resourceful Ho, became quite apprehensive that, unless appropriate precaution was taken, their Vietnamese friends would be eventually eliminated. They, therefore, sought to place DMH and VNQDD elements in positions of power by constraining Ho to include more nationalists in his government.

Confronted with an increasingly violent anti-Viet Minh campaign and faced with mounting Chinese pressure, the old fox temporarily yielded. On October 23, an agreement between Ho Chi Minh and Nguyen Hai Than was concluded under which the DMH pledged to support the government in its struggle for independence and against colonialism in return for Ho's promise to admit nationalist members to his cabinet. The accord, however, was short-lived. The VNQDD, ever mindful of Ho's treacherous maneuvers in the past, rejected the pact. Instead, it continued to clamor for a thorough reshuffling of the government to include a large number of nationalists, attacking Ho where he was most vulnerable, namely, that his government was controlled by the Indochinese Communist Party (ICP). Finding himself on the defensive, the worried DRV President hastily convened the Central Committee of the ICP for a three-day conference, from November 9 to 11, 1945. With a view to disarming his opponents, Ho made a startling move. At the close of the conference, the ICP announced its own dissolution. The Communist resolution read:

1. Whereas, in consideration of the given historical situation, both internationally and internally, the present moment is precisely an exceptional occasion for Vietnam to reconquer her unitary independence;

2. Whereas, in order to complete the Party's task in this immense movement of the Vietnamese people's emancipation, a national union conceived without distinction of class and parties is an indispensable factor;

3. Wishing to prove that the Communists, in so far as they are advance guard militants of the Vietnamese people, are always ready to make the greatest sacrifices for national liberation, are always disposed to put the interest of the country above that of classes, and to give up the interests of the Party to serve those of the Vietnamese people;

4. In order to destroy all misunderstandings, domestic and foreign, which can hinder the liberation of our country, the Central Executive Committee of the Indochina Communist Party in meeting assembled on

November 11, 1945, has decided to voluntarily dissolve the Indochina Communist Party.

Those followers of Communism desirous of continuing their theoretical studies will affiliate with the Indochina Association of Marxist Studies.

Central Committee Indochina Communist Party
November 11, 1945[22]

Ho's strategy was also calculated to reassure the Chinese command of the nationalist nature of the Viet Minh government and to make it more appealing to non-Communist Vietnamese. In reality, however, the dissolution of the ICP was just another Ho trick. "In truth," as Truong Chinh was to reveal candidly later, "it continued its activities underground."[23] Ho immediately issued numerous appeals to individuals and organizations, urging everyone to unite in the common struggle against French colonialism. The government simultaneously announced that a draft of a democratic constitution would shortly be submitted to the people for consideration. Basically, it would provide for an elected President of the Republic, an elected National Legislature, and a set of rights and duties of citizens.

The DMH and the VNQDD, however, refused to be misled by Ho's new move. The Viet Minh chief's unwillingness to reshuffle his government did nothing but stiffen the nationalist opposition. From their headquarters located in the Chinese-occupied sections, they launched repeated attacks against Ho's militia. Hanoi was a city at war. Ho, who had made tortuous attempts to convince the Chinese that he favored cooperation with his opponents but always backed out, deemed that the situation had become too serious to postpone a compromise. The Chinese command, on their part, hoped that a Viet Minh-nationalist coalition would work this time. The Liuchow experiment of October, 1942,[24] was again repeated. General Siao Wan brought together the opposition forces and pressured them to reach an agreement. An accord was concluded between the Viet Minh, the DMH, and the VNQDD, which provided for:

a. A government of national union;
b. Participation by all three parties in the policy-making process;

c. The fusion of the three militias;

d. A pledge not to use force to settle disputes;

e. A cessation of mutual attacks through the press;

f. The creation of a unified army to liberate the South.

No sooner had it been reached than the agreement of November 19 proved worthless. Having made a pledge which he did not intend to honor, the old fox decreed elections for a Quoc Dan Dai Hoi or National Assembly to be held on December 23.[25] In violation of his solemn promise, Ho postponed the formation of a new coalition government on the grounds that it should take place only after the people had expressed their will at the polls. Ho's maneuver greatly worried his opponents who had good reasons to believe that the Viet Minh would rig the elections. In their view, a Communist victory was ensured by two main factors: (a) the nationalists' exclusion from the government, which, in the eye of the predominantly illiterate masses, had been primarily responsible for Vietnam's independence, and (b) the Viet Minh readiness to take advantage of the administrative machinery both during the short campaign and at the polls. Pushed into a corner, the DMH and the VNQDD reacted with increasing violence and effectiveness. Besides organizing large antigovernment demonstrations, they thrust all their forces on the Viet Minh militia, and went so far as to kidnap important Communist officials, including Minister of Interior Vo Nguyen Giap, and Propaganda Minister Tran Huy Lieu. Another top leader, Tran Van Giau, who had just arrived from Cochinchina, barely escaped assassination. Simultaneously, the nationalists vigorously clamored for the formation, without delay, of a coalition government, calling on the people to boycott the announced elections. Peace and order had vanished from the capital. The situation kept deteriorating. Unable to suppress the opposition and restore order, the Ho government found itself in a precarious existence.

Thereupon, Lu Han stepped in. Lest their interests be seriously affected by prolonged chaos, the Chinese command forced the warring parties to negotiate their dispute. Another round of talks began. Aware that they could not oppose elections, the nationalists tried to have them postponed on the grounds that their candidates needed time to conduct an adequate campaign. On December 19, Ho yielded, agreeing to postpone the elections until January 6. This concession, however, did not satisfy the Chinese and their protégés, who stressed that their exclusion from the government had been an insurmountable handicap in the campaign. A compromise formula was finally accepted by both sides. Ho acquiesced in the nationalist demand for seventy seats in the National Assembly (twenty for the DMH and fifty for the VNQDD), regardless of the outcome of the elections. On December 25, Ho also complied with his opponents' request that a coalition government be formed immediately. It would be composed of ten members: four Viet Minh, four nationalists, and two independent. At the nationalists' request, Vo Nguyen Giap and Tran Huy Lieu, two of Ho's closest and most effective associates, were not to be included in the new government.

Why did Ho make such important concessions? Several factors might have influenced his decision:

a. General Siao Wan's forceful pressure;

b. The chaotic conditions in the capital;

c. Ho's fear that his opposition would sabotage the elections, which he desperately wanted;

d. Ho's realization that the 70 seats promised to his competitors would give them little or no influence in a 350-member National Assembly;

e. Mutual agreement that the provisional coalition government would resign after the elections, which the Viet Minh would inevitably win.

Therefore, Ho's acceptance of the nationalist conditions should not be interpreted as a Viet Minh setback. While the concessions appeared to be a significant gain for the DMH and the VNQDD, they had no concrete or lasting effects. Most importantly, they assured the survival of the Ho government and made possible the elections which were to put a cloak of legitimacy upon the Viet Minh regime. Far from weakening his influence, the coalition government increased Ho's appeal among the masses. In fact, in his address to the people following the formation of the new government, the astute revolutionary was able to say:

With a view to winning complete independence and bringing about a close cooperation between the various political parties to further strengthen the Government, it is now named the Provisional Government. At this moment, if the parties unite together, the Government can overcome difficulties. All the Vietnamese people want the Provisional Government to hold office until the election of the National Assembly, which will change it into a definite Government.[26]

In this declaration, Ho also informed the Vietnamese that the various armed forces would be unified under the government, that is, under Viet Minh control, and that political parties were not permitted to maintain standing armies. These were essentially the terms of the Viet Minh-nationalist agreement, which the old fox intended to make public to convince the people of the reasonableness of his position and to deny his opponents any pretext to resort to violence should the events turn against them. A very shrewd move, indeed!

The crisis temporarily weathered, Ho turned his attention to the elections. On the eve of the election, the calculating revolutionary launched a last appeal to his people with a twofold purpose in mind: (*a*) to turn out as many voters as possible who would put a seal of approval on the Viet Minh regime, and (*b*) to show to the world that the Vietnamese were closely united behind Ho's government:

Tomorrow will be January 6, 1946.

It will take our people to a new path.

It will be a happy day for our compatriots, because it is the day of the general election, the first day in Vietnamese history on which our people will begin to enjoy their democratic rights.

Tomorrow our people will show to the southern fighters that while in the military field they are using weapons to oppose the enemy, in the political field we are using our votes to consolidate our forces.

Tomorrow our compatriots will show to the world that the Vietnamese people are determined to: unite closely, fight the colonialists, and regain independence.

Tomorrow they will freely choose and elect worthy people to represent them in the management of State affairs. . . .

Tomorrow all voters will not fail to go to the polls. Tomorrow everybody will enjoy the rights granted to independent and free citizens.[27]

Since its coming to power, the Viet Minh had indefatigably and successfully built up a legend for Ho Chi Minh, picturing him as an intrepid patriot whose daring exploits had inspired a generation of revolutionaries, a fearless nationalist who had confounded both the French and the Japanese, the Liberator of Vietnam, the Founder of the republic, the benign Uncle of the people. The legend had captivated the imagination of the largely illiterate masses. Thus, in order to win, a candidate simply needed to hang on to Uncle Ho's coattail. Just as in the United States, during the 1956 electoral campaign, many candidates, exploiting President Eisenhower's popularity, came up with buttons and slogans such as "I Like Ike," and "Ike Likes Me," Viet Minh candidates in 1946 had also resorted to the same practice. Everyone claimed that he liked Uncle Ho or Uncle Ho liked him, that he had been a friend or an associate of the Viet Minh chief. This, however, was not necessary as the events were to illustrate. A Ho Chi Minh-organized election would inevitably lead to a Communist victory.

The campaign and first national election proceeded as expected. Many candidates, whom the regime labelled as "undesirable," such as those who had criticized or would challenge the Communist leadership and those who were justly and unjustly accused of collaboration with the French or the Japanese, were disqualified. Only government-approved names were permitted to present themselves as candidates. With a view to conveying the impression of widespread participation, Ho arranged to have a few prominent non–Viet Minh personalities run and be elected here and there. In a country where an overwhelming majority of the people were illiterate and unfamiliar with the democratic process, the general election was nothing but a farce. The following excerpt from an article in *Viet Nam* (January 8, 1946), the VNQDD official newspaper, correctly reflected the popular attitude toward the unusual election:

I met a dyer. In reply to my question "Whom are you going to vote for tomorrow," he said: "I know only Ho Chi Minh; therefore, I will vote for him." A barber also told me: "I will vote for Ho Chi Minh. I don't have to worry about the other candidates for I don't know them. But the election officials must know them, and they will tell me whom I should vote for." An employee of the Water Company said to me: "I did not want to go to the polls, but my neighbor who is a Tu Ve (Viet Minh militiaman) kept pestering me until I agreed to go. I don't know how to write. I will ask someone at the voting station to help me mark my ballot." A resident of Nam Dinh confessed to me: "I had already voted in Nam Dinh, but I wanted to see the election in Hanoi. So I arranged to obtain another ballot here." At another polling station, a woman asked the three young girls sitting at the desk: "Would you please write down the names of the candidates I must vote for? I don't have much time for politics, and I don't know all the candidates either."[28]

As a former member of the Vietnamese resistance movement describes, "the names of official candidates (the majority of whom were communists and party sympathizers, including the ex-Emperor Bao Dai) were versified and also inscribed in three lists called A, B, and C. When illiterate voters who then formed 80 per cent of the population arrived at the ballot box, the official responsible for marking the ballot paper on their behalf would ask them: 'For whom do you want to vote?' All they had to do was simply to recite the verse they had memorized or to say 'A, B, and C,' and that did the trick."[29]

Similar stories could be told *ad infinitum*. While too young to vote, the author, who then lived in the village of Phu Ninh, District of Quang Trach, Province of Quang Binh, accompanied his mother out of curiosity to the village hall where the voting took place. In the center of the hall, there was a big table over which a huge portrait of Chairman Ho looked down, and around which sat two solemn-faced election officials, who were also Viet Minh agents. This was the polling "booth." Although a list of five candidates who were to run for the five seats alloted to the area had been circulated among the people who were expected to memorize the names, the predominantly illiterate villagers were unable to remember them. To those who forgot the candidates' names, the officials would ask: "Are you voting for A, B, X, Y, and Z?" Invariably, the answers were "Yes" or "Of course." To accelerate the process, one of the officials came up with an ingenious idea. He asked the voters to gather in groups of ten, collected the ballots, then asked one group after another the same question he had put to individual voters: "Are you voting for A, B, X, Y, and Z?" The answer, of course, was always affirmative.

It was about noon. Some one hundred persons, who had been busy chatting with each other, had not voted. The presiding election official told them to leave their ballots on the table, promising to mark them as soon as he had time. The people obligingly thanked him for his helpfulness. The voting was over. Everyone was satisfied. A "sophisticated" villager, who had been to the city several times, earnestly observed: "We should have a typewriter with a lot of carbon paper. It would be much faster to mark lots of ballots, all at the same time, with a typewriter." He then proceeded to explain to his friends how a typewriter worked and how carbon copies were made. Very impressed, his friends nodded approvingly. The election in Phu Ninh was typical of what went on in the rest of the country on January 6, 1946, the day on which Vietnamese, as Ho said, "freely choose and elect worthy people to represent them in the management of State affairs." The old revolutionary thus thoroughly "prepared" his countrymen to enjoy their first democratic right and fulfill their first democratic duty. Generally, the voter was spared the trouble of having to make a choice as there was only one candidate for each seat available. Needless to say, the election officials were also government agents or Viet Minh sympathizers. In view of the illiteracy of the majority of the voters and of the lack of secrecy in the casting of ballots, these officials were free to mark the ballots as they pleased. Ho, who ran in Hanoi, received 98 per cent of the votes cast, while Vo Nguyen Giap was elected in Nghe An, Ho's native province, by a 97 per cent majority, and Pham Van Dong handily carried Quang Ngai, his birth place. In such an election, it was only natural to expect Viet Minh candidates, who ran under various party labels, to win by an impressive margin.

The first national election in Ho's republic was thus marked by glaring irregularities:

1. The party in power was so confident of the outcome of the election, or was so ready to fabricate returns, that it gave its opposition, in advance, seventy seats in the National Assembly;

2. The DMH and the VNQDD, aware of their ineffective organization, chose not to challenge the Viet Minh, but were accorded representation anyway;

3. In spite of the postponement of the election until January 6, 1946, it was held in many localities as originally scheduled, on December 23, 1945;[30]

4. Although no voting took place in the Tonkinese provinces controlled by the nationalists (Vinh Yen, Viet Tri, Yen Bay, Lang Son, Dap Cau, etc.), Viet Minh candidates were officially declared elected from these areas;

5. While the National Assembly held its opening session on March 2, 1946, the results of the election were not officially published until six weeks later, on April 13, long after the Assembly had recessed;

6. The importance or insignificance of the popularity "elected" National Assembly was well reflected in the length of its lightning session, which lasted five full hours, from 8 A.M. to 1 P.M.!

In any case, the election officially gave the Viet Minh a clear majority in the National Assembly, legitimized the Ho Chi Minh government, and transformed it into a permanent one. With such a popular "mandate," Ho, as he had usually done in the past, conveniently ignored the agreement he had concluded with the opposition. While publicly advocating unity, cooperation, and collaboration, the calculating Communist leader ordered military operations to "liberate" those areas controlled by the DMH and the VNQDD. At the outset, the mopping-up activities, which began on January 13, were not very successful. Whenever the situation turned against their Vietnamese friends, the Chinese stepped in. This Chinese intervention, however, did not deter Ho from pursuing his plan to eliminate his nationalist opponents. Not until July, 1946, after the Chinese troops' departure from Indochina, did the Viet Minh succeed in clearing the Red River Valley of nationalist elements. The last VNQDD frontier stronghold in Lao Kay fell in November of that year. Thus vanished all the vestiges of DMH and VNQDD military resistance to the Ho regime.

Meanwhile, in spite of extensive Chinese financial, military, and moral backing, the DMH and the VNQDD continued to be outmaneuvered by the astute revolutionary master from Nghe An. Losing, at last, all interest in supporting a lost cause, the Chinese command devoted their energy on more profitable pursuits. While waiting for the outcome of the Sino-French negotiations going on in Chungking, the Kuomintang generals carried on their predatory activities in Tonkin and North Annam. Finally, on February 28, 1946, a Franco-Chinese treaty was signed. Anxious to reoccupy, Indochina, the French acquiesced in most of the Chinese demands. Under the terms of the treaty, France agreed to:

a. Return to China the French concessions in Shanghai, Tientsin, Hankow, and Canton;

b. Reserve in the port of Haiphong a special zone for the free transit of goods coming from or bound for China;

c. Exempt from customs and transit duties all goods coming from or bound for China;

d. Transfer to China the ownership of the branch of the Indo-china-Yunnan Railroad situated in Chinese territory;

e. Respect the rights and privileges which Chinese nationals had traditionally enjoyed in Indochina.[31]

In return for these considerable concessions, Chungking promised to turn over to the French command the responsibility for guarding the Japanese, maintaining peace and order and protecting Chinese nationals north of the 16th parallel, and to withdraw its armies from Indochina within the month of March.

In spite of the Chungking treaty, the Chinese command in Indo-china, unable to prevent a French return, still made futile attempts to delay the landing of French troops in Haiphong on the grounds that they had not received specific instructions from their government to this effect. When Leclerc's troops attempted to disembark in Haiphong on March 6, they were greeted with fire from Chinese shore batteries. Not until two days later, after Chungking had directly intervened, did French troops go ashore. Greatly disappointed, the local Kuomintang commanders dragged their feet. It was not until the end of May that the first contingents of the Chinese armies begin to withdraw. By the middle of June, while the last Chinese troops nonchalantly left Tonkin, members of the Chinese Commissariat services and government departments still stayed on to take care of the sale and transportation of booty. Before their departure, the rapacious Chinese generals, whose main concern was financial gain, sold to Ho large quantities of

American weapons which had been given them under the Lend-Lease agreements and the Japanese stocks which they had acquired following their arrival in Vietnam.

In retrospect, the Chinese occupation of North Indochina, far from endangering the Viet Minh position, strengthened it considerably. By delaying the French return, the Chinese gave Ho the much-needed time to consolidate his gain, North Vietnam, and, at the same time, eliminate his nationalist competitors. Moreover, the Chinese supplied Ho with weapons which he had been unable to obtain from other sources.

The Foreign Front

If the election had the immediate effect of legitimizing Ho's government, it did not make its external problems any easier. Ho had hoped that the big powers would extend recognition to his regime and give moral support to an independent Vietnam. The United States, and more specifically the American OSS (Office of Strategic Services) officers in Tonkin, had expressed strong sympathy for the Viet Minh revolution. Major Patti, head of the OSS team that arrived in Hanoi in August, 1945, General Gallagher, head of the Combat Section South China Command, who entered Indochina as adviser to the Chinese Army, and Major Buckley, a representative of the State Department with the OSS, in addition to those officers who had been parachuted into Ho's jungle headquarters in the summer of that year, all honestly believed that both the Potsdam Agreement and the United States government opposed a French return in Indochina. Their sympathy for Ho's regime was repeatedly denounced by Jean Sainteny, in whose view the naïve Americans had been fooled by the revolutionary fox.[32] According to many French observers,[33] whose resentment against the Americans for the latter's alleged noncooperation often impaired their judgment, OSS officers in Tonkin were engaged in promoting American imperialism, showing the Vietnamese the wealth and power of the United States that could be used to bring democracy and economic prosperity to Vietnam. While Major Buckley founded the Vietnamese-American Friendship Association, Major Patti reportedly offered to support the DRV in exchange for economic concessions to the United States, and General Gallagher allegedly proposed that the building of railroads, roads, and airfields be given to the Donovan financial group.[34] Ho Chi Minh, as Chesneaux maintains, rejected these advances. Ho was known to be eager to enlist American help against the French and the Chinese and obtain U.S. recognition for his regime. He had in the past collaborated with the French, the British, and the Chinese, and with whoever would help his cause. Vo Nguyen Giap, too, was much in favor of "particularly intimate relations" with the United States. One is inclined, therefore, to believe that the shrewd DRV President would not have rejected such American offers had they been made.

The OSS officers, Sainteny writes, flattered by the Viet Minh government, inflated by a sense of importance accorded them by the French, but utterly ignorant of the Indochinese realities, played into Ho's hands. The Americans, Sainteny complains, did not even bother to conceal their dislike for the French. In spite of the absence of any evidence to support their argument, many influential Frenchmen[35] conveniently attributed the Viet Minh success to American intrigues. In any case, Ho did not enjoy official U.S. support. After an initial period of ambiguity, Washington, perhaps increasingly aware of Ho's Communist connections, informed its men in Tonkin that the United States would take a neutral position and would not oppose a French return in Indochina.

On his part, while trying to enlist American support, Ho was aware that it might not be forthcoming. During his conversations in December, 1945, with Frank White, then an OSS major, Ho candidly expressed his hopes and fears. The two men had an undisturbed talk for two hours. Of this meeting between two friends, White writes:

The conversation began in French, but he begged my pardon and said he would like to use his English, which was better than my French. He wondered if Americans knew how strongly the Vietnamese desired independence. He went back to the early Chinese invasions, then the French occupation and finally the past five years under the Japanese. But Ho really wanted to talk about the future, and he mentioned the need of help from France, the Soviet Union and the U.S., in that order.[36]

Referring to the agreements he was negotiating with the French representatives in Hanoi, he expressed doubt that they

would be honored either in Saigon or Paris. Further, he did not believe that the Soviet Union could or would make a real contribution to building a new Vietnam. The U.S. was probably in the best position to do that, but Ho doubted that the U.S. could be counted on.[37]

At Ho's invitation, White returned to the palace for a reception at 7 P.M. Of this dinner, which nobody except the Chinese guests enjoyed, the ex-OSS officer gives the following account:

There were three other Vietnamese with Ho. Two were elderly men in mandarin robes; the third, much younger, was introduced as the provisional minister of national defense. This was Vo Nguyen Giap; the name meant nothing then.

Suddenly through the big double doors burst the whole French military first team: Generals Leclerc, Valluy and Salan. I knew them well and they knew me; the French never concealed their dislike of OSS. But even the French were startled by the next arrivals: the field commander of Lu Han's Chinese army and his chief of staff, followed shortly by the British chief of MI-5 in Hanoi.

When dinner was announced I didn't know what to do. If there had not been an empty chair, I was prepared to slink away. But there was— next to Ho's. I sat down. The dinner was a horror. The French scarcely spoke to the Chinese, who in turn got drunk. At one point I said to Ho, "I think, Mr. President, that there is some resentment over the seating arrangement." I meant of course, my place next to him. "Yes," he replied, "I see that. But who else could I talk to?"[38]

Thus, in spite of his expressed doubts, Ho stubbornly clung to the hope that the United States would help him. With individual Americans the old revolutionary laboriously cultivated friendship, hoping that their reports to Washington would cause the United States to adopt a more favorable position toward his regime.

If Ho did not count on American support, neither did he bank on Soviet help. This view was echoed by leading Communist cadres.

Even the most orthodox among them, like shaggy-haired Tran Van Giau, the partisan organizer, granted that the Russians went out for "an excess of ideological compromise," and said he expected no help from that quarter, no matter how distant or verbal it might be. "The Russians are nationalists for Russia first and above all," another Annamite Communist said with some bitterness. "They would be interested in us only if we served some purpose of theirs. Right now, unfortunately, we do not seem to serve any such purpose."[39]

Moscow was, in fact, preoccupied with its effort to consolidate Soviet gains and extend Soviet influence in Europe, and, aware of the growing importance of the French Communist party, refrained from taking any step that might impair its good relations with Paris. Contrary to what it has been doing recently vis-à-vis the National Liberation Front and the so-called Provisional Government of South Vietnam which she promptly recognized, the Soviet Union was reluctant to extend official recognition to the DRV. Such acknowledgement did not come until January 30, 1950, more than four years after Ho had proclaimed Vietnam's independence.

When Ho referred to French help, he apparently did not have in mind the de Gaulle government, whose policy was the restoration of the old order in Indochina, but seemed to think of the French Communist party, which had then enjoyed considerable influence in France. A penetrating observer of French politics, Ho nevertheless did not lay all his hope on his French comrades, who were "Frenchmen and colonialists first and Communists after."

One of the top ranking Annamite Communists spoke contemptuously of Thorez, who in a Paris speech had said he was in favor of the Annamites "finally arriving at their independence." He laughed sourly: "A fine rubber phrase, is it not? You can stretch it into any shape or any meaning. No, I am afraid we cannot depend on these fine gentlemen. They are the dominant party in France now. And look what Frenchmen are doing now in Indochina."[40]

Ho was thus less successful on the foreign front than on the domestic front, where his ruthlessly effective ICP decisively eliminated the nationalist opposition in spite of Chinese interference. The Americans, while entertaining much sympathy for the Viet Minh revolution, were deterred by Ho's Communist connections. His Soviet and French comrades, to whom national interests and political ambitions took precedence over ideological considerations, were of no use to the old fighter.

The French Problem

While the British suppressed the Nam Bo Committee and systematically carried out a war against the Viet Minh on behalf of
the French in the South, the Chinese appeared ready to replace the
Ho Chi Minh government in the North with one led by their
Vietnamese protégés. Ho's problem was further complicated by
Paris' attempt to negotiate a settlement with Chungking regarding
the withdrawal of the Chinese armies from, and the return of
French troops to, North Indochina. Faced with this dilemma, Ho
desperately appealed to the Allies to recognize his regime and to
the French to negotiate with him. The French, however, aware of
Ho's revolutionary background and experience, ignored his advances. Instead, they sought out other nationalist leaders whom
they believed to be more malleable. On October 12 and 15, 1945,
for instance, Sainteny approached Nguyen Hai Than, the DMH
leader. The Vietnamese impressed the French representative as a
dull person, lacking an effective organization and a solid power
base. While the intransigent VNQDD refused to have anything to
do with the French, ex-Emperor Bao Dai, aware of his own precarious existence and convinced that a wrong move would be fatal
for him, frustrated Sainteny's efforts to establish contact with
him.[41]

Meanwhile, Admiral Georges Thierry d'Argenlieu, the French
High Commissioner for Indochina, who arrived in Saigon on October 31, 1945, conceived of his mission as the restoration of
French rule in Indochina. A Carmelite monk on leave from his
monastery as well as a high-ranking naval officer, d'Argenlieu was
a loyal friend of de Gaulle, then head of the French provisional
government, with whom he shared the unshakable belief in
France's grandeur. Upon his arrival, the Admiral immediately revealed his intention to restore, at any cost whatever, French sovereignty in Indochina. In this "sacred" duty, "we will never give up,"
the High Commissioner reportedly said. D'Argenlieu naturally lent
a favorable ear to the French administrators and colons in Saigon
who emphasized that France should not negotiate with any one
but Bao Dai and the mandarin elite. The most urgent task, in their

view, was to get rid of the Vietnamese nationalist "pirates" and restore the old order. The authoritarian High Commissioner strongly disagreed with Leclerc, the commander of the Expeditionary Corps, as the French forces in Indochina were called. General Leclerc repeatedly stressed the necessity of an agreement with the Viet Minh government that would permit a peaceful return of French troops in the territory north of the 16th parallel. The idea was vetoed by d'Argenlieu on the grounds that negotiation with the Ho regime, which had come to power by force and with Japanese assistance and which had unilaterally proclaimed Vietnam's independence, would amount to legitimizing it. Furthermore, it would endanger the plan for a French Union. The proposal caused such a commotion in Saigon that d'Argenlieu, for a moment, thought of reporting Leclerc's "defeatist tendencies" to General de Gaulle.[42] It should be noted that Leclerc was not less concerned than d'Argenlieu with France's grandeur. The military operations conducted to "pacify" Cochinchina, however, had convinced him that the independence movement was nationwide and that France lacked the military power to suppress it. "We never intended to launch an armed conquest of North Indochina," the general wrote. "The Cochinchinese experience demonstrated that to accomplish that, we need forces much stronger than those which we now have,"[43] Leclerc's primary interest was the peaceful return of French troops to Tonkin. And to this end, he was prepared to make a compromise with the Viet Minh.

Thus, instead of negotiating in earnest with Ho, d'Argenlieu and his entourage even toyed with the idea of installing Bao Long, Bao Dai's eldest son, as Emperor and appointing Nam Phuong, the young prince's mother, as Regent. As the story goes, the Catholic ex-Empress refused to receive the High Commissioner's emissaries. Only at the insistence of the Apostolic Delegate did she agree to see them. Unwilling to dignify the French overture with an answer, Nam Phuong went to her piano and played the new Vietnamese national anthem.[44]

The absence of an alternative to Ho, in addition to the latter's readiness to make considerable concessions, therefore, persuaded Sainteny that the Viet Minh chief was the only man they could deal with.

Accord of March 6, 1946

Before delving into the Franco-Vietnamese discussions, it might be helpful to consider the background of the French representative in the negotiations leading to the March 6, 1946, Accord. Jean Sainteny had lived in Indochina for three years before the war. In April, 1945, he was sent to China to direct the activities of Mission 5, an intelligence-gathering group headquartered in Kunming, Yunnan. On the basis of the information he had about Chiang Kai-shek's design, Sainteny warned his government, early in August, 1945, to oppose any Allied plan that would permit the Chinese to enter Indochina.[45] At the news of Japan's surrender, Sainteny, in view of the absence of a French representative in Hanoi, immediately made attempts to reach the Tonkinese capital to defend his country's interest. After a brief delay for which the impatient Frenchman unfairly held the OSS team responsible, Sainteny and his small staff arrived in Hanoi, on an American plane, on August 22. Though given no official assignment, he took upon himself the task of promoting French interests and restoring the old order in North Indochina. This energetic French representative repeatedly urged Paris to conclude an accord with Chungking, while he himself tirelessly attempted to reach an agreement with Ho Chi Minh that would permit French troops to enter the territory north of the 16th parallel. Although it was the Viet Minh, aided by the Chinese, who kept the French out of Tonkin, Sainteny conveniently attributed his mission's failure to both American hostility and Chinese obstruction.[46] His book, *Story of a Lost Peace*, published in 1953, contains abundant evidence of his anti-American bias, which seriously affected his generally sound judgment. Unfortunately, he has been faithfully quoted by French authors who held the United States responsible for Ho's success in 1945 and France's humiliating defeat in 1954.[47] While it was true that the OSS officers, whose sympathy for the Viet Minh revolution enraged Sainteny, did not give active support to the French in the North as the British did in the South, it was not the Americans who frustrated Sainteny's maneuvers.

Ho Chi Minh, on his part, had always expressed his willingness to come to terms with the French. Aware of his own limitations, the pragmatic revolutionary abhorred the thought of using force against France, and believed that he could reach his goal more safely through negotiation. To France he was ready to make concessions which he considered to be much less costly than a bloody conflict. Through the good offices of OSS Major Patti, a meeting was consequently arranged on August 27, five days after Sainteny's landing in Hanoi, between the French representative and Ho's Minister of Interior Vo Nguyen Giap. The initial encounter was courteous. Both sides cautiously laid the ground work, exploring each other's position. Not until September 28 did the DRV President participate in the Franco-Vietnamese negotiation. In their first meeting, Ho impressed Sainteny as an ascetic, intelligent, energetic, and shrewd individual, "a personality of the first order." In view of the frantic state of mind of the masses, whom the propaganda machine of Tran Huy Lieu, Ho's Propaganda Minister, had effectively aroused against the French, and in view of the opposition of the Chinese command and their Vietnamese friends to any deal with France, Ho and Sainteny agreed to hold strictly secret meetings. The fact that their residences were close to each other greatly facilitated their contact. In order not to be seen, the French representative usually went to meet Ho and Giap at night, accompanied by his political adviser Léon Pignon. Often taking part in these talks was the socialist Hoang Minh Giam, who was to become the DRV Minister of Foreign Affairs following the Fontainebleau Conference. These secret meetings went on intermittently for nearly seven months.

Throughout these negotiations, Ho felt completely alone, deserted even by his comrades in the French Communist party, a party which he had helped found in 1920 and in which he put high hopes. The small group of French Communists in Saigon, in fact, bluntly warned the Viet Minh to be patient and cautious, to make sure that their position be in agreement with that of the Soviet Union, who was one of France's firm allies at that time. In brief, they suggested that Ho should not take any action that might be an embarrassment to either Paris or Moscow. Furthermore, the French Communists urged their Vietnamese comrades to wait until the French elections in October, in which their party would certainly make an impressive showing, had taken place. The additional strength it would thus acquire, argued the metropolitan Communist party, could be used to help the Viet Minh obtain a more favorable settlement.[48] This bold warning greatly disturbed Ho, who was to note with increasing dismay Paris' unchanging position in spite of the growing influence of the French Communist party following the October election.

As negotiator, Ho was besieged with seemingly insoluble problems. Everywhere he turned he saw only intransigent faces: the French, the Chinese, the anti-Viet Minh nationalists, and even leading members of the Tong Bo (Viet Minh Central Executive Committee). The French had no intention of changing the status of Indochina. The Chinese opposed any Franco-Viet Minh compromise without their approval. The DMH and the VNQDD were dead set against any Sainteny-Ho deal, which would amount to a French recognition of the Viet Minh regime. The Tong Bo leaders, angered by the French suppression of the independence movement in Cochinchina, had no faith in French promises.

For months, Ho had been engaged in a frantic effort to save his fragile regime. For a moment, the prospect of its survival appeared quite bleak. After having labored against great odds for a quarter of a century, the old revolutionary was confronted with a most serious challenge which could undo his lifework. He was deeply worried. "Ho Chi Minh had become an old man," said an American reporter who had met him in Shanghai twelve years earlier and who saw him again in mid-November, 1945. "His hair had turned gray. He wore now a scraggly little moustache and a beard of thin long strands. His cheeks were hollow, his skin like old paper. His brown eyes shone with a quizzical brightness. He wore a faded khaki jacket and trousers, a white shirt and old slippers."[49] Such was the man who negotiated with Sainteny. There are ample reasons to believe that both the French representative and the Viet Minh leader wanted a settlement. Sainteny, advised by Leclerc that France could not reconquer North Indochina without much stronger forces, wanted an agreement with the Viet Minh government that would permit French troops to enter Tonkin peacefully to relieve the Chinese armies. Ho, on his part, apprehensive that a Sino-French deal, which had been negotiated in Chungking, would squeeze him out of power, wanted to reach an accord with the French that would save his regime.

If the magic word *doc lap* (independence) had united the people behind the Viet Minh government and motivated the indigent Vietnamese to make generous contributions during the Gold Week, it was also a stumbling block in the Franco-Viet Minh negotiations. Disagreements on the meaning of the term *doc lap* often caused the negotiators to call off their talks for days, and even weeks. The French government, through d'Argenlieu, adamantly refused to grant independence to Vietnam or to agree to the unity of the three *ky*.[50] The "pacification" of Cochinchina and the arrival of Leclerc's prestigious Armored Division, in addition to the Chinese willingness to replace Ho, indeed strengthened the French position. Without a trump card, the old fox tried to play out his hand as cautiously as possible. Furthermore, the impending signing of the Sino-French treaty in Chungking, which would lead to the departure of the Chinese armies and leave Indochina open to the French Expeditionary Corps, put Ho under greater pressure. The DRV President, painfully aware that time had run out for him, was prepared to acquiesce in Sainteny's demand, going as far as to recognize France's privileged economic and political position in Vietnam in return for her recognition of Vietnamese autonomy, not independence, within the French Union. "Why not?" said he matter-of-factly. "We have been paying out our life's blood for decades. Suppose it costs us a few hundred million more piasters to buy our freedom?"[51] Ho entertained no illusions whatsoever about his regime's precarious existence and military capability. The thought of pitting his infantile militia against the vastly better-equipped French troops profoundly unsettled him. As he had advised the Nam Bo Committee to negotiate with the French, Ho undoubtedly preferred peaceful negotiation to armed resistance. War would be the last resort, to be undertaken only after all peaceful means of preserving Viet Minh rule had been exhausted.

In spite or because of the mounting pressure from various quarters (Chinese, nationalist, and Viet Minh Tong Bo), Ho became increasingly conciliatory toward the French. Max André, a member of one of the parties (MRP or Mouvement Républicain Populaire) participating in the Paris coalition government, who arrived in Hanoi early in 1946 to discuss, on his party's behalf, the terms of an agreement with the Viet Minh, was surprised by Ho's moderation.[52] The DRV President accepted the principles of "a division of powers between France and Vietnam in security matters, with national defense the joint concern of the two," and of Vietnamese exclusive control of internal affairs. He also conceded that "independence (which no French representatives were authorized to offer) was not only impossible if Vietnam were to remain within the French Union, but also impracticable."[53]

In an interview granted to Pierre Maurice Dessinges, special correspondent of the Paris daily *Résistance*, on January 6, the first national election day in the DRV, Ho also said:

> We entertained no hatred whatsoever for France or the French people. We greatly admire them and do not want to break the ties which have so strongly united our two peoples. We demand, however, that France make the first sincere and concrete move. We wish for it even more when we realize that other countries are attempting to meddle in the affairs which we consider to be our own. Our two peoples must not give these countries the opportunity to preach to us. We want to, and we must, reach a settlement by ourselves. But, remember, if we are forced to fight, we will fight to the finish.[54]

Ho's moderation, or more exactly his readiness to make concessions that would guarantee his regime's survival, was corroborated by Sainteny, who believed that the Viet Minh leader's proposal, actions, and attitude at that time conveyed the impression that he was firmly opposed to a solution by force, and that he aspired to be the Gandhi of Indochina.[55] In view of the Viet Minh's precarious existence at that time, one could hardly disagree with Sainteny on the first point. Ho's past and future actions, however, eloquently denied the second point. As far as the use of brute force was concerned, the pacific Indian mahatma and the ruthless Vietnamese revolutionary were a world apart.

Meanwhile, in contrast to the virulent anti-French campaign launched by the Chinese who actively sought to prevent a Franco-Vietnamese rapprochement, the Viet Minh press, which had aroused the people to fight for immediate and complete *doc lap*, began to reverse itself. Instead of independence, it emphasized the need for Franco-Vietnamese understanding. Making a 180-degree turn, Ho engaged in a frantic effort to prepare his people to accept the concessions he was to make to the French.

On February 16, exactly six weeks before the signing of the Sino-

French treaty in Chungking, a breakthrough in the Ho-Sainteny talks seemed to be within grasp. After a long meeting, the DRV President clarified his position, explaining both his concessions and conditions for the return of French troops to the North. Ho no longer insisted on immediate independence. A very important concession, indeed. Sainteny hurriedly departed for Saigon to confer with his immediate superior, General Leclerc, who had assumed the functions of High Commissioner in the absence of d'Argenlieu. The Admiral had left for Paris on February 13 following the resignation of President de Gaulle. A new government had been installed under the premiership of the Socialist Félix Gouin. Another Socialist, Marius Moutet, had replaced the Gaullist Jacques Soustelle at the Ministry for Overseas France, the former Ministry of Colonies. These changes had profoundly disturbed d'Argenlieu, who became apprehensive that Paris would no longer support his plan. These fears, however, were soon dissipated. The Socialist Moutet, to the High Commissioner's relief, did not deviate from the policy adopted by the Gaullist Soustelle.

Upon his arrival in Saigon, on February 18, Sainteny gave Leclerc a detailed report on the Franco-Viet Minh negotiations. The acting High Commissioner, aware of the necessity of an agreement, had in fact requested his government, on February 14, to go as far as to recognize Vietnam's independence. He immediately telegrammed the main points of Ho's position to Admiral d'Argenlieu, urging an instant counterproposal from Paris. "I repeat," insisted the General, "it is vitally important that concrete proposals be immediately forwarded by the French government, otherwise the opportunity might be lost."[56]

Upon notification of Paris' favorable reaction, Sainteny returned without delay to Hanoi to inform Ho of the French government's position. Only a few points remained to be clarified before the drafting of the agreement. As regards Vietnam's status, Ho himself defined it as a "Free State within the Indochinese Federation and within the French Union." In essence, the French government agreed to recognize the DRV as an autonomous state within the Indochinese Federation and the French Union, to supply Vietnam with advisers and technicians, and to carry out the decision to be taken by the population of Cochinchina regarding the latter's position vis-à-vis Vietnam. The Ho Chi Minh government, on its part,

pledged to guarantee France's economic and cultural privileges
and to accept amicably the French army which, in conformity with
the treaty to be signed in Chungking, was to relieve the Chinese
forces.

With a view to maintaining himself in power, the calculating
revolutionary thus settled for considerably less than what his people had clamored for. Was it pragmatism or opportunism? It was
both. Ho had been known both as a cold realist and as a ruthless
opportunist all his life. His readiness to compromise and to accept
the French return in spite of the events in Cochinchina, however,
aroused a storm of criticism. Even the most devastating appellation
of *Viet gian* (traitor) was hurled at him. Increasingly vociferous in
their attack, the DMH and the VNQDD called for the resignation
of Ho Chi Minh and the formation of a government of union and
resistance under Vinh Thuy, the ex-Emperor Bao Dai. On February 19, a big demonstration was organized to this end.

Aware of the prevailing ugly mood, Sainteny called Ho's attention to the fact that, to be acceptable to both sides, the agreement
they had negotiated must be signed, not by a government composed exclusively of Viet Minh members, but by one which included spokesmen for all shades of opinion.[57] Sainteny's position
happened to coincide with Ho's evaluation of the situation. Sensing
the mounting influence of the opposition, unwilling to assume sole
responsibility for any concession to France, and anxious to neutralize the nationalist groups by implicating them in the deal he
had been making with Sainteny, Ho again executed one of his
dexterous maneuvers. After keeping his opponents out of the government for months, in spite of agreements to the contrary, the
cunning DRV President suddenly invited them to join his cabinet.
Fearing another Viet Minh trick and opposing the Communist
compromise plan, the pro-Chinese elements refused to participate
in Ho's government. In an attempt to counter the DMH and
VNQDD opposition, the old fox sought to enlist the support of
other prominent nationalist leaders. His effort met only with rebuff. One of the men contacted by Ho was Ngo Dinh Diem,[58]
whom the Viet Minh had seized early in 1946 and subjected to the
rigors of hunger and illness in the Tonkinese mountains. Beside his
own mistreatment at the hands of Ho's men, Diem had other rea-

sons to distrust the old Communist. One of his brothers, the influential anti-French governor Ngo Dinh Khoi had been killed, "mistakenly," by the Viet Minh. In return for his cooperation, Diem, therefore, insisted on obtaining additional information on Ho's activities and plans, far more than the Viet Minh leader was prepared to give. Upon Diem's refusal to cooperate, Ho reportedly said: "Well, I see it is useless to discuss matters with you while you are so irritable, but stay around a little while."[59] Diem stayed on. Neither he nor Ho, however, changed his position. Shortly afterwards, the Viet Minh master, for political reasons, released his prisoner.

The violent criticism from within his own party and the ferocious attack from the pro-Chinese groups, in addition to the rebuff by other nationalist leaders, threw Ho into a state of utter perplexity. Visibly confused, the old fighter even considered resignation from the presidency. According to a well-informed source, on February 23, 1946, at 7 A.M., a dejected Ho Chi Minh paid an unexpected visit to his Supreme Counsellor Bao Dai. The situation had taken a dangerous turn, said the DRV President. The Viet Minh, in view of its Marxist connections, might be a hindrance in the struggle for national independence. Therefore, a change in the leadership of the republic was necessary. Consequently, Ho proposed that the ex-Emperor take over the government to allay the big powers' distrust of Communism. Ho suggested that he and Bao Dai switch positions, i.e., Ho would become Supreme Counsellor and Bao Dai would step up into the presidency. Although taken aback, Bao Dai realized that it was not the first time the calculating Communist had made such a proposal. Afraid that he might walk into a trap, Bao Dai insisted that he had no political ambitions and that power did not appeal to him. He would, however, do whatever the national interest required. Meanwhile, he would like to have a little time to think and to consult with the Americans and the Chinese.

At 1 P.M., Ho returned, pressing the Supreme Counsellor for an answer. Fearful that the Viet Minh would use the proposed leadership change as a pretext to start a guerilla war against the new government, which would sign the unpopular agreement with France, Vinh Thuy inquired whether the Viet Minh would partici-

pate in the new government. Answering in the affirmative, Ho
further assured Bao Dai that it would not be difficult to prevail
upon the newly elected National Assembly to vest authority in the
man who had so "skillfully" performed his functions of Supreme
Counsellor. Again, the Viet Minh chief asked the ex-Emperor to
consider the suggestion seriously.

At 7 P.M., Ho again reappeared at Bao Dai's residence. This
time, however, the DRV President asked his host to forget all that
had been discussed during the day, apologizing for having considered relieving his burden on another person when things went
wrong. He had realized his weakness and decided to carry on his
responsibilities. After the crisis, and under more propitious circumstances, Ho continued, he would relinquish power in favor of Vinh
Thuy and would withdraw from the scene.[60]

What caused such a sudden change of heart on Ho's part? The
Chinese, again, played an important role. Aware of Ho's dilemma
and anxious to have the agreement ratified by a coalition government, Sainteny interceded with Siao Wan, urging him to put pressure on his Vietnamese friends. The Chinese general, who had
been working for the inclusion of the DMH and the VNQDD in
the Viet Minh government and had been deeply distressed by their
inefficiency and ineffectiveness, persuaded his Vietnamese protégés
to join Ho's governing coalition and exploit their chance to share in
the exercise of power. The nationalist parties reluctantly gave in.
The incompetence of their Vietnamese friends had finally convinced the Kuomintang commanders of the futility of setting up a
pro-Chinese government in Hanoi and led them to stake their interests on the Ho regime. A well-run government in Tonkin and
North Annam would leave them undisturbed in their plundering
activities and, at the same time, strengthen the Chinese position in
the Sino-French negotiation then going on in Chungking. This was
the only time when Chinese, French, and Viet Minh interests
seemed to harmonize with each other. By forcing their Vietnamese
proteges to enter the coalition, the Chinese command made it possible for Ho to remain in power.

On February 24, under the watchful eyes of General Siao Wan,
another Viet Minh-nationalist accord was signed. A new government of national union was formed along the lines defined in the

December 22, 1945, agreement. The Viet Minh and its affiliate, the Dan Chu Dang or Democratic Party, retained the Ministries of Finance, Education, Communications and Public Works, and Justice, while the DMH and the VNQDD took over the portfolios of Foreign Affairs, National Economy, Agriculture, and Social Affairs. The crucial Ministries of Interior and Defense went to "nonpartisans" or "neutrals." As expected, Ho remained President of the Republic, while the old DMH leader Nguyen Hai Than was offered the newly-created post of Vice-President. At the nationalist insistence, two of Ho's most effective and trusted lieutenants, former Interior Minister Vo Nguyen Giap and former Propaganda Minister Tran Huy Lieu, were not included in the new government.

These Viet Minh concessions, however, were more apparent than real. Instead of causing a shift in power and diminishing the Communist influence, they strengthened Ho's hands. By creating the superfluous vice-presidency for Nguyen Hai Than, whose organization had never been a match for the Viet Minh, the old fox handily neutralized the DMH opposition. The acceptance of the vital Ministry of Foreign Affairs, far from giving the VNQDD any significant influence, actually implicated it in the deal Ho had been making with Sainteny and thus compelled it to defend a policy it had violently condemned. The retention of the key portfolios of Education and Communication also permitted the Viet Minh to monopolize the communication media and continue their propaganda as usual. Of the two "nonpartisans" or "neutrals" who headed the Ministries of Interior and Defense, Huynh Thuc Khang, a respected old nationalist, had been secretly won over to the Communist cause, and Phan Anh, a widely-admired youthful lawyer, entertained considerable sympathy for the Viet Minh league. Vo Nguyen Giap, though nominally outside the government, nevertheless enjoyed more power than any one else, with the exception of Ho himself. As Chairman of the newly-created Superior War Council, which exerted direct control over the army, Giap was in fact the Minister of Defense and Commander-in-Chief of the armed forces.

Thus, without making any significant concessions, Ho shrewdly tied the opposition to his bandwagon. Having disarmed his nationalist critics, the DRV President casually announced the agreement he had made with the French. A communiqué, issued on February 26, read:

> On February 25, President Ho Chi Minh discussed with Mr. Sainteny, the French representative, the possibility of opening official negotiations between Vietnam and France. The President reiterated that the Vietnamese position was "independence and cooperation." Mr. Sainteny indicated that France agreed to recognize the right of Vietnam to have its own government, parliament, army, and finances within the French Union. The two interlocutors exchanged views on the question of Viet-namese representation abroad. They agreed that, before negotiation began, two necessary conditions must be created: first, an atmosphere of detente and concord, and second, immediate armistice on all fronts.[61]

In any case, the Viet Minh needed time to explain their volteface to the people, who had been told to prepare themselves for a struggle to the finish and to reject any compromise short of independence. The Communications (Propaganda) Ministry made a frantic attempt to convince the masses that it was the French who, exhausted by their military operations in the South, begged for negotiation.

Meanwhile, in Saigon, Leclerc impatiently waited for a signal from Chungking. On March 1, upon receiving a wire informing him of the signing of the Franco-Chinese treaty on the previous day, the general issued orders to his troops to leave immediately for Haiphong. The sudden departure of Leclerc's army from Saigon caused Ho to convene the newly-elected National Assembly on March 2, one day ahead of schedule. At its first session, the Assembly accepted the seventy members of the pro-Chinese parties who had not been elected, but were entitled to serve as a result of the December 22, 1945, agreement. The Viet Minh-controlled legislature also requested Ho, who had tendered his resignation, to form a "Government of National Union." The old leader obligingly complied with the demand. Within half an hour, the formation of the "Government of Union and Resistance" was announced as follows:

President: Ho Chi Minh (Viet Minh or VM)
Vice-President: Nguyen Hai Than (DMH)
Justice: Vu Dinh Hoe (VM)

Education: Dang Thai Mai (VM)
Finance: Le Van Hien (VM)
Public Works: Tran Dang Khoa (VM)
Foreign Affairs: Nguyen Tuong Tam (VNQDD)
Economy: Chu Ba Phuong (VNQDD)
Health: Truong Dinh Tri (DMH)
Agriculture: Bo Xuan Luat (DMH)
Interior: Huynh Thuc Khang (nonpartisan)
Defense: Phan Anh (nonpartisan).

The resignation of the old government and the formation of the new one were mere formalities. There was no change in membership or division of powers. After voting the investiture of the new government, the Assembly set up a number of committees that were to function during its recess, and of which the most important were:

a. the High Consultative Council, headed by ex-Emperor Bao Dai;

b. the National Resistance Committee, which replaced the Superior War Council, under the chairmanship of Vo Nguyen Giap;[62]

c. the Permanent Committee, composed entirely of Viet Minh members, which was to function while the National Assembly was not in session;[63]

d. the Constituent Committee, entrusted with the task of drafting a constitution for the Democratic Republic.

At the close of its session, which lasted from 8 A.M. to 1 P.M., the National Assembly issued a proclamation calling on Vietnamese to devote all their energy to the defense and reconstruction of the fatherland. With the exception of those members who served on the various committees and in the government, all the people's representatives immediately returned to their respective constituencies to prepare for the impending struggle against France.

Having implicated the opposition and gotten rid of the National Assembly, which had provided his regime with a democratic façade and lent support to its claim to legitimacy, Ho was ready to conclude his agreement with Sainteny. With the pending arrival of Leclerc's troops, who were scheduled to land in Haiphong between March 5, and 7, both Ho and Sainteny realized the urgent need of an accord. Unless an agreement were reached, war would inevitably break out upon the arrival of French troops. For a few days, hectic negotiations went on. Ho, encouraged by the Chinese command, decided to bargain until the end, hoping to wrest a few concessions from France that would make the treaty less repugnant to his people. While agreeing to accept the status of a *free* state for Vietnam, he insisted on the unification of the three *ky*. Sainteny and Pignon, however, refused to move an inch, emphasizing that Cochinchina should be free to decide its own position vis-à-vis Vietnam. As time was running out, the French fleet inexorably moved closer to the Tonkinese waters. The situation was further aggravated by the failure of the Chinese and the French in Chungking to reach an agreement concerning the relief of the Kuomintang armies in Indochina. General Ma Ing, chief of staff of Lu Han, who was in Chungking at that time, declared that since he had not received any instructions from his government permitting a French landing in Haiphong, he would order Chinese shore batteries to fire at the French fleet if such a landing were attempted. Furthermore, the Chinese command argued, by letting the French disembark, they would incur the wrath of the Vietnamese, who would undoubtedly take reprisals on the Chinese residents in Tonkin. Unless they received further notice from Chungking, and until a Franco-Vietnamese accord was reached, they would continue to prevent French troops from setting ashore in Haiphong.

Meanwhile, the French fleet entered the Gulf of Tonkin, slowly proceeding toward Haiphong. Unwilling to risk a confrontation with Leclerc's army, General Chiao Pe-chang, Lu Han's deputy, called on Ho, on March 5, urging him to reach an agreement with Sainteny. Greatly annoyed by this abrupt Chinese volte-face, the Viet Minh chief protested against Chiao's interference. Ho met with Sainteny, hoping to find a solution. Franco-Vietnamese negotiations went on until past midnight without an agreement. An atmosphere of despair permeated the conference room. The tired negotiators finally agreed to recess. Before parting, Sainteny and Pignon earnestly requested Ho to think over and make a decision before it was too late. French warships had been in sight from the Tonkinese coast. War was on the verge of becoming a reality.

Then, on March 6, at dawn, Hoang Minh Giam, who had been with Ho throughout the negotiation, called on Sainteny to inform him that "the President had accepted his conditions."[64] It was immediately agreed that they should meet again at noon to draft the agreement and that the signing of the accord should take place at 4 P.M.

The signing ceremony, however, started at 4:30 P.M. In a shrewd move, Ho appointed the VNQDD leader Vu Hong Khanh, whose anti-French sentiment had been well known, as special delegate from the Council of Ministers and co-signer of the treaty.

Under the accord of March 6, 1946, France recognized Vietnam as a *free* state within the Indochinese Federation and the French Union, having its own government, parliament, army, and treasury, and pledged to carry out the decision taken by the population through a referendum concerning the unification of the three *ky*.[65]

The DRV, on its part, agreed to accept the French army when it came to relieve the Chinese forces in Tonkin and North Annam. A military annex to the agreement provided for a relief force of 25,000 (10,000 Vietnamese and 15,000 Frenchmen), "under supreme French command with the assistance of Vietnamese representatives." The French units in charge of the Japanese were to be repatriated as soon as their mission was completed following the evacuation of Japanese prisoners, with a deadline of ten months. As to those units that shared with the Vietnamese army the responsibility for order in North Indochina, they were to withdraw in five annual installments.[66] Finally, the length of the mission of the units guarding air and naval bases was to be determined in later conferences.

As far as diplomacy was concerned, the March 6, 1946, Accord was a veritable compromise. While the French had to renounce, on paper, their ambition to restore the old order in Indochina, the Viet Minh too had to give up their insistence on Vietnam's immediate and complete independence. Both parties, however, achieved their immediate objective. For Sainteny, it was the peaceful entry of French troops into Tonkin and North Annam; for Ho Chi Minh, it was the French recognition of his government as the only legitimate authority in the "Free State of Vietnam." At any rate, the French Commissioner[67] was satisfied with the agreement, which prevented the armed confrontation he had feared. Ho, however, had mixed feelings. "I am not happy," confided he to Sainteny after the signing of the accord, "for basically it is you who have won. You know very well that I wanted more than that. . . .

Anyway, I understand that you cannot have everything in one day."[68]

Ho, indeed, was not happy about the concessions he had made. How could he, who had come to power under the slogan "Independence or Death," explain to the highly aroused Vietnamese that he had bowed to the French? How could he explain the return of French troops, who, all Vietnamese believed, hiding behind empty promises, were prepared to retake possession of the whole country. Leclerc's men and armored tanks were already on their way to Hanoi! How could Ho avoid the dreadful label of *Viet gian* (traitor)? With a view to soothing his highly agitated fellow countrymen, the old revolutionary proposed a joint Franco-Vietnamese proclamation, which was immediately issued as follows:

> Since the French Government has recognized Vietnam's right to have its own government and dispose of its administration, the Government of Vietnam will not oppose the peaceful arrival of the French units called on to relieve the Chinese occupation forces in Indochina north of the 16th parallel.
>
> In consequence of this preliminary accord, hostilities will cease throughout Indochina within twenty-four hours following the broadcast of this proclamation over Radio Hanoi and Radio Saigon.[69]

Such a declaration, however, was clearly inadequate. The Vietnamese expected a more convincing clarification from their government. The task of explaining the seemingly suicidal concession Ho entrusted to his articulate lieutenant Vo Nguyen Giap, a lawyer by training. On March 7, at a huge rally in Hanoi, attended by some 100,000 people, the Commander of the DRV Army, speaking for Ho, eloquently defended the agreement. Under the then existing conditions, reasoned Giap, there were three alternatives: (a) a protracted resistance, (b) a short war of resistance, and (c) negotiation. The first proposition was rejected because of the unfavorable international situation. Paris had signed a treaty with Chungking, while Great Britain and the United States had sided with France:

> Besides, in certain areas, where the revolutionary movement has not taken root, many people do not take it seriously. If we prolonged the resistance war, a number of sectors would collapse or lose the fighting spirit. By continuing the military struggle, we would lose our forces and,

gradually, our land. We would be able to hold only a few regions. Though this would be a heroic resistance, no one could say whether or not the terrible sufferings it would inflict upon our people could be ever compensated.

As to the second alternative, Giap candidly admitted that the poorly-equipped DRV forces would not be a match for the French Expeditionary Corps, equipped with all kinds of modern weapons. Negotiation, therefore, was the most correct step. It would restore peace and create conditions leading to complete independence. Most importantly, Giap emphasized,

Negotiation has already led to a cessation of hostilities and prevented a bloodshed. We have negotiated primarily to protect and strengthen our political, military, and economic position. Our country is a free country. All the liberties are in our hands. We have all the power and all the time needed to organize our internal administration, to strengthen our military means, to develop our economy, and to raise the living standard of our people. Soon, the three *ky* will be reunited. Rice will flow from Cochinchina to Tonkin, and the spectre of famine will vanish.

To strengthen his argument, Giap, the good Marxist, continued:

In considering world history, one sees that many people in bad situations have been able to overcome difficulties by knowing when to wait for an occasion more favorable to their progress. Russia, in 1918, for example, signed the Brest-Litovsk Treaty to stop the German invasion in order to strengthen her army and her political power. Did Russia not become very strong thanks to this strategy?[70]

Before this very crowd, which had been won over by Giap's forceful arguments, suddenly appeared a slender man whose tiny stature was well accented by a huge gold-starred red flag in the background. A thunderous ovation exploded. "Ho Chu Tich Muon Nam!" (Long Live President Ho). Having sufficiently savored this popular tribute, Ho slowly stretched his arms to calm the excited crowd, then said:

Though we have been independent, in fact, since August 1945, no powers have yet recognized our independence. The agreement with France will open the way to international recognition of our country. It will lead us into a firmer international position, and this is a great political victory. French troops will come, under Allied command. There will be only 15,000 of them, and they will stay only for five years. . . To negotiate rather than to fight is an indication of political wisdom. Anyway, why should we sacrifice 50 or 100,000 men when we can achieve independence within five years through negotiation?

In an apparent attempt to satisfy Lu Han and his Vietnamese protégés of Ho's "pro-Chinese" sentiments and to warn the French that Chinese assistance would be sought should they renege on their promise, the DRV President continued:

Keep your calm and your discipline. Do not be discouraged. We must be watchful and ready. We have friends, however. We know that we can count on the friendship of the Chinese people. China and Vietnam are like lips and teeth.

To conclude his speech, the old fox made an emotional appeal to his aroused audience:

I, Ho Chi Minh, have always led you on the road to liberty and have fought all my life for the independence of our fatherland. You know that I would rather die than betray our country. I swear that I have not betrayed you.[71]

Ho, indeed, did not betray his countrymen at this juncture. Painfully aware of the might of Leclerc's armored divisions for which his infantile army was not a serious match, the pragmatist revolutionary sincerely wanted to avoid an armed clash, which would both annihilate his forces and devastate his country. It should be emphasized again that Ho was not only a dedicated Marxist, but also an ardent nationalist. Throughout his life or, more specifically, for nearly half a century, from 1920 when he joined the French Communist party to 1969 when he passed into history, Ho was constantly obsessed with two main ideas, which remained the two basic objectives of his life: national independence and Communist rule over a unified Vietnam. As these two aims were intertwined, the thought of treating them separately had never entered Ho's mind. The Viet Minh leader knew exactly what he wanted; he knew equally well what the French were after. Their ambitions were irreconcilable. The March 6, 1946, Accord, therefore, was not a definite settlement, but simply a postponement of the inevitable. At the very best, Ho might stave off for a short time the ultimate bloody confrontation, but he entertained no illusion of preventing what was destined to happen. This postponement would enable the Viet Minh to strengthen their political and military position for an eventual showdown.

The issue of war and peace, however, would not be decided by Ho, but by the French who had revealed, in word and in deed, their intention to hang on to their colonies. Leclerc had, in fact, warned his soldiers that they were fighting for the restoration of French greatness.[72] And to the Vietnamese delegation that greeted him upon his landing in Haiphong, on March 7, 1946, the French commander, referring to the agreement that had just been signed, arrogantly said: "I had left (Saigon) and would have come anyway, with or without your accord."[73] On the following day, Leclerc also remarked to Vo Nguyen Giap: "Tell the Vietnamese that they can count on me. But I am French, and in regard to your aspirations I will, of course, act as a Frenchman, first as a Frenchman."[74]

Admiral d'Argenlieu, on his part, promptly criticized the accord signed by Sainteny. "I am amazed," said he, on March 8, "yes, that is the word, I am amazed that France has such a fine expeditionary corps and, yet, its leaders would rather negotiate than fight."[75] Twelve days later, at a reception in honor of the King of Cambodia then visiting Saigon, the High Commissioner, again, publicly condemned the Ho-Sainteny accord, comparing it with the 1938 Munich agreement between Great Britain, France, and Germany. In any case, the French position had been clarified by Cedile, Commissioner for Cochinchina. On March 12, with the Admiral's approval, he had assured the French administrators and colons in Saigon that the March 6 Accord was only a preliminary agreement, stressing the following points:

1. The reference to the Ho Chi Minh regime as the government of Vietnam was simply a matter of courtesy. It did not imply a recognition by France of a single government for the three *ky*;
2. Tonkin, Annam, and Cochinchina would each decide its own status vis-à-vis Vietnam through a referendum;
3. The referendum would not take place before order was completely restored;
4. The March 6 Accord was only a "local agreement" between the Hanoi authorities and the French Commissioner for Tonkin and North Annam;

5. The Accord had no bearing on Cochinchina, which was a French colony.

In conclusion, Cedile again emphasized:

I wish to declare that the French government intends to establish in Cochinchina, as well as in the other countries of the Indochinese Federation, a free regime similar to that which exists in Cambodia and has been envisaged for Tonkin. . . . Cochinchina, too, will soon have its own government, parliament, army, and finances. It will have the same rights and the same advantages as the other members of the Federation.[76]

This French renegation of the March 6 Accord was confirmed two days later by Paris. On March 14, Marius Moutet, the Socialist Minister for French Overseas Territories, announced that Cochinchina would be given the constitution of a free state. The French position was clear. The unification of Cochinchina with Tonkin and Annam should be prevented. Steps had to be taken to set up a separate Cochinchinese state under French control. Immediately, Cedile turned his attention to the Advisory Council for Cochinchina. This group, which had been set up on February 4, 1946, and consisted of four Frenchmen and eight Vietnamese of whom seven were French citizens, was the logical choice as an instrument of French policy. Under Cedile's guidance, the Advisory Council conveniently declared itself entitled to speak for the people of Cochinchina. At a meeting, on March 26, it discussed the formation of a provisional autonomous government with Dr. Nguyen Van Thinh, a physician and wealthy landowner, as Prime Minister. While the idea appealed to a handful of wealthy landowners, businessmen, and intellectuals, who had long cast their lot with the French, the overwhelming majority of the Cochinchinese population, who identified themselves with their fellow countrymen in Tonkin and Annam, rejected it as an absurd French attempt to divide the people and weaken the independence movement. French-supported publications and demonstrations in favor of an autonomous Cochinchina failed to stir the masses. Slogans such as "Cochinchina for the Cochinchinese" fell only on deaf ears.

As far as the Saigon authorities were concerned, the March 6 Accord would apply only to the Viet Minh forces. Leclerc unceremoniously rejected Ho's proposal regarding the establishment of a mixed Franco-Vietnamese commission to restore peace in Cochinchina, suggesting, instead, that the DRV President give order to his men to cease all hostile actions. The French also arrested Ho's emissaries to the South, and ordered local Vietnamese commanders to surrender their arms and prisoners during the month of March. Such a demand for capitulation, of course, was not complied with. Thereupon, the French took "police action" against members of the resistance whom they considered as bandits, bombed and burned entire villages, made mass arrests, and executed captured guerillas. The Vietnamese retaliated by attacking French outposts, and as- sassinating *Viet gian* (traitors), that is, those who collaborated with the French. The March Accord, far from ending the fighting in Cochinchina, intensified it. Paris, at last, concurred with d'Ar- genlieu that the use of force was the only logical solution to the Indochina problem.

Meanwhile, in spite of his unchivalrous treatment of Ho, Le- clerc, one of the leading defenders of the March Accord, became increasingly anxious to bring his mission to a fruitful conclusion. With the entry into the North of his troops who would soon occupy every strategic position, the general considered the military prob- lem half solved. Only the political questions raised by the Accord remained to be settled. To this end, Leclerc made untiring at- tempts to promote a Ho-d'Argenlieu meeting. The High Commis- sioner finally agreed to invite the Viet Minh chief to visit him on board the cruiser *Émile Bertin* in the Ha Long Bay, a most pic- turesque site near Haiphong. The historic encounter took place on March 24, 1946. Ho arrived on board the French warship, accom- panied by his Minister for Foreign Affairs Nguyen Tuong Tam (VNQDD), his gray eminence Hoang Minh Giam, and Commis- sioner Sainteny. D'Argenlieu and his entourage, including Leclerc, gave the Vietnamese delegation an "impressive" welcome. Ho was treated with a review of the French Far East Fleet, which the High Commissioner had ordered into the Tonkinese waters for the occasion. D'Argenlieu undoubtedly intended to impress his guests with the might of the French navy. Ho, understandably, felt ill at ease during the entire ceremony. The sight of the French naval power, like that of Leclerc's armored division during his trip from Hanoi to Haiphong, was greatly discomforting to Ho.

After a rather long exchange of civilities, the Vietnamese and the French representatives finally settled to serious business. In contrast to Ho, who was quite anxious to begin negotiations immediately, d'Argenlieu remained noncommittal, trying to postpone the conference promised in the March 6 Accord. The basic issues raised in the agreement, such as the diplomatic relations of Vietnam with foreign states, the future status of Indochina, and French cultural and economic interests in Vietnam, had to be settled before any one could know what the "free State" of Vietnam was about. According to Ho, Vietnam, under the terms of the Accord, was a sovereign state having control over its domestic and foreign affairs, and a member of a loose Indochinese Federation and of the French Union. The French, apparently, had another concept of the "free State" of Vietnam. It would be like Cambodia, where the Commissioner of the French Republic was responsible for public order, served as adviser to the King, and had access to Cabinet meetings, and where government ministers were not allowed to make official pronouncements without French approval. D'Argenlieu firmly believed that time was on his side. The French Expeditionary Corps, which had entered Tonkin, would soon control the strategic points and, consequently, be in a position to convince Ho to be less demanding.

Since the March 6 Accord provided that "Hanoi, Saigon, or Paris may be chosen as the location of the conference," the DRV President proposed that discussions should be held in the French capital. Ho's preference for Paris was clearly based on several factors:

a. In the metropolis, French negotiators would be less exposed to the pressure of the colons and administrators than in either Hanoi or Saigon;

b. The Paris political circles would be more sympathetic to the Vietnamese cause than would the Saigon authorities, notably the intransigent Gaullist d'Argenlieu;

c. A conference in Paris would help focus world public opinion on the Vietnamese struggle for independence.

Ironically, it was these very considerations that caused d'Argenlieu, who abhorred the idea that a Franco-Vietnamese conference should take place outside his jurisdiction, to oppose Ho's proposal. The High Commissioner reminded his interlocutor that he could not go to Paris without an invitation from the French government, suggesting, instead, a preliminary meeting in Indochina in preparation for an ultimate conference in Paris. For this purpose, d'Argenlieu proposed Dalat, a resort town in southern Annam, which he considered to be "neutral" ground but which, in practice, was under French control. In spite of serious misgivings, Ho nevertheless realized that he had no choice but to accept the Admiral's proposal. The Viet Minh chief, however, insisted that the French delegation to the Dalat conference be composed of negotiators from metropolitan France and include some representatives from the Ministry of Foreign Affairs. Ho left d'Argenlieu, deeply disturbed and more convinced than ever of the French resolve to postpone a definite settlement until they became strong enough to impose a solution of force.

Meanwhile, it might be remembered, the Cochinchinese Advisory Committee, under Commissioner Cedile's guidance, had nominated, on March 26, Dr. Nguyen Van Thinh as head of the "Provisional Government of the Republic of Cochinchina." This crude maneuver removed any remaining doubt regarding the good faith of the French in negotiating the March 6 Accord, which they had arrogantly flouted. It was an uncalled-for provocation. The Viet Minh immediately retaliated. A reign of terror began. Kidnappings and assassinations of *Viet gian* (traitors), i.e., Vietnamese separatists and collaborators, multiplied. As a countermeasure, the French arrested, imprisoned, and executed scores of terrorists or Viet Minh agents. Brutality was met with brutality. If a French soldier was killed in a village, the whole area was searched or burned to ashes while suspects were unceremoniously shot. In the meantime, French troops landed in Tourane (now, Danang, Central Vietnam) and in Hue, occupying strategic points.

The Dalat Conference

It was in the midst of rising tension that the Dalat Conference was convened on April 17, 1946. In view of the unsettling situation in the North following the landing of Leclerc's troops, of the explosive events in the South, and of his disappointing encounter with d'Argenlieu, Ho decided not to attend the Dalat Conference but to entrust the negotiation to his loyal associate Vo Nguyen Giap.

Although on paper, Nguyen Tuong Tam, the VNQDD Minister of Foreign Affairs, was the head of the Vietnamese delegation, in practice it was Giap who dominated the discussions. From the opening session presided over by Admiral d'Argenlieu, it became clear that the Dalat Conference would lead to nowhere but an impasse. The French High Commissioner, intent on minimizing its importance, sent to Dalat a small group of bureaucrats. In contrast to the Vietnamese delegation,[77] which was composed of leading political figures who could speak for the Ho government, the French team[78] was composed mainly of colonial administrators from d'Argenlieu's office and a number of technicians from France, none of whom was authorized to speak for the Paris government. Worse still, the head of the French delegation, Max André, was closely associated with the Bank of Indochina, a monument of French colonialism.

From the beginning, Giap insisted that in view of the hostilities in the South the Cochinchina question should be discussed first. The French delegates demurred on the ground that the issue was not within their competence to discuss. Besides, they argued, there were no hostilities in Cochinchina, only "police action." The basic Franco-Vietnamese disagreement centered upon the divergent concepts of the Indochinese Federation and of the "free State" of Vietnam. The French delegates viewed the Indochinese Federation as a super-government presided over by the French High Commissioner, who would direct the federal services and execute federal laws with the assistance of federal commissioners appointed by, and responsible to, him alone. The High Commissioner would also be the intermediary between the federated states and the French government. An Assembly of States, in which the five political divisions of Indochina and French interests were to be equally represented and which was to enjoy limited legislative and budgetary powers, would cooperate with the High Commissioner in the exercise of his functions. The French clearly wanted Cochinchina, with its rich rice fields and profitable rubber plantations, to be a separate political entity, for without the Cochinchinese granary, Vietnam would not survive as an independent state. In the Assembly of States, Vietnam, which would embrace only Tonkin and Annam, would be outvoted by Cochinchina, Cambodia, Laos, and French interests. As to Cochinchina's status, the French monotonously expressed their willingness to arrange a referendum after peace had been restored in the South! This promise appeared highly derisory as d'Argenlieu had put in motion his scheme to set up the "Republic of Cochinchina."

Ho's representatives, on their side, rejecting the French concept of the Indochinese Federation, envisaged it as a loose federation of independent states, each having its own armed forces, finances, and diplomatic service, an organization designed primarily to coordinate the economic interests of its members. They agreed, nevertheless, to recognize France's economic and commercial privileges in return for French technical and financial assistance. Regarding Cochinchina, the Vietnamese strongly criticized the French disregard of the armistice agreement and their operations against nationalist members of the resistance, condemning d'Argenlieu's plan to set up a separatist "republic" in the South. For Ho, Cochinchina was an integral part of Vietnam and, consequently, its political status was not open to question. The referendum provided by the March 6 Accord was designed simply to settle an administrative issue—the degree of autonomy Cochinchina was to enjoy within the state of Vietnam.

The irreconcilable positions of the two delegations thus precluded any agreement. On May 11, the Dalat Conference came to an end. It was a disappointing diplomatic failure. Seized with emotion, the Vietnamese left the conference room in tears. The only palpable accomplishment of the Franco-Vietnamese discussions was the clarification of the French position, which was to restore the old order in Indochina.

Upon his return to Hanoi, Giap had long talks with Ho. Confronted with the stubborn French determination to impose a solution of force, the dejected DRV President agreed with Giap that preparations must be made for a long drawn-out war. At the same time, he made tireless efforts to prevent or, at least, to postpone it. In an apparent attempt to create a better atmosphere for the ensuing meeting in France, Ho, the born diplomat and the consummate actor, issued an optimistic statement after the Dalat Conference:

Both our delegations have recognized the need to form an Indochinese Federation. In this federation all the states concerned will be linked not with hampering bonds, but with unifying and strengthening bonds. We agree on the principle of the creation of a federal organism providing it allows the members of the federation to prosper freely while remaining independent. . . . We must still determine the methods by which this Federation is to be realized.[79]

Realizing that he would not get anywhere with d'Argenlieu, Ho became more impatient than ever to depart for France. This time, the High Commissioner found himself without a pretext to oppose such a move. A joint communiqué issued at the close of the Ho-d'Argenlieu meeting at Ha Long Bay had in fact stated that a Vietnamese delegation would leave for Paris in the second half of May to take part in the official and definite negotiations. The Viet Minh chief was very anxious to enter into direct contact with the French government and to renew his friendship with the French Socialist and Communist leaders who, he hoped, would lend support to his cause. Aware of Ho's plan and fearful that he might succeed, d'Argenlieu paid an unexpected visit to Hanoi, on May 18, trying to convince the Viet Minh President to postpone his departure for Paris on the ground that the political instability then reigning in France was not conducive to a fruitful negotiation. Besides, Ho's presence in Vietnam was necessary to settle certain internal problems. Otherwise, the High Commissioner warned, it might soon be impossible for him (d'Argenlieu) to oppose the Cochinchinese aspirations for autonomy. Obviously shocked by such an insolent threat of blackmail, Ho, however, maintained his sangfroid. Staring at his host, the Viet Minh chief firmly informed his affronting visitor that a Vietnamese delegation had been appointed and was ready to leave for Paris as soon as possible.

Upon his return to Saigon, d'Argenlieu gave green light to the Cochinchinese Advisory Council to accelerate its preparations for the declaration of the autonomous republic in the South. On May 26, through a hastily-passed motion, the Cochinchinese provincial councillors, who had been summoned to Saigon for the occasion, gave their support to the Advisory Council's proposal regarding the formation of a provisional government that was to be entrusted with the responsibility of establishing a republican regime. On May 30, just one day before Ho's departure for Paris, the authoritarian High Commissioner, in the name of the French government, recognized the Republic of Cochinchina as a free state, having its own government, parliament, army, and finances, forming part of the Indochinese Federation and the French Union. Two days later, the autonomous Republic of Cochinchina was officially proclaimed. Of the nine members of the provisional government, seven were French citizens, including President Nguyen Van Thinh, and Vice-President and Minister of Defense Nguyen Van Xuan, who was also a colonel in the French army.

5 ☆ *The Diplomat*

~~~~~~

SINCE HIS last meetings with d'Argenlieu, Ho had the premonition that the temerarious High Commissioner was resolved to do everything within his power to prevent a Franco-Vietnamese settlement short of restoration of the old order in Indochina. Therefore, it became imperative that Ho personally negotiate with the responsible leaders in Paris. Having entrusted the direction of the government to his loyal and able lieutenant Vo Nguyen Giap, Ho and his delegation left Hanoi on the closing day of May. The news of the proclamation of the Republic of Cochinchina reached Ho while his plane was flying over Syria. Noticeably upset, the seasoned revolutionary, however, rapidly regained his composure. To General Raoul Salan, the French commander in North Indochina who accompanied him, Ho diplomatically minimized the incident, ascribing d'Argenlieu's action to a "misunderstanding," which would soon be solved in Paris.

The Charming Visitor

Ho's scheduled arrival in the French capital was most inopportune. France was in the midst of a political campaign. Pending the outcome of the general election to be held on June 2, a caretaker government had been installed to manage the routine business. The Vietnamese delegation thus would have to cool their heels since no negotiation could begin before a new government was formed. Apprehensive that Ho's presence would cause a commotion in Paris' political circles and provide him with an excellent opportunity to renew his friendship and contact with important leaders, the French authorities requested that Sainteny keep him away from the capital. Meeting the Viet Minh chief at the Orly airport, Sainteny embarrassingly informed his guest that the Franco-Vietnamese conference had to be postponed for at least a month, and that arrangements had been made for Ho and his delegation to relax in Biarritz, a picturesque sea resort in southwestern France. Consequently, the two planes carrying the Vietnamese delegation, instead of unloading at Orly, took off for Biarritz with an additional passenger, Sainteny, who served as Ho's official guide during his stay in France.

Upon their arrival at the resort town, the Vietnamese delegates were installed at Carlton, the area's biggest hotel. At the beginning, Ho was unusually reticent and appeared quite nervous. He asked Sainteny whether he should return to Hanoi. Since France had unilaterally decided the status of Cochinchina in contravention of the March 6 Accord, Ho argued, it would be useless to proceed with another Franco-Vietnamese conference. Patiently, the French official tried to persuade the Viet Minh chief that d'Argenlieu's action was of a provisional nature and did not seal the fate of Cochinchina, which would be subject to a referendum as provided in the March agreement. The impending talks would settle this thorny question in addition to the other problems of Franco-Vietnamese relations. Apparently satisfied with Sainteny's explanation, the old revolutionary found his smile again. While most of the members of his delegation left for Paris, Ho remained, making good use of his unofficial stay on the Basque coast. Peope flocked to see him, talk with him, or shake his hand. Important people, humble people, politicians, fishermen, workers, men, women, and children all were charmed by the old Vietnamese with a gentle look, a wispy goatee, and a simple attire. Ho impressed the workers with his understanding of their problems. He amazed the fishermen, with whom he went fishing, with his unconcern for seasickness. He endeared himself to the mothers whose children he patted

or embraced. Very soon, Ho became a popular local celebrity.
Besides roaming the countryside and visiting Lourdes, the affable
and simple revolutionary also played pelota, attended receptions,
and chatted freely with the people he met. Many Vietnamese residents in France also came to visit him. As a shrewd militant who
had the habit of making gains out of losses, Ho turned his forced
stay in Biarritz into a personal triumph. Thus, when three leading
French Communists, including the Air Force Minister, for political
reasons, complained of the "indescribable" conditions in which the
DRV President was "sequestered" in Biarritz, Ho good-humoredly
declared that he was enchanted with his stay on the Basque coast.[1]

Meanwhile, the June 2 election resulted in a setback for the
Communists and a slight victory for the MRP (Mouvement Républicain Populaire) led by Georges Bidault, who formed a new government on June 19. The new Premier immediately declared the
period from June 22 to July 4 as that of Ho Chi Minh's state visit in
France. The DRV President was finally allowed to come to Paris.
On June 27, after thanking the people and officials of Biarritz for
their hospitality, Ho took off for the capital, accompanied by
Sainteny. In flying over Tours, Sainteny recalls, the old revolutionary looked down with apparent nostalgia at the city where he
had, twenty-five years earlier, participated in the founding of the
French Communist party. Late in the afternoon, Ho's plane landed
at Le Bourget airport, where a very large crowd, including the
Minister for Overseas Territories, Marius Moutet, and many other
leading civilian and military officials, had been waiting. The sight
of such an impressive group of people and of the colorful airport
decorated with French and Vietnamese flags touched Ho so deeply
that he became ill at ease. Turning pale, he stared at the crowd,
lost for words. As his plane came to a stop, Ho nervously grasped
Sainteny's arm. "Above all, don't leave me," said he to the French
official, "there are so many people."[2] Hesitantly, Ho got off the
plane. The official greeting began. The Vietnamese and French
national anthems were played. With his inseparable colonial cork
hat in his hand, Ho stood stiff at attention, his mind, perhaps,
wandering. . . . Twenty-three years earlier, as an outlaw, he had
unceremoniously left Paris to attend the Peasants' International
Congress in Moscow. Now, he returned to the same city, honored
as a head of state!

Ho's official stay in Paris was filled with the routine diplomatic receptions and activities: visits to the Arc de Triomphe, the Versailles Palace, and the City Hall, deposition of a wreath at the Tomb of the Unknown Soldier, attendance at the Opera, etc. Very soon, the fragile, little man with fulgurant eyes, the wispy goatee, the cork hat, and the high-buttoned linen work suit became a familiar figure in the French capital. On July 2, Ho and Bidault met for the first time. At the luncheon given in his honor, the DRV President, in reply to the French Premier's welcome address, paid a glowing tribute to France and the heroic city of Paris, and expressed his enthusiasm for the French Union by drawing a parallel to it:

Before officially greeting the French Government, I had the opportunity to visit the Basque provinces, a very beautiful region of France. The contact with the Basques taught me many lessons. While maintaining their peculiarities, dialect, and customs, the Basque people continue to be French citizens. Though France has many provinces which differ from each other, it remains unified and indivisible. In the future, the French Union will astonish the world with its solidarity and unity. The French Union that we will establish on a democratic basis can be set up only under a good omen. It is here in Paris, a heroic and generous city which proclaimed the principles of liberty, equality, and fraternity, a city which has the tradition to champion the equality of other peoples, it is in this very city that I solemnly declare that Vietnam will join this humanitarian organization.

Paris is the city which discovered the eternal ideals for the 1789 Revolution; it has remained loyal to its ideals in the bloodshed between the democratic and fascist blocs.

Attributing the harmonious relations between France and Vietnam to Paris' efforts, and voicing his firm belief that all obstacles would be overcome at Fontainebleau, Ho continued:

Paris has made no small contributions to the concord of Vietnam and France within the French Union including free and equal nations which cherish the same democratic ideals and are all for freedom. It is here in Paris that Vietnam will step forward to the path of independence. I am convinced that it will not be long before independent Vietnam plays its worthy role in the Pacific. No doubt many difficulties are awaiting the Fontainebleau Conference which has the responsibility to lay down the foundation for the relations between new France and new Vietnam. But sincerity and mutual confidence will level all obstacles. Have we not done away with aggressive imperialism and narrow chauvinism which are no longer fit for the present world? We are all stimulated by the same spirit. The Confucian philosophy and the Western philosophy alike uphold an ethic principle which is "Do as you would be done by." I believe that in those conditions, the forthcoming conference will achieve satisfactory results.[3]

At the Royal-Monceau Hotel where he stayed, Ho gave countless receptions and interviews to reporters, politicians, government officials, representatives of commercial and financial interests. As he had done in Biarritz, Ho, the born diplomat and the consummate actor, easily charmed the sophisticated Parisians with his apparent simplicity. Chivalrously distributing roses to woman reporters, fondly caressing children, and seizing every opportunity to condemn extremism and violence, the shrewd revolutionary passed for a man of peace. "As soon as one approaches this frail man," recalls one admiring reporter, "one shares the admiration of all men around him, over whom he towers with his serenity acquired from wide experience."[4] Equally flattering is the remark of another newsman who notes that "his wit, his Oriental courtesy, his savoir-faire, his mixed profundity and playfulness in social intercourse, his open love for children, above all his seeming sincerity and simplicity captured one and all."[5] Thus, in spite of his ruthlessness, there was a genuine warmth in Ho that inspired friendship, confidence, and loyalty in the people he came in contact with. It was this warmth that often caused observers to forget the cunning and ruthless aspects of Ho's personality. Always charming and conciliatory, the old fighter painstakingly tried to avoid conveying the impression that he was a doctrinaire, but studiously attempted to project himself as a pragmatic revolutionary. "Everyone has the right to his own doctrine," said he to a number of Western correspondents. "I studied and chose Marx. Jesus said two thousand years ago that one should love one's enemies. That dogma has not been realized. When will Marxism be realized? I cannot answer. . . . To achieve a Communist society, big industrial and agricultural production is necessary. . . . I do not know when that will be realized in Vietnam, where production is low. We are not yet in a position to meet the conditions."[6]

During his stay in Paris, Ho carefully cultivated friendly relations with the French Left, the press, and, to the dismay of the French government, foreign diplomats. Sainteny, who had been assigned the role of intermediary between the DRV President and the host government, complained that Ho, often disregarding protocol, went over his head to obtain what he wanted.

The Fontainebleau Conference

Paris' decision to force Ho to cool his heels in Biarritz was the first in a series of humiliations inflicted upon the old revolutionary. In an obvious gesture to further embarrass Ho, Premier Bidault refused to permit the Franco-Vietnamese talks to be held in Paris. The French Prime Minister understandably was anxious to remove the Vietnamese from the capital where they had established contact with liberal political circles, the press, and the public, which had shown considerable sympathy for their cause, and to prevent the kind of publicity that a Paris-based conference would generate. Fontainebleau, a community located some 35 miles from Paris, was chosen instead as the meeting place. To add insult to injury, Premier Bidault, on June 29, appointed a French delegation which, composed primarily of men who had attended the Dalat Conference, did not include any cabinet member or leader of consequence. Worse still, this team was to be headed by the archaic High Commissioner for Indochina. Only a violent protest from Ho himself caused the French government to replace d'Argenlieu with Max André,[7] the man who had led the French delegation at Dalat. Bidault's maneuvers, which clearly indicated that the French government had no intention of budging from its position at Dalat, dissipated any lingering hope that Paris and Saigon had been at odds. To deal with this French team Ho put forth an impressive delegation which included seven ministers and deputy-ministers, leaders of the anti-Viet Minh parties that had been part of the Government of National Union, and even a member of the royal family.[8] While entrusting the conduct of the negotiation to his loyal associate Pham Van Dong, Ho chose to stay away from the conference.

If the Vietnamese were desirous of a definite settlement, the French were intent on procrastinating it. With a view to minimiz-

ing the importance of the Fontainebleau talks, wrecking the conference, then blaming Ho for its failure, Premier Bidault thus pur-
posefully sent a subcabinet level delegation, whose main concern
was "strict discipline" and rigorous adherence to majority views. In
this regard, Paul Rivet, a member of the French delegation, writes:

. . . it is certain that the choice of M. Max André could not please the
Vietnamese delegates, who were not unaware of his links with the
Franco-Chinese Bank and, consequently, with the Bank of Indochina.

However that may be, M. Max André invited to his home, on July 5,
1946, all the French delegates in order to make contact before the first
official Franco-Vietnamese conference, which was to take place the next
day at Fontainebleau. I accepted this invitation. I was surprised not to
find among the delegates men whom I knew for their profound knowledge of the Indochinese scene. . . . I asked as soon as the meeting opened
for the text of the agreements of March 6, which would serve as the
basis of the discussions and I hoped to be able to study them that
evening. My question appeared inopportune and I was told that this text
would be communicated to me later. On the contrary, they insisted more
on the necessity for strict discipline in the delegation and a rigorous
adherence to decisions made by the majority of the members. From this
moment, my role was a silent one. I listened to the comments that the
delegates exchanged and, when I took leave of M. Max André, I announced to him that I was resigning.

Condemning the French approach to the conference, Rivet gave
additional insights into the French motives:

That evening I communicated this decision to M. Marius Moutet in a
long letter in which I said that I intended to be neither dupe nor accomplice nor hostage, and in which I denounced the large-scale maneuver
which was to be undertaken with rare tenacity during long months: to
bring the Fontainebleau conference to an impasse, to profit from the
discredit that the failure of the negotiations was supposed to cast on the
negotiators, in particular on Ho Chi Minh, and to propose the Bao Dai
combination; if necessary, to impose it, by depriving Tonkin of rice
supplies from Cochinchina and thus provoking famine.[9]

The Fontainebleau Conference, which opened on July 6, was
thus doomed to fail. Misjudging both the strength and the intention of the French Socialist and Communist parties, whose main
concern was victory in the next general election and whose knowledge of the Indochina problem was mediocre, Ho made the mis-

take of identifying his cause with the French Left and, consequently, alienating the more influential and responsible political
parties. On the opening day of the conference, Ho committed an
inexplicable blunder. To the embarrassment of the Socialist Minister of Overseas Territories, Marius Moutet, Ho, who had maintained contact with nationalist leaders from the French colonies,
received a delegation led by the Algerian Ferhat Abbas, emphasizing the common problems confronting Algeria and Vietnam.
With the exception of these flaws, Ho's conduct in Paris reflected a
very shrewd and calculating mind. In spite of Premier Bidault's
rebuff, Ho diplomatically and optimistically spoke of a French
Union of free and equal nations, of the "sincerity and mutual confidence" prevailing at the Fontainebleau Conference, and of the
"friendly cooperation" between France and Vietnam that would be
"a great example for the world to realize that with mutual confidence, free and equal nations can always solve the most difficult
problems."[10] In instructing Pham Van Dong to take a strong stand
at the conference while he himself minimized the Franco-Vietnamese differences, Ho had several objectives in mind: (a) to have
the Vietnamese delegation present the Vietnamese position as it
should be, (b) to appear as a very flexible man ready to compromise, and (c) in case of an impasse, to put the blame on the
intransigent elements, both French and Vietnamese.

At Fontainebleau, as at Dalat, the French delegates apparently
were not interested in discussing the points raised by the March 6
Accord, but in retrieving some of the concessions that had been
made under that agreement. They refused to budge an inch from
their previous position. A distressed Ho soon learned that the rigid
policy he had deplored was not d'Argenlieu's alone but also that of
the French government. While Ho's objective was Vietnam's independence and unity within the French Union, Paris' aim was the
restoration of French rule in a different form. Thus, the items on
the agenda—the status of the "free State of Vietnam" within the
Indochinese Federation and the French Union, the union of the
three *ky*, Vietnam's diplomatic representation, and France's cultural and economic interests—instead of being points of discussion,
became stumbling blocks because of the archaic French position.

In contrast to Bidault's concept of the French Union as a group
of states closely bound to each other by common organs and mov-

ing toward a federal system, Ho, during his press conference on July 12, said:

On the political level, the relations between France and Vietnam must proceed from a treaty. This treaty rests on a fundamental principle: the right of people to decide their own fate. On the economic and cultural level, we are partisans of an association with France within the framework of a French Union. There will be solidarity whenever common interests are involved.

The existence of the Indochinese Federation is justified by the necessity of coordinating the activities of Vietnam, Laos and Cambodia. It must be essentially economic. Vietnam, on its part, being more favored in this respect than its neighbors, is prepared to lend them assistance if requested. It is determined, however, to prevent the Federation from becoming a kind of disguised General Government.[11]

In spite of the High Commissioner's blunder in calling a Conference on Indochina on August 1, Ho, the shrewd calculator, still remained conciliatory on the question of Cochinchina, which he unequivocally declared to be Vietnamese territory, "the flesh of our flesh, the blood of our blood." To a *Franc-Tireur* reporter, the Viet Minh chief said:

Ethnically, historically, Cochinchina is part of Vietnam inasmuch as Brittany and the Basque country are part of France. However, since these facts are disputed, we are ready to wait for the result of a plebiscite. The main thing is to organize it under normal conditions. . . . While we do not recognize the "de facto government" of Saigon, it exists . . . and we are prepared to collaborate with it to prepare a plebiscite by creating a mixed Commission.

To show his understanding of the problem and his eagerness to promote Franco-Vietnamese rapprochement, Ho continued:

If we cannot forget the wrong done to us, can we forget what we owe France? We need her, culturally and economically. We want her technicians and her capital to help Vietnam become prosperous. A fruitful cooperation is possible. France has everything to gain from it.

I came to make peace. I do not intend to go back to Hanoi with empty hands. I want to return there in France's company, that is, to bring to the Vietnamese a concrete evidence of the collaboration we are seeking.[12]

While the delegates pursued their futile talks in Fontainebleau, Admiral d'Argenlieu again opened his bag of tricks. With a view to administering the coup de grâce to the Franco-Vietnamese negotiation, the obnoxious High Commissioner announced, on July 25, that the question of an Indochinese Federation could not be settled by a conference attended only by delegates from Paris and Hanoi. Therefore, a second Dalat Conference was scheduled for August 1 to which representatives from Cambodia, Laos, Cochinchina, and observers from South Annam and the mountainous region of South Indochina were invited to discuss the future of the federation. By excluding representatives of the Hanoi regime, d'Argenlieu conveyed the impression that only leaders from French-controlled areas were qualified to speak for the people of Indochina. The High Commissioner's defying maneuver profoundly disturbed Ho and enraged the Vietnamese delegation in France. Pretending to be imperturbable, the Viet Minh chief nevertheless ordered Pham Van Dong to lodge a violent protest at Fontainebleau and to request, on August 1, that the conference be suspended until a satisfactory explanation was given. In an interview with Philippe Devillers on August 3, the Admiral, gratified by the suspension of the Fontainebleau talks, flatly said: "I can assure you that if General de Gaulle were President of the Republic at this moment, Mr. Ho Chi Minh would not be given so much freedom nor permitted to trifle that way. He would have been forced to stay within his rank."[13]

Meanwhile, Max André, the chief French negotiator at Fontainebleau, informed the Vietnamese delegation, on August 9, that the second Dalat Conference was designed simply to ascertain the views of the other populations of Indochina regarding the proposed federation and, consequently, should not be permitted to interfere with their own negotiation. Soon, the two delegations resumed their discussions. In the evening of September 9–10, a limited *modus vivendi* on economic and financial questions, which was essentially a Vietnamese concession, was reached. On the following day, however, Phan Van Dong, aware that the agreement was nothing but a Vietnamese acceptance of the French conditions regarding Vietnam's membership in the Indochinese Federation without a French guarantee to recognize Vietnam's independence and unity, demanded that the *modus vivendi* be discussed again and that France make a definite commitment concerning the referendum in Cochinchina. Max André refused to comply with Dong's request. The Fontainebleau came to a close. As Devillers and Lacouture aptly explained,

France had not been prepared to lead a confederation of sovereign and equal nations of which she would be the guide, the "elder nation." This was what the Hanoi delegates to the Franco-Vietnamese Conferences at Dalat (April 1946) and Fontainebleau (August 1946) must have felt. They understood that for almost all their interlocutors, Vietnam could only be a satellite within the framework of an Indochinese Federation, whose services would be controlled exclusively by Paris and whose arbiter would be the French High Commissioner.[14]

On September 13, the Vietnamese delegation, their heads high, unbowed and uncowed, left Paris for Toulon, whence they sailed for Haiphong three days later. Ho, however, decided to remain in the French capital for a little longer. Since the middle of August, he had left Royal-Monceau Hotel for the villa of a French comrade, Raymond Aubrac, in Soissy-sous-Montmorency.

During his stay in France, Ho, who had "come to make peace," and who would not return to Hanoi without "France's company," feverishly sought to achieve an agreement with Paris. Meanwhile, in Hanoi, numerous demonstrations took place against the Fontainebleau Conference during the second half of August. The highly aroused public vehemently condemned the intransigent attitude of the French authorities in both Saigon and Paris. Worried by these events which might get out of hand, Sainteny discussed the situation with Ho, who, for the first time, agreed with the French official that his absence from Hanoi should not be prolonged much longer. "I know what you are referring to," said the old revolutionary, "but what could I do if I return empty-handed?"[15] In an obvious attempt to remind the French government that he was the moderate leader with whom it should reach a settlement, Ho let it be known that unless he returned with an agreement, the extremists in Tonkin would gain the upper hand. The telegram he asked Sainteny to transmit to Hanoi on September 2, the first anniversary of Vietnam's "independence," was intended for both the Vietnamese and the French governments:

From President Ho Chi Minh to Vietnam Government in Hanoi: I have learned that commemoration of Independence Day takes place in our country. I want the ceremonies to be free of unfriendly demonstrations against France thus permitting her representative to eventually take part in them.[16]

The day following the closing of the Fontainebleau Conference, which had ended in total failure, Ho, the seemingly incurable optimist, still remarked to an Associated Press reporter that there was no real discord between France and Vietnam, and that their disagreements were of the kind one found in every family!

The modus vivendi *of September 14, 1946*

After the departure of the Vietnamese delegates, who were justifiably proud of their conduct at Fontainebleau, a hesitant and perplexed Ho stayed on, trying to salvage something from the wreckage in order not to return empty-handed. On September 14, he called on Marius Moutet, the Socialist Minister of Overseas Territories, and Premier Bidault. As Sainteny describes, Ho, refusing to admit failure, was resigned to accept a "poor *modus vivendi* hastily drawn up in my office." The former French Commissioner for Tonkin recalls the breakfast at his home bringing together Ho Chi Minh, Marius Moutet, and himself, at which the old fighter again said: "Do not leave this way. Arm me with something against those who seek to outdo me. You will not regret it."[17] Fearing the worst, an armed conflict, which had already loomed on the horizon, Ho continued with resignation: "If we must fight, we will fight. You will kill ten of our men, and we will kill one of yours. Yet, in the end, it is you who will tire."

It was midnight, September 14, 1946. A frail, little man in military tunic hesitantly walked toward the residence of Minister Marius Moutet. It was none other than Ho Chi Minh. In spite of his lively eyes, he looked very tired, very perplexed. After a day of meditation and calculation, Ho had decided to sign the *modus vivendi*. Fearing that any further delay would cause either him or Moutet to change his mind, the old revolutionary, ignoring protocol, went straight to the Minister's bedroom, insisting that the agreement be signed at once. It was an unusual diplomatic ceremony. It took place in a bedroom. Of the two officials present, one was dressed in pajamas and the other wore an ill-fitting tunic. It was also a brief ceremony. Moutet wanted to go to sleep, and Ho was anxious to return to his hotel. With mixed feelings, Ho murmured to the police inspector who escorted him back to his residence: "I just signed my death warrant."

A death warrant for Vietnam, it was indeed. Without making any concessions, the French obtained almost everything they had asked for at Dalat and at Fontainebleau. French citizens in Vietnam were to enjoy the same freedom of establishment as natives, "freedom of opinion, of teaching, of commerce, of circulation, and more generally all democratic liberties." The consent of the French government was to be required for any change in the status of French property and enterprises, which were not to be "submitted to a stricter regime than that accorded property and enterprises of Vietnamese nationals." All French property requisitioned or confiscated by the Vietnamese government was to be returned to its owners or representatives. French schools and scientific institutes were to function freely in Vietnam, and the Pasteur Institute and the School for Far Eastern Studies returned to the French government. Hanoi also agreed to give priority to French advisers, technicians, and experts. Pending a final agreement, the piaster issued by the Bank of Indochina was to be the currency in Vietnam, which would form a customs union with the other Indochinese states. A mixed committee was to study the problem of restoring and improving communication between Vietnam and the other members of the Indochinese Federation and the French Union. Until a final accord was concluded, a Franco-Vietnamese commission was to arrange for Vietnamese consular representation in neighboring states and for Vietnamese relations with foreign consulates.

For Cochinchina, Paris agreed only to restore public order, promote democratic liberties, and cooperate with Hanoi in bringing about a cease-fire. The *modus vivendi* was thus less advantageous to Ho than the March 6 Accord. No mention was made of a referendum in Cochinchina; no reference was made to the status of the "free State of Vietnam." The crucial political questions were not settled.

What did Ho receive in return for these considerable concessions? Nothing; nothing but a French promise "to seek together the conclusion of special agreements on all questions which may arise" and to resume negotiations for a final treaty no later than January, 1947.

Why, then, did the old fox sign such an unfavorable agreement? Ho was apparently anxious to avoid a rupture with France, a rupture which, he feared, would lead to a military confrontation. He wanted to gain additional time to prepare his country for a war which the intransigent French government seemed resolved to impose on it. Perhaps the Viet Minh leader also believed that the coming November elections in France would result in additional strength for his French Communist comrades, who would be in a position to influence Paris to go half-way to meet the Vietnamese demands. Above all, the opportunistic Ho, once convinced of France's determination to stay in Indochina, decided to play the French game in order to maintain himself in power. In signing the *modus vivendi* Ho hoped to persuade Paris that it had everything to gain by negotiating with him for he was willing to accommodate the French with almost everything they wanted. Did he not ask the Minister of Overseas Territories, Marius Moutet, to arm him with something against the Vietnamese extremists who sought to outdo him?

Instead of flying back to Hanoi, Ho chose to sail, on the ground that air travel tended to impair his health. Sainteny, however, believes that the Viet Minh leader was afraid of an attempt on his life, in which case flying would make him more vulnerable to an attack than sailing.[18] Ho's utter disregard for dangers throughout his life seemed to lend little weight to such an argument. A more plausible explanation of Ho's decision to sail would be his desire to gain time. Aware of the deep consternation caused by the *modus vivendi* among the Vietnamese, who had begun to accuse him of betrayal, the DRV President apparently wanted to prolong his trip as long as possible, hoping that tempers would subside when he landed in Haiphong. Thus, Sainteny's efforts to convince Ho to avail himself of the fastest means of transportation remained futile. At the Viet Minh chief's request, Paris put at his disposition the French sloop *Dumont-d'Urville*.

Ho's last days on French soil were discouragingly unpleasant.

On September 16, the man who had entered Paris full of hopes nearly three months earlier left the capital in a state of perplexity. Sainteny, who escorted Ho to Toulon, gives the following account of the old revolutionary's discomforting experience during his trip from Paris to the French port. At Montelimar, the train carrying Ho and Sainteny made a brief stop. A crowd, composed mostly of Vietnamese workers in the area, had been waiting for the Viet Minh leader. In contrast to the spontaneous acclamation given a few days earlier to Pham Van Dong and the Vietnamese delegation, who had refused to yield to the French at Fontainebleau, the reception extended Ho was embarrassingly lukewarm. The shouts of "Viet Nam Doc Lap Muon Nam!" (Long Live Independent Vietnam) hardly dominated those of "Viet Gian" (traitor) that were intended for Ho. From the steps of his car, Ho made a short address in which he explained his reasons for signing the unpopular *modus vivendi,* and asked his countrymen to leave politics to him and make good use of their stay in France by working beside their "French brothers" and learning a trade. Vietnam had a great need for skilled workers and experienced technicians.

At Marseilles, where lived the largest Vietnamese colony in France, the welcome was not any more encouraging for the tired revolutionary. The dreadful appellation of "Viet Gian" was again hurled at him. Ho, however, remained calm, spoke with moderation, stressing Franco-Vietnamese friendship and expressing hopes for the future. While Ho emphasized cooperation, two Communist members of the Marseille City Council exhorted Vietnamese to carry their struggle to the finish against oppressive French colonialism.[19] The shouts of "Viet Gian," like the "Open Letter to Comrade Nguyen Ai Quoc, April 1946,"[20] in which a group of Vietnamese immigrants in France, remnants of the handful of men trained by Ho in 1925, accused him of treason, profoundly upset the usually imperturbable revolutionary.

On September 18, upon his arrival in Toulon, Ho went aboard the *Dumont-d'Urville.* On the following day, at dawn, the warship left the French port for the high seas. Ho Chi Minh had stayed in France for a little over three months.

Meanwhile, Admiral d'Argenlieu, greatly enchanted by the *modus vivendi,* wanted to discuss the state of Franco-Vietnamese relations with Ho. At the High Commissioner's request, the DRV

President stopped to see him in the bay of Cam Ranh. The meeting took place on October 18 on the cruiser *Suffren*. After a long talk, the two men appeared in a conciliatory mood. To the reporters gathered for the occasion Ho complained of the fierce tone of the Saigon and Hanoi newspapers, and expressed his wish that the press would help achieve a detente instead of arousing people's feeling. Ho also condemned the acts of terrorism in the South, and optimistically remarked that a faithful adherence to the *modus vivendi* would greatly help improve Franco-Vietnamese relations. In this the High Commissioner naturally concurred.

Triumphant Return

After almost five months' absence, Ho arrived in Haiphong on October 20, noticeably perplexed and worried. The *modus vivendi* had caused widespread indignation among the people who had expected a better deal from Ho Who Enlightens. Numerous were those who had accused him of selling out to the French. "When one remains in foreign countries for a long time, one becomes their slave," said some of the tracts circulated in Hanoi and Haiphong. Criticism of the agreement found expression even in the government-controlled press. Thus, opposition to the unsatisfactory accord was not limited to the extremist elements as many authors have claimed, but was shared by Vietnamese from all walks of life and from all political groupings. Illustrating the popular feeling was the tumultuous welcome given Pham Van Dong and his delegation upon their return on October 3. They had stood firm at Fontainebleau, and the people were behind them.

Ho, however, had reversed the Vietnamese delegation's position at Fontainebleau. He had given the French almost everything they wanted for nothing tangible in return. What kind of reception was waiting for him? Visibly confused, the wispy-bearded, little man nervously paced the deck of the French sloop as it approached the port of Haiphong. Ho was prepared to face the same kind of welcome as those that had been given him in Montelimar and Marseilles. From the ship he saw a huge crowd, the gold-starred red flags, and the banderoles carrying slogans which he was unable to read from such a distance. He appeared markedly ill at ease. He had no choice but to land. As he stepped ashore, however, the thunderous shouts of "Ho Chu Tich Muon Nam!" (Long Live President Ho) nearly knocked him off balance. Slowly, Ho took out a large red handkerchief. Slowly, he wiped his eyes. The consummate actor again used his favorite trick! What caused such a change of heart among those Vietnamese who, two months earlier, had violently condemned and protested against the unreasonable French position at Fontainebleau, a position in which Ho had finally acquiesced? Why did these same people, who had so strongly supported the Pham Van Dong delegation's firm stand in France, give such an ovation to the man who had reversed it? The answer to these questions is simple. There was no change of heart among Vietnamese. Aware of the popular sentiment against any concession to France, Pham Van Dong had made strenuous efforts to convince the Vietnamese that, pending a definite and more favorable settlement, the *modus vivendi* which averted a military confrontation was the only possible agreement under the existing conditions. The effective Viet Minh propaganda had proved, once again, up to its challenge.

During his train journey from Haiphong to Hanoi, Ho was given similarly enthusiastic receptions. At every station, from the port to the capital, along the sixty-mile route, youth, peasants, men, women, whom the local Viet Minh committees had gathered for the occasion, deliriously cheered Uncle Ho. Each time, the old actor mechanically took out his red handkerchief and wiped his eyes, which, finally, became red from repeated rubbing. The simple peasants were deeply moved.

In Hanoi, where he arrived in the evening, Uncle Ho enjoyed the same elaborate and enthusiastic welcome. Extolling Franco-Vietnamese friendship, the shrewd Communist requested that both the Vietnamese and French national anthems be played. At the first press conference following his return, Ho, explaining the *modus vivendi*, said: "While resolved to obtain independence and unity for our country, we are equally determined to live within the French Union. Since France loves democracy and liberty, there is no reason why she should not give them to Vietnam. I can assure you that the Paris Government intends to adhere faithfully to the recent accord. This *modus vivendi* was necessary to facilitate Franco-Vietnamese relations pending the resumption of negotiations in January 1947."[21] At the same time, the DRV President appealed to both French and Vietnamese reporters to respect the spirit of the accord and refrain from making provocative and divisive statements.

Similarly, in his address to the nation on October 23, Ho reported on the Franco-Vietnamese relations as follows:

On my way to France, during my stay in France, and on my way back from France, the French Government, to show its desire to cooperate with Vietnam, received me ceremoniously. Out of sincere friendship for our people, the French people received me fraternally. . . .

Thanks to the understanding of French personalities in the North and Center of Vietnam, most of the difficulties arising between the Vietnamese and the Frenchmen have lately been settled.

I hope that from now on cooperation between the two peoples will be closer. . . .

. . . I went to France with the purpose of solving the question of Vietnam's independence and the unification of the North, Center, and South. Due to the present situation in France, these two questions have not yet been settled. We have to wait. But I dare to vouch that sooner or later Vietnam is sure to be independent, and its three parts, the North, the Center, and the South, will be unified.

Ho gave an account of his activities in France that might sound trivial to readers but was very important to the Vietnamese, whose country had not been treated as a member of the international community:

We took Vietnam's flag to France. The French Government and people and foreign residents there looked on our flag with respect.

We drew greater attention from the French Government and people and made them understand the question of Vietnam better than before. We also drew the attention of the world and made it understand the question of Vietnam better than before.

We caused a great many Frenchmen to become friends of the Vietnamese people and approve of Vietnam's independence and sincere Vietnamese-French cooperation on an equal footing.

We further heightened the position of the Vietnamese youth, women's, and workers' organizations because respective international organizations have recognized our organizations as members.

The *modus vivendi*, Ho stressed, had, first, "permitted the Vietnamese and French to carry out their business easily," and second, "paved the way for the next Conference to be conducted in a friendly manner."

Referring to the unity of Vietnam and the status of Cochinchina, the DRV President reiterated his position by drawing a parallel to France:

Compatriots in the South and the southern part of Central Vietnam! The North, Center, and South are part and parcel of Vietnam. We have the same ancestors, we are of the same family, we are all brothers and sisters. Our country has three parts, which are the North, the Center, and the South. They are just like three brothers in the same family. They are just like three regions of France: Normandy, Provence, and Beauce.

No one can divide the children of the same family. No one can divide France. Likewise, no one can divide Vietnam. . . .

So long as the Fatherland is not yet unified and our compatriots are still suffering, I can neither eat with an appetite, nor sleep in peace. I solemnly promise you that with your determination and that of the entire people, our beloved South will surely come back into the bosom of our Fatherland.

To conclude his address, the "benevolent Uncle Ho" appealed to Vietnamese to forget their differences and avoid violent actions, which, as events were to illustrate, were freely resorted to by the Viet Minh organization:

Acts of reprisal are forbidden. Toward those who went astray, our compatriots must display a generous policy. We must let them hear the voice of reason. Everybody loves his country. It is only for petty interests that they forget the great cause. If we use the right words, they will certainly listen to us. Violent actions are absolutely forbidden. This is what you have to do at present to create a peaceful atmosphere, paving the way democratically to reach the unification of our Vietnam.[22]

Things had changed considerably during Ho's extended absence from Vietnam. While the pro-Chinese nationalists had been reduced to impotence, the French had convincingly strengthened their military position north of the 16th parallel and become increasingly menacing and provocative. It should be recalled that for nearly a year, from August, 1945, to the summer of 1946, numerous prominent non-Communist leaders had supported the Viet Minh-led revolution or had not publicly opposed it. Ho had adroitly made use of Bao Dai, exploiting the prestige of the ex-Emperor who still commanded considerable respect and loyalty among the tradition-bound Vietnamese. On March 18, however, Bao Dai, availing himself of an unexpected opportunity to leave the country, decided to put an end to his farcical role as Ho's Supreme Counsellor. Dutifully complying with the DRV President's request that he take part in a mission entrusted with the task of seeking Chinese military and economic assistance for the Viet Minh government, the ex-Emperor departed for China. Once out of Vietnam, however, Bao Dai, instead of going to Chungking, took off for Hong Kong. The flight of Ho's Supreme Counsellor caused a great commotion inside the country. The opposition intensified its attack on the regime, again condemning the March 6 Accord and other Viet Minh maneuvers. Ho decided that persuasion should give way to assassination.

Consequently, during the DRV President's absence and on his instructions, Vo Nguyen Giap proceeded with a systematic elimination of anti-Viet Minh nationalists. Ironically, the French cooperated with Giap in his relentless effort to suppress these "saboteurs" of the March Accord. Both separate and joint Viet Minh-French military operations were launched against the VNQDD and DMH partisans on the heels of the departing Chinese troops. If the French helped Giap get rid of the nationalist elements, they also fortified their position, arriving in the North in greater numbers than agreed under the March Accord, and freely occupying buildings and areas without bothering to consult the Hanoi government. Such was the situation Ho found upon his return. Soon, the DRV President proceeded to reshuffle his government in preparation for a showdown with the French. On October 31, the entire cabinet resigned. The Constituent Assembly, which had been convened for the express purpose of approving the government's policies, immediately requested the Viet Minh chief to form a new government. Three days later, Ho presented his new cabinet, which was composed almost entirely of Viet Minh and "nonparty" hardliners. President Ho also took over the portfolio of Foreign Affairs while Vo Nguyen Giap was officially appointed Minister of Defense. On November 9, the Constituent Assembly adopted the draft of the Constitution that affirmed, without reservation, Vietnam's independence and unity.

Beginning of a Conflict

While there was no doubt regarding Ho's desire to avoid an armed conflict with France, all evidence indicated that the French were determined to go ahead with their solution of force. Ever since the French unloaded their modern weapons at Haiphong, on March 8, Ho had become obsessed with the fear of a French attack. Contrary to the March 6 Accord, the French in fact brought in enormous quantities of arms and more troops than allowed, set up military installations, recruited Vietnamese for military construction work, occupied public buildings, and transformed cities into veritable French military strongholds. More seriously, on April 10, just a little over a month after the signing of the Franco-Vietnamese agreement, General Valluy, d'Argenlieu's deputy in Saigon, directed the French garrisons north of the 16th parallel to undertake "the study of measures which would have the effect of progressively modifying and transforming the plan of action for a *coup d'état.*"[23] The directive clearly indicated bad faith on the part of the French authorities, who had signed a treaty with Ho, then shamelessly sought to destroy him.

Meanwhile, in the face of d'Argenlieu's refusal to admit Hanoi's representatives into Cochinchina and of continued military actions against the Viet Minh units in the South, Ho eluded the French proposal to form a joint Franco-Vietnamese force which, under the military agreement of April 3, was to be responsible for public security in the territory north of the 16th parallel.

In addition to frequent clashes between French troops and Viet Minh militia men, in which each side accused the other of provocation, the incidents in Haiphong augured ill for the course of Franco-Vietnamese relations. In reply to the Vietnamese attempts to enforce customs control in Haiphong, General Morlière, the acting Commissioner for Tonkin, announced, on September 10, his decision to establish temporary control over imports and exports. Ho lodged a sharp protest against such violation of Vietnamese sovereignty. The French, in disregard of the *modus vivendi*, refused to change their position. Tension was running high. It reached a climax on November 20. Two armed clashes took place on the same day, one in Langson which ended in a French "victory," and the other in Haiphong which precipitated the ultimate showdown. Early in the morning, a French patrol boat cruising in the harbor of Haiphong seized a Chinese junk with contraband cargo. Vietnamese soldiers intercepted the French boat and detained its three-man crew. Instead of having the local liaison commission settle the incident, the local French commander, Colonel Dèbes, decided to use force to free the French "prisoners." Heavy fighting broke out in the city. Frustrated in their attempt to break the barricades erected by the Vietnamese around their areas, the French attacked and expelled the Viet Minh guards stationed in the French quarters.

Upon hearing of the incident, Ho immediately ordered the Vietnamese members of the liaison committee to meet with their French counterparts. The Vietnamese, accepting a cease-fire, agreed to release the French prisoners and remove the barricades. The French, however, while refusing to permit Vietnamese guards to return to their posts in the French quarters, insisted on remaining in the Vietnamese sections. At 2 P.M., accusing the Vietnamese of failing to remove all barricades as agreed—it would take at least a day to finish the job—French armored cars and bulldozers moved into the Vietnamese quarters. Heavy fighting resumed. Ho and General Morlière, the acting Commissioner, promptly intervened. A cease-fire again was agreed upon. On November 21, the fighting came to a halt. The incident seemed to have been settled when Saigon stepped in. With Paris' approval, General Valluy, the acting High Commissioner—d'Argenlieu was in France to sell his plan of using force to overthrow Ho's regime—decided to teach the Vietnamese a lesson. Enraged by Ho's lack of respect for French might, Valluy ordered Morliere to use force to gain full control of Haiphong and to crush any Vietnamese resistance. Morlière painstakingly assured the acting High Commissioner that the incident had been satisfactorily settled and that any further exploitation of the situation could lead to a large-scale conflict. Unmoved, Valluy, ignoring the established procedure by going over the head of General Morlière, who was then the principal French representative north of the 16th parallel, wired a message to Colonel Dèbes, the French commander in Haiphong and Morlière's subordinate, urging him to take action. "It appears clear," read the telegram, "that we are up against premeditated aggressions carefully staged by the Vietnamese regular army, which no longer seems to obey its government's orders. Under these circumstances, your commendable attempts at conciliation and division of quarters, as well as the inquiry that I asked you to make, are out of season. The moment has come to give a severe lesson to those who have treacherously attacked you. Use all the means at your disposal to make yourself complete master of Haiphong and so bring the Vietnamese army around to a better understanding of the situation."[24]

With such an encouragement, the irascible Dèbes issued, on November 23, an ultimatum to the local Vietnamese authorities, ordering the withdrawal of all Vietnamese troops from Haiphong within two hours or face consequences. When the time was up, the French, true to their promise, deployed everything they had against the Vietnamese in Haiphong: troops, armored tanks, heavy artillery, bombers, and the guns of the cruiser *Suffren*, the warship on which Ho and d'Argenlieu had had a friendly meeting on October 18! "At ten o'clock," writes Devillers, "Dèbes began the attack with artillery. The French units who entered the Chinese quarters were immediately met with a brisk fire. Dèbes called on the naval battery. The *Suffren* . . . , at the colonel's express request, opened fire on the targets in the Vietnamese quarters. Compartments and straw-huts began to burn. The people, driven by fear, ran over one another trying to reach the countryside. Grenades mowed everything down: houses, women, children, old men, and adults. In the acrid and dark smoke through which the odor of blood began to rise, the slaughter of the fugitives who unfurled on the streets to Do Son and Kien An was horrible."[25] As the dead and the wounded lay unattended, the survivors flocked to the countryside. According to reliable French estimates,[26] at least 6,000 Vietnamese were killed. The Haiphong carnage episode was undoubtedly the turning point in the history of Franco-Viet Minh relations.

To add insult to injury, d'Argenlieu, on November 24, had the temerity to send a message supporting his deputy's action. "I have learned with indignation of the recent attacks at Haiphong and Langson," said the cable. "Once again, our troops were victims of criminal premeditation. I bow before our great dead. I salute our wounded men. To all commanders and soldiers I convey from Paris my painful sympathy and the assurance that the Government of the Republic and the country, sadly moved by these attacks, realize the extraordinary difficulties you have met and the exceptional merits of the Expeditionary Corps which will overcome them. You have my esteem and confidence. We shall not retreat nor give up."[27]

In contrast to such a provocative and arrogant attitude, Ho's reaction was astonishingly subdued. Apprehensive that an armed confrontation with the French would destroy his ambition of staying in power, Ho appealed to his indignant countrymen to remain calm. With a view to settling the Haiphong incident and discussing measures to reduce tension, the calculating Communist leader sent Giap to see General Morlière on November 25. Ho stubbornly clung to the already vanishing hope of reaching an understanding with the French. After a two-day delay, during which he consulted with acting High Commissioner Valluy, Morlière received Giap to put forth the French position: (a) evacuation of all Vietnamese troops from Haiphong, and (b) French control of Haiphong and its surroundings and of all roads connecting French garrisons, notably the Haiphong-Do Son route. Confronted with this new ultimatum, Giap suggested the formation of a mixed commission to study the question. Thereupon, Morlière informed his interlocutor that he had received definite instructions from Saigon and that the French conditions were not negotiable.

In spite of his seemingly incurable optimism and his readiness to make concessions to save his regime, Ho began to realize that war could no longer be avoided. While trying to talk peace, he ordered Giap to keep his troops ready for war. On November 28, Ho again appealed to his people to remain patient and calm. On the following day, however, the Viet Minh Tong Bo (Central Executive Committee) issued a stern statement criticizing the politics of appeasement, and asked the DRV President to take a firmer stand.

Meanwhile, Sainteny, at the request of his government, agreed to return to Indochina to resume his duties as French Commissioner for Tonkin and North Annam. He landed in Saigon on November 26. The hardliner Valluy, fearful that Sainteny might frustrate his scheme to reduce Ho to impotence, retained the Commissioner in Saigon until the Haiphong incident was settled to his satisfaction. After a week's sojourn in the South, Sainteny finally prevailed over Valluy to let him go to Hanoi. On December 2, the

French Commissioner arrived at the Gia Lam airport, where he was greeted by Allied, French, and Vietnamese officials. In vain, Sainteny tried to seek out the familiar face of his friend Ho Chi Minh, whom he had expected to see upon his landing. The President was sick, Vo Nguyen Giap explained. To Sainteny, Ho's absence from the welcome ceremony was a bad omen. Immediately, the French official requested a meeting with the Viet Minh leader. Hoang Minh Giam, one of the main participants in the negotiations leading to the March 6 Accord, patiently assured Sainteny that the President was still confined to bed but would receive the French representative as soon as his condition permitted. On the following day, a note from Ho reached Sainteny's office. "I would be very happy to receive you this afternoon, between 5 and 6 o'clock," said the brief message. "In view of the present state of my health, this would be, of course, a visit between old friends."[28] Of this meeting, which dissipated his suspicion that Ho was not really ill and that the extremists had taken over the government in Hanoi, Sainteny writes:

I found Ho Chi Minh in bed: his eyes shone; his hands which held mine for a long while were feverish. Hoang Minh Giam and Nam, who were with him, did not leave the room and he did not ask them to leave us alone as he usually did. We talked about his health, my trip, . . . common places. Finally, he made reference to the events in Haiphong and appeared deeply upset by them. He hinted that these grave incidents were not unconnected with the illness which kept him in bed.

"You see," I said to him, "I was right when I expressed concern in Paris over your decision to prolong your absence from your country."

"Right," he replied, "but you too had delayed your return too long."

We stopped at that, and I never saw the President of Vietnam again.[29]

Following this last meeting of the two main authors of the March 6 Accord, Franco-Vietnamese relations steadily moved toward the breaking point. Sainteny had many discussions with Hoang Minh Giam, Ho's gray eminence, during which both sides tried to perform the impossible task of achieving a detente and restoring mutual confidence. Giam demanded that French troops withdraw back to the positions they had occupied before November 20, while Sainteny insisted that all anti-French propaganda be stopped and that the Vietnamese population that had fled Haiphong and Hanoi in large numbers for the safety of the countryside return to their homes in the two cities. Both Sainteny and Ho, however, realized that the time for a political solution had long passed and that military men had taken over the reins.

On December 6, in a desperate move, Ho made a radio appeal to the French National Assembly, in which he reaffirmed the sincere desire of the Vietnamese people and government to collaborate with France and to be part of the French Union, and attributed the deteriorating situation to a number of Frenchmen in Indochina who had disregarded the Franco-Vietnamese agreements. "In the name of the interests of both the French and Vietnamese people," concluded Ho, "I urgently appeal to the French National Assembly and Government to direct the French authorities in Vietnam to restore in Haiphong and Lang Son the conditions which had prevailed prior to November 20, with a view to applying the *modus vivendi* of September 14 and creating a base for a sincere and lasting Franco-Vietnamese collaboration. . . . The war has shed too much French and Vietnamese blood and caused too much destruction. Such a situation must not last."[30]

In an interview, given to Bernard Dranber, correspondent for the *Paris-Saigon* daily, Ho again said, on the following day:

I want you to know that my countrymen and I sincerely want peace. We do not want war. . . .

We do not want war, and the French people . . . do not want war. This war, we want to avoid at any cost. While we have a passion for independence, it is independence within the French Union that we want. War does not pay. . . .

If war is forced on us, we will fight. We are not unaware of what is in store for us. France disposes of terrifying weapons. The struggle will be atrocious, but the Vietnamese people are willing to endure everything rather than give up their freedom. However, I hope and wish with all my heart that we would not reach that decision. Neither France nor Vietnam can afford the luxury of a bloody war.[41]

Meanwhile, the formation of a Socialist government in Paris by Léon Blum, who had favored a settlement based on independence for Vietnam, suddenly revived Ho's hope for a Franco-Vietnamese understanding. On December 15, the Viet Minh chief made a last "concrete" proposal to the French government, which included three important parts:

1. The Vietnamese government would urge the evacuated population to return the cities, take all necessary measures to the normal economic life in the cities, help bring an end to the protective measures taken by the population in the cities, and ensure the return to normalcy of the Hanoi-Haiphong and Hanoi-Lang Son routes;

2. The French would assure the return of the French and Vietnamese troops to the positions they had occupied in Lang Son and Haiphong before November 20, withdraw the reinforcement they had recently sent into Tourane in violation of the Franco-Vietnamese agreements, and put an end to their so-called mop-up operations and campaign of repression in Cochinchina and southern Annam;

3. Both sides would immediately put in motion the organs provided to implement the *modus vivendi*, one commission in Hanoi and another in Saigon, and cease all propaganda over the radio and in the press.[32]

Ho's proposal did not get the attention it deserved in Saigon, where the authorities were interested only in a Viet Minh surrender. For eleven days, the communication was held up in the High Commissariat. When it finally reached Paris on December 26, it was already much too late. War had erupted.

During the hectic weeks preceding the outbreak of the war, Ho was very ill. He had suffered from a serious bout of malaria and was confined to bed for several weeks. Fearing an attempt on his life by those Viet Minh and nationalist elements who had condemned his eagerness to compromise with France in order to save his regime, the Hanoi authorities tightened security measures and kept the DRV President under virtual house arrest. In spite of his physical condition, the Viet Minh chief continued to work hard and try to postpone the inevitable collision with France, and to receive foreign visitors to explain his position. On December 16, consequently, the ailing President gave an interview to two American reporters, Foster Hailey of *The New York Times* and Robert Trumbull of *Newsweek*. The latter gives the following account of the meeting, which took place in the old revolutionary's bedroom:

Ho then approaching 60, was one of the few Asian leaders I have met who looked older than his years, which may have been the effect of his illness. He received us propped against two pillows in a large bed, with his wispy black beard hanging over his pajamas. He was living in the former residence of the French governors, which had been redesignated as the Presidential palace. Foster and I sat in chairs on one side of the bed; after French champagne was served to us, we asked questions for more than an hour. We were to be the last Western correspondents to see Ho in many years, during which false rumors emanated from French circles from time to time that he was dead.

The vicious eight-year struggle that was to be known as the Indo-China War was to begin three days later, but Ho gave us no hint of that.[33]

Having faced countless odds which he had generally overcome, Ho apparently still hoped that he could at least postpone the inevitable showdown.

On December 17, General Valluy paid a surprise visit to Haiphong where he met with Sainteny and General Morlière. As aggressive as ever, Valluy made it clear that if the "cowards" (Vietnamese) wanted a fight, they should have it. On the same day, a serious incident took place in Hanoi. A French truck was attacked by the Tu Ve (Viet Minh militia), and three French soldiers were killed. Enraged by this assault on French honor, the usually calm Sainteny, who had just returned from his meeting with the irascible Valluy, ordered the liquidation of a nearby Tu Ve post. The houses surrounding the garrison were also flattened. As a result, fifteen Vietnamese were killed. The following morning, about one hundred French paratroopers invaded the Vietnamese quarter to search for the body of one of their comrades who had allegedly been killed on December 12. The search was conducted with undue roughness. Men, women, and children were thrown out of their houses. Shouting was mixed with screaming. Suddenly, a grenade exploded. A French paratrooper was killed. Another was wounded. The "cowards" were at it again! Promptly, the French retaliated by massacring twenty Vietnamese. Claiming that shots had been fired from the Ministry of Finance, the French occupied that government building. As barricades went up in the city, Sainteny immediately requested that the Vietnamese government order the removal of these obstructions. Impatient with the Vietnamese slowness, the French Commissioner sent out bulldozers to clear the streets. General Morlière, on his side, demanded that the Hanoi authorities disarm, without delay, the Tu Ve and turn over all security duties to the French. Viewing Morlière's request as another ultimatum, Ho became convinced that the French were about to repeat the Haiphong experiment. Still confined to bed with high fever, Ho sent his Foreign Minister Hoang Minh Giam to see Sainteny, begging the French Commissioner to exert his influence to help ease tension. Sainteny's attitude, however, had already stiffened. French honor could not tolerate any more challenge.

Meanwhile, Morlière ordered his troops back to their barracks and put them on the alert. At 6 P.M., according to Devillers, the French received an intelligence report that the Tu Ve were going to launch an attack that evening. Morlière immediately dispatched his troops and tanks to occupy the strategic points.

At 8 P.M., a thunderous explosion shook the city. The power station had been blown up. Hanoi suddenly plunged into darkness. Firing started. The war which Ho had tirelessly tried to prevent began at last. Immediately, all French fingers pointed at Ho as the aggressor. The French conveniently brushed aside the argument that the Vietnamese, who had been pushed to the edge of an abyss, had to strike back. In any case, d'Argenlieu, Valluy, and company, finally got what they had so eagerly sought: a war to annihilate Ho Chi Minh and teach the Vietnamese a lesson about French might.

On whose shoulders should the responsibility for the eight-year Franco-Vietnamese war rest? On Hanoi, which allegedly fired the first shot on the night of December 19, 1946? Or on the Saigon authorities, who had systematically disregarded the March 6 Accord, established a puppet autonomous "Republic of Cochinchina," torpedoed the Fontainebleau Conference, ignored the September 14 *modus vivendi*, mercilessly bombarded Haiphong on November 23, 1946, then repeatedly issued ultimatums to Ho to surrender?

Violent condemnation of the Vietnamese "treacherous" attack of December 19, 1946, was promptly heard from all French circles. Stories of atrocities perpetrated upon French nationals were widely circulated, and the number of Frenchmen killed grossly exaggerated. These groundless accusations were to be refuted by many well-informed French observers. After careful investigation, Paul Mus, a leading French scholar on Vietnam, for instance, affirmed that only thirty-seven Europeans had fallen victim during the attack. "I am today in a position to state and prove," wrote Professor Mus in November, 1949, "that four-fifths of the stories or reports of awful atrocities inflicted by the Vietnamese on our compatriots in Hanoi, on December 19, 1946, are either made up or in error."[34] The cruelty of the Vietnamese "aggressors" on that fateful night of December, 1946, which caused so much indignation among the French, was, however, a mere shadow of what the French Expeditionary Corps had done in Haiphong on November 23, 1946, and were to do in Hanoi following their occupation of the capital on December 20. Thousands of Vietnamese civilians were indiscriminatly killed.

Having overrun Hanoi on December 20, the French captured Ho's residence in the afternoon. The malaria-stricken DRV president had been carried away to a remote hideout in the countryside. That evening, he issued the historic appeal to his compatriots, informing them that the resistance war had begun:

Compatriots all over the country!

As we desired peace, we made concessions. But the more we made concessions, the further the French colonialists went because they are resolved to invade our country once again.

No! We would rather sacrifice all than lose our country. We are determined not to be enslaved.

Compatriots! Rise up!

Men and women, old and young, regardless of creeds, political parties, or nationalities, all the Vietnamese must stand up to fight the French colonialists to save the Fatherland. Those who have rifles will use their rifles; those who have swords will use their swords; those who have no swords will use spades, hoes, or sticks. Everyone must endeavor to oppose the colonialists and save his country.

Armymen, self-defense guards, and militiamen!

The hour for national salvation has struck! We must sacrifice even our last drop of blood to safeguard our country.

Even if we have to endure hardship in the Resistance War, with the determination to make sacrifices, victory will surely be ours.

Long live an independent and unified Vietnam!

Long live the victorious Resistance![35]

As Ho's address to his people implied, only a minuscule number of Vietnamese possessed rifles. Very few owned swords. The majority, however, possessed spades, hoes, and sticks. The Vietnamese army was not much better equipped. And it was against these men that the powerful Expeditionary Corps fought.

On the following day, Ho again issued a message to the Vietnamese people, the French people, and the peoples of the Allied nations, in which he explained the position of the Vietnamese people who were "facing two alternatives: either to stay with hands bound and heads bowed as slaves again, or to struggle to the end to win back freedom and independence."

To the French people the Viet Minh chief said:

We have affection for you and sincerely want to cooperate with you within the framework of the French Union because we have a common ideal which is freedom, equality, and independence.

It is the reactionary French colonialists who have blemished France's honor and are seeking to divide us by provoking a war. As soon as France acknowledges our independence and unification and calls back home the bellicose French colonialists, friendly relations and cooperation between the peoples of Vietnam and France will be restored immediately.

Calling on the members of the Expeditionary Corps not to sacrifice their lives to promote the selfish interests of the colons, Ho continued:

There is no grudge or rancor between us. It is for the sake of their selfish interests that the reactionary colonialists provoked clashes. Profits will be theirs, death yours, and medals of victory will be conferred on the militarists. But for you and your families, there is only suffering and poverty. Think it over and think again. Can you be content with sacrificing your bones and blood and your lives for the reactionaries? In joining us you will be treated as friends.

Appealing to the people of the Allied countries to intervene on the Vietnamese behalf, the old revolutionary added:

After the recent World War, peace was restored by the democratic countries. However, the French reactionaries trampled underfoot the Atlantic and San Francisco Charters. They are waging an aggressive war in Vietnam. They must bear the responsibility. The Vietnamese people ask you to intervene.

Ho concluded his message by reminding his compatriots that

The Resistance War will be long and fraught with sufferings. Whatever sacrifices we have to make and however long the Resistance War will last, we are determined to fight to the end, until Vietnam is completely independent and unified. We are 20 million against 100,000 colonialists. Our victory is firmly guaranteed.[36]

Meanwhile, after establishing their mastery over Hanoi, the French came up with an ingenious scheme: to bring their forces to bear on Ho and crush him decisively in a single blow. To this end, the French command made meticulous preparations, assembling all available shock troops and war materiel. It was a combined operation involving all three branches of the service: army, navy, and air force, and planned in the minutest details by the most resourceful strategists of the French Expeditionary Corps. Airborne troops were to be parachuted over Bac Kan, a little jungle town near the Chinese frontier that served as Ho's headquarters. At the same time, two columns were to race forward and make contact with the paratroopers: one armed column was to proceed along Colonial Route 4, while the other waterborne was to go up the Clear River. The painstakingly-planned operation was launched amid great enthusiasm and optimism. D'Argenlieu, convinced that Ho's regime was nearing its end, sat back and waited. Everything had been proceeding smoothly when, unexpectedly, two "minor" flaws marred the otherwise perfect expedition: (a) the boats could not get up the Clear River and (b) the paratroopers entrusted with the mission of seizing Ho dead or alive descended on Bac Kan sixty minutes too late![37] The old fox had vanished into the thick jungle.

6 ☆ *President Ho Against France*

~~~~~~~~~~~~~~~~~~~~~~~~~~~~~~~~~~~~~~

THE OUTBREAK of the war had the immediate effect of rallying Vietnamese behind Ho Chi Minh. Many of those who had accused him of selling out to the French seemed now ready to accept his argument that the signing of the *modus vivendi* was only one of his desperate attempts to avert the conflict. And those who had opposed negotiations with the French suddenly found themselves on the same side with Ho. Thus, France's determination to impose a military solution in Indochina strengthened Ho's image as the champion of Vietnam's independence. France's refusal to recognize the Vietnamese national aspirations made it impossible for the nationalists to dissociate from the Communists in a struggle in which nationalist imperatives outweighed all others.

The Persistent Conciliator

When war broke out in Indochina, metropolitan France was undergoing quite an unsettling political phase. Léon Blum, a Socialist and long-standing critic of French colonial policies, was heading a caretaker government that was to last only four weeks. In a speech on December 23, 1946, three days following the French capture of Hanoi, Blum, declaring that the old colonial system founded on conquest and maintained by force was finished, emphasized that Vietnam must be accorded freedom and that lasting and friendly Franco-Vietnamese relations could derive only from negotiations, not from war. Unfortunately, Blum justified his government's policy of force on the grounds that it was the Viet Minh who had started the war and that France had to fight in self-defense. The French Premier, apparently, was badly misinformed and unaware of Ho's December 15 peace proposals, which had been withheld in Saigon.

Although the Communists and the Socialists were the only groups in France that consistently criticized d'Argenlieu's policy of confrontation, the latter, with almost equal consistency from 1945 to 1953, acted contrary to their expressed views by going along with the parties of the Right, which stubbornly insisted that there could be no negotiations before public order had been restored. In a speech in the Chamber of Deputies on March 18, 1946, Marius Moutet, the Socialist Minister of Overseas Affairs, went so far as to say: "What I reproach Admiral d'Argenlieu for is not that he did not follow the directives of the government. I reproach him for having anticipated them."[1] As the Minister of Overseas Affairs during this critical period and the official who signed the September 14, 1946, *modus vivendi* with Ho Chi Minh, Moutet, undoubtedly, was primarily responsible for France's policy in Indochina.

In any case, Premier Blum, shortly after the outbreak of the war, did make a serious attempt to reach a settlement with Ho. To this end, he dispatched Moutet and General Leclerc, the popular military leader who had played a vital role in the negotiations leading to the signing and acceptance of the March 6, 1946, Accord, on a fact-finding tour in Indochina. While refusing the command of all French forces in Indochina which Blum had offered him, Leclerc agreed to serve on the Moutet mission. Leclerc's appointment was made against the wish of Admiral d'Argenlieu, who had strongly condemned the general's "defeatist" tendencies. Moutet and Leclerc arrived in Saigon on December 26 and 28, respectively. In a serious attempt to establish contact with the French officials, the Viet Minh radio announced, on the very day of Moutet's arrival, that Ho had set up his headquarters in Ha Dong, approximately six miles from Hanoi, and wished to have a meeting with the French Minister. Upon his arrival, Leclerc immediately flew to Hanoi to inspect both the military and political situations. Moutet, on the contrary, displaying a lack of concern for the pressing Vietnamese problem, indulged in leisurely visits and receptions in Cambodia and Laos. Upon landing in Pnom Penh on December 29, the Minister casually remarked that if Ho had any proposals to make, they would be given careful consideration. On the same day, the Viet Minh radio announced that the DRV President had sent a message to Premier Blum in which he expressed satisfaction with the French decision to dispatch a fact-finding mission, requested the return of French troops to the positions they had occupied prior to December 17, 1946, and proposed a cease-fire. On New Year's Day, 1947, the same radio broadcast a warm message from the DRV President to the French government and people and to the Minister of Overseas Affairs, and renewed the proposal for a Moutet-Ho meeting.

These repeated Viet Minh requests, however, fell on deaf ears. The Socialist Minister had no intention of seeing the old revolutionary in spite of his statements to the contrary. Although before departing from Saigon for Hanoi Moutet had stressed that the purpose of his mission was to seek a peaceful settlement of the Indochina problem and to work toward the observance of the September 14, 1946, *modus vivendi*, he did little to acquaint himself with the situation during his thirty-hour stay in the Tonkinese capital. Not only did he ignore Ho's appeals for a meeting, he also took care that no members of his entourage come into contact with Viet Minh representatives. Encouraged by the Minister's indifference to Ho's overtures, the High Commissariat decided to withhold two very important letters which the DRV government had addressed to him. In these messages dated December 29 and 31, the Viet Minh leader proposed an immediate cease-fire and release of prisoners, a Moutet-Ho meeting to discuss, on the basis of the March 6, 1946, Accord, a detailed outline for a definite treaty to be drafted in Paris.[2]

While in Tonkin, Moutet called on Sainteny, who was recuperating from a wound suffered during the December 19 fighting and whose patience with the Viet Minh had run low since their assault on France's grandeur, and also inspected French military posts and hospitals. During one his tours around the city, the French Minister was fired on. This unfortunate incident markedly upset Moutet, whose sympathy for Ho rapidly reached the vanishing point. "Before any negotiations today," declared a bellicose Moutet upon leaving Hanoi, "it is necessary to have a military decision. I am sorry, but one cannot commit such acts of madness as the Vietnamese have done with impunity."[3] In view of his preconceived ideas and of the briefing he had received from those French officials, whose strong prejudices against the Ho regime was a matter of record, Moutet went away absolutely convinced that the war had been premeditated by the Vietnamese.

Thus the Moutet mission, instead of helping bring about a cease-fire, lent support to d'Argenlieu's policy of force. In spite of all evidence to the contrary, the Minister of Overseas Affairs conveniently put all the blame for the outbreak of the war on his good old friend Ho Chi Minh, and reported to the French government that the Viet Minh chief had made no effort to establish contact with him during his stay in Hanoi. What about the Viet Minh broadcast appeals? "Such appeals cannot be taken seriously," Moutet explained. "They were obviously acts of propaganda. . . . In view of the fanciful nature of all the declarations broadcast by Vietnamese stations, one cannot attach too much attention to them. . . . I am certain that those who hold real power in the Vietnamese government do not want an accord."[4] The Minister's view, however, was not shared by Léon Boutbien, a member of the Executive Committee of the French Socialist party, who had accompanied Moutet during the latter's visit to Hanoi. Offering a completely different interpretation of the conflict, Boutbien affirmed that the Viet Minh government had contacted the Moutet mission and that he, himself, had met with some of Ho's representatives.[5]

Why did Moutet, whose mission was to appraise the Indochinese situation and seek a way out of the impasse, take such an uncompromising stand? According to Max André, the head of the French delegations at both the Dalat and Fontainebleau Conferences, Premier Blum first had sent Moutet to Indochina to negotiate a settlement; later, succumbing to the mounting pressure of the pro-colonial MRP (Mouvement Républicain Populaire), Blum directed the Minister to avoid negotiations with Ho.[6] Such irresolution, unfortunately, was to be the attitude of the French government throughout the war. Even the Socialists, who had advocated a peaceful settlement, were won over to the military solution. On January 21, 1947, the Socialist Paul Ramadier succeeded his fellow Socialist Léon Blum as Premier of France. Hoping to salvage the situation, Paris once again offered Leclerc the post of High Commissioner with extensive military and civil powers. Though not interested in the offer, the popular general nevertheless set forth his conditions for acceptance: an army of 500,000 men, full military and civil powers, negotiation with Ho Chi Minh, and independence for Vietnam within the French Union. "In 1947," warned Leclerc, "France will no longer put down by force a grouping of 24 million inhabitants which is assuming unity and in which there exists a xenophobic and perhaps national ideal." Stressing the need for a settlement with all Vietnamese factions, including the Viet Minh, the general added: *"The capital problem from now on is political.* It is a question of coming to terms with an awakening xenophobic nationalism, of channelling it in order to safeguard, at least in part, the rights of France."[7]

Even if his conditions had been granted, Leclerc would not have accepted the offer for he knew that Paris had already decided the course of action to be followed in Indochina and that the High Commissioner, whoever he might be, would not be able to change it. Leclerc's refusal to be an instrument of French colonial policies was motivated primarily by his keen understanding of the Indochinese situation and his opposition to Paris' futile attempt to impose a solution of force. De Gaulle's warning did not seem to play a significant part in the general's decision. "They want to use you," the future President of the Fifth Republic had told his former comrade-in-arms. "You don't know politics. . . . They will make you take the responsibility for abandoning Indochina. . . . They will make you an instrument of capitulation."[8] De Gaulle, who had emphatically stated at the Brazzaville Conference in January, 1944, that "the aims of the work of civilization which France is accomplishing in her possessions exclude any idea of autonomy and any possibility of development outside the French Empire bloc. The attainment of 'self-government' in the colonies, even in the most distant future, must be excluded," had actually opposed Premier Ramadier's offer to Leclerc, whose liberal views greatly alarmed him.

Although disturbed by Leclerc's frank and accurate appraisal of the situation, French politicians continued to quarrel over the war issue. With the exception of the Communists, who halfheartedly advocated negotiations with the Viet Minh government, the parties of the Right and the Center steadfastly opposed further talks with Ho Chi Minh or recognition of Vietnam's right to independence, insisting that it was the Viet Minh "aggressors" who had rejected a peaceful settlement. In addition to this ill-conceived approach, the despairingly unstable situation in Paris helped prolong the war. From 1945 to 1954, there were fifteen governments that handled the complicated Indochina problem on a day-to-day basis without firm guidance or a continuous policy. One after another, the fifteen French cabinets wandered aimlessly without being able to define either the cause or the purpose of the costly war. As the influential paper *Le Monde* aptly stated, Paris seemed to follow a plan designed to eliminate all possibilities of negotiation and to prolong indefinitely the conflict which was the principal source of revenues for certain political groups.[9]

After only a few months of fighting in Indochina, French policymakers began to realize that the quick victory they had hoped for was sheer chimera. The debate then centered upon the question of whether the war should be fought to the finish or be settled through negotiations. With the exception of the Communists, all parties opposed talks with the Viet Minh regime on the grounds that it was dominated largely by Communist extremists and, consequently, not entitled to speak for the Vietnamese people. With which government, then, should France negotiate? Logically, it should be one that would, as General Leclerc had suggested, represent all factions of the Vietnamese people. Since no such government existed, the French reasoned, it had to be created. In the French view, however, a government entitled to speak for the Vietnamese people had to be one that would include only the anti-Viet Minh groups. It would compete with the Ho regime for popular support and foreign recognition. To this government France would make a few minor concessions such as recognition of Vietnam's "independence" within the French Union. Once this step had been taken, Ho would be deprived of the only legitimate pretext under which he was fighting, and the Viet Minh appeal would lose all its force among the Vietnamese masses. Should Ho choose to challenge the French-backed government by continuing the armed struggle, the colonial war, which had been ignited by the French, would be transformed into a civil war, a contest between nationalist and Communist forces and, consequently, a part of the global East-West conflict. An ingenious scheme! In view of the deteriorating international situation as evidenced by the impasse at the Moscow Conference held in March, Paris was quite confident that Washington would support its effort to check the Communist expansion in Asia. On March 12, President Truman had in fact appeared before the Congress to ask for $400,000,000 in military and economic aid for Greece and Turkey,[10] stressing that "it must be the policy of the United States to support free peoples who are resisting attempted subjugation by armed minorities or by outside pressures."

Meanwhile, in Indochina, with Ho back in the jungle, d'Argenlieu, still convinced that events had turned in his favor, advocated the return of the traditional institutions, that is, a docile monarchy under French guidance and protection. Early in 1947, the High Commissioner sent an emissary to discuss the French plan with Bao Dai, who had taken refuge in Hong Kong since March, 1946. The ex-Emperor, however, aware of the nationalist fervor of his people and of the strength of the Viet Minh, refused to be a tool in the French scheme. At about the same time, anti-Viet Minh forces, once again, attempted to form a coalition that would seek to achieve independence through other means. On February 17, they announced the formation in Nanking of a "Vietnam National Union Front." The new organization immediately established contact with other groups inside Vietnam such as the Cao Dai of Pham Cong Tac, the Hoa Hao of Huynh Phu So,[11] and the Social Democratic Party of Nguyen Van Sam, proposing a congress to be held in Canton in the following month. At the close of their weeklong meeting, from March 15 to 22, the delegates adopted a resolution placing the National Union Front under Bao Dai's leadership, stressing that the Vietnamese resistance was the collective effort of many parties and organizations, not of the Viet Minh alone which represented only the Vietnamese Communists, and expressing their willingness to cooperate with France on the basis of national independence and equality. While the Front lent weight to d'Argenlieu's thesis that Bao Dai was the only person capable of rallying the anti-Communist forces of nationalism and least susceptible of endangering French interest, it was marked by personal rivalries and the absence of a well-defined program.

As the Vietnamese nationalists needlessly wasted their energy,

Paris began to give serious consideration to the "Bao Dai solution." In order to win the cooperation of the Vietnamese nationalists and to convey the impression that it was embarking upon a new, constructive policy, Paris, on March 5, 1947, recalled the "imperious" d'Argenlieu who had so effectively discredited the French government in the eyes of most Vietnamese. The removal of the disastrous admiral and the appointment of the civilian Emile Bollaert as High Commissioner did indeed arouse false hopes among Vietnamese, both in the jungle and in the cities. Ho apparently believed that Franco-Viet Minh negotiations would soon be resumed. Premier Ramadier's declaration of March 18 further strengthened the DRV President's hope. Addressing the National Assembly, the French leader said:

The Indochina problem shall not be settled by force. Neither shall be any other problem of Overseas France. There will be nothing but political solutions. . . . There will be no domination, no subjection, but association. . . . This means that we respect the independence of people. . . . That was the reason why, on January 21, I pronounced before you the words "Independence within the French Union." It means the right of the Vietnamese people to administer and conduct their affairs, to choose their government, and to determine the framework within which they want to live. I also said: unity of the three Vietnamese countries if the Vietnamese people so desire, and . . . in the manner they desire.[12]

On the same day, Ho made preliminary preparations for a Franco-Vietnamese parley by relinquishing the Foreign Affairs portfolio in favor of Vice-Minister Hoang Minh Giam. In addition to being a Socialist who enjoyed good rapport with his fellow Socialists in Premier Ramadier's party, Giam had been one of the architects of the March 6, 1946, Accord. Then, on March 21, Ho issued the following statement:

If the French government made an official and frank declaration recognizing Vietnam's unity and independence and gave adequate guarantees to this effect, all other questions would be easily settled. . . . Once again, we solemnly declare that the Vietnamese people desire only unity and independence within the French Union and pledge to respect France's economic and cultural interests in Vietnam.

A mere word from France will suffice to immediately bring an end to the present hostilities, to save so many lives and so much property, to resume friendship and restore confidence. If, in spite of our sincere desire for peace, France decides to continue the war, she will lose everything and gain nothing for war will only breed hatred and rancor between our two peoples. We beg the French government to let us know its policy toward Vietnam. We beg the French people to let us know their feeling in regard to this bloody and stupid conflict.[13]

Simultaneously, Tran Ngoc Danh, Ho's representative in Paris, offered to contact his government with a view to reopening negotiations. In spite of this urgent plea, the French Socialist Party of Premier Ramadier and Minister Moutet, on the same day, passed a resolution calling for negotiations with "qualified representatives of Vietnam," and thus ruling out direct talks with the Ho regime. Thus, the French Prime Minister's pronouncement of March 18 was nothing but a distasteful hoax.

On April 1, the new High Commissioner arrived in Saigon to begin the "constructive phase" of French policy toward Vietnam. Upon his arrival, Bollaert immediately lifted both the censorship in Saigon and the state of siege in Hanoi and Haiphong, removed Léon Pignon and Albert Torel, two of d'Argenlieu's most trusted associates, and appointed as his Political Adviser Professor Paul Mus, a renowned Vietnam specialist, who had entertained considerable sympathy for the Vietnamese aspirations. These conciliatory gestures, unfortunately, were soon negated by the High Commissioner's own declarations, which specified that France could not negotiate with the Viet Minh regime since it was controlled by the Communists, who constituted only a minor segment of the nationalist movement. Paris, however, emphasized that Bollaert was willing and ready to make concessions to a government representing all Vietnamese political factions.

From his jungle hideout, the old guerilla leader followed the new High Commissioner with great interest. Not deterred by the French declarations, Ho, on April 25, sent Bollaert a message in which he reaffirmed Vietnam's friendship for the French people and government, and proposed an immediate cease-fire and a resumption of talks with a view to reaching a peaceful settlement of the conflict. The French government was thus caught in its own net for, on April 3, it had expressed its willingness to examine any armistice proposal from the Viet Minh. Though not spelled out in specific details, Ho's letter was in essence a peace proposal. This episode, important as it might appear, was only one in a series of lost opportunities. Had France wished, she could have ended the war then. Paris, however, wanted a cease-fire, not a settlement with the Viet Minh. In any case, the French Command in Indochina had already set forth its minimum conditions for an armistice: the Viet Minh were to free all prisoners, cease all acts of hostility, terrorism, and propaganda, surrender half of their weapons to the French, and give French troops complete freedom of movement behind the Viet Minh lines.[14]

Meanwhile, Paris was in the midst of a political crisis. On May 4, the Communist Ministers left the Ramadier government. With their departure, the hardliners were in complete control of the cabinet, all opposed to renewed negotiations with the Ho regime. In Saigon, however, Bollaert, advised by Paul Mus, favored a resumption of talks with the Viet Minh. The High Commissioner thus found himself in a distressing dilemma. Should he carry out his government's policy, which he knew would lead to disaster, or should he attempt to negotiate a settlement with Ho Chi Minh that would undoubtedly be rejected by Paris? General de Gaulle, who was in the process of building the RPF (Ralliement du Peuple Français) as the spokesman for French nationalism, had already issued a stern warning that anyone responsible for the loss of any French overseas possessions should be prepared to suffer the consequences. Under these circumstances, Bollaert sent the reluctant Paul Mus to meet Ho Chi Minh to inform him of the French position. Early in May, Mus left for Tonkin to establish contact with the Viet Minh leader. On May 9, he had a rendezvous with Hoang Minh Giam, the DRV Foreign Minister, at the Bridge of Rapids approximately forty miles from Hanoi. Since his mission was to communicate to Ho the French conditions for a cease-fire, Mus asked Giam whether he could meet with the Viet Minh leader. The request was granted.

After covering roughly forty miles in Viet Minh territory, the French emissary arrived in Thai Nguyen on May 12. Full of hope, the old guerilla left his secret hideout to meet his visitor. Ho and Mus were no strangers to each other. They had met in 1946 and, through an exchange of ideas, had come to admire each other. As the two exchanged civilities, one could not fail to contrast Ho's cheerful appearance with Mus' grave look. Hesitantly, the French emissary delivered the message. As the French conditions were spelled out, Ho's smile vanished and his face quickly froze. The Viet

Minh leader was asked to (a) hand over to the French all of his troops' weapons, (b) confine his disarmed forces within the areas to be defined by the French Command, (c) recognize the right of French troops to move freely throughout Vietnam, (d) return all hostages, both French and Vietnamese, and (e) surrender all foreigners who had served in the Viet Minh ranks.[15] The French Command, aware that the foreign technicians—Japanese, German, and other deserters from the Foreign Legion—were the only men capable of instructing Viet Minh troops in the use of Japanese, French, and American weapons,[16] had specifically advised Mus that the last point in the proposal was not negotiable under any circumstances. This also was the very point on which Ho could not give in. To turn over the foreign technicians would not only deprive the Viet Minh of desperately needed military instructors, but would also amount to betraying those who had sought asylum, cast their lot, and cooperated with the Ho regime. If the other conditions were unacceptable, the demand for the surrender of the foreign personnel in the Viet Minh Army was outrageous. "The failure of this negotiation [the Mus mission]," Paul Coste-Floret, Minister of War, was to complain on March 11, 1949, "resulted from the clause on the surrender of foreigners in the ranks of the Viet Minh."[17] There was no negotiation, however, as Mus was to explain later. His mission was to communicate, not to discuss, the conditions for a cease-fire which Ho had proposed on April 25.[18]

After hearing the French proposal, which was in effect an ultimatum for an unconditional Viet Minh surrender, the disturbed guerilla leader stared at his embarrassed visitor. Slowly, he asked the French emissary whether he would, were he in Ho's place, accept those terms. Mus admitted that he would not. "In the French Union," continued Ho in a grave voice, "there is no place for cowards. If I accepted those conditions, I would be one."[19] Aware of the Viet Minh situation and sensing that the war was going to last for a long time, Mus hesitantly asked his host: "Do you think that in spite of this war, there will be a common future for us?" "Yes, in spite of that," replied the imperturbable guerilla, "we need help, and we are used to you."[20] Thereupon, Ho shook hands with Mus. Then, slowly, the old fox disappeared in the thick jungle, forgetting to open the champagne bottles he had brought along for celebration. He had thought that a cease-fire agreement was forthcoming!

Following this disappointing encounter with Paul Mus, Ho sen ʋ message to his people in which he, once again, reported that tne French had rejected his effort to stop the war through negotiatiõn:

For the sake of humanity and peace, for the maintenance of the sympathy with France, our Government has proposed to the French Government to find ways and means to stop war by negotiations on the basis of our people's aspirations for unity and independence.

But the French colonialist militarists are used to atrocity, inhumanity, and impoliteness. They hold our Army and people in contempt. They put forth arrogant and unacceptable conditions.

They asked us (1) to surrender them all our weapons, (2) to give the French Army freedom to move everywhere in our country, etc.

This means that they want us to surrender.

To persuade the Vietnamese to continue their effort to liberate the fatherland, Ho shrewdly aroused them against the French abuses:

They want to strangle our fatherland. They want us to give them a free hand to burn down villages, plunder our property, massacre our people, rape our women, and destroy temples, pagodas, and churches. This means that they want all our compatriots and our offspring to kneel down and bow our heads and be their everlasting slaves.[21]

In view of the unacceptable conditions he proposed to the Viet Minh, and his generally uncompromising position, Bollaert apparently did not contemplate negotiations with Ho Chi Minh. Why, then, did he send Paul Mus to meet with the Viet Minh leader? The Mus mission might be interpreted as a shrewd maneuver on the High Commissioner's part. By establishing contact with Ho and presenting him with an ultimatum, Bollaert attempted to allay the fears of both the French Left and Right. The former would be satisfied that Saigon had got in touch with Ho while the latter would be content that no serious negotiations with the Viet Minh had been planned. Such contact would also warn Bao Dai that if he refused to cooperate with the French, they might deal with the Viet Minh. Finally, through a Ho-Mus meeting, Saigon wanted to check the rumors that had been circulated, namely, that the old revolutionary had lost control of his government and had been replaced by younger extremists. In any case, the Mus mission did accomplish one thing. It convinced the French that Ho, as always, was still in complete command of the situation and quite capable of making instant decisions without having to consult with the Viet Minh Tong Bo.[22]

Three days following the Ho-Mus meeting, Bollaert proceeded to give the Vietnamese a glimpse of France's "new" policy:

France will remain in Indochina and Indochina will remain within the French Union. That is the first axiom of our policy. It would be detrimental to the interest of peace to think otherwise. The maintenance of the French presence in Indochina is a fact from now onward, and it would be a mistake not to take this into consideration. . . . It is up to the people of this country to obtain peace. Let the representatives of all parties come to us. I say all parties because we do not admit that any group has a monopoly on representing the Vietnamese people.[23]

Bollaert's pronouncement profoundly disturbed the Vietnamese people, who had expected a real departure from the antiquated d'Argenlieu line, and who were suddenly reminded of the popular French adage *plus ça change, plus c'est la même chose* (the more it changes, the more it is the same thing)! Thus Paris' policy remained unchanged. Determined to maintain their presence in Indochina, the French tried every alternative short of granting independence. Resorting to the traditional method of "divide and rule," they proceeded to split the independence movement into nationalist and Communist factions and appealed to the anti-Communism of the non-Viet Minh elements. They tried to create an alternative government to the Ho regime. Bollaert's initial contacts with anti-Communist leaders were discouraging. One after another, the Vietnamese unequivocally informed the High Commissioner that they, too, were after what France had refused to grant to Ho Chi Minh, namely, Vietnam's unity and independence. Among the political figures approached by the French official were Ngo Dinh Diem, the well-known patriot, who had resigned from the Bao Dai government in 1933 in protest against oppressive colonial rule, and Nguyen Manh Ha, the competent Minister of National Economy in the first Ho Chi Minh cabinet. Bollaert's attempt to bring nationalists of solid reputation into a government headed by Bao Dai, who still enjoyed considerable prestige among the tradition-bound masses, was met with failure.

Meanwhile Paul Mus, following his mission to Ho, was sent to Hong Kong to make overture to Bao Dai. As citizen Vinh Thuy,[24] the ex-Emperor nominally was still a member of the DRV government. Ho had, in fact, sent Ho Dac Lien, a prominent nationalist, to Hong Kong to propose in the name of national interest that Bao Dai negotiate with the French on the Viet Minh behalf. Aware of Ho's ruthless and calculating mind, the ex-Emperor rejected his proposal. Mus' mission to Hong Kong did not fare any better. Cautioned by his entourage that the French might use him as a threat to force Ho into a compromise, and convinced that his people, whose passion for *doc lap* (independence) had reached the boiling point, would disavow any government that collaborated with the French at their expense, the much-abused Bao Dai refused to be a pawn in a French intrigue again. The thought of reigning over his country under French auspices did not appeal to him. As he had told d'Argenlieu's emissaries in January, the former Emperor informed Mus that unless the French were ready to satisfy the Vietnamese fundamental aspirations by making those concessions they had refused to Ho, he would not be able to rally enough support for whatever government he might lead. As a price for his cooperation, Bao Dai unequivocally asked the French to dissolve the separatist Cochinchinese government and to recognize Vietnam's unity and independence. Unless this demand was satisfied, Bao Dai emphasized, no nationalist leader could compete with Ho Chi Minh. Both of Mus' missions thus ended in failure. He had not been able to scare the old revolutionary into surrender; neither could he talk the ex-monarch into cooperation with France.

Since the French plan hinged on Bao Dai, Bollaert decided to try personal diplomacy upon the former Emperor. Early in June, he himself journeyed to the British Crown colony. In an attempt to allay Bao Dai's suspicion of a Franco-Viet Minh deal, which had been aroused by the Ho-Mus meeting, the High Commissioner assured him that no Franco-Viet Minh negotiations had been or would be contemplated, and gently cautioned his interlocutor against any move that would associate him with the Viet Minh. In view of the grave situation in Vietnam and of the rising red tide everywhere, Bollaert argued, Bao Dai should return to head a nationalist government and prevent the Communists from misleading the masses. In spite of the French official's eloquence, the ex-Emperor still insisted that he could not return without a formal guarantee of Vietnam's unity and independence, refused to take a stand against the Viet Minh or to become involved in political quarrels, and continued to refer to the Ho regime as the resistance government, stressing that not all Vietnamese in the *maquis* (anti-French guerilla movement) were Communists.

In a subsequent interview given to a Saigon newspaper, on July 5, Bao Dai, for the first time since his abdication, publicly stated his position, implying that he was ready to serve as mediator between the French government and the Vietnamese political parties to bring about a peaceful settlement of the conflict:

> If the Vietnamese place their trust in me, if my presence can help restore friendly relations between our people and the French, I shall be happy to return to Indochina.
> I am neither for the Viet Minh nor against them. I belong to no party. Peace will rapidly return when the French realize that the spirit of our people is no longer the same today as it was ten years ago.[25]

Bao Dai's statement was heard with considerable relief in the Viet Bac jungle.[26] Upon being informed of the ex-Emperor's unexpectedly firm attitude toward the French and favorably neutral toward his regime,[27] the old guerilla again toyed with the thought that Bao Dai could be persuaded to join forces with him. Ho's most serious problem then appeared to be his inability to remove the Communist label from his government in spite of the many concessions he had made to his nationalist competitors. It was indeed wishful thinking on the old revolutionary's part to believe that, despite his usual record as a ruthless agent of international Communism, he could still inspire trust among the non-Marxist leaders of his country. In any case, old Ho continued to try and hope.

Apprehensive that the masses would rally behind the pro-Bao Dai groups, which then seemed to be more successful in obtaining concessions from France, the old fox reshuffled his cabinet on July 19. With a view to making it more appealing to non-Viet Minh elements and more acceptable to the French, Ho allowed greater nationalist representation in the new government. Furthermore, he quietly removed from his cabinet two of his closest associates, Vo Nguyen Giap and Pham Van Dong, who were *personae non gratae* to the French and, consequently, obstacles to any Franco-Viet Minh rapprochement. While Giap, the articulate negotiator at the Dalat Conference, was considered by the French as the instigator of the

Hanoi incident of December 19, 1946, Dong, the inflexible head of the Vietnamese delegation at Fontainebleau, was viewed as the symbol of Viet Minh intransigence. The affable Hoang Minh Giam, one of the principal negotiators of the March 6, 1946, Accord, retained the Ministry of Foreign Affairs, while the "nonpartisan" Ta Quang Buu headed the Ministry of National Defense. In the Ministry of Interior, the extremist Ton Duc Thang, the future DRV President,[28] was replaced by the conciliatory Phan Ke Toai, the former Imperial Delegate for Tonkin who had handed power to the Viet Minh, on August 17, 1945, in Hanoi. The new twenty-seven-member cabinet included three (instead of six) Communists, four Democrats, four Socialists, two Nationalists, three Catholics, one Buddhist, eight "independents," and two former mandarins. Bao Dai, again, was appointed Supreme Counsellor. Since the key positions were held by Communists, Socialists, and Democrats, who were all Viet Minh, this cabinet change was merely a tactical move and, thus, did not inconvenience Ho in any way. As he had outmaneuvered his competitors in the past, the shrewd guerilla had no doubt whatsoever about his ability to outfox them again. With a team composed of men who apparently held moderate views, Ho hoped to attract more nationalists to his cause and induce the French to negotiate with his regime.

Meanwhile, the Viet Minh cease-fire proposal of April 25 became known to the French public. Paris and Saigon unhesitatingly blamed Ho for rejecting their "reasonable" conditions. In the face of this unscrupulous distortion of the truth, the Viet Minh radio began to broadcast the French terms for a cease-fire. In July, the DRV mission in Paris also released the content of Ho's April message to the French government, which stressed that "in order to prove Vietnam's sincere desire for peace and friendship for the French people, the Vietnamese Government proposes to the French Government an immediate cessation of hostilities and resumption of negotiations with a view to reaching a peaceful settlement of the conflict." The Socialists wanted a cease-fire as soon as possible, while the other parties wanted to make it conditional on certain Viet Minh concessions. Although all agreed that negotiations should follow a truce, they disagreed on the question of which party France should negotiate with. Naturally, France would not negotiate with the Ho Chi Minh government.

Attempts were then made to find an acceptable opponent for France. Of the anti-Viet Minh groups, only one was organized that might be able to compete with the Ho regime, the United National Front. The leaders of the Front, such as Nguyen Tuong Tam (VNQDD) and Nguyen Van Sam (Social Democratic Party), however, were intransigent nationalists who had refused to collaborate with the French and who could count on the support of other prominent anti-French leaders. Certainly, they would not settle for less than what Ho had aksed from the French. And France could not expect them to join forces with her against the Viet Minh without granting them the concessions she had withheld from the DRV leader. Thus France eliminated the Ho regime and the United National Front as acceptable representatives of the Vietnamese. The only remaining party that might be able to rally nationalist support and which would not work against French interest was Bao Dai. In view of the ex-Emperor's past docility and of his present shortage of funds in Hong Kong, where he found escape in a life of pleasure, the French were confident that they could again use him as a tool to carry out their scheme. Should Bao Dai insist on independence for his country, the French reasoned, France could easily satisfy his demand with a "solemn" declaration making Vietnam an "independent" state within the French Union. Bao Dai's unexpectedly firm stand, however, greatly astonished the French, who had thought of him only as a playboy.

Franco-Vietnamese relations had thus reached an impasse: Paris refused to negotiate with the Viet Minh regime, Ho was not ready to surrender, and the nationalists, including Bao Dai, would not cooperate with France without a firm guarantee of Vietnam's unity and independence. The prospect of a peaceful settlement of the conflict was dimmer than ever. Determined to break the deadlock, Bollaert, following his encounter with Bao Dai, left for Paris. In order to maintain and protect French interests in Indochina, explained the High Commissioner to his government, France had no choice but to negotiate with both the Viet Minh and the pro-Bao Dai groups and even to go so far as to grant Vietnam a semblance of independence within the French Union. The threat of France negotiating with both Ho Chi Minh and Bao Dai would force the two Vietnamese leaders to abandon their rigid stand and seek a compromise with France, Bollaert stressed. Though divided on the issue of negotiation, the vacillating French government agreed to let Bollaert test his new strategy. With such support, the confident High Commissioner went back to Saigon on July 21. At his press conference, on the day following his arrival, Bollaert caught everyone off guard, the Viet Minh, the pro-Bao Dai organizations as well as the French colons. In a startling announcement, he said that the senseless war must stop before serious negotiations could take place. "We intend that there will be neither victors nor vanquished at the conclusion of this conflict," stressed the High Commissioner. "It is with all parties and groups in a vast upsurge of patriotism that we shall work out a lasting peace. Colonialism is dead, and France is the first to renounce it."[29]

In reply to Bollaert's unexpected pronouncements, the Viet Minh radio emphasized that if such was the French position, a peaceful settlement of the conflict could easily be reached. A few days following the High Commissioner's declaration, the Viet Minh leader, too, held a press conference. Expressing satisfaction with the French position, Ho said:

The High Commissioner is a clear-sighted politician. He certainly is aware that there is only one way to achieve friendly relations between France and Vietnam: it is to recognize Vietnam's real independence and unity within the French Union. That was the reason why Mr. Bollaert declared that colonialism was dead. I wholeheartedly agree with the High Commissioner that a cessation of hostilities is a necessary condition for the opening of peaceful negotiations. Thus, the Government of Vietnam has, since April 25, proposed a cessation of hostilities. Following this proposal, Professor P. Mus, representing the High Commissioner, came to see us. . . . He told us that the French Government would give us an official answer. Up to this date, no such reply has reached us.

Taking up Bollaert on another point, Ho continued:

The High Commissioner said that there would be neither victors nor vanquished at the end of the conflict. I share his view on this.

In reference to the last part of Bollaert's statement, Ho, who had just brought many non-Viet Minh members into his government, challenged the French official to keep his words:

The High Commissioner added that he wanted to lay the foundations for a lasting peace with all parties, and that the Government of Vietnam was composed not only of representatives of all parties but also of patriots belonging to no party. If the High Commissioner wishes to establish contact with all political parties worthy of the name, he certainly would not have to go elsewhere to look for them.[30]

When questioned about Bao Dai, Ho gave a shrewd answer, which was, in effect, an appeal to the ex-Emperor to join forces with the resistance government:

Many members of the Government, including myself, all friends of Counsellor Vinh Thuy, are anxious to see him again and hope that he will soon return to join us in the management of the affairs of state. Counsellor Vinh Thuy, however, cannot leave Hongkong at this time. We are separated from him in space, but not in thought. The Government and the people of Vietnam have full confidence in the loyalty of Counsellor Vinh Thuy who, while abroad, continues to work for the national Government of which he has never ceased to be a part.[31]

Ho's latest tactical move—his decision to include many non-Viet Minh members in the resistance government, his conciliatory reply to Bollaert's declaration, and his praise of Bao Dai—created a favorable impression on many Vietnamese, who began to give serious consideration to a "Ho Chi Minh-Bao Dai Solution," to end the war. The Viet Minh maneuver, however, worried the French Command and the colons, who had already opposed Bollaert's plan.

The DRV President, on his side, eagerly explored the possibility of a cease-fire and negotiations. In August, he ordered Tran Van Giau, head of the Viet Minh delegation for Southeast Asia, to establish contact with the French Minister in Bangkok, Thailand. Informing the French representative of Ho's sincere desire for peace, Giau, on behalf of the Viet Minh chief, proposed a resumption of Franco-Vietnamese negotiations on the basis of Vietnam's unity and independence within the French Union, close Franco-Vietnamese collaboration on cultural and economic matters, close association in foreign affairs and diplomatic representation, and the presence of French bases in specific areas for the defense of the French Union.[32] Ho's terms were immediately forwarded to Paris, which, as usual, disregarded them.

In the meantime, in Saigon, Bollaert proceeded with the first phase of his plan, which called for a cessation of hostilities. Specific instructions about the cease-fire were transmitted in sealed envelopes not to be opened until noon, August 15, to all French commanders in the field. It was not by sheer coincidence that this date was chosen. August 15 happened to be the day on which Great Britain was to officially recognize India's and Pakistan's independence. As if Paris acted in unison with London, Bollaert was scheduled to announce on that day France's decision to cease all military actions in Indochina and to grant Vietnam independence within the French Union. This independence, however, would not confer upon Vietnam the right to have its own army or diplomacy. In spite of this severe limitation, Bollaert's plan aroused strong opposition among the French colonial society and the High Command, notably, General Valluy, the ever-confident Commander-in-Chief of the Expeditionary Corps in Indochina, who seemed to be always ready to "wipe out" (but, alas, never did!) the Viet Minh forces, and whose characteristic move was to issue ultimatums to Ho's armies to surrender. Furious, Valluy hurriedly left for Paris to plead with his government to postpone the execution of Bollaert's plan. With understandable ease, the general convinced the French cabinet that the projected cease-fire was ill-timed since the offensive he had been preparing for the dry season would, once for all, crush the Viet Minh forces. Premier Ramadier immediately summoned Bollaert to Paris to inform him that the French government, at that juncture, definitely opposed a truce that would strengthen Ho Chi Minh's, not Bao Dai's, hands. Under no circumstances, stressed Ramadier, should the word "independence" be used. Thus Bollaert's plan, if not shelved, was postponed and so drastically revised that it became meaningless. The projected cease-fire was called off. Lost was another opportunity to end the unfortunate war!

Ho and the "Bao Dai Solution"

Following his frustrated attempt to break the impasse in Indochina, Bollaert announced that he was going to deliver a very important speech on September 10 in Ha Dong.

Meanwhile, on August 19, Nguyen Van Sam, on behalf of the United National Front, made a formal request to Bao Dai urging the ex-Emperor to form a provisional government with the qualified representatives of all political parties with a view to guiding the people in their struggle for independence and unity. From Saigon the Front cabled, three days later, a similar request to the former monarch. Thereupon, Bao Dai sent his spokesman Tran Van Tuyen to Saigon to explore the situation. In an interview given to the press on August 25, Tuyen announced that Bao Dai's position had not changed: He would not return to head a government unless the people requested it, and until France agreed to recognize Vietnam's unity and independence. "His Majesty Bao Dai no longer considers himself the Supreme Counsellor to the Ho Chi Minh government," said Tuyen. "He is not opposed to any understanding with Ho Chi Minh in regard to negotiations with France, on condition that this understanding shall be made on the basis of equality and that the Viet Minh shall not consider itself superior to the other parties."[33] On August 30, in order to emphasize that the Viet Minh was merely a faction in the resistance movement and, consequently, not entitled to speak for the entire Vietnamese population, Tuyen warned that if France dealt with Ho Chi Minh, the Vietnamese nationalists would turn against both France and Ho Chi Minh.[34]

On September 4, Bao Dai finally made a move by inviting the leaders of all political parties to come to Hong Kong to inform him about the situation and thus help him take the appropriate steps to ensure an honorable and lasting peace. In answer to this invitation, twenty-four delegates went to see Bao Dai on September 9, the eve of Bollaert's Ha Dong speech. The French authorities, who issued exit visas, had taken care that the Vietnamese delegation would not be composed entirely of intransigent nationalists by including men whose attachment to the mother country was beyond doubt. Bao Dai's move provoked immediate reaction from Ho, who stressed that only the resistance government, not the ex-Emperor, was given the mandate to enter into negotiations with France.

Both Ho Chi Minh and Bao Dai, their supporters and competitors, had been waiting impatiently for the Ha Dong speech. Anxiously, they had been asking themselves: "Will the French announce a cease-fire?" "Will the war be over?" "Will France recognize Vietnam's *doc lap*?"

Finally, it was September 10! At last, the High Commissioner delivered his eagerly awaited speech! A cruel farce! Bollaert had nothing new to offer. The "new" policy actually was a rehash of d'Argenlieu's worn-out scheme. It conspicuously avoided any refer-

ence to the word "independence." In pompous words, Bollaert
handed out an empty promise:

1. Vietnam would be a "free" state within the French Union;
2. The question of unity of the three *ky* would be decided by the
populations concerned in a free referendum:
3. The "common services," i.e., customs, public works, immigration, issuance of currency, etc., and the budget would be in French
hands.

"The offer I am tendering in the name of the Government of the
Republic," the High Commissioner concluded with the solemnity of
a comic actor, "is an indivisible whole which must be either fully
accepted or wholly rejected. We cannot permit a haggling which
would verily be unworthy of such a noble cause."[35]
An ill-conceived speech! In view of Bollaert's previous statements,
this pronouncement was both deceiving and startling. It caused
widespread disappointment throughout the country. Both the Viet
Minh and other nationalist groups unanimously rejected Bollaert's
offer of "liberty within the French Union." Ho's disenchantment,
however, was caused not so much by the French refusal to recognize Vietnam's independence as by the High Commissioner's decision, to discredit the Viet Minh. While appealing to "all spiritual
and social families of Vietnam" to send to the conference table their
most capable men who could inspire confidence, Bollaert emphasized that the Viet Minh, "authors of the aggression of December
19," had considerably discredited themselves in the eyes of the
French people. Their presence in the negotiations, therefore, would
not be in the best interest of the Vietnamese people.
Two days following Bollaert's speech, Pham Ngoc Thach, the Viet
Minh Vice-Minister for Foreign Affairs, sent a letter to the United
Nations Secretary General Trygve Lie, requesting the Security
Council "to put an end to the war of aggression that France has
undertaken these last two years against Vietnam," and proposing
the opening of negotiations, under United Nations auspices, between France and the Ho Chi Minh government on the basis of
Vietnam's independence and territorial integrity, respect for French
economic and cultural interests, and the withdrawal of French
forces from Vietnam. Thach's letter went unanswered.
On September 15, Hoang Minh Giam, the DRV Minister for

Foreign Affairs, expressing the Viet Minh reaction to the Ha Dong speech, stated that although his government wanted peace, friendly collaboration with France, and independence within the French Union, it considered the High Commissioner's policy too narrow-minded. In view of Bollaert's September 10 declarations and of General Valluy's systematic preparations for the autumn offensive, Ho became painfully aware that the French had turned their back to his regime and decided to continue their solution of force.

In Hong Kong, where he had been assured by Bollaert's emissaries that France would make "liberal" concessions to Vietnam, Bao Dai heard the Ha Dong speech with profound disappointment. Although the French made clear that they were no longer interested in negotiations with the Viet Minh, Bao Dai could not accept the French terms and still compete with Ho, who was fighting for independence and unity. The ex-Emperor suddenly found himself in a difficult situation. Should he, or should he not, negotiate with the French now that a Franco-Viet Minh deal had been clearly ruled out and that Bollaert had made an outrageous "offer," which "must be either fully accepted or wholly rejected"?

It was under trying circumstances such as this one that Bao Dai, who had occasionally shown evidence of political acumen and patriotism, failed to provide firm leadership. In Hong Kong, besides the advocates of collaboration with France, there were well-meaning nationalists such as the head of the United National Front Nguyen Van Sam, the prominent journalist Nguyen Phan Long, the Catholic spokesman Tran Van Ly, the VNQDD leaders Nguyen Hai Than and Nguyen Tuong Tam. Although unanimously opposed to Bollaert's terms, they were sadly divided in regard to a common action to be taken in the face of the French challenge. Bao Dai, unfortunately, failed to hold his supporters together. While the dismayed VNQDD leaders, who had given up any hope of working out a compromise with France, went back to their exile in China, and while Nguyen Van Sam categorically rejected Bollaert's "new" policy, other nationalists still deemed it possible to negotiate with the French on the following grounds:

a. In view of Bollaert's appeal to "all spiritual and social families" of Vietnam and rejection of the Viet Minh, Bao Dai was the only person qualified to speak for the Vietnamese people;

b. In view of French preparations for the autumn offensive, which, according to General Valluy, would once for all crush the Viet Minh forces, Bao Dai could no longer use the threat of cooperation with Ho to wrest concessions from the French;

c. An outright rejection of the French "offer" would isolate Bao Dai and his supporters, and might prompt the French to negotiate only with their Vietnamese collaborators;

d. The course of international events would work in Bao Dai's favor. Since the United States had just intervened on behalf of the Indonesians against the Dutch, it would very likely support a Vietnamese independence movement, provided it was not led by Communists.

In addition to these political considerations, another personal reason seemed to have influenced Bao Dai to break with Ho and move closer to the French. The Viet Minh reportedly had stripped the ex-Emperor of his Vietnamese citizenship and condemned him to death *in absentia*.[36]

On September 18, against Ngo Dinh Diem's advice, Bao Dai made a fateful move. Addressing his people for the first time since his abdication, the former Emperor expressed his readiness to examine with the French authorities the proposals that had been made at Ha Dong:

To avoid bloodshed, I renounced the throne of my ancestors. Since you wished to entrust your destiny to new leaders, I voluntarily withdrew. . . . Today, in spite of the dictatorship that stifles your voice, I hear your appeals and your cries of distress. Thus have vanished all your hopes for happiness which a skillful propaganda and a new ideology had once kindled in your hearts. In your distress, you come to me. . . . Answering your appeal, I accept the mission which you entrust me and am ready to enter into contact with the French authorities. I want, first of all, to obtain independence and unity for you. . . . Then I will exert the full weight of my authority to mediate in the conflict which has set you one against the other.[37]

The die was cast. The ex-monarch and the old revolutionary finally parted company. Shortly after issuing his proclamation, Bao Dai received an important visitor, William C. Bullitt, wartime U.S. ambassador to France and an influential member of the Republican Party, who had just completed his visit to Indochina. As he was to write shortly afterward in *Life*, Bullitt told the ex-Emperor that a French "surrender to Ho Chi Minh and his Communist comrades" would be "the worst disaster which could befall the French, the Annamites and the civilized world." He expressed the wish that France would recognize Vietnam's independence within the French Union, send back to Vietnam the delegation then representing the Ho regime in Paris, "permit the non-Communist nationalists . . . to prepare complete political, economic and military organizations for control of the country," and "leave the Annamite nationalists the task of winning over the nationalist elements which compose two thirds of the forces of Ho Chi Minh and cooperate with the nationalist forces in crushing the irreconcilable Communists."[38] Though Bullitt's article, published after his visit with Bao Dai in Hong Kong, represented the opinion of a private citizen, Paris' political circles, among which the former American ambassador still enjoyed considerable prestige, viewed it as an expression of official U.S. policy. Washington, the French believed, was behind the "Bao Dai solution." The stage was thus set for the ex-Emperor's entrance.

To prevent the formation of an anti-Viet Minh government, Ho resorted to his familiar strategy—physical elimination of opponents. Orders were given for the execution of prominent pro-Bao Dai leaders, among whom were Nguyen Van Sam, head of the United National Front, and Dr. Truong Dinh Tri, chairman of the Tonkinese Administrative Committee and once a Minister in the DRV government. These two men were assassinated by Ho's agents late in October, within twenty-four hours of each other.

Meanwhile in Paris, on November 21, the pro-colonial-MRP Robert Schuman took over the reins of government from Premier Paul Ramadier, while the Socialist Marius Moutet gave up the Ministry of Overseas France to Paul Coste-Floret, whose anti-Viet Minh views were sledom concealed. And in Saigon, the High Commissioner made preparations for the ex-Emperor's return, dispatching emissaries to Hong Kong to arrange a Bollaert-Bao Dai meeting.

The ex-Emperor, however, was not very anxious to meet with any French representative or emissary. Since issuing his proclamation on September 18, which he later regretted, Bao Dai had been made aware that a Viet Minh defeat would strengthen the French position and encourage Bollaert to shove the Ha Dong formula down his throat, and that, in order to successfully compete with the Viet

Minh for leadership of the nationalist movement, he, Bao Dai, must succeed in obtaining from France what Ho had been fighting for, namely, unity and independence. A depressed Bao Dai now refused to meet with Bollaert unless the French were ready to acquiesce to these basic Vietnamese demands. This, precisely, was the ex-monarch's dilemma. The French preferred him to Ho simply because they assumed he would be less nationalistic and less demanding than the old revolutionary. Bao Dai was thus caught between the French, who wanted him to be a malleable instrument of their colonial policy, and the Vietnamese, who expected him to be an intransigent defender of their cause.

Anxious to overcome the Vietnamese leader's scruples, Bollaert asked Paris for, and received, the permission to go so far as to pronounce the word "independence" as a bait to bring Bao Dai into the game. A French emissary was immediately sent to Hong Kong to propose a Bollaert-Bao Dai meeting, the purpose of which, the High Commissioner emphasized, was to discuss Vietnam's "independence." With such French assurance, the ex-Emperor accepted the invitation. Before leaving Hong Kong for Ha Long Bay, where the rendezvous was to take place, the Vietnamese leader was warned by his entourage against any premature agreement. "Above all, do not sign anything," he was cautioned. At the end of their two-day meeting on board the flagship *Duguay-Trouin,* Bao Dai and Bollaert agreed on the terms of a joint declaration, which recognized Vietnam's "independence," and a secret protocol, which imposed severe restrictions on independence. Bollaert stressed the need to authenticate these documents. Bao Dai hesitated. Not until after the French official had given him formal assurance that the protocol was nothing more than the minutes of their discussions and, consequently, would not bind him in any way did Bao Dai initial the two documents. Elated that France had finally conceded "independence" to Vietnam, Bao Dai returned to Hong Kong. The ex-Emperor's joy, however, was short-lived. While approving the declaration, his advisers, unanimously, rejected the restrictions mentioned in the protocol. It soon dawned upon Bao Dai that Bollaert had used tricks to obtain his signature. Greatly indignant that his good faith had been abused, Bao Dai requested that the protocol be modified. The High Commissioner, however, proud of his "diplomatic shrewdness" and determined to exploit the Bao Dai-signed document, naturally refused to comply with the Vietnamese request.

After futile attempts to obtain satisfaction from Bollaert, Bao Dai left Hong Kong, visited Paris, London, and finally settled down in Geneva. In order to extricate himself from the French trap, the ex-monarch declared that he had signed the December 7 Protocol simply as a private individual, not as a representative of any party, group, or government. Furthermore, the protocol was considered by the leaders of political and religious groups as totally inadequate. Bao Dai was quickly criticized by the right-wing politicians in Paris for his refusal to compromise on the issue of independence and unity, and by the left wing, which considered him unqualified to speak for the Vietnamese people.

Meanwhile, Bollaert, hard pressed to break the Franco-Vietnamese deadlock, and determined to frighten Bao Dai into accepting the French conditions, made another ingenious move. In March, news was carefully leaked that Saigon again was considering negotiations with Ho Chi Minh, and that a French emissary would soon be sent to confer with Viet Minh representatives in Hong Kong. In April, Louis Caput, a member of the French Socialist Party who had played a significant role in the negotiations leading to the March 6, 1946, Accord, and who was firmly opposed to the Bao Dai solution but strongly in favor of a settlement with Ho Chi Minh, left for the British Crown colony presumably to make the contact. Caput, however, did not meet with any Viet Minh representatives in Hong Kong. Although he had undertaken the "mission" in good faith, he later realized that he had been misused by Bollaert. "I am more and more convinced," wrote Caput on September 18, 1948, "that I was asked to go to Hong Kong only in order to facilitate his [Bollaert's] rapprochement with Bao Dai and hasten the conclusion of the accords of June 5 [1948]."[39] Bollaert's maneuver caused quick reaction from Bao Dai.

In a renewed attempt to obtain more acceptable conditions from the French, the ex-Emperor sent another emissary, Dr. Phan Huy Dan, to Saigon to negotiate with Bollaert. The unyielding High Commissioner simply reiterated what he had said on several previous occasions, namely, that the Ha Long Protocol would be generously interpreted. Apprehensive that Saigon might reopen negotiations with the Viet Minh, Bao Dai welcomed his advisers' proposal for a provisional central government to bring about Vietnam's military, administrative, and economic reunification and to maintain contact with France. Informed of this move, Bollaert, who was as anxious as the Vietnamese to prevent a Franco-Vietnamese rupture, agreed to obtain Paris' approval for the plan, on condition that Bao Dai officially endorse the proposed government and countersign the protocol, which it would have to sign, and which the High Commissioner had steadfastly refused to amend.

At a meeting in Saigon on May 20, representatives from the three *ky* passed a motion entrusting Nguyen Van Xuan, former head of the separatist Cochinchinese government and a recently-promoted brigadier general in the French army, with the task of forming a provisional central government. Only after prominent nationalist leaders such as Ngo Dinh Diem had refused to serve under the unsatisfactory conditions imposed by the Ha Long Protocol was Xuan given the assignment. Shortly after his election, the General formally notified the High Commissioner that Vietnam had declared its unity and that he had been given the responsibility of forming its first government. On May 27, in presenting his cabinet to Bao Dai in Hong Kong, Xuan pledged to follow the ex-Emperor's instructions and directives.

Meanwhile, Paris, which had consistently opposed the unification of the three *ky*, naturally was not prepared to give recognition to any government that claimed to speak for a united Vietnam. Reluctantly, it "took cognizance" of the constitution of the Xuan government. In the face of the French refusal to accord official recognition to the new government, Bao Dai announced that it could not act in his name. Through his spokesman, the former monarch emphasized that the Xuan government was a step in the Franco-Vietnamese negotiations, that, although the provisional central government did not owe its existence to him, he would maintain close contact with it, and that he would not return to Vietnam until he received firm assurances from France that the legitimate aspirations of the Vietnamese people, namely, true unity and real independence within the French Union, would be satisfied.

The ex-Emperor's "intransigence" was not what the French had bargained for when they decided on the Bao Dai formula. In any case, the resourceful Bollaert was confident that he had caught Bao Dai in his net. Stressing, once again, that Paris was ready to offer generous concessions under the Ha Long protocol and to give assurance of Vietnam's unity and independence, the High Commissioner prevailed upon the former monarch to reach a formal agreement with France. Again, against the advice of his nationalist supporters, notably, Ngo Dinh Diem, Bao Dai gave in.

On June 5, 1948, on the French cruiser *Duguay-Trouin* anchored in the historic and ever-picturesque Ha Long Bay, the protocol was signed by Bollaert and Xuan in the presence of Bao Dai, who countersigned it. As agreed, only the joint declaration, which opened with the following most eagerly-awaited words, was made public: "France solemnly recognizes the independence of Vietnam whose right it is to bring about freely its unity. Vietnam, on its part, proclaims its adhesion to the French Union as a state associated with France. The independence of Vietnam has no limits other than those emanating from its membership in the French Union."[40]

Other "special agreements" were to be made on cultural, economic, financial, technical, and diplomatic matters. Basically, the Ha Long Bay Agreement, which did not spell out the terms of independence, the status of an associated state, etc., was as vague as the March 6, 1946, Accord, which had required endless and futile follow-up discussions. The French again resorted to their familiar tactic of procrastination. In any case, Bao Dai, confident that Bollaert had negotiated in good faith, was satisfied. "You just acknowledged Vietnam's unity and independence in the bosom of the French Union," he solemnly told the High Commissioner. "Vietnam will regain her internal sovereignty and traditional boundaries. I am leaving Hong Kong for good. For me as well as for Vietnam, the Hong Kong episode is over."[41] That very evening, the ex-Emperor was on his way to France, apparently convinced that he had wrested from the French what Ho had been unable to obtain through patient negotiations and bloody fighting.

The news of the signing of the Ha Long Protocol was received with mixed feelings in Vietnam. While admitting that the formal recognition of Vietnam and of its right to bring about unity were quite significant French concessions, many Vietnamese remained skeptical. "Didn't the French, who had concluded a number of agreements with the Viet Minh regime, unscrupulously disregard them?" they asked themselves.

In the Viet Bac jungle, however, the DRV leaders were worried. Fearful that a central government, which received from France what he had failed to obtain, would be in a most advantageous position to compete with the Viet Minh regime for popular support and draw the nationalist elements from the resistance ranks, Ho, in May, had actually asked Bao Dai to withhold investiture from the Xuan government. The old guerilla had good reason to believe that the war-wearied people of Vietnam would welcome the Ha Long Bay Declaration of June 5, which promised unity and independence, and turn their back to the Viet Minh slogans of struggle to the finish. Therefore, Ho lost no time branding the Xuan cabinet a puppet government "ready to commit every kind of treason in the service of its foreign masters," declaring that "the Government of Vietnam reserves for itself the right to try these quislings in accordance with national laws," and considered "null and void any document signed by these puppets with any foreign country."[42] Furthermore, General Xuan was tried and sentenced to death.

The Ha Long Bay Agreement, in a sense, represented a significant gain for the Vietnamese nationalists, who had prevailed on the French to recognize Vietnam's independence. Had the agreement been honored, it would have been another turning point in Franco-Vietnamese relations. France's duplicity, alas, negated the promise she had so "solemnly" made, nullified the Bao Dai solution, which she had herself proposed, and pulled the rug from under the non-Viet Minh nationalists' feet! Ho's fear of widespread dissatisfaction and defections from the Viet Minh ranks was soon removed by the French themselves. No sooner had the Ha Long Bay Agreement been concluded than Coste-Floret, the Minister for Overseas France, made a statement to allay the French misgivings about the concessions. Addressing the National Assembly on June 8, Coste-Floret assured the Deputies that nothing had changed in Indochina, that the June 5 Accord did not mean an immediate return to peace but a step toward the pacification of the country. Lest there should be any misunderstanding, the Minister emphasized that France would retain control of the foreign relations and defense of the French Union. In regard to Cochinchina, Coste-Floret added, the Ha Long Bay Agreement did not imply an automatic recognition of its union with Tonkin and Annam. France merely promised not to oppose the union of the three *ky* if their people really wanted it. In the meantime, Cochinchina remained a French colony, whose status could not be altered without an act of the French Parliament.[43] To further confuse the situation, the Schuman government did not deem it necessary to submit the Ha Long Bay Agreement to the National Assembly for ratification. And the majority of the French political parties also made it clear that they would approve the Bao Dai formula only if it did not involve major concessions to the Vietnamese.

Not until August 19 did the Radical André Marie, who had succeeded Premier Schuman, take the necessary step. Reluctant to repudiate the efforts of his party colleague Bollaert, the new Premier announced the government's approval of the agreement. In addition to that consideration, André Marie had been convinced that the Ha Long Bay Agreement, hedged in with so many restrictions, would not cause any departure from the French position.

In the meantime, Bao Dai, distressed by the French devious maneuvers, remained aloof from the Xuan government. In a letter to Bollaert on July 11, the ex-Emperor went so far as to dissociate himself from the June 5 Agreement, declaring that his role at Ha Long Bay had been simply that of a witness. The protocol, he repeated, could not bring peace to Vietnam and could not provide a basis for a lasting understanding between the French and Vietnamese people. Since the Bao Dai solution required Bao Dai's presence in Vietnam, Bollaert engaged in tireless attempts to persuade the former Emperor to return to his country. In their last encounter in St. Germain on August 25, 1948, Bao Dai, once again, made it clear to Bollaert that he would not go back to Vietnam before the liquidation of the colonial regime in Cochinchina and before receiving sufficient guarantees in regard to his country's independence. When he resigned from his post of High Commissioner and left Indochina in October, 1948, Bollaert sadly realized that the Ha Long Bay Agreement, of which he had been the principal architect, had not helped resolve the Franco-Vietnamese impasse. And ironically, his successor was none other than Léon Pignon, d'Argenlieu's trusted adviser, whom he had removed from the High Commissariat, upon his arrival in Saigon in April, 1947, to improve Franco-Vietnamese relations!

Paris' lack of good faith had encouraged the colons in Saigon to agitate even against the Ha Long Bay Agreement. General Xuan was denounced as a dangerous nationalist, and Bollaert was accused of selling out to the Vietnamese! French short-sightedness and duplicity considerably simplified Ho's political problems. The first formal opposition to the Viet Minh regime collapsed as soon as, or even before, it took shape, thanks to French maneuvers. Instead of luring non-Viet Minh combatants from the *maquis*, the Ha Long Bay Agreement hardened their anticolonial feeling and strengthened their resolve to cast their lot with Ho Chi Minh.

From his jungle headquarters in the Viet Bac, the old guerilla followed the latest development in Saigon with unexpected relief. Sensing that the French were not prepared to give Bao Dai what they had denied him, the calculating DRV President attempted, once again, to mollify the French by projecting himself as a conciliatory opponent who would settle for considerably less than the ex-Emperor. On October 27, 1948, speaking through Tran Ngoc Danh, head of the Viet Minh delegation in Paris, Ho patiently renewed his peace overture to the French, declaring that the DRV still remained "faithful to the principles which governed the signature of the preliminary Convention of March 6, 1946 and the *modus vivendi* of September 14, 1946." In an apparent attempt to create an atmosphere of detente by absolving Paris from any responsibility for the war, Ho reiterated that he viewed "the events of November and December 1946 and the following prolongation of the present hostilities as the responsibility of French colonial authorities who were determined to recapture Indochina by a colonial war contrary to the spirit and the letter of the French Constitution." The Viet Minh government further reaffirmed its "readiness to cooperate, on the basis of reprocity of rights and duties, with all members of the French Union within the framework of the Union and with all democratic nations within the framework of the United Nations Organization." To this end, it emphasized, it was ready, as it had always been, to conclude with France a just and lasting agreement.[44]

Less than a month later, Ho took another diplomatic step to obtain international recognition. On November 22, the Viet Minh Republic in the jungle applied for membership in the United Nations, emphasizing that *a.* it had been an independent state since September 2, 1945, following the Allied victory over Japan to which it had heavily contributed;

b. it had been recognized by France through the Accord of March 6, 1946;

c. it had been appointed by the Vietnamese National Assembly following the January 6, 1946 general elections;

d. it had made considerable political (Constitution of November 9, 1946), economic (campaign against famine and endemic undernourishment), social (institution of social legislation), and cultural (anti-illiteracy campaign) progress; and

e. it was ready to accept, without any reservation, the principles of the United Nations Charter, and was capable of fulfilling the obligations deriving from it.[45]

Ho's timely moves provoked favorable reaction in the French capital. Early in 1949, claiming to speak for the former imperial family, Prince Buu Hoi, a cousin of Bao Dai, who had taken part in the Fontainebleau Conference, warned Paris against creating and supporting artificial governments, and urged the French to negotiate with "the government of President Ho Chi Minh" in order to seek a peaceful settlement of the conflict. At about the same time, his father, Prince Ung Uy, left the French-controlled area in Indochina for the Viet Minh zone.

In addition to the Communists, who had always opposed negotiations with any group other than the Ho regime, the Socialists began to have second thoughts about the Bao Dai solution. "The negotiations with Bao Dai cannot result in an agreement with the people of Vietnam," wrote Guy Mollet, General Secretary of the Socialist Party, in January, 1949. "The ex-Emperor enjoys no authority in the country." Therefore, France must "try everything to put an end to the war through negotiations with all the political and cultural factions of the Vietnamese people and, in the first place, with the government of Ho Chi Minh."[46]

Ironically, the parties of the Right (for different reasons) were equally critical of the ex-Emperor because of his insistence on French recognition of Vietnam's unity and independence. Faced with such opposition from both the Left and the Right, the irresolute French government kept postponing decisions. As usual, it had neither the desire to negotiate a compromise nor a plan to effectively pursue the war. Contrary to General de Gaulle's assertion that France should not rush anything and that sooner or later the French solution would have to be accepted,[47] time worked for Ho Chi Minh. While in France politicians engaged in futile debates, in China the rising red tide steadily and inexorably engulfed the country. One after another, Chiang Kai-shek's bastions crumbled. In January, 1949, Mao Tse-tung's troops overran Peking. The collapse of the Kuomintang armies was imminent. With the Communist victories in China, the situation in Vietnam suddenly changed. Ho's jungle republic would soon have a powerful friend across the border.

Distressed by the prospect of a gigantic Communist Chinese state in the rear of the Viet Minh, which would inevitably frustrate France's effort to stay in Indochina, and hard pressed by the rising cost of the war, which had severely drained France's resources, Paris became anxious to create an effective anti-Viet Minh government that would involve Vietnamese participation in the struggle. To this end an "independent" state of Vietnam susceptible of international, notably, American, recognition must be created. France would then join forces with Vietnam against the Viet Minh. The colonial war would be transformed into a civil war, a struggle between nationalist and Communist forces, and thus a part of the worldwide struggle between the East and the West. The United States, in view of her containment policy, would not relish the prospect of a Viet Minh victory in Indochina, which would threaten the security of non-Communist Southeast Asia. Washington, reasoned the French, would be compelled to give them moral, financial, and military support to defeat the Viet Minh. Convinced that Vietnam's "independence" as interpreted by the French would not compromise France's presence in Indochina in any way, Paris no longer hesitated to give in to Bao Dai. The ex-Emperor, for his part, believed that the victories of the Chinese Communists, who would undoubtedly give moral and material support to the Ho regime, actually improved the anti-Viet Minh nationalists' position vis-à-vis the French. The nationalists could now use the threat of joining the resistance or of noncooperation with the French to force Paris to make *bona fide* concessions.

Thus, with different interpretations of the same events, both the

French and the Bao Dai forces began to reassess their position. On January 16, 1949, High Commissioner Pignon journeyed to Cannes to talk with Bao Dai. Shortly afterward, the two men met again in Paris. It was finally decided that the principles of June 5, 1948, should be formalized and clarified in an exchange of letters between President Vincent Auriol of France and Bao Dai. Under the Élyseée Agreement of March 8, 1949, as the letters came to be known, France went as far as to reaffirm "her decision not to raise any *de jure* or *de facto* obstacle to the admission of Cochinchina within the framework of Vietnam," provided that the people of Cochinchina be first consulted. While renouncing its special rights to the cities of Hanoi, Haiphong, and Tourane, the French government still claimed to have incurred "particular duties" toward the mountaineers in the South and the Thai highlanders in the North, whose special status was to be the subject of further negotiations.

While Vietnam's unity was not questioned, her independence was quite limited. The French would retain control over defense and foreign relations, a stipulation which the Pham Van Dong delegation had firmly rejected at Fontainebleau in 1946. Although Vietnam was to enjoy internal sovereignty, French nationals were to be tried only under French law, and citizens of the French Union and of the states enjoying a privileged status were to be tried before mixed tribunals. Vietnam's economic and financial independence was similarly limited by the proviso that her national currency would remain tied to the French monetary zone and to that of the other two Indochinese states, with which she was to form a customs union. Property and enterprises belonging to citizens of the French Union would not be subject to expropriation without the consent of the French government. And the vital question of how much control the Vietnamese were to have over their own treasury, immigration, postal and telegraphic service, and economic planning was to be decided in a later conference.

While apparently more advantageous to the Vietnamese than the previous accords, the Élyseée Agreement did not imply any fundamental change in the French position. On March 9, three days following the signing of the Agreement, Defense Minister Paul Ramadier informed the Council of the Republic that "expenditures for Indochina are more necessary than ever because a new phase is beginning which does not permit us to slow down our military efforts."[48]

In the meantime, Bao Dai, reluctant to face his people without any concrete concession from France, informed Paris that he would return to Vietnam only after the French had effectively put an end to Cochinchinese separatism. Bao Dai's wish was granted. Under the French Constitution, however, the status of a member of the French Union could be changed only by an act of Parliament following a request by the territorial assembly of the member in question. Since no such assembly existed in Cochinchina, one had to be created. On April 23, in Saigon, the freshly constituted Territorial Assembly voted for Cochinchina's accession to Vietnam.

Two days later, without waiting for the French National Assembly to pass on the Cochinchinese decision, Bao Dai quietly left France for Vietnam. He had been away from his country for more than three years. His unheralded arrival in Indochina was matched only by his quiet departure from France. Shy and unsure of the support and welcome he would receive from his people, the former Emperor preferred to avoid any possible embarrassment. Upon his arrival in Indochina, Bao Dai bypassed Saigon and flew immediately to the resort city of Dalat, where, three years earlier, Vo Nguyen Giap had clashed with the French delegation. The town had not changed since he last saw it as His Majesty the Emperor. The flowers were still beautiful, the hills still green, the lakes still clear, the villas still lovely, the air still fresh, the weather still cool, and the people still hospitable. Here, among the weeping willows, the former monarch waited.

On May 21, the French National Assembly finally passed a bill recognizing Cochinchina as part of Vietnam. In the crazy fashion of French politics, which has often dizzied many a foreign observer, the Communists and the Socialists, for "good" reasons, voted against the act which was to become law on June 4.

Saigon was no longer the capital of the Cochinchinese Republic, but a city of Vietnam. On June 13, Bao Dai arrived in Saigon amidst colorful flags and an indifferent population. Ho had ordered his agents to keep the people off the streets. At a formal ceremony on June 4, the ex-Emperor and the High Commissioner exchanged letters giving effect to the Élyseée Agreement. On this

occasion, while announcing his decision to retain the title *Duc Quoc
Truong*, His Majesty Chief of State, in order to have a legal international status, Bao Dai "solemnly" proclaimed that "the people who
had fought heroically for the independence of their homeland"
would decide the future constitution of the country. An honored
place in the State of Vietnam was thus reserved for members of the
resistance.

At the end of the month, the Cochinchinese government tendered
its resignation to His Majesty Chief of State. Separatism came to an
end. Vietnam, at last, recovered her unity!

Painfully aware that his regime would not survive without the
support of genuine nationalist elements, Bao Dai made cautious
attempts to ingratiate himself with the anticolonial leaders by re-
serving a number of posts in his cabinet for men in the resistance.
During his summer visit to Hanoi, the Chief of State went so far as
to lay a wreath on the monument to the Vietnamese who had been
killed by the French after December 19, 1946. Many prominent
nationalists in both the *maquis* and the French-controlled area, including those most opposed to the Viet Minh, however, chose to
wait to see whether the French would honor their agreements with
the ex-Emperor. Invited to head Bao Dai's cabinet, Ngo Dinh Diem
again declined the offer, reiterating that he would participate in the
government only after the aspirations of the Vietnamese people
were satisfied, or when Vietnam obtained a political status similar
to that of India and Pakistan within the British Commonwealth.
Then, emphasized Diem, the best posts in new Vietnam should be
reserved for those who had merited most of the country, the members of the resistance.[49]

Faced with such refusal, Bao Dai had to assume the post of Prime
Minister himself. With the exception of Nguyen Phan Long, a journalist of renown, who held the portfolios of both Interior and Foreign Affairs, Bao Dai's cabinet failed to attract or impress the Vietnamese people. His Majesty made the mistake of appointing to the
post of Deputy Premier General Nguyen Van Xuan, a man who had
been closely identified with Cochinchinese separatism. Xuan, however, was soon dropped when Bao Dai reshuffled his government in
February, 1950.

Nguyen Phan Long, Premier in the second Bao Dai cabinet, was eased out of office at the insistence of the High Commissioner, who had been irritated by his request that American military and economic aid be given directly to the Vietnamese and that the Élyseée Agreement be interpreted in a most liberal way. Of the next three Prime Ministers who "governed" the State of Vietnam until the fall of Dienbienphu, Tran Van Huu was a reliable collaborator of the French, Nguyen Van Tam, a French "patriot," and Prince Buu Loc, a cousin of His Majesty.

Although, on paper, Vietnam was an independent Associated State within the French Union, in practice, its status had not changed in any significant way. Power still remained in French hands. The French still controlled the police, while the Bao Dai government had no army and no independent finances. The High Commissioner, with the Expeditionary Corps at his disposal, was the master of Indochina. Bao Dai, the Chief of State, enjoyed little popular support, partly due to the lack of an effective organization and mostly due to French maneuvers. A well-meaning man, Bao Dai had tried hard to wrest from the French what his people aspired to, namely, unity and independence. In the process, he neglected to build up a political organization within his own country. Without a power base, Bao Dai failed to rally the Vietnamese nationalists behind his government, even after he had obtained from the French what they had denied to Ho. While sincerely concerned about his country's interests, Bao Dai was a pacific man, not a perseverant fighter—the kind of leader Vietnam needed in that critical period of her history. Instead of remaining intransigent toward the French as he had been prior to his return to Vietnam, Bao Dai, once in his country, bent too easily under French pressure. A prisoner of the French and of his opportunist advisers, the Chief of State found escape in hunting tigers in the southern highlands.

From June to December, 1949, the Bao Dai government and the French authorities wasted considerable time in interminable discussions regarding the status of the State of Vietnam. By the end of the year, Pignon and Bao Dai had signed twenty-seven complementary agreements governing the transfer of internal power from French to Vietnamese hands. No sooner had they been concluded than they proved irrelevant or inapplicable. By resorting to various devices to postpone the transfer of power, the French effectively and irreparably undermined the regime they had helped establish and, consequently, strengthened Ho Chi Minh's government. As one of Bao Dai's former advisers aptly pointed out:.

The Vietnamese people considered Bao Dai's regime as a puppet regime, created and supported by the French for the sole purpose of endorsing French colonial policy and lending it an appearance of legality. Vietnam had no national assembly and no constitution. Bao Dai's successive governments were all created out of sheer arbitrariness, under French inspiration. And the treaties they negotiated and signed with the French were all for the maintenance of French colonial privileges. . . .

Consequently the Communists not only enjoyed the neutrality of the great majority of the Vietnamese population, but also the active support of many sincere nationalists, who fought along with the Viet Minh against French colonialism.[50]

Meanwhile, Ho became less and less interested in negotiations with the French. His hardening attitude could be attributed to several factors: (*a*) the definite division of the world into Communist and non-Communist blocs, (*b*) the return of Bao Dai to Vietnam, and the subsequent (July 1, 1949) proclamation of the State of Vietnam as rival of the DRV, and (*c*) the Communist victories in China. On August 7, 1949, Ho withdrew from Paris the delegation he had left behind upon his departure from France at the close of the Fontainebleau Conference in 1946.

As the prospect of a peaceful settlement of the conflict had vanished out of sight, Ho devoted all his energy to the military struggle.

Guerilla Leader

At the outset, the Viet Minh were in a precarious situation. By the end of March, they had lost control of the towns in Tonkin and northern Annam. The ill-equipped and inadequately trained local militias were no match for the Expeditionary Corps. It was they, however, who bore the brunt of the fighting, while Vo Nguyen Giap's regular army withdrew into the Viet Bac, the Viet Minh political and military headquarters.

Aware that his forces had to be further increased and better trained before they could face the French, Ho, for the first three years, refrained from throwing them against the Expeditionary Corps in large-scale battles. The arrival of the Chinese Communist troops at the border in 1949 offered Ho an excellent opportunity to strengthen his army. The Chinese supplied the Viet Minh with large amounts of artillery and also two practice ranges at Tsingsi and Longchow. Viet Minh officers were sent to China for further military education, while Chinese advisers and technicians arrived in the Viet Bac to train the Vietnamese. Chinese aid permitted Giap to announce in February, 1950, that the people's war[51] was entering a new phase and that the war of movement was to replace guerilla activities. This, however, did not mean that the guerilla war was over. While the *chu luc* or regular army prepared for a large-scale offensive, the local militias, composed of men who were peasants or laborers by day and guerillas by night, and the regional forces, those in charge of the defense of the areas in which they lived, continued their disruptive activities. These consisted of blowing up bridges, destroying roads connecting French outposts, ambushing French patrols and convoys, attacking French positions and, thus, immobilizing large numbers of the Expeditionary Corps, or assassinating *Viet gian* or Vietnamese traitors (those suspected of collaboration with the Bao Dai government).

Ho wanted complete control over the central and eastern parts along the Sino-Tonkinese border, from which area the Viet Minh would have easy access to China and launch attacks against the French. In order to achieve his aim, he must effectively eliminate all the French border outposts. Ho asked his military commander Vo Nguyen Giap if the Viet Minh forces were ready to meet this challenge. With more supplies and ammunition, more manpower, his army should be able to carry out the assignment, replied the Viet Minh general. Since military supplies would come from China, Ho concentrated on the personnel problem. On November 4, 1949, the DRV President decreed nationwide conscription of all citizens, male and female, above the age of eighteen. Vietnamese had to "volunteer" either for military service or for transportation duties. During the long preparation period, Ho, unwilling to take any chance, frequently went over the Viet Minh military plans with his top lieutenants, Vo Nguyen Giap, Pham Van Dong, and Truong Chinh.

In the summer of 1950, with Chinese arms and advice, Giap organized his forces into five infantry divisions numbering 12,000 each. They were designated as the 304th, 308th, 312th, 316th, and 320th divisions. At the approach of autumn, Giap began to move. The time was most propitious. The wet season was over. And as the United States had been deeply involved in the Korean conflict since June, further American assistance to the French was unlikely. In addition, the French morale was low. In spite of the urgent pleas of General Carpentier, the Commander-in-Chief in Indochina, for reinforcements, the French government had decided, on August 14, to reduce the Expeditionary Corps by 9,000 men. The French National Assembly had also made its support of the government's policy and military operations in Indochina conditional on the assurance that no draftees would be used in the war.

In September, Giap ambitiously undertook to drive the French out of the frontier ridge. Moving out of his protected terrain with a force that outnumbered the enemy about 8 to 1, Giap attacked Dong Khe, a key French garrison on Route 4 between Cao Bang and Lang Son. After two days of ferocious fighting, the Viet Minh overran Dong Khe. Deeply worried, General Carpentier ordered the evacuation of Cao Bang. In October, a French column of 3,500 left That Khe to escort the 1,500-man Cao Bang garrison to safety. Both the Cao Bang force and the reinforcing column, in addition to a paratroop relief battalion, were ambushed and decimated by the waiting Viet Minh divisions. Giap then directed his men against the remaining French outposts on Route 4. One by one, they were evacuated in a great hurry. As Giap was closing in on them, the French, in panic, abandoned their main base in Lang Son on the night of October 17–18, leaving behind huge stocks of arms, ammunition, and vehicles.

The dispersion of the French and French-led troops on the Cao Bang Ridge had been one of the worst disasters in French Colonial history. Out of 10,000 troops disposed along that ridge, the losses were calculated to be 6,000 men, 13 guns, 125 mortars, 950 machine-guns, 1,200 sub-carbines, and over 8,000 rifles. In addition some 450 trucks were either lost or left behind. The majority of the 6,000 soldiers were taken prisoner, and to look after them Viet Minh POW camps were installed along the Chinese frontier zone.[52]

Following their retreat from the Cao Bang Ridge, the thoroughly-demoralized French successively relinquished Thai Nguyen, Hoa Binh, the French stronghold on the supply route connecting the Viet Bac and the Viet Minh-controlled northern Annam, and Lao Kay, the last French outpost near the Chinese border. By December, 1950, Ho had become the undisputed master over the frontier area stretching from the coastal town of Mon Cay near Ha Long Bay to the Laotian border, adjacent to friendly Chinese territory. The military situation, suddenly, became irreversible. Equally irreversible was the red tide that was to engulf Tonkin and northern Annam.

The French had lost the Cao Bang Ridge, and Ho Chi Minh had won the war. The ensuing battles merely prolonged the French agony until Giap finally administered the coup de grace at Dienbienphu. Victims of their own illusion, the overconfident French had entertained the mistaken notion that the inferior Viet Minh guerillas were both unwilling and unable to confront them in conventional warfare.

Following Giap's Cao Bang victory, the Viet Minh radio and leaflets began to announce that Ho Chi Minh would be in Hanoi to celebrate *Tet*, the Vietnamese lunar New Year, which fell in February, 1951. Panic-stricken, the French made preparations to evacuate French women and children from Tonkin.

On the French side, soldiers and politicians blamed each other for their disaster. General Alessandri, the Commander of the French forces in Tonkin, was fired. Also dismissed were Marcel Carpentier, the Commander-in-Chief of the Expeditionary Corps in Indochina, and Léon Pignon, the High Commissioner. The Cao Bang defeat seriously wounded French pride. To salvage the situation, Paris appointed General Jean de Lattre de Tassigny, France's most illustrious soldier, High Commissioner and Commander-in-Chief in Indochina. An egocentric and overbearing man, de Lattre was nicknamed *le roi Jean*, or King John, in the French Army because of his fondness for the "regal elegance" and the "military ceremonial recalling the more civilized days of the eighteenth century,"[53] and his insistence that all local civil and military officials, with contingents of troops, should be present any time he was due to arrive at or leave from an Indochinese airfield.[54] Upon his arrival in Saigon on December 17, 1950, de Lattre took measures to raise the sagging

French morale. The General shuffled the military command and sent back to France the ships that had been ordered to evacuate French women and children, arguing that as long as their families were with them the men would hold on to Indochina better. De Lattre's presence indeed dispelled the panic that had struck the French population in Tonkin. To defend the delta, the new Commander-in-Chief ordered the construction of 1,200 concrete strong points around it. These static defense positions came to be known as the "de Lattre line." As events were to illustrate, not only did these strong points fail to prevent Viet Minh infiltration, they tied down a substantial portion of the Expeditionary Corps that de Lattre badly needed for effective action against the Viet Minh. Thus, in answer to Giap's strategic offensive the French commanders from then onward clung to their static defense concept, immobilizing their forces in fixed positions and, consequently, providing convenient targets for Viet Minh assaults. According to General Henri Navarre, the Commander-in-Chief at the time of Dienbienphu, at least 100,000 of the 190,000-man Expeditionary Corps were tied down in strategic defense duties around the delta.[55] In any case, de Lattre succeeded in stemming the Viet Minh tide and gave Giap a few invaluable lessons which the Viet Minh general would not soon forget.

Meanwhile, encouraged by his troops' exploits, the old guerilla cut out for himself a more ambitious task. In order to reestablish Ho's authority and enable his DRV to compete favorably with Bao Dai's State of Vietnam for popular support and international recognition, the Viet Minh must bring a greater part of the population under their control. Of the two main population centers, the Mekong River delta in Cochinchina was definitely out of reach, but the Red River delta in Tonkin was within perfect striking distance for Giap's armies. In view of the recent spectacular victories of his men and of the low morale of the Expeditionary Corps, Ho decided that the time had come for him to dislodge the French from the coveted area. For the execution of this daring plan Ho turned to Giap.

On January 13, 1951, the Viet Minh Commander launched two divisions, the 308th and the 312th, against the fort of Vinh Yen, thirty miles northwest of Hanoi. Things went sour for General Giap this time. The French were ready. Following his inspection tour in

Tonkin, de Lattre, aware of the strategic importance of the Red River delta, had made preparations for its defense. And he made a point to be at Vinh Yen to welcome Giap! After five days of bitter fighting, during which de Lattre used all the firepower he could muster and inflicted heavy casualties on the Viet Minh forces, Giap withdrew, leaving 6,000 dead and 600 prisoners captured by the French.

Undaunted, on March 23, Giap attacked another French strong point in Mao Khe, about twenty miles northwest of Haiphong. The savage six-day battle took its toll. Giap's battered 316th division retreated, suffering 3,000 casualties, of whom 400 were dead.

In spite of these heavy losses, Ho decided that the offensive campaign must continue. The prospect of leaving the inhospitable jungle for the sunny city of Hanoi had perhaps caused the malaria-afflicted revolutionary to lose patience. In order to force the French out of the delta, another big Viet Minh victory was necessary.

On May 29, therefore, the 304th, 308th, and 320th divisions began another campaign. This series of Day River battles ended on June 18 with another smarting defeat for Giap. Viet Minh casualties again ran high, about a third of the men involved, including 1,000 taken prisoner.

By June, Giap became painfully aware that his attempt to reconquer the Red River delta for Ho had been foiled by de Lattre de Tassigny. Ho's return to Hanoi had to be postponed for many more *Tet*. Meanwhile, Giap retreated to the Viet Bac jungle to lick his wounds. While on the French side command frequently changed hands in what became known as the "carnival of generals," Giap continued to direct the Viet Minh military operations in spite of his defeats. His privileged situation might be attributed to at least two factors: (*a*) Giap did not make military decisions alone; it was the Tong Bo, or, more specifically, Ho Chi Minh, that was in charge of the war; and (*b*) there were no Viet Minh commanders with sufficient political prestige and military experience to take Giap's place.

Learning from their costly lessons, Ho and Giap decided not to engage the French in frontal attacks again. Instead, they quietly infiltrated thousands of their troops into the Red River delta, behind the de Lattre line to harass the French and prepare the people for a final showdown. The Viet Minh also concentrated on the Tonkinese highlands, the Thai country, and eventually spread into Laos in 1953.

In sending his men into the Lao kingdom, Ho, the guerilla leader, acted in unison with Ho, the dedicated agent of international Communism. The former intended to divert French attention from the Viet Minh buildup in Tonkin, force the French to send their mobile reserve into Laos to meet the Viet Minh threat, and thus foil their attempt to build up offensive strength. The latter decided to set up a "resistance government" that would spread Communism in Laos and weaken the French hold over the country.

Thus, Ho's immediate objectives and long-range goals harmonized perfectly. Ever since 1930, when he founded the Indochinese Communist Party (ICP) in Canton, Ho had been preoccupied with the thought of leading a successful revolution in the three Indochinese states. The name of the party itself, Indochinese, not Vietnamese, testified to his ambition. Ho's instructions to the ICP regional executive committees on November 25, 1945, included a plan for the formation of a United Front against French colonialism in Vietnam, Laos, and Cambodia. To implement his plan in Laos, Ho had at his service Prince Souphanouvong, a half brother of Prince Souvanna Phouma, the present Laotian Prime Minister. Souphanouvong, or the Red Prince, as he has been called, whom Ho had befriended in 1945, joined the Viet Minh leader at his jungle headquarters in the Viet Bac in 1949. At this very hideout, a congress of Lao rebel leaders took place on August 13, 1950. Under the aegis of Comrade Ho Chi Minh, the Neo Lao Issara or National United Front was created, and a "Government of National Resistance" of the Pathet Lao (State of Lao) proclaimed. Souphanouvong became President of the Front and Prime Minister of the new "government."

On March 3, 1951, the Lao Issara met with its sister organizations in Vietnam (Lien Viet) and Cambodia (Khmer Issarak) to coordinate their fight against the French. At this conference, writes the Australian Communist journalist Wilfred Burchett,

It was decided to set up a Vietnam-Khmer-Lao Alliance which called on the people of the three countries to coordinate their fight to defeat the colonialists. It was on the basis of these decisions, published on March

11, 1951, that Vietnamese volunteers later entered Cambodia and Laos to fight side by side with the Khmer Issarak forces—by then the Khmer National Liberation Army—and the Pathet Lao.[56]

At about the same time, the ICP, which had gone underground, was reconstituted under the name of the Vietnam Workers' Party. To allay the fear that, by renaming itself Vietnam Workers' Party instead of Indochinese Communist Party, the organization had given up its interests in Lao and Cambodia, Ho affirmed that the direction of the resistance movements in Laos and Cambodia continued to remain in Vietnamese hands, stressing that

The creation of a separate party for each of the three states does not prejudice the revolutionary movement in Indochina. . . . The Vietnamese Party reserves the right to supervise the activities of its brother parties in Cambodia and Laos.

The Central Executive Committee of the Vietnamese Workers' Party has designated a Cambodian and Laotian bureau charged with assisting the revolutionary movements in these countries. It organizes periodic assemblies of the three parties in order to discuss questions of common interest; it works toward the creation of a Vietnamese-Khmer-Laotian United Front. Militarily, Vietnam, Cambodia, and Laos constitute a combat zone; Vietnam has substantially assisted Cambodia and Laos militarily as well as from all other points of view.[57]

Thus, in the 1952–53 winter, Ho's men entered Laos to collect intelligence and stocks of rice, which they were to bury together with depots of arms in preparation for future offensives, to force the French to disperse their mobile reserve, and to harvest a very valuable opium crop.

Again in April, units of the 308th, 312th, and 316th Divisions reentered Lao, took over Sam Neua where they staged a public trial of the provincial governor and a district official. The victims, found guilty of collaboration with the French, were summarily executed. Upon their departure, the Viet Minh handed over Sam Neua to Souphanouvong, who made it the seat of his "Resistance Government," leaving behind two regiments, the 108th and 803rd of the 308th Division, to assist the Red Prince. During this incursion, Ho's soldiers surrounded several French outposts, which then had to be supplied by air, and thus temporarily tied down the French transport aircraft needed for service in Tonkin. After roaming freely over

the country, the Viet Minh suddenly withdrew on May 7. Ho's
ventures in Laos caused deep concern in the French High Command and prompted them to make preparations for the defense of
the little kingdom.

To further confuse the French, Ho made other diversionary
moves in Cambodia in the summer of 1953 by ordering his agents to
engage the Expeditionary Corps in minor skirmishes in the western
and northeastern parts of the Khmer kingdom. Here again, Ho
played the double role of Vietnamese guerilla chief and Indochinese
Communist leader. As previously discussed, Ho's interest in Cambodia dated as far back as 1930 and was clarified in 1945 in his
instructions to the ICP regional executive committees. In 1946, Viet
Minh agents helped the Khmer Issarak or Free Cambodian movement organize guerilla units against the French. And the President
of the Cambodian "Government of National Resistance," proclaimed
in 1950, was Son Ngoc Minh, a Cambodian of Vietnamese extrac-
tion, who was also in charge of the Viet Minh propaganda in the
Khmer kingdom. Another Vietnamese Cambodian, Sieu Heng,
headed the "Central Office South," which was responsible for all
Viet Minh operations in Cambodia, Cochinchina, and southern
Annam.

Thus, in his fight against the French, Ho, who disposed of a well-
oiled and far-reaching organization, was able to mobilize not only
the Vietnamese but also the Laotians and Cambodians.

From the time of de Lattre's arrival in Indochina in December,
1950, to the moment of his death from cancer in Paris in January,
1951, neither the French nor the Viet Minh made any progress.
While successfully repelling Giap's attacks and inflicting heavy
casualties on his men, the French were unable to pursue him or to
invade his stronghold. Neither side was strong enough to dislodge
the other. It was, consequently, a military stalemate, a sort of deadlock that favored Ho Chi Minh. Although it is true that de Lattre
succeeded in halting Giap's advances, it is unlikely that *le roi Jean*
could have won the Indochina war even had he lived longer.[58] The
tide had already turned against the Expeditionary Corps before the
famous French general arrived in Indochina.

De Lattre was succeeded as Commander-in-Chief by General
Raoul Salan, his deputy, and as High Commissioner by Jean
Letourneau, who had been first Minister of Overseas France, then

Minister for the Associated States. In spite of the shift of the military balance in Ho's favor, the French still refused to give wider freedoms to the State of Vietnam.

Meanwhile, freed from his involvement in the Korean conflict, which had ended in July 1953, Mao Tse-tung augmented his aid to the Ho regime. "The Chinese now were able to spare greatly increased quantities of materiel in the form of guns and ammunition (largely supplied by the Soviets) for use in the Indochinese battle front," wrote General Eisenhower in his *Mandate for Change.* "More advisers were being sent in and the Chinese were making available to the Viet Minh logistical experience they had gained in the Korean war."[59] The Viet Minh, consequently, with the inflow of instructors and equipment from China, rapidly built up their forces to push forth their strategic offensive, hoping to win a few spectacular victories, which would intensify the already growing antiwar sentiment in France and, thus, force Paris to negotiate on Ho's terms. A penetrating observer of French politics, the old guerilla wasted no time drawing conclusions from the developments in France. The public had been aroused against *la sale guerre* (the dirty war), a seemingly endless war that had cost too many French lives and drained France's resources in face of a resurging Germany. It had been incensed at the abuses committed in its name. Thousands of Frenchmen and Vietnamese in high positions had been making a fortune by engaging in illegitimate money transactions involving the Indochinese piaster, which was grossly overvalued, 17 French francs for 1 piaster.

Any one willing to enter into this unholy partnership of trading piaster who had, say, 10,000 piasters to spare, only needed permission to transfer this sum to France, at the official rate of 17 francs. Permission was obtained through the right connections from an office effectively controlled by the Bank of Indochina. . . . Receiving permission for the transfer meant that the original sum was doubled. But this was only the beginning of the operation. The 10,000 piasters, after being turned into 170,000 francs, were now used to acquire piasters at their real value of 7 or 8 francs. This could be done legally by importing goods into Indochina, or illegally by changing the francs into dollars and by buying with these dollars the cheap piasters on the black market. The 10,000 piasters have now become 20,000–30,000, and if retransferred to France, 250,000–300,000 francs, four times their actual value. Theoretically, this operation could go on forever, and in fact went on long enough to produce quite a number of new French and Vietnamese multimillion-aires, at the expense of the French treasury, which bought piasters for 17 francs that could be sold only for 7 or 8.[60]

The piaster traffic benefited not only French and Vietnamese specu-lators but also Ho Chi Minh, who bought the black market dollars which he used to obtain arms and supplies.[61]

The left-wing press published whatever it pleased about the war, giving facts and figures, which provided the Viet Minh with invalu-able information. A number of papers and periodicals carried arti-cles written expressly to hit at low morale. The French Communist party and left-wing organizations did not limit their protest to verbal pronouncements. It was reported that sometimes up to 40 per cent of the consignments of war materiel were sabotaged before they reached Indochina.[62]

Not only did the Viet Minh witness these developments, they had predicted them. Truong Chinh, Ho's leading theoretician, had in-deed said:

. . . the general Confederation of Labour organized throughout France many demonstrations embracing millions of people with the slogan: "Immediate negotiations with Vietnam."

In the future, the anti-war movement in France will certainly grow extensively. . . . The opinion of honest people in the world against French colonialist aggression will gradually isolate France in the interna-tional arena. . . . If France does not negotiate with us soon, these difficulties will grow to such an extent that France will be powerless to overcome them. Why? Because the more France fights Vietnam, the more she will suffer losses in manpower and material resources, the more hardships the French people will endure, the more the anti-war move-ment in France and the revolutionary movement in the French colonies will develop, and the more severely the democratic world will condemn French colonial policy.[63]

As if they had heeded Truong Chinh's warning, many a French politician, notably Pierre Mendès-France, a Radical Socialist leader, had, since 1950, urged large concessions to Ho Chi Minh.[64] Even conservative Premier Antoine Pinay undertook, in 1952, to explore the possibility of ending the war through negotiation with the Ho regime. To this end, he chose Prince Buu Hoi, a man whose impartiality could not be questioned either by the Right or by the Left. Although he had been a member of the DRV delegation at the Fontainebleau Conference in 1946, Buu Hoi later severed relations with the Ho government when the Viet Minh extremists gained the upper hand. The Pinay cabinet, however, collapsed before Buu Hoi could carry out the mission. In February 1953, at the request of the new Premier, René Mayer, the Prince, accompanied by Jacques Raphael-Leygues, a Radical Socialist, journeyed to Rangoon, Burma, where the DRV had maintained a diplomatic mission. Although Buu Hoi's message was acknowledged, no reply was given. Ho apparently was waiting for the reaction of the French High Command in Indochina to his incursion into Laos.

Meanwhile, Premier Joseph Laniel, a Conservative Independent, announced on July 3, 1953, that his government was prepared to "perfect" the independence of the three Associated States of Indochina in accordance with the Pau Agreements (signed in December, 1950, between France and the State of Vietnam, Cambodia, and Laos), and to discuss whatever problem might remain. Premier Laniel's announcement was received with skepticism in both Paris and Saigon. "We have granted Vietnam 'full independence' eighteen times since 1949," exclaimed the Radical Deputy François Mitterand. "Isn't it about time we did just once, but for good?"[65] Similarly, Bao Dai is reported to have complained in private: "What do they mean 'perfect'? What's the matter with the French—they're always giving us our independence. Can't they give it to us once and for all?"[66]

In any case, Bao Dai made preparations to go to Paris. The news that the Chief of State would again negotiate with the French caused the nationalists in the French-controlled area to demand unqualified independence for Vietnam. Ngo Dinh Nhu, a trade union leader and brother of future President Ngo Dinh Diem, organized an unofficial Congress for National Union and Peace, which met in Cholon on September 6. At the end of its two-day session, it passed a resolution calling for, among other things, unconditional independence for Vietnam and the immediate summoning of a national assembly.

The publicity given this Congress and the strong position it had adopted forced Bao Dai to convene an official one, purposedly to remove the impression of disunity on the nationalist side and to appoint delegates to take part in the forthcoming negotiations with France. On October 16, after tumultuous sessions, the Bao Dai-sponsored Congress, too, demanded a constitution and a national assembly elected by universal suffrage, and insisted on an independent Vietnam outside the French Union. The last part of the motion, however, was amended the next day to specify that Vietnam would not participate in "the French Union in its present form." In addition, the Congress refused to appoint any delegates to negotiate with France.

The Bao Dai Congress drew sharp reaction from the French government. On October 27, Premier Laniel, deploring the Vietnamese incident, stated that while France would "never abandon her friends . . . she would have no reason to prolong her sacrifices if . . . the significance of these sacrifices were misunderstood or betrayed," i.e., if the Associated States decided to leave the French Union. In an apparent warning to Bao Dai and invitation to Ho Chi Minh, Laniel expressed his government's readiness to negotiate a settlement, stressing that France did not fight the war for seven years for the sake of fighting. It was Ho, however, who did not want to negotiate, the Premier continued. It was Ho who had declared, on September 2, that only a complete Viet Minh victory would lead to peace.[67]

On the following day, while recommending that the armies of the Associated States be further developed, the Prime Minister again said that steps should be taken to negotiate a peaceful settlement of the Indochina problem.

During the first week of November, Laniel again emphasized that France was "ready to seize all occasions to make peace whether in Indochina or elsewhere," reiterating in the clearest and most categorical fashion that the conflict should not necessarily require a military solution. "No more than the Americans in Korea," the Premier stressed, "do we demand an unconditional surrender of the enemy in order to discuss with him. . . . If an honorable solution were in sight, either on the local or international level, France would be happy to welcome a diplomatic solution of the conflict."[68]

Since their hope for a military victory had vanished, most political leaders of France finally agreed that negotiation was the only way out of the Indochina quagmire. They disagreed, however, on the negotiation format. Should it be a bilateral Franco-Vietnamese parley, or an international conference in which the Big Powers would be called upon to play a conciliatory role? Since it was a question of France's grandeur and honor, the majority settled for the second alternative.

Having witnessed the debates in the French National Assembly and discussed the Indochina situation with various French officials and leaders, Sven Löfgen, the Paris-based correspondent for the Swedish paper *Expressen*, one day decided to make his contribution to international diplomacy. Through the DRV *chargé d'affaires* in Peking, Löfgen relayed a questionnaire to Ho Chi Minh on the war and the prospect of a settlement. No words came from the Viet Bac jungle. Then, on November 29, 1953, *Expressen* startled the world by publishing Ho's answers to the questions that had been submitted to him. The old guerilla said:

> If the French Government has drawn a lesson from the war they have been waging these last years and wants to negotiate an armistice in Vietnam and solve the Vietnam problem by peaceful means, the people and Government of the Democratic Republic of Vietnam are ready to meet this desire. . . .
>
> The French Government's sincere respect for the genuine independence of Vietnam must be the basis of the armistice.
>
> If there are neutral countries which try to speed up a cessation of hostilities in Vietnam by means of negotiations, they will be welcome. However, the negotiation for an armistice is mainly the concern of the Government of the Democratic Republic of Vietnam and the French Government.

Being a shrewd agitator, who seldom let an opportunity slip by without making a propaganda statement, Ho warned the French people against the sinister American imperialists:

> I have constantly showed my sympathy, affection, and respect for the French people and the French peace fighters. Today not only is the independence of Vietnam seriously jeopardized, but the independence of France is also gravely threatened. On the one hand, the U.S. imperialists egg on the French colonialists to continue and expand the aggressive war in Vietnam, thus weakening them more and more through fighting, in the hope of replacing France in Indochina; on the other, they oblige France to ratify the Eruopean defense treaty that is to revive German militarism.[69]

Ho was thus ready to talk peace. His position was reaffirmed again and again by the Viet Minh radio in the following weeks. Ho's statements should not have come as a surprise, however. Although many observers had thought that a continuation of the war would benefit Ho, the critical situation in Ho's country did not corroborate this belief. The war had taken its toll. Eight years of fighting had exhausted the DRV meager resources, devastated much of the country, drained the patience of the Vietnamese people who were longing for peace to improve their miserable lot, dampened the enthusiasm of the resistance fighters who had seen too many of their comrades fall in an increasingly demanding and seemingly endless war, and put a heavy strain on the malaria-afflicted Viet Minh leader. Furthermore, a cease-fire would provide Ho with an excellent opportunity to use his effective, well-entrenched organization to bring about a peaceful disintegration of the State of Vietnam.

In addition, both the Soviet Union and Communist China had been laying ground for peace talks in Indochina. Since the armistice in Korea, Moscow and Peking had taken a position clearly in favor of a peaceful settlement of the Indochinese problem. In their discussions of the Vietnam conflict, Soviet and Chinese radios frequently mentioned the possibility of an armistice on the Korean model. And on November 27, two days before Ho's replies to the *Expressen* questionnaire were published, the Soviet government had accepted a Western proposal, which had been made five months earlier, for a Big Four (France, Great Britain, the United States, and the Soviet Union) meeting to discuss German reunification and demilitarization, with the proviso that the Russian delegate would raise the question of a five-power conference, to which China would be invited, to settle the pending Asian problems.

Subsequently, at the Big Four meeting, which opened on January 25, 1954, in Berlin, the Soviet Foreign Minister, convinced that France was anxious to discuss a settlement of the Indochina conflict, urged France to stay out of the European Defense Community and to accept Communist China at the peace talks in return for the Soviet effort to arrange an armistice in Indochina. Although no decisions were reached on the German questions, the Big Four agreed to call a five-power conference in Geneva in April to discuss the Korea and Indochina problems.

Meanwhile in Paris, in answer to Ho's overture, Defense Minister René Pleven suggested that Alain Savary, a Socialist Deputy, establish contact with the Viet Minh. Savary agreed, on condition that the government support his effort. The Deputy's wish was soon satisfied by Premier Laniel, who, in the name of the French government, asked him to sound out Ho's intention. An obstacle, however, suddenly arose. Foreign Minister Georges Bidault, who had never concealed his dislike for the Ho regime, vetoed the project. "Ho Chi Minh is about to capitulate," confided Bidault to Savary, whom he received at the beginning of March after a delay of three months. "We are going to beat him. Don't strengthen him with that kind of contact."[70] By the time Laniel and Pleven prevailed upon the Foreign Minister to change his mind, it was already too late. The battle of Dienbienphu had begun. Savary's voyage abruptly ended in Moscow in April.

Ho's display of a readiness to negotiate was followed by a determined effort to strengthen his bargaining position. Convinced that his armies must score more decisive victories before he could dictate the peace terms, Ho ordered Giap to throw all available forces against the Expeditionary Corps. The French Commander-in-Chief, General Navarre, obligingly offered Giap an excellent target.

In view of the Viet Minh incursions into Laos early in 1953, and in view of the presence of Giap's divisions in Tonkin near the Laotian border, Navarre became increasingly worried that Giap would make deeper penetrations into the Lao kingdom when the rainy season was over. In Navarre's view, the defense of Laos was necessitated by two basic considerations: (*a*) A Viet Minh arrival in force on the Mekong would endanger central and southern Indochina, and (*b*) the Franco-Laotian Agreement of October 22, 1953, which provided for Laos' adherence to the French Union, imposed upon France the duty to protect that kingdom against the Viet Minh.

Since Laos could not be defended by a war of movement because of the nature of the terrain itself and of the lack of adaptation of the French forces, Navarre reasoned, its protection could be achieved through the establishment of fortified areas astride the Viet Minh route to the kingdom. While this method would not prevent light enemy units from roaming through the countryside, it would permit the French to control essential points and, consequently, prevent an outright Viet Minh invasion of Laos.[71] Thus, on November 20, the French Commander-in-Chief dropped several battalions of troops to seize and hold Dienbienphu, a saucer-like base inside the Viet Minh territory, 10 miles from the Laotian border and 170 miles from Hanoi. A complex of strongly defended areas was immediately built. The French garrison gradually increased until it numbered a little over 18,000.

According to Giap,

Dien Bien Phu was a very strongly fortified entrenched camp. But on the other hand, it was set up in a mountainous region, on ground which was advantageous to us, and decidedly disadvantageous to the enemy. Dien Bien Phu was, moreover, a completely isolated position, far away from all the enemy's bases. The only means of supplying Dien Bien Phu was by air. These circumstances could easily deprive the enemy of all initiative and force him on the defensive if attacked.[72]

However well entrenched it might appear, Dienbienphu was quite vulnerable to a Viet Minh attack, as Giap was to point out:

On our side, we had picked units of the regular army which we could concentrate to achieve supremacy in power. We could overcome all difficulties in solving the necessary tactical problems; we had, in addition, an immense rear, and the problem of supplying the front with food and ammunition, though very difficult, was not insoluble.[73]

What happened at Dienbienphu is history. Ho had to win since he was determined "to wipe out at all costs the whole enemy force" in the French fortress. This famous battle began on March 13 and ended on May 8, 1954, just one day before the armistice talks were to commence in Geneva. After fifty-five days and nights of ferocious fighting, the exhausted defenders surrendered. Over the corpses of Giap's death volunteers, who had thrown themselves into the mouths of the French guns until they were blown up to lie in piles on the ground, the surviving Viet Minh human waves advanced, and advanced, until they engulfed the French bastion.

What did Dienbienphu cost to both sides? The victors suffered 23,000 casualties, of whom 8,000 were killed. The vanquished lost 7,184 dead and wounded, in addition to the 11,000 survivors who were marched into captivity.

Thus ended Dienbienphu, the grave of France's colonial ambitions!

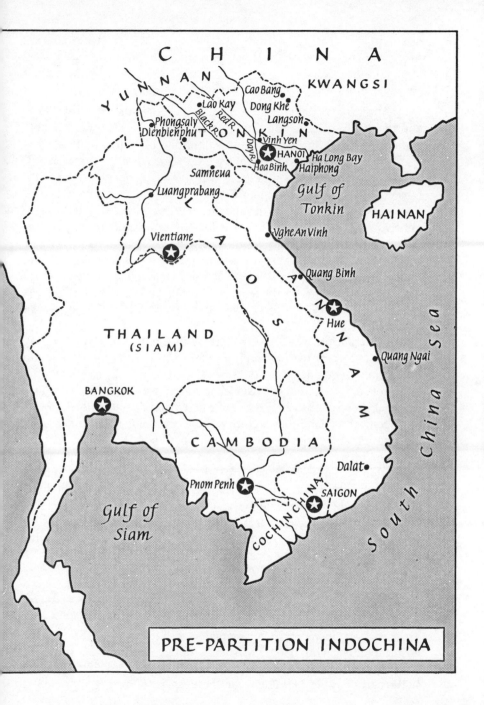

PRE-PARTITION INDOCHINA

The Victor

In April, 1954, delegates from nine states—France, Great Britain, the United States, the Soviet Union, the People's Republic of China, Ho Chi Minh's Democratic Republic of Vietnam, Bao Dai's State of Vietnam, Cambodia, and Laos[74]—arrived in the peaceful city of Geneva for a conference, which was to open on the 26th. Since the first part of the meeting dealt with the thorny problem of Korean reunification, the discussions on Indochina did not begin until May 8, twenty-four hours after the commandant of the besieged fortress of Dienbienphu, Brigadier General de Castries, radioed his last message to his commanding officer in Tonkin, Major General Cogny. "The end is approaching," said de Castries with resignation. "We will fight to the finish. We will destroy our cannons and radio equipment. Good bye, General. Long live France!"[75]

Ho's delegation was led by Pham Van Dong, the DRV Deputy Premier and Minister of Foreign Affairs, who had been the main Viet Minh negotiator at Fontainebleau in 1946. Throughout the Conference, co-chaired by Soviet Foreign Minister Molotov and British Foreign Minister Eden, Dong was to display the same intransigence and diplomatic ability, which had not been affected by eight years of deprivation in the inhospitable Viet Bac jungle. As Ho had intended, the appearance of Dong as head of the DRV delegation was a bad portent for the French. The inflexible man of 1946, whom the French had to contend with, now approached the conference table as a hardened victor. And to their greater dismay, the charming goateed visitor in Paris in 1946, the conciliatory leader who had signed the September, 1946, *modus vivendi* with France, was not here, in Geneva!

Besides the Viet Minh victories on the battlefield, Ho was to enjoy another advantage over his opponent: disunity in the French camp. While in the United States, President Eisenhower and an overwhelming majority of Senators of both parties were deadset against American involvement in a colonial war, Secretary of State John Foster Dulles, who had consistently opposed any concessions to Asian Communism, advocated the use of force to deny Ho a victory. In the early days of Dienbienphu, the desperate French approached the United States for help. During his visit to Washington on March 20, 1954, General Paul Ely, the French chief of staff, gloomily told his American counterpart, Admiral Arthur Radford, of the possibility of a French defeat at Dienbienphu and of its disastrous consequences in Indochina. Dulles assured Ely that American air power would be brought in to prevent such eventuality. Thus assured, General Ely reported to his government about the American promise. Dulles, however, soon found himself in a dilemma. Both the President and the Senate opposed his plan. In an attempt to extricate himself from such an untenable position, Dulles proposed that the United States and Great Britain take "united action" against Asian Communism, knowing that Prime Minister Churchill would veto the idea. Subsequently, in answer to an urgent plea by the French for help, Dulles informed them that the United States would intervene in Indochina only if the British government approved the "united action" plan. This unfortunate episode put a severe strain on the relations between Washington, Paris, and London, preventing them from presenting a united stand in Geneva.

Displaying an obvious lack of enthusiasm for the Conference, Dulles appointed his Under Secretary of State Bedell Smith to head the American delegation, and left Geneva for Washington on May 5, three days before the discussions on Indochina were scheduled to begin. During his stay in the Swiss city, he completely ignored Chou En-lai, the Communist Chinese Premier and Minister of Foreign Affairs. Similarly, French Foreign Minister Bidault, whose dislike for the Viet Minh had blinded him to the Indochinese realities, acted as if Pham Van Dong did not exist, refusing to have any contact with Ho's chief delegate. While half-heartedly presenting his government's plan, he rejected the Dong proposal as soon as it was made. British Secretary Eden, who had opposed Dulles' plan for "united action" against the Communists "in advance of the results of Geneva," seemed to be the only Western head of delegation who was really interested in a successful conference.

In the face of Western disunity, the Communists appeared closely united. Long before the Conference opened, Moscow, Peking, and the DRV had agreed on the objectives to be reached and the strategy to be followed at Geneva. Throughout the Conference, Molotov maintained firm control over the Communist delegations.

At the opening session, after mentioning the civilizing mission of France in Indochina and giving a distorted interpretation of the war, Bidault proposed a plan that was strictly military in nature, leaving untouched the political questions that were the roots of the conflict. It called for the cessation of all hostilities in Indochina and for the withdrawal of Viet Minh troops from Laos and Cambodia. As to the legitimate authority, Bidault stressed, France recognized only the State of Vietnam. It was up to the government of that state to find a solution to its political problems.

Showing no emotion, except boredom, Pham Van Dong listened to the French speech. When his turn came, the DRV Foreign Minister, without reference to Bidault's statements, insisted, in a brusque voice, that the Khmer and Pathet Lao "Resistance Governments," which Ho had helped create in 1950, should be invited to participate in the work of the Conference, on the ground that these "governments" had "liberated" vast areas of Cambodia and Laos and "exerted all their efforts in creating a democratic power and in raising the living standard of the population in the liberated areas."[76]

"Are we going to discuss the admission of phantom governments?" asked the French Foreign Minister, whose patience seemed to run out. "Mr. Bidault has used the same terms in the past to refer to the Government of the Democratic Republic of Vietnam," Dong curtly retorted.

Thereupon, Sam Sary, the representative of the Royal Cambodian government, intervened. Denying knowledge of a "Free Khmer Government," and of the vast territories it had allegedly liberated, Sary emphasized that such governments existed only in the imagination of the Ministers of the Eastern bloc. And to ridicule Dong's claim, he asked Molotov, the co-chairman of the Conference, whether the Soviet Minister would agree to the participation, in an international meeting, of a representative of the Polish government in London.

In his turn, Sanakikone, the head of the Laotian delegation, rejected the Viet Minh contention. Stressing that the Lao Issara movement had been dissolved in October, 1949, and that the so-called Pathet Lao, successors to the Lao Issara and led by expatriate Prince Souphanouvong, represented nothing, Sananikone said:

Mr. Pham Van Dong has told us that a "free Lao administration" was being installed in the occupied zones. For the good of the inhabitants, I wish it were so. But alas, that is far from being the case. The so-called Government does not exist apart from the Viet Minh, and has no seat other than the Viet Minh military command posts.[77]

Undaunted by the ridicule of his extravagant demands, Dong refused to yield. Only after both Molotov and Chou En-lai had applied pressure on him did Ho's chief delegate drop his demand and thus avert a deadlock at the Conference.

On May 10, following a violent tirade against American intervention in Indochina, the Viet Minh Foreign Minister unveiled his government's plan for a cease-fire. It included recognition by France of the independence and territorial integrity of the DRV, the Khmer and Pathet Lao states, an agreement for the withdrawal of foreign troops from the three states, free general elections under the supervision of local "consultative committees," a DRV declaration of its willingness to consider the question of membership in the French Union, recognition by the DRV, Laos, and Cambodia of French economic and cultural interests in Indochina, prohibition against persecution of persons who had collaborated with either party during the war, and exchange of prisoners of war.

Dong's proposal provoked immediate negative reaction from Bidault. In an ensuing press conference, the French Foreign Minister's spokesman noted that the Viet Minh were less interested in a cease-fire than in the total conquest of Indochina, and that, if the Dong plan went through, all three Indochinese states would be ruled by Communist governments. This apparent rejection of the Viet Minh formula caused a cabinet crisis in Paris. A series of interpellations took place in the National Assembly. The Laniel government, however, was saved by a majority of two votes.

Meanwhile, Bao Dai found himself in a precarious situation. In the face of the Viet Minh growing strength and the vanishing French influence, his government would have to accept whatever compromise the French might decide to make. Painfully aware that he was on his own from then onward, the Chief of State tried to save the nationalist cause as best as he could. On May 12, his Foreign Minister Nguyen Quoc Dinh, sensing that an agreement was in the making to divide Vietnam, expressed strong opposition to any proposal that contemplated either a permanent or temporary, *de facto* or *de jure* partition of the country. Dinh also specified that any settlement must provide for international supervision of the execution of the cease-fire terms, recognition of the state headed by Bao Dai as the only one qualified to speak for Vietnam, and general elections under United Nations auspices. The Dinh plan, of course, was not well received, even by the French, who were then interested only in a cease-fire.

The Conference seemed to come to a standstill. Bidault's persistent refusal to have contact with Pham Van Dong greatly irritated Molotov. On June 8, the Soviet Minister's anger exploded in the open. In an obvious attempt to bring down the Laniel government and, consequently, effect the recall of Bidault, Molotov, who was aware of the strong popular desire in France for an end to the war, launched a virulent attack on the French Foreign Minister, accusing him of deliberately attempting to delay a settlement. Molotov's attempt was well rewarded. On June 12, the Laniel government fell.

Two days following the Soviet Minister's invective, and while Bidault was in Paris, the Geneva Conference reached the turning point. In a secret meeting between the French and Viet Minh military delegates in the evening of June 10, Ta Quang Buu, the DRV Vice-Minister of Defense, was asked by his French interlocutors, General Delteil and Colonel de Brebisson, to clarify certain statements by Pham Van Dong on May 25, namely, the term "exchange of territories." It implied a provisional partition of Vietnam pending a general election to reunify the country, explained Buu. As soon as the meeting was over, General Delteil called on Frédéric-Dupont, Minister for the Associated States, and Jean Chauvel, French ambassador to Switzerland, both members of the French delegation in Geneva, to inform them of the important Viet Minh message. Paris was immediately alerted of the latest development.

In France, in the meantime, Pierre Mendès-France, the Radical Socialist who had, since 1950, advocated major concessions to Ho Chi Minh, was asked by President René Coty to form a new cabinet. "I am ready to resign," said Mendès-France on June 17, when he presented his government to the National Assembly, "if by July 20, I have not obtained a cease-fire in Indochina." It appeared foolhardy

for a Prime Minister of France to make such a statement so soon
after Dienbienphu, unless he was prepared to surrender unconditionally to the Viet Minh. "How could he expect to settle an eight-
year-old war in a month? Why should he tie his own hands in the
negotiations he was going to conduct with Pham Van Dong?", the
puzzled French people worriedly asked themselves. Mendès-France,
however, seemed quite confident. His confidence in his ability, or
his determination, to end the Indochina war might be attributed to
two main factors: (*a*) aware of the Viet Minh partition plan,
which had been communicated to him,[78] he was willing to negotiate on that basis, and (*b*) in view of Molotov's repeated infer-
ences that an armistice in Indochina could be arranged in exchange
for a French promise to stay out of the European Defense Community (EDC), there is reason to believe that Mendès-France, a well-
known opponent of the EDC, under whose premiership the Treaty
of Paris was to be rejected by the French National Assembly by a
single vote on August 30, 1954, decided to make a deal with his
Soviet counterpart.

As a warning to Molotov and his Viet Minh comrades to honor
the terms of the bargain, Mendès-France also announced in the
National Assembly that if he failed at Geneva, he would, before
resigning, request the dispatch of draftees to Indochina. To make
good his threat, the new Premier ordered the French troops stationed in Germany to be inoculated against yellow fever in preparation for duties in Indochina.[79]

With such conviction, Mendès-France left for Geneva, acting
as his own Foreign Minister. The congenial French Premier imme-
diately established contact with Pham Van Dong and Chou En-lai.
The negotiations proceeded smoothly until, suddenly, Ho's chief
delegate stalled. In return for abandoning the "Khmer Resistance
Government," Dong insisted that France recognize the "Pathet
Lao Government." Unable to move the DRV Foreign Minister,
Mendès-France sought help from the suave Chou En-lai.

It may be of interest to note that early in July, during the recess of
the Conference, Chou, who had engaged in serious discussions
with Mendès-France on June 23, left for a tour in Asia to consult
with such Asian leaders as India's Nehru, Burma's U Nu, and, of
course, Ho Chi Minh. During their three-day meeting (July 3–5) on
the Sino-Vietnamese border, Chou, in addition to informing Ho of

the French position, discussed the terms of a settlement which Molotov and he himself had considered acceptable.

This Sino-Viet Minh consultation had been arranged by the Chinese Premier and Foreign Minister, who was to persuade the old guerilla to postpone his ambitious plan for Vietnam, Laos, and Cambodia until a later date. Chou, actually, had been urged by Molotov, whose primary concern was a French guarantee to stay out of the EDC in exchange for a Soviet-arranged settlement of the Indochina conflict, to have a conference with Ho. In view of Mendès-France's proposal in the French National Assembly for a more vigorous pursuance of the war should the negotiations fail, and in view of Dulles' rigid stand on Indochina, Molotov argued, an unyielding Viet Minh attitude would give the United States a pretext to intervene in the war. Although convinced that Ho was in a position to demand more than what Molotov thought possible, Chou obliging accepted the Soviet view, which, coincidentally, also served the Chinese interest. While Peking wished to Communize all three Indochinese states and, eventually, Southeast Asia, it dreaded the prospect of an Indochina ruled by the resourceful Vietnamese Communists, who would be a certain threat to China's hegemony in the area. Furthermore, a Chinese refusal to acquiesce in the Soviet view would very likely lead Moscow to refuse technical and economic aid, which Peking needed to implement its first Five Year Plan. Chou En-lai, therefore, did not undertake this mission without enthusiasm.

As his regime was indebted to China for military and technical aid, which had been a main factor in the Viet Minh victories over the French, and as Chou promised further Chinese support for his cause, Ho had no choice but to agree to the Peking Prime Minister's suggestions. The joint communiqué issued at the end of their meeting merely stated that the two leaders had had a full exchange of views on the war and the Geneva Conference.[80]

Understandably, Ho, who had set out to settle the conflict on his own terms without making significant concessions, resented this Soviet-Chinese interference. "A number of members of the Viet Minh delegation," wrote *The New York Times* correspondent Tillman Durdin, "have openly declared Chinese and Molotov pressure forced them to accept less than they rightfully should have obtained."[81] Ho would have liked to prolong the Geneva Conference. In another month, his armies would have scored more victories and brought almost the entire country as well as Laos and Cambodia under Viet Minh control and influence. In any case, Ho must have said to himself as he had told Sainteny after the signing of the March 6, 1946, Accord: "I am not happy for basically it is you who have won. . . . I wanted more than that. . . . Anyway, I understand that you cannot have everything in one day."

Thus, with active Soviet and Chinese assistance, Mendès-France delivered his promise of obtaining peace in a month. In a "clearance sale," the French Premier hurriedly disposed of Indochina. On July 20, three separate cease-fires were signed by Brigadier General Dalteil, on behalf of the Commander in Chief of the French Forces in Indochina, and the Viet Minh Vice-Minister of Defense, Ta Quang Buu, on behalf of the "Commander in Chief of the Units of the Khmer Resistance Forces" and the Commander in Chief of the Vietnam People's Army. These were the only documents signed at Geneva. The Agreement on the Cessation of Hostilities in Vietnam provided for the provisional partition of the country along the 17th parallel, with Ho controlling the North and Bao Dai the South, the regrouping of the regular armed forces in the respective zones, and an International Control Commission (ICC), composed of representatives of India (chairman), Canada, and Poland, to supervise the execution of the cease-fire.

Another document, dated July 21, 1954, and called Final Declaration, was merely "noted" by the participants in the Conference. Stating that the military demarcation line was only provisional and should not be construed as a political or territorial boundary, it provided for general elections to be held in July, 1956, under the supervision of the ICC with consultations "to be held on this subject between the competent representative authorities of the two zones from 20 July 1950 onwards."

Thus, Ho obtained half of Vietnam, a promise of a general election to reunify the country, and a provision recognizing the right of the Pathet Lao fighting units to regroup in the provinces of Phongsaly and Samneua, "pending a political settlement."

In the face of the French and Communist decision to divide the country, Tran Van Do, who had succeeded Nguyen Quoc Dinh as Foreign Minister of the State of Vietnam following the appointment of Premier Ngo Dinh Diem, condemned the armistice as "catastrophic and immoral," and stated that his government reserved "complete freedom of action to guarantee the sacred right of the Vietnamese people to territorial unity, national independence and freedom."[82]

Dissociating itself from the Agreements, the United States issued a unilateral declaration stressing that it would "refrain from the threat or use of force to disturb them," and would "view any renewal of aggression in violation of the . . . agreements with grave concern and as seriously threatening international peace and security." And

In the case of nations now divided against their will, we shall continue to seek to achieve unity through free elections supervised by the United Nations to insure that they are conducted fairly.[83]

In the final analysis, only Ho Chi Minh won. He obtained the departure of the French from Indochina.

In his report to the Vietnamese people on the day following the Final Declaration, Ho was able to say:

The Geneva Conference has come to an end. It is a great victory to our diplomacy. . . .

This great victory is also due to the support given us in our just struggle by the peoples of our brother countries, by the French people, and by the peace-loving people of the world.

Thanks to these victories and the efforts made by the delegation of the Soviet Union at the Berlin Conference, negotiations were opened between our country and France at the Geneva Conference. At this conference, the struggle of our delegation and the assistance given by the delegations of the Soviet Union and China have ended in a great victory for us. The French Government has recognized the independence, sovereignty, unity, and territorial integrity of our country, it has agreed to withdraw French troops from our country, etc.

Sounding a martial note, the victorious guerilla issued another call to arms:

From now on, we must make very effort to consolidate peace, and achieve reunification, independence, and democracy throughout our country. . . .

North, Central, and South Vietnam are territories of ours. Our country will certainly be united, our entire people will surely be liberated. . . .

The struggle to consolidate peace and achieve reunification, independence, and democracy is also a long and hard struggle. . . .

I call on all our compatriots, armymen, and cadres to follow strictly the lines and policies laid down by the Party and the Government, to struggle for the consolidation of peace and the achievement of national reunification, independence, and democracy throughout the country.[84]

The last French soldier left Hanoi on October 9, 1954. On the following day, the VPA (Vietnam People's Army) divisions that had fought at Dienbienphu triumphantly entered the capital to begin an impressive victory parade. Hanoi was in the true sense of the word a red city. It was decorated with innumerable gold-starred red flags and mostly red banners welcoming the returning heroes. The people's enthusiasm was both sincere and simulated. While young children, wives, mothers and fathers had reason to be happy to see their brothers, fathers, husbands, and sons come back safe and sound from the battlefield, intellectuals, merchants, and people of means who had not been able to decide whether or not they should move to the South had mixed feelings. Although aware of the ways in which Communists treated nonproletarian classes, they were reluctant to give up their possessions which they had labored so long and so hard to acquire. They also entertained the illusion that if they shouted their support and enthusiasm for the Ho regime they would be tolerated. No matter how he felt, however, almost everyone in Hanoi was curious to have a glimpse of the men who had conquered the French at Dienbienphu. Almost everyone was waving flags and brought flowers for the troops. These proud men sat in neat rows in powerful trucks or marched "with disciplined swinging steps, battle-hardened veterans, but not hardened enough to prevent tears from rolling down their cheeks at the sight of a beloved face not seen for eight years, the voice of a mother, father, wife or child in a gasping shout of recognition as the trucks and columns of marching men swept on."[85] To the onlookers it was indeed an impressive hero's welcome.

Finally, on October 15, almost three months after the signing of the armistice in Geneva, Ho, the Victorious Guerilla Leader, quietly reentered Hanoi. No big reception. No tumultuous cheering. Since his fighting men had already received a well-deserved welcome, Ho had ordered that official victory celebrations be postponed until the

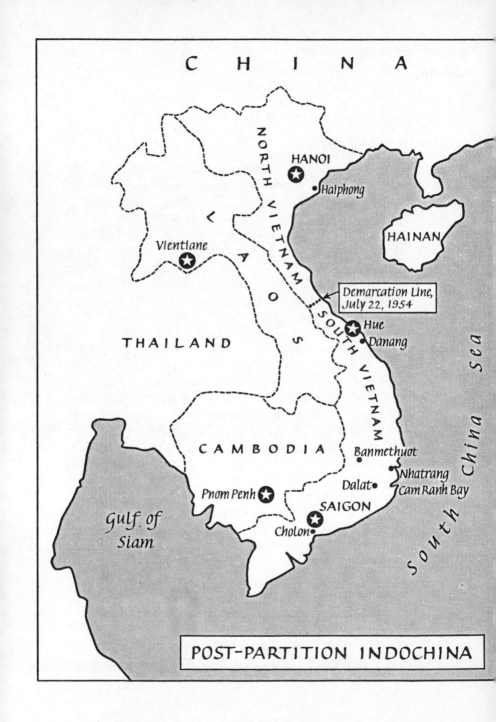

C H I N A

NORTH VIETNAM

HANOI

Haiphong

Vientiane

L A O S

HAINAN

THAILAND

Demarcation Line,
July 22, 1954

Hue
Danang

SOUTH VIETNAM

CAMBODIA

Banmethuot

Nhatrang
Cam Ranh Bay

Dalat

Pnom Penh

SAIGON

Cholon

Gulf of
Siam

South China Sea

POST-PARTITION INDOCHINA

following New Year's Day.'In his usual simplicity, the old revolutionary returned to the capital, not in a shiny limousine, but in an old French army truck which the VPA had captured from the enemy. Although his hair was a bit thinner and his cheeks paler, his eyes were still amazingly lively and his military tunic still wrinkled. And he still looked awkward before a crowd. Smiling timidly, the old fighter whose legend had fired the imagination of millions of people in various lands greeted members of the International Control Commission, "discussed the Geneva settlement over tea at a long table outdoors, and then made a brief appearance before a gathering of veteran co-workers and friends. Popping almost coyly from behind a curtain in a large reception hall, Ho smiled and reminded his audience: 'I am an old guerilla fighter, you know.' "[86]

But his guerilla days were over. From now on, Ho Chi Minh, President of the Democratic Republic of Vietnam, would not have to leave Hanoi for the inhospitable jungle again!

7 ☆ *Chairman Ho Against the United States*

~~~~~~

ALTHOUGH THE FRENCH, due to their smarting defeats on the battle-field and mounting opposition to the war at home, were most eager to extricate themselves from the Indochina quagmire, the Viet Minh, in spite of their military victories but in view of Soviet and Chinese pressure, had to content themselves with considerably less than what they had expected. The result, however, was a compromise, which was quite favorable to Ho's DRV but in which Bao Dai's State of Vietnam and the United States refused to acquiesce. While Ho failed in his attempt to impose his protégés, the Pathet Lao and Khmer "Resistance Governments," on the Geneva con-ferees, he won a major concession that permitted the Pathet Lao forces to regroup, pending a political settlement, in Phongsaly and Samneua, the two northeastern provinces of Laos contiguous to China and North Vietnam. Thus, the Pathat Lao possession of Samneua, which the Vie Minh had handed over to Souphanouvong in 1953, was sanctioned by the Geneva Conference. As regards Vietnam, Ho obtained the partition of the country and a promise of "free general elections" to reunify it.

The Geneva Agreements of 1954

The Geneva Accords of 1954, which included three cease-fire agreements—one for each Indochinese state—and a Final Declaration, was a peculiar diplomatic document. Of the three Agreements on the Cessation of Hostilities, the one on Vietnam was signed by the DRV Vice-Minister of Defense Ta Quang Buu, on behalf of the Commander-in-Chief of the VPA and Brigadier General Delteil representing the Commander-in-Chief of the French Union Forces in Indochina; the one on Cambodia also signed by Ta Quang Buu, on behalf of the Commander-in-Chief of the Khmer Resistance Forces, the Commander-in-Chief of the Vietnamese Military Units, and General Nhiek Tioulong representing the Commander-in-Chief of the Khmer National Armed Forces; the third on Laos signed by Ta Quang Buu on behalf of the Fighting Units of the Pathet Lao, the Commander-in-Chief of the VPA, and General Delteil representing the Commander-in-Chief of the French Union Forces! Although they decided the fate of the State of Vietnam, which opposed them, and Laos, representatives of their governments were not asked to sign the documents.

The validity of the Accord on Vietnam, in particular, was open to question from the very beginning. The delegation of the State of Vietnam in Geneva registered its "solemn protests" against (*a*) the armistice agreement which had been concluded in haste between "the French and Viet Minh High Commands," and which contained many provisions of a nature to "compromise the political future of the Vietnamese people," (*b*) the fact that it abandoned to the Viet Minh certain areas which it considered essential for the defense of Vietnam against further Communist aggression, (*c*) the French High Command's decision, without consultation with the State of Vietnam, to fix the date of future elections, and (*d*) "the manner in which the armistice has been concluded and the conditions of the armistice which took no account of the aspirations of the Vietnamese people." In addition, it "reserved," as previously noted, "complete freedom of action to guarantee the sacred right of the Vietnamese people to territorial unity, national independence and freedom." On July 22, Premier Ngo Dinh Diem also ordered all flags to be flown at half mast for three days in protest against the "catastrophic and immoral" accords.

Under the Agreement on the Cessation of Hostilities in Vietnam, withdrawals of the military forces, equipment, and supplies to the respective zones along the 17th parallel were to be completed within 300 days without hindrance, destruction or sabotage of any public property, injury to the life and property of the civil population, or interference in local civil administration (Article 15). Both parties pledged to refrain from reprisals and discrimination against persons or organization on account of their activities during the hostilities, guarantee their "democratic liberties," and recognize the right of civilians to choose, within a period of 300 days, up to May 18, 1955,[1] the zone in which they wished to live (Article 14). While prohibiting "the introduction into Vietnam of any troop reinforcements and additional military personnel (Article 16) and the establishment of new military bases (Article 18) and the maintenance of foreign-controlled based (Article 19)," the Agreement permitted, under inspection, the rotation of military units (Article 16a) and the replacement of destroyed, damaged, or worn-out war material, arms, and munitions (Article 17b). An International Control Commission (ICC), composed of representatives of India (chairman), Canada, and Poland, was set up to supervise the execution of the cease-fire. While it had the power to decide certain issues by majority vote (Article 41), the Commission's decisions on "questions concerning violations, or threats of violations, which might lead to a resumption of hostilities . . . must be unanimous" (Article 42). Thus the most important clause of the Agreement, the one requiring unanimity on the part of the ICC in regard to violations or threats of violations, had the immediate effect of nullifying the entire document. It was indeed wishful thinking to expect Canada (Western), Poland (Communist), and India (neutralist) to agree unanimously on such vital issues of Communist-nationalist confrontation in Vietnam. Only her eagerness to extricate herself from an untenable position and her awareness that she would not be involved in any further negotiation on Vietnam could have prompted France to acquiesce in such an extravagant Viet Minh demand.

Besides taking "note" of the cease-fire agreements, the Final Declaration stressed that "the military demarcation line is provisional and should not in any way be interpreted as constituting a political or territorial boundary." With reference to the political question, which had been the main cause of the war, the Declaration gave an extremely confusing explanation:

The Conference declares that, so far as Vietnam is concerned, the settlement of political problems, effected on the basis of respect for the principles of independence, unity and territorial integrity, shall permit the Vietnamese people to enjoy the fundamental freedoms, guaranteed by democratic institutions established as a result of free general elections by secret ballot. In order to ensure that sufficient progress in the restoration of peace has been made, and that all the necessary conditions obtain for free expression of the national will, general elections shall be held in July 1956, under the supervision of an international commission composed of representatives of the Member States of the International Supervisory Commission [Paragraph 7].

The second part of this statement defies any logic. The Conference did not settle the political question; it merely visualized a solution through elections "in order to ensure that sufficient progress in the restoration of peace has been made. . . ." There would be no reason to assume that the participants at Geneva really believed there would be free elections in a Communist-controlled country, in this case, in the Vietnamese territory north of the demarcation line, or gave much thought to the fact that the partition of Vietnam along the 17th parallel gave Ho a decisive advantage in any elections. There were 15 million people in the North as against 12 million in the South.

In the final analysis, the Geneva Agreements were definitely advantageous to the Ho regime. It was Mendès-France himself, the man who had negotiated the Franco-Viet Minh settlement, who admitted it with considerable candor. "I want no one to have any illusions about the contents of the Accords that were just signed in Geneva," said the French Premier on July 22, 1954, when he represented the document to the French National Assembly. "Much of the text is cruel because it confirms facts that are cruel. It could not have been otherwise."[2]

As Mendès-France made that sobering remark to his fellow legislators, Ho called on his people, soldiers, and cadres from North to South to "make every effort to consolidate peace and achieve national reunification, independence, and democracy" throughout the country. Ho immediately set his plan in motion. In contravention of the cease-fire accord, which required the withdrawal of all military equipment and supplies within 300 days, the Viet Minh, upon their departure for the North, left behind an estimated 10,000 guerillas and cadres and large hidden ammunition dumps and arms depots. The Viet Minh cadres were to organize in 1955 the "Army of Liberation" and carry on their kidnapping, terror, and guerilla operations against the Saigon government.

Upon the French High Command's complaint that the Viet Minh arms caches had been left behind expressly for subversive purposes, the ineffectual ICC, which had been marred from the beginning by disagreements between the Canadian, Indian, and Polish members, visited seven depots that had been discovered in the northern province of Quang Tri. The Commission, however, did not take any action. According to a former Public Relations Officer of the ICC, B. S. Murti, the local authorities failed to prove to the Commission's satisfaction that the war material had been left by the VPA "with specific subversive intentions."[3] It is difficult to understand the ICC insistence on that kind of evidence. The Commission should, at least, have requested an explanation from the VPA High Command. Following this incident, added Murti, the French military authorities, feeling that further investigations in other provinces of similar charges would serve no useful purposes, decided to drop their complaints.

Although pledged to permit and help the people to choose their zone of residence within a period of 300 days, Ho made every attempt to prevent and punish those who sought to leave the DRV. On complaints about obstacles to free movement from North to South, the ICC sent inspection teams to various areas and found that (*a*) the "machinery giving permits and transport facilities were not adequate to deal with the situation," (*b*) the local authorities in the DRV were ineffective in implementing the provisions of the Geneva Accords pertaining to freedom of movement, (*c*) contrary to the Agreements, which permitted civilians to move freely any time to either zone within a 300-day interval, many applications had been rejected simply because the applicants did not give the date of their departure, (*d*) the billeting of VPA troops on the villagers to "advise" them not to go South, which had led to armed clashes causing loss of lives, was not persuasion as claimed by the DRV government but pressure against the people, and (*e*) the implementation of Article 14d (free choice of zone of residence) in the Red River Delta, the Nghe An (Ho's native province), and Ha Tinh provinces were "not very satisfactory."[4]

In spite of Ho's unscrupulous attempts to stop the mass exodus from the DRV, nearly 900,000 of whom 500,000 were Catholic, had left his zone by July 25, 1955, in contrast to approximately 80,000 guerillas and their dependents who had departed for the North.

Both the DRV and the State of Vietnam were guilty of contravening the section dealing with reprisals and discrimination against former enemy supporters or combatants. The bitterness and distrust engendered by eight years of war could not be easily overcome. In the North, suspected or actual former collaborators of the French or the Bao Dai government and individuals who had opposed Communism were arrested, reeducated, or simply eliminated, while in the South former VPA cadres and resistance workers were arrested and detained without trial.

Ho had begun to have some misgivings about holding elections since the signing of the cease-fire agreements. Convinced that he would win as he had in January, 1946, when the first national election was held in Vietnam, he had demanded at Geneva that elections should take place within a few months after the cessation of hostilities. He wanted to exploit the chaotic conditions in the South where, he thought, the Bao Dai government would not have sufficient time to establish itself or would be strong enough to assert its independence from the French and thus would be a very vulnerable target for Viet Minh attacks. As the symbol of Vietnamese resistance to and victory over France, the DRV government would be more appealing to Vietnamese throughout the country, Ho reasoned. However, the State of Vietnam's demand for free elections under United Nations auspices, its subsequent condemnation of the Geneva Agreements in which it had not taken part, and its insistence on "complete freedom of action to guarantee the sacred right of the Vietnamese people to territorial unity, national independence and freedom" gave Ho deep concern. The exclusion of the State of Vietnam from the cease-fire negotiations, a decision which Ho had forced upon the French, was not a Viet Minh diplomatic victory as Ho had thought but a serious mistake. Though it proved, as the Viet Minh chief had intended, that there were only two parties involved in the Indochina conflict, France and the Ho-led DRV, it gave the State of Vietnam a legitimate excuse not to implement the Geneva Agreements. Aware of the stubbornness and reputation of Premier Ngo Dinh Diem, whom he had met and tried in vain to bring into his government in 1946, Ho became increasingly apprehensive that in two years Diem might succeed in building an effective government and obtaining the departure of the French from South Vietnam. More importantly, the Saigon Premier, in view of his well-known anti-French and anti-Communist position, would undoubtedly receive considerable support from Washington. On the very day of the Final Declaration of the Geneva Conference, President Eisenhower in effect had emphatically stated that

the United States has not itself been a party or bound by the decisions taken by the Conference, but it is our hope that it will lead to the establishment of peace consistent with the rights and the needs of the countries concerned. The agreement contains features which we do not like, but a great deal depends on how they work in practice.

. . . the United States will not use force to disturb the settlement. We also say that any renewal of Communist aggression would be viewed by us as a matter of grave concern. . . .

The United States is actively pursuing discussions with other free nations with a view to the rapid organization of a collective defense in Southeast Asia in order to prevent further direct or indirect Communist aggression in that general area.[5]

Therefore, Ho began to make preparations to assure himself of a victory in 1956 by ordering measures designed to sap the State of Vietnam.

Ho and the U.S. Imperialists

The United States of America are a Republic which has no territorial interests in this country. They have paid the greatest contributions to the Vietnamese fight against fascist Japan, our enemy, and so the Great American Republic is a good friend of ours.

Statement by Vo Nguyen Giap,
Ho's Minister of Interior, on
Independence Day, September 2, 1945

To achieve national reunification, independence, and democracy throughout the country, we must first of all preserve and strengthen peace. . . . We must unite in a monolithic bloc against the maneuvers of peace wreckers, the U.S. imperialists . . . and their henchmen.

Statement by Ho Chi Minh on
Independence Day, September 2, 1954

The above statements reflected Ho's changing attitude toward the United States. Within an interval of nine years, Ho had, at least in appearance, changed from an ardent advocate of friendship with the United States to a bitter enemy of America. The revolutionary of 1945, who pretended to be a pure nationalist, needed American support for international recognition while the conqueror of the French in 1954, a professed Communist, not only resented American assistance to the French during the Indochina war, but also had little sympathy for the leading exponent of a system which Marx had condemned.

Secretary of State Dulles' proposal for "united action" greatly disturbed Ho. It was this threat of American intervention that Molotov used to pressure Ho to settle for less than what he had expected. While Pham Van Dong dictated the Viet Minh terms to Mendès-France in Geneva, Ho, condemning American interference, said on July 15, 1954:

With the coming of the Geneva Conference and faced with our victory of Dienbienphu the United States plotted to issue a "joint communiqué" with France, Britain and other countries to threaten China, charging it with intervention in the Indochina war. The move has come to grief owing to the opposition of Britain and other countries. Then the Americans proposed a "joint action" to save France at Dienbienphu but Britain and other countries again disagreed, and this scheme, too, failed. They used every means to prevent the holding of the Geneva Conference to wreck peace. Despite the departure of the U.S. Secretary of State the work of the Conference continued and has brought some results.

Referring to the U.S. plan to use "Asians to fight Asians," Ho continued:

For all its [sic] setbacks, the Americans still prove to be obdurate and are speeding up the formation of the S.E.A.T.O. Their failure means success for our camp. U.S. imperialism is the main enemy of world peace, consequently we must muster our forces to oppose it.[6]

Ho's reaction to American policies in the aftermath of the Geneva Conference was conditioned by his interpretation of Washington's intention:

After the Dienbienphu Campaign the U.S. intention and plan for intervention have also undergone changes towards protracting and internationalizing the Indochina War, sabotaging the Geneva Conference, ousting the French by every means, whereby to occupy Vietnam, Cambodia and Laos, enslave the people of these countries, and create tension in the world situation.

Therefore the U.S. imperialists have become not only the enemy of the world peoples but also, gradually, the main and direct enemy of the Vietnamese, Cambodian and Lao peoples.[7]

Ho's open break with Washington had actually come before both the Geneva Conference and Dulles's proposal for "united action" against the Viet Minh. Following the proclamation of the People's Republic in Peking on October 1, 1949, Ho, who had diligently tried to wear his nationalist mask, succumbed to the mounting pressure of the extremist members of the Tong Bo, then openly declared his allegiance to international Communism. This was indeed a significant move since Ho had, as late as March, 1949, vehemently denounced the charge that his government was Communist-dominated as pure French imperialist fabrication.[8]

Subsequently, in answer to Ho's announcement on January 14, 1950, of his readiness to establish diplomatic relations with all states on the basis of equality, mutual respect for independence, and territorial integrity, the People's Republic of China, on January 18, recognized the DRV in the Viet Bac jungle as "the legal government representing the will of the Vietnamese people."[9] Similarly, on January 30, the Soviet Union announced its decision to establish diplomatic relations with the Ho regime on the ground that it represented "the overwhelming majority of the population of the country."[10] North Korea and the East European states soon followed suit. Ho's DRV had, at last, cast its lot with the camp of the people's democracies.

Having shed his nationalist pretense, Ho began his verbal attack on the United States. On May 8, 1950, Washington

convinced that neither national independence nor democratic evolution exist in any area dominated by Soviet imperialism, considers the situation [in Indochina] to be such as to warrant its according economic aid and military equipment to the Associated States of Indochina, and to France in order to assist them in restoring peaceful and democratic development.[11]

Ho immediately condemned this "direct" American intervention in Vietnam, declaring that the Vietnamese from then onward had to face two opponents, the "French bandits" and the "American interventionists."[12] According to Ho, "the first American reactionary who arrived in Vietnam to prepare for U.S. intervention . . . was W. Bullitt, a notorious spy and Truman's friend and representative. Since then Vietnam has witnessed the uninterrupted coming and going of congressmen, spies, generals and admirals, businessmen, bankers and even a bishop."[13]

The increased American aid to the French both irritated and worried Ho. In an article published in April, 1952, under the pen-name of Din, the old guerilla wrote:

From the beginning of the war, the Americans have been supplying France with money and armaments. To take an example, 85 per cent of weapons, war materiel and even canned food captured by our troops were labelled "made in U.S.A." This "aid" had particularly increased since U.S. intervention in Korea in June 1950. It includes airplanes, boats, trucks, military outfits, napalm bombs, etc.[14]

Ho's grief was quite justifiable. While from 1946 to 1954 the French appropriated nearly $7.6 billion for military purposes in Indochina, the United States contributed approximately $4.2 billion in aid through France and directly to the State of Vietnam.[15]

Following the signing of the Geneva Agreements Ho directed his efforts against the "U.S. imperialists and their henchmen" in Saigon. Having left behind in South Vietnam cadres and weapons, the DRV President bided his time, confidently waiting for the elections scheduled for July, 1956.

Meanwhile, in South Vietnam, Ngo Dinh Diem proved to be a thorn in Ho's flesh. Asked by Bao Dai to form a government on June 16, 1954, when the ship of state was sinking, Diem accepted the unenviable task of running South Vietnam during those desperate months or, as most observers said, of presiding over the collapse of the State of Vietnam. Convinced, however, that if the French withdrew from his country a strong nationalist government could stem the Viet Minh advances, Diem assumed his office on July 7 when the fate of Vietnam had been decided at Geneva. Strongly opposed to the agreements which his government had neither negotiated nor signed, the stubborn Premier served notice to Ho that the southern regime would be free to safeguard the right of the Vietnamese to unity, independence, and freedom. Diem went so far as to call on the people in the North to rally to their southern compatriots to continue their struggle for independence and liberty. Confident that Washington, which had expressed serious reservations about the Geneva Accords, would support a strong nationalist government in Saigon, Diem approached his task with considerable zeal. His first challenge was to disband or bring under the government's control the private armies of the Cao Dai and Hoa Hao politico-religious sects and to suppress the Binh Xuyen bandits to whom Bao Dai had sold the police and the secret service.

In addition, there were many other problems that seemed to defy any solution. Nearly one million refugees had to be fed, resettled, and employed. The National Army, commanded by a French citizen, had to be reorganized and made subservient to the government, the Viet Minh courts and tax collecting services in the countryside to be discontinued, and the confidence of the South Vietnamese to be restored!

In their attempt to keep the Bao Dai regime powerless, the French had armed and supplied the private armies, and permitted them to remain independent from Saigon. Even in the aftermath of Geneva, they continued to pursue this "divide and rule" practice allegedly to protect their interests in South Vietnam. Ironically, in the execution of this policy General Paul Ely, the last French High Commissioner and Commander-in-Chief, had the cooperation of the U.S. Ambassador in Saigon, General Lawton Collins, who considered the aloof Diem a failure. Diem fought the Binh Xuyen against the advice of General Ely, who then threw his troops and tanks around Saigon to protect his Binh Xuyen protégés from the National Army and denied Diem gasoline and ammunition which the French still controlled. Contrary to the gloomy prediction of political pundits, Diem defeated the Binh Xuyen, then the Hoa Hao, and won over the Cao Dai. In the process he also dismissed the rebellious Chief of Staff, General Nguyen Van Hinh, deposed Bao Dai, the absent Chief of State and "playboy Emperor," in a referendum, and proclaimed the Republic of Vietnam. Not until then did Diem convince Washington that he deserved American support.

While Diem was able to overcome the obstacles created by the French, he had greater difficulty with the problems carved out for him by Ho Chi Minh. Immediately after the signing of the Geneva Accords, Viet Minh cadres who had been left behind in the South began to form "peace movements," "democratic fronts," and publish newspapers clamoring for democratic freedoms. In all fairness to Diem one should realize that unless he was prepared to throw South Vietnam into chaos he could not remove all restrictions on democratic liberties during those troubled years.

Meanwhile, on June 16, 1955, Ho's government announced its readiness to hold consultative conference with representatives of the authorities in the South to discuss the organization of general elections.[16]

Not until July 16 did the Saigon regime give an answer to the DRV proposal. In a broadcast to the nation, Diem reiterated that the State of Vietnam was not bound in any way by the Geneva agreements which had been signed against the will of the Vietnamese people. While his government did not reject the principle of free elections as a peaceful and democratic means of bringing about reunification of the country, Diem stressed, it would refuse to consider any proposal from the Viet Minh until they ceased to violate their obligations under the Geneva Accords and put the interests of Communism above those of the nation. He also called on the people in the North to have confidence, promising to bring them "independence in freedom."[17]

This Southern rejection of elections without United Nations supervision was what Ho had feared. Anxious to push forth the elections he knew he could use fraudulent methods to win, Ho again sent notes on July 19 to the Saigon and Paris governments and the ICC requesting a consultative meeting between Northern and Southern representatives. Thereupon, the British and French governments advised Diem to arrange for consultations with the DRV in preparation for general elections. On August 9, Diem again emphasized that his government did not consider itself bound by the Geneva Accords which it had not signed, that it was the Viet Minh who had recommended partition against the objection of the

State of Vietnam, and that "conditions of freedom of life and of voting must be assured before free elections could take place."[18]

In a subsequent press conference, Secretary of State Dulles agreed with Diem that the conditions in North Vietnam prevented the holding of free elections.[19]

There was good reason to believe that falsified votes in the North, which had a larger population, would nullify the votes in the South, even in the very unlikely event in which all Southern votes went to Diem.

Thus, the first deadline fixed by the Geneva Conference, July 20, 1955, passed without incident.

Disturbed by Diem's successes in the South and his refusal to participate in a consultative conference, Ho sent back to the South many of the Viet Minh cadres who had gone North. By November, 1955, an estimated 6,000 Communist agents, including a VPA general, had slipped into Diem's Republic to organize guerilla warfare.[20] Viet Minh agents also distributed propaganda literature signed by the Patriotic Front in the DRV, which was controlled by the Lao Dong Party (Communist) and allegedly embraced all Vietnamese working for national unity and independence.

The second deadline fixed by the Geneva Accords, July 20, 1956, also passed without incident. Ho lodged a protest to the British and Soviet co-chairmen of the Geneva Conference. Having timidly urged the authorities in both North and South Vietnam to properly implement the Accords, the co-chairmen decided to extend indefinitely the functions of the ineffectual ICC and requested the Ho and Diem regimes to inform them as soon as an agreement was reached on the dates for consultation and elections. In addition, Peking proposed that another conference be convened in Geneva.

Much had taken place between July, 1954, and July, 1956. To Ho's dismay, Diem's position had been greatly strengthened by American support. On June 1, 1956, Assistant Secretary of State Walter Robertson announced that

President Diem and the Government of Free Vietnam reaffirmed on April 6 of this year and on other occasions their desire to seek the reunification of Vietnam by peaceful means. In this goal, we support them fully. . . . For our part . . . we support President Diem fully in his position that if elections are to be held, there first must be conditions which preclude intimidation or coercion of the electorate.[21]

This "U.S.-Diem clique" collusion, Ho would not soon forget. Frustrated in his attempt to annex South Vietnam through Communist-style elections, Ho turned his wrath on the United States. As he had successfully exploited the feeling of Vietnamese against French colonialism during the Indochina war, the shrewd revolutionary now attempted to arouse them against American imperialism. In his message to Vietnamese all over the country on July 6, 1956, Ho said:

the U.S. imperialists and the pro-American authorities in South Vietnam have been plotting to partition our country permanently and prevent the holding of free general elections as provided for by the Geneva Agreements. They have been acting against the interests of our fatherland and people.

The conqueror of the French, however, would not tolerate American interference. Announcing what was to be done, Ho continued:

Vietnam must be reunified. Our compatriots in both the South and the North will certainly live under the same roof again. Let them be resolved to unite closely and on a broad basis in accordance with the Programme of the Vietnam Fatherland Front, participate eagerly in the patriotic emulation movement, endeavour to consolidate the North and struggle with determination and perseverance for a peaceful, unified, independent, democratic, prosperous and strong Vietnam.[22]

In contrast to his forceful exhortations, Ho's protest to the co-chairmen of the Geneva Conference was markedly feeble. Having so consistently flouted the agreements he had signed, Ho apparently did not expect the participants of the Conference to give serious consideration to his complaint. A study of the domestic conditions of the DRV in 1956 indicates that Ho, the pragmatic revolutionary, took the only logical step available to him. An extremely severe crisis, which almost tore North Vietnam apart and which required the entire energy of all Lao Dong Party members, prevented Ho from devoting too much time to the South. The land reform campaign begun in 1953 had backfired. Far from increasing agricultural production as Ho had promised, it seriously aggravated the food shortage problem. Instead of happiness, it was terror. It was the period of execution of landlords. The countryside was crowded with

mourners. In despair the peasants revolted. Battle-tested veterans of
the resistance war were called on to quash the rebellion.

Regarding elections, it is interesting to recall here a remark by the
late President Eisenhower, which has been often incorrectly interpreted or intentionally misconstrued. Writing in his memoirs, the
President said:

I have never talked or corresponded with a person with knowledgeable
experience in Indochinese affairs who did not agree that had elections
been held *as of the time of the fighting*, possibly 80 per cent of the
population would have voted for the Communist Ho Chi Minh as their
leader rather than *Chief of State Bao Dai* [emphasis supplied].[23]

First of all, during the fighting most Vietnamese were disgusted
with Chief of State Bao Dai, the absentee "Majesty" whose time was
divided between seeking pleasures in the French Riviera and, during
his short visits to Vietnam, hunting tigers in the Southern highlands, while Vietnamese whose loyalty to France was beyond doubt
ran his government in Saigon. Not until July 1, 1954, when the
outcome of the war and the fate of Vietnam had been decided at
Geneva, did Ngo Dinh Diem, a nationalist opponent of both the
French and the Bao Dai solution, take over as Premier of the State
of Vietnam. Thus, had elections been held "as of the time of the
fighting" between Bao Dai and any unknown opponent, the discredited Bao Dai would have lost. Ho, of course, would have won such
a contest, too.

Secondly, had *free* elections been held in July, 1956, between Ho
Chi Minh and Ngo Dinh Diem—Bao Dai had been deposed as
Chief of State in a referendum held on October 23, 1955—the vote
would have gone against Ho for several reasons: (*a*) the Ngo Dinh
Diem of 1956 was a respected and admired nationalist leader, who
had successfully defied the French by defeating the obnoxious Binh
Xuyen bandits and the Cao Dai and Hoa Hao private armies, (*b*)
sent to France the rebellious Chief of Staff and French citizen
Nguyen Van Hinh, (*c*) gotten rid of the "playboy Emperor," (*d*)
proclaimed a republic, and (*e*) obtained the withdrawal of all
French troops from Vietnam. In brief, Diem had strengthened the
people's faith in him as a man qualified to build a regime capable of
competing with Ho's DRV.

While these events worked for Diem in the South, other factors conspired against Ho in the North. The Communist methods of silencing opposition had profoundly horrified the masses. The brutality with which the Lao Dong party, that is, the Communist party, had carried out the land reform campaign had convincingly warned the people what was in store for them. In spite of a halt in the terror in 1954, nearly 900,000 Vietnamese had "voted with their feet" against the Ho regime by going South. At the end of the agrarian reform campaign, an estimated 100,000 persons had lost their lives in what a leftist French professor who lived in Hanoi until 1959 referred to as an "undescribable butchery."[24] Landlords, those who owned an acre or more of land and whose alleged crime had been exploitation or mistreatment of the poor, were tried by people's tribunals composed entirely of peasants before which defendants were not permitted to defend themselves. Their signed "confession" was enough to prove their guilt. Those who received the death penalty were shot immediately after the sentence was given, then dumped in a hole that had been dug before the trial began.[25] Among the victims were many resistance heroes who had been decorated by Uncle Ho and members of the Lao Dong Party. Although the law permitted those sentenced to death to appeal to the DRV President for clemency, Uncle Ho did not raise a finger to pardon one single "nephew" or "niece," not even loyal members of the Lao Dong Party who, before they were cut down by bullets, still felt enough loyalty to Uncle Ho to shout: "Long live Ho Chi Minh!"[26]

Another half million, whose lives had been spared, spent their days in prison or at hard labor. Hundreds of thousands of others, perhaps ten times the number condemned to death by the people's courts,[27] women, children, old people, members of the condemned or executed landlords' families, were effectively isolated, prevented from working or having any contact with their fellow human beings and, thus, condemned to a slow, horrible death from starvation. All in all, 12,000 Lao Dong Party members were committed to prison. The brutality had reached such a proportion that even Hanoi's papers began to carry gruesome stories about the campaign and the executions. In a speech before the Lao Dong Central Committee in October, 1956, General Vo Nguyen Giap, the man who presided over the rectification of "errors" campaign, candidly admitted the excesses of overzealous party workers:

We . . . executed too many honest people . . . and, seeing enemies everywhere, resorted to terror which became far too widespread. . . . When reorganizing the Party we paid too much importance to the notion of social class instead of adhering . . . to political qualifications alone. Instead of recognizing education to be the first essential, we resorted exclusively to organizational measures such as disciplinary punishments, expulsion from the Party, executions, dissolutions of Party branches and cells. Worse still, torture came to be regarded as a normal practice during Party reorganization.[28]

Tales of gruesome murders and assassinations of landlords, party members, and innocent people of all ages soon found widespread circulation in the South where people became paralyzed with fright. Even those who had admired the revolutionary Ho Chi Minh for his selfless dedication began to abhor his inhuman methods. Thus, the speculation that Ho would win a *free* election in 1956 apparently did not take into consideration the feeling of the Vietnamese people in both the North and the South, which, in the final analysis, should have been the determining factor.

But Ho, as usual, blamed everything on the "U.S. imperialist-Diem fascist clique."

The "Liberation" of South Vietnam

With the two dates fixed by the Geneva Conference receded into history without any incident, Ho ordered the Viet Cong,[29] i.e., the Viet Minh cadre who had remained behind during the freedom of movement period and those who had reinfiltrated back into the South, to intensify their agitation and propaganda efforts to bring about the collapse of Diem's Republic.

In 1957, on the twelfth anniversary of the August Revolution, Le Duan, the actual Secretary General of the Lao Dong Party,[30] explained Ho's desire to "liberate" the South. In a speech delivered on that occasion, Le Duan said:

We have won the day, but liberated only half of our country. The other half still lies in the hands of the U.S. imperialist and Diem feudalist clique. The revolutionary task of all of us is to achieve national independence and independence all over the country. This task lays ahead of us two concrete works: to build the North and take it vigorously to socialism and to step up the revolutionary movement in South Vietnam against U.S. imperialism and Diem's feudalism.

In order to carry through these two tasks, it is necessary to accelerate the patriotic movement among the population. . . . In the South this patriotism must be concretely manifested in the movement opposing the enslavement policy of the U.S.-Diem clique, claiming national independence, fighting the fascist policies, repression and oppression by the U.S. clique, demanding democracy, improvement of the people's livelihood, thwarting the U.S.-Diem's bellicose policy and claiming peaceful reunification of the country.[31]

The following year, more vigorous steps were taken to accelerate the "revolutionary movement" in the South. With a view to paralyzing the Saigon government and immobilizing the people, the Viet Cong resorted to terror, executing informers and assassinating village chiefs, local officials, and teachers. By December, armed bands roamed the countryside, which the Diem government, even with a much larger army, could not protect. Not until the *Tet* (Vietnamese lunar New Year) of 1959 did the Viet Cong begin large-scale raids and attacks against army outposts in strength while continuing their sabotage and murder activities. An estimated 1,700 local officials and teachers were murdered in 1959 and 4,000 in 1960.

As the Diem regime grew increasingly oppressive and dictatorial, as more and more people became disenchanted with the Saigon government, Ho concentrated on exploiting popular grievances and laying the ground for an armed uprising. Instead of direct aggression, the shrewd Lao Dong Party chairman chose subversion and war from within, which was more difficult for Saigon to deal with and would not provoke American intervention. On April 20, 1960, in a speech delivered at a meeting for the commemoration of Lenin's ninetieth birthday, Le Duan, Ho's faithful spokesman, re-emphasized the theme that "the liberation of the South is not only a task for the southern people, but also of the entire people, of the South as well as of the North. The northern people will never neglect their task with regard to one half of their country which is not liberated."

In view of the peace offensive of the Communist bloc, however, an outright military attempt by the North was not desirable. As Le Duan explained, in the present conjecture, when the possibility exists to maintain a lasting peace in the world and create favourable conditions for the world movement of socialist revolution and national independence to go forward, we can and must guide and restrict within the South the solving of the contradiction between imperialism and the colonies in our country.[32]

In order to guide the socialist revoltuion in the South, the Lao Dong Party must coordinate the insurgents' activities. A plan, which had been prepared since the summer of 1959, was finally unveiled to the delegates at the Third Congress of the Lao Dong Party in September, 1960. In a statement apparently designed to prepare the delegates for what was to be announced, Ho reminded them that

the U.S.-Diem clique is now partitioning our country and trampling on the South of our country. So long as we have not driven the American imperialists out of the South, liberating it from the barbarous rule of the U.S.-Diem clique, our people can know no peace of mind.[33]

Le Duan, the newly elected Party First Secretary, then recom- mended that the South Vietnamese people, "under the leadership of the Marxist-Leninist Party and the working class, should endeavor to build a worker-peasant-army coalition bloc and set up a broad national united front."[34]

The liberation of the South was to be "a two-stage affair: first, the elimination of the U.S. imperialists and the Ngo Dinh Diem clique, . . . then the establishment of a national democratic coalition government . . . that would negotiate with the North for reunification."[35] On September 10, consequently, the Party passed a resolution describing the united front to be formed:

To ensure the complete success of the revolutionary struggle in South Vietnam our people there must strive to establish a united bloc of workers, peasants, and soldiers to bring into being a broad, united national front, directed against the U.S.-Diemists and based on the worker-peasant alliance. The front must carry out its work in a very flexible manner in order to rally all forces that can be rallied, win over all forces that can be won over, neutralize all forces that can be neutralized, and draw the masses into the general struggle against the U.S.-Diem clique for the liberation of the South and the peaceful reunification of the Fatherland.[36]

Three months later, on December 20, a *Mat Tran Gian Toc Giai Phong Mien Nam*, or National Front for the Liberation of South Vietnam, known briefly as the National Liberation Front (NLF), was formed "somewhere in Nam Bo" (Cochinchina). Its ten-point Manifesto bore a marked resemblance to the resolution of the Lao Dong Party Third Congress. It advocated, among other things, a government of "broad and progressive democracy," "a foreign policy of peace and neutrality," and normal relations between North and South Vietnam as a first step toward peaceful reunification of the country. On May 18, 1961, the Liberation Front Radio also announced that the resolution of the Third Congress of the Lao Dong Party had been correctly implemented by the delegates of the Party in South Vietnam.

As anti-French nationalists had joined the Viet Minh during the Indochina war, a number of non-Communists opposed to the U.S.-supported Saigon regime were attracted to the Front. No nationalist of renown, however, even those most critical of the Diem and succeeding governments, have joined the NLF. Its most important non-Communist member, Nguyen Huu Tho, was an obscure southern provincial lawyer until his election as Chairman in 1962, a move designed to give the Front an appearance of nationalism and independence from Hanoi. The key post of Secretary General, however, went to the Communist Nguyen Van Hieu, who held it until 1964 when Huynh Tan Phat, another Communist, took over. Whatever postions they might occupy in the NLF, non-Communists did not play any significant role but served merely as tools of Hanoi. As a directive from the Lao Dong Party illustrated,

In the present situation of South Vietnam, the Central Committee supports integration of these elements into the Front, not because the Party is going to entrust these classes with heavy responsibilities in the revolutionary liberation of South Vietnam, but only to utilize their abilities and their prestige in order to push forward the revolution and to give more prestige to the People's Front for the Liberation of South Vietnam.

This line of conduct is only a temporary policy of the Party. When the revolution is crowned with success, this policy will be revised. Then the Party will act overtly to lead the revolution in South Vietnam.[37]

Although the NLF has claimed that it was created by thirty parties and organizations with a seven-million membership,[38] most of them existed only in the imagination of the Front leaders. While it is true that a number of peasants voluntarily supported the NLF, the majority were gradually talked into giving food to a few soldiers now and then, make traps to be used against government and Allied troops, or participating passively or actively in antigovernment propaganda, etc. until they found themselves so implicated that they could no longer refuse to cooperate with the Front. Those who did would soon learn that their names and pro-Viet Cong activities had been leaked to the Saigon police who wasted no time arresting them. With the peasants the Viet Cong used both persuasion and terror, with the latter in increasingly large doses.

The Front's subservience to Hanoi was further evidenced by the presence in its midst of the People's Revolutionary Party (PRP), whose formation was announced in January, 1962. Although described as an independent Marxist-Leninist party, the PRP, according to a captured Communist document, "is nothing but the Lao Dong Party of Vietnam, unified from North to South, under the direction of the central executive committee of the party, the chief of which is President Ho."

The document also explains the PRP position as follows:

In regard to the foundation of the People's Revolutionary Party of South Vietnam, the creation of this party is only a matter of strategy; it needs to be explained within the party; and to deceive the enemy, it is necessary that the new party be given the outward appearance corresponding to a division of the party (Lao Dong) into two and the foundation of a new party, so that the enemy cannot use it in his propaganda.

Within the party, it is necessary to explain that the founding of the People's Revolutionary Party has the purpose of isolating the Americans and the Ngo Dinh Diem regime, and to counter their accusations of an invasion of the South by the North. It is a means of supporting our sabotage of the Geneva agreement, of advancing the plan of invasion of the South, and at the same time permitting the Front for Liberation of the South to recruit new adherents, and to gain the sympathy of the non-aligned countries in Southeast Asia.[39]

Thus, war has again engulfed South Vietnam. It was initiated by Ho Chi Minh who wanted to "liberate" the South and "peacefully" unify the country. As the North Korean Communist Party said in its tribute to the departed revolutionary, on September 4, 1969, "under the skillful leadership of Comrade Ho Chi Minh, the people of

Vietnam have successively inflicted heavy defeats on the U.S. imperialists."[40] Whatever opinion one may have about victories and defeats on the battlefields of Vietnam, one could not help being frightened by the staggering death toll on both sides. From the time Ho set up the NLF to launch the "revolutionary war" to "liberate" South Vietnam until he agreed to peace talks in Paris, countless civilians and hundreds of thousands of combatants had lost their lives. Of the soldiers killed in action from 1960 to 1967, 16,022 were American, 55,398 South Vietnamese, and 255,356 Viet Cong and North Vietnamese.[41] And the face of South Vietnam had been badly distorted!

The Irreconcilable Chairman

From the autumn of 1963, when the Vietnam conflict threatened to develop into a large-scale war, to the spring of 1968, when Ho agreed to peace talks, innumerable peace overtures were made with a view to a negotiated settlement of the Vietnam problem. Unlike the requests for negotiation during the Indochina war, which had almost invariably come from Ho's Viet Bac jungle headquarters, peace proposals this time were primarily initiated by Washington. Ho, the persistent conciliator of yesteryear, had become Ho, the irreconcilable bargainer. It is estimated that more than 2,000 efforts to mediate were made by the United States, third-party governments, and individuals.[42]

The first initiative, however, came from the Viet Cong, just two days after the collapse of the Diem regime, which threw South Vietnam into a nearly chaotic state. On November 3, 1963, a statement broadcast over the NLF radio vaguely proposed that all parties concerned should meet to discuss South Vietnam's future. Since it was not further elaborated, the suggestion was not seriously considered. More importantly, the unsettling situation in Saigon precluded any negotiations.

Instead of simmering down, the conflict expanded into the DRV. On August 2, 1964, the U.S. warship *Maddox* was allegedly attacked in international waters off the coast of North Vietnam by DRV torpedo boats. Two days later, similar attacks took place against the American destroyers *C. Turner Joy* and *Maddox* by North

Vietnamese PT boats. In retaliation, President Johnson ordered air action against gunboats and other supporting facilities in the DRV. At this juncture, United Nations mediation was suggested. In reply to a Soviet proposal that a DRV representative be invited to give the Vietnamese side of the story to the Security Council, Hanoi maintained that the United Nations had no right to interfere and that any decision by the Security Council would be considered "null and void."

In the face of North Vietnamese aggressive intent, the U.S. Congress passed a joint resolution on August 7, approving and supporting the President's determination "to take all necessary measures to repel any armed attack against the forces of the United States and to prevent further aggression."

The war escalated. On February 7, 1965, U.S. bombers again struck targets in the North in retaliation against Viet Cong attacks on American billets in the South. The war was finally brought home to Ho. Both sides began to strengthen their position. The United States augmented its forces in Vietnam from 23,300 in 1964 to 125,000 by early fall and 208,800 by the end of 1965, while the Viet Cong and North Vietnamese forces rose from 170,200 to 222,800 during the same period, including the 12,400 men who had infiltrated from the North in 1964.[43]

Alarmed by this spiral buildup, U.N. Secretary General U Thant, in February, 1955, proposed international negotiations on Vietnam, in or out of the United Nations. Two weeks later, Ho flatly rejected Thant's suggestion, stating that the DRV would consider peace negotiations only if all American troops were withdrawn from South Vietnam. Washington took a similar position on March 9, stressing that the United States would not enter into talks until North Vietnam stopped its aggression against South Vietnam.

Following the failure of Thant's effort, Yugoslavia's President Tito sponsored a meeting of heads of state and government of seventeen nonaligned nations in Belgrade. At the close of their conference on March 15, they issued "an urgent appeal to the parties concerned to start negotiations, as soon as possible, without posing any preconditions, so that a political solution to the problem of Vietnam may be found in accordance with the legitimate aspirations of the Vietnamese people and in the spirit of the Geneva Agreement on Vietnam." Washington endorsed the proposal, stressing that it was ready to negotiate without conditions while Hanoi called the appeal "a peace fraud and a big bluff" masterminded by Tito, the "stool pigeon" of the U.S. imperialists.

One week after the Belgrade appeal, the NLF broadcast a set of conditions which it called a "five-point peace program." The Front's demands included withdrawal of U.S. support from the Saigon government and troops from South Vietnam, and recognition of the NLF as the only "genuine representative" of the South Vietnamese people.

On April 7, in his speech delivered at Johns Hopkins University, President Johnson, reiterating U.S. willingness to negotiate without conditions, went so far as to promise a one billion-dollar American investment in the development of Southeast Asia and invite North Vietnam to "take its place in the common effort just as soon as peaceful cooperation is possible."[44]

On April 8 and 11, respectively, Peking denounced the Johnson peace offer as a trick while Hanoi described it as a "ludicrous swindle." Ho's answer to the American proposal was given in a speech in the DRV National Assembly on April 10:

The U.S. imperialists must respect the Geneva Agreements, withdraw from South Vietnam, and immediately stop the attacks on North Vietnam. That is the only measure to settle the war in Vietnam, to implement the 1954 Geneva Agreements, to defend peace in Indochina and Southeast Asia. There is no other solution. And that is the answer of our people and government to the U.S. imperialists.[45]

At about the same time as President Johnson gave his Baltimore speech, Premier Pham Van Dong presented the Hanoi position in a four-point plan similar to the NLF proposal:

1. Withdrawal of U.S. troops, military personnel, and weapons, dismantling of all U.S. bases, cancellation of U.S. military alliance with South Vietnam, cessation of all acts of war against North Vietnam;

2. Temporary continuation of the partition of Vietnam, adherence to the military provisions of the Geneva Agreements regarding the ban on military alliances, foreign military bases and personnel;

3. Settlement of "internal affairs of South Vietnam" by the South Vietnamese people themselves in accordance with the NLF program;

4. Peaceful reunification of Vietnam to be settled by the Vietnamese people without any foreign interference.[46]

Both Communist plans sounded more like a set of conditions which a victorious DRV would impose upon a defeated United States than a peace proposal. Such were the plans which, for more than two years, Ho persistently insisted that Washington must accept in full before Hanoi would consider peace talks. One could not help wondering whether Ho, the student par excellence, was merely applying here a lesson which he had learned from the French High Commissioners for Indochina. Ho had apparently lifted a page out of Emile Bollaert's diplomatic manual. On September 10, 1947, speaking for a "highly conciliatory France," the High Commissioner in effect said in a speech which Ho had been waiting eagerly in the Viet Bac jungle: "France will remain in Indochina and Indochina will remain within the French Union," and "the offer I am tendering in the name of the Government of the Republic is an indivisible whole which must be either fully accepted or wholly rejected. We cannot permit a haggling which would verily be unworthy of such a noble cause."[47]

Following the disclosure of the Dong plan, Patrick Gordon Walker, a special British envoy, was rebuffed in his attempt to meet with Hanoi's and Peking's officials with a view to exploring the possibility of peace talks. The six-day bombing pause in North Vietnam, from May 13 to 19, initiated by the United States as a conciliatory gesture to mollify Ho's attitude, was promptly ridiculed by the DRV as just another imperialist "trick." On July 1, Ho again rejected a request by a four-nation (Britain, Ghana, Nigeria, and Trinidad-Tobago) British Commonwealth mission on Vietnam for talks in Hanoi, stating that "Mr. Wilson has not correctly carried out his obligations as a Co-Chairman of the 1954 Geneva Conference on Vietnam. He has tried to support United States imperialist aggression in Vietnam. He cannot engage in peace negotiations since he has himself supported the United States policy of aggression and expansion of the war."[48]

Subsequently, however, Harold Davies, British Labor member of Parliament, was permitted to visit the North Vietnamese capital. Following his discussions with several top DRV officials, Davies returned to report that Hanoi would not budge from its four-point proposal.

Efforts to bring the belligerents to the conference table continued. On July 28, President Johnson sent a letter to U.N. Secretary General U Thant, requesting "all members of the United Nations, individually and collectively, to use their influence to bring about unconditional discussions."[49]

A most dramatic event took place on October 4 when Pope Paul VI flew to New York to address the United Nations and make a plea for an end to the Vietnam war. It was the first appearance of a Roman pontiff before the world assembly.

On October 15–16, the student National Coordinating Committee to End the War in Vietnam organized a series of demonstrations in the United States, while similar protests were staged in foreign cities. These were followed by a march sponsored by the National Committee for a Sane Nuclear Policy on November 23 during which an estimated 15,000 to 35,000 persons gathered in front of the White House to demand peace in Vietnam. To further dramatize their opposition to the war, the Quaker Norman R. Morrison burned himself to death in front of the Pentagon on November 2 while Roger Allen LaPorte of the pacifist Catholic Worker Movement committed suicide by fire in front of the U.N. headquarters in New York a week later. From Hanoi, Ho followed these developments with great interest, convinced that mounting public pressure would force Washington to swallow Hanoi's formula.

Meanwhile, a peace feeler was initiated by Giorgio La Pira, a former mayor of Florence, Italy, and a professor of Roman law at the University of Florence. La Pira was received by Ho himself on November 11. Upon his return, the professor through his friend Amintore Fanfani, the Italian Foreign Minister who was then serving as President of the U.N. General Assembly in New York, communicated Ho's terms to Washington. In order to have negotiations, La Pira reported, Ho demanded (*a*) a complete cease-fire in both North and South Vietnam, and (*b*) a declaration of adherence to the Geneva Agreements on the basis of Hanoi's four points, which included the settlement of South Vietnam's internal affairs in accordance with the NLF five-point program.

In answer to Ho's proposal, Washington (*a*) reaffirmed its readiness for negotiations without preconditions, (*b*) stated that it was willing to negotiate on the basis of the Geneva Agreements, (*c*) was prepared to accept a mutual cease-fire, and (*d*) would be willing to discuss Hanoi's four points although it did not agree that they were an authoritative interpretation of the Geneva Agreements. The United States, in addition, considered the DRV insistence on a prior declaration of acceptance of the NLF program as a precondition.

Washington's reply reached Hanoi on December 13, two days before U.S. bombers struck a power plant in Uong Bi, close to Haiphong. On December 17, the *St. Louis Post-Dispatch* published a report on the La Pira peace probe. It has been said that both the bombing near Haiphong and the disclosure by the St. Louis paper of the demarche killed it altogether. On December 18, the DRV issued a statement describing the report of Hanoi's peace feeler as "sheer groundless fabrication."

Again, on Christmas Eve, the United States suspended all air strikes against North Vietnam. In addition to the bombing pause which was to last 37 days (until January 30, 1966), President Johnson dispatched a team of high-ranking emissaries headed by veteran diplomat W. Averell Harriman to 34 capitals to deliver his message to representatives of 115 governments and explore with them the possibility of a negotiated settlement of the war. While, according to Peking, "these monsters and freaks of all description are scurrying hither and thither and raising a lot of dust with their sinister activities,"[50] Hanoi launched its own "peace offensive." On January 24, Ho sent letters to the heads of state of the Communist countries and several non-Communist nations such as Canada and India, both members of the ICC. Referring to the Johnson move, Ho said:

> While intensifying and extending the war of aggression in Vietnam the U.S. imperialists are clamoring about their "desire for peace" and their "readiness to engage in unconditional discussion" in the hope of fooling world and American public opinion. . . .
>
> At the very moment when the U.S. Government puts forward the so-called new "peace efforts," it is frantically increasing the U.S. strength in South Vietnam. . . .
>
> Obviously, the U.S. "search for peace" is only designed to conceal its schemes for an intensified war of aggression. The Johnson administration stand remains: aggression and expansion of the war.

Having ridiculed the U.S. move, Ho reiterated:

If the U.S. Government really wants a peaceful settlement, it must accept the four-point stand of the Government of the Democratic Republic of Vietnam, and prove this by actual deeds, it must end unconditionally and for good all bombing raids and other war acts against the Democratic Republic of Vietnam. Only in this way can a political solution to the Vietnamese problem by envisaged.

Ho then called on these governments to increase their support and assistance to his people's "just struggle," and to "resolutely condemn the U.S. Government's sham peace tricks."[51]

In March, Canada's Prime Minister Lester Pearson, who had received Ho's January 24 letter, decided to sound the North Vietnamese attitude toward negotiations while the channel was still open. With Washington's encouragement, Pearson sent Chester Ronning, a veteran diplomat and one of Canada's most respected specialists on Asian affairs, to Hanoi on March 7. During his four-day stay in the DRV capital, Ronning had long talks with high ranking officials, including Premier Pham Van Dong and Foreign Minister Nguyen Duy Trinh. Upon his return, the Canadian diplomat informed Washington that Hanoi refused to depart from its four-point program.

In June, Ronning set out for another journey to the DRV. Again, he spent four days in Hanoi, from June 14 to 18, talking with the same officials. Ronning's second mission accomplished as much, or as little, as his first one. Ho's message was clear: he would negotiate only on his own terms.

Meanwhile, undaunted by North Vietnam's repudiation of his efforts, U.N. Secretary General U Thant submitted, on March 14, 1967, a three-point plan calling for (*a*) a general standstill truce, (*b*) preliminary talks, and (*c*) the reconvening of the Geneva Conference.[52]

On March 18, the United States announced its acceptance of the Thant proposal, reiterating that it had been always "willing to enter into discussions without preconditions with Hanoi at any time."

On March 27, Hanoi as usual rejected the Secretary General's suggestion, stressing again that the DRV four-point stand and the NLF five-point statement must be accepted as a basis for the settlement of the conflict, and reemphasizing that "the Vietnam problem has no concern with the United Nations and the United Nations has absolutely no right to interfere in any way in the Vietnam question."[53]

Nothing significant developed until September 29, when President Johnson delivered a speech in San Antonio, Texas, in which he offered to "send a trusted representative of America to any spot on this earth to talk in public or in private with a spokesman of Hanoi," and to "stop all aerial and naval bombardment of North Vietnam when this will lead promptly to productive discussions," assuming that "while discussions proceed North Vietnam would not take advantage of the bombing cessation or limitation."[54] This was indeed a very important American concession. The United States no longer insisted on a halt in North Vietnamese infiltration in return for a bombing pause.

There was no immediate reaction from Hanoi although *Nhan Dan,* the Lao Dong Party official paper, rejected the last American peace feeler as another "trick." Then on December 29, Foreign Minister Nguyen Duy Trinh issued the following statement:

> The U.S. Government has unceasingly claimed that it wants to talk with Hanoi but has received no response. If the U.S. Government truly wants to talk, it must, as was made clear in our statement on 28 January 1967, first of all stop unconditionally the bombing and all other acts of war against the DRV, the DRV *will* hold talks with the United States on questions concerned [emphasis supplied].

Since it affirmed that talks "will" follow a bombing halt, Trinh's statement indicated a softening in Hanoi's position. The DRV Foreign Minister, however, prefaced his remark with a serious qualification, which was, in effect, a precondition: "The stand of the Vietnamese people is quite clear," said Trinh. "That is the four-point stand of the DRV Government and the political program of the NFLSV. That is the basis for the settlement of the Vietnam question."[55]

Thus Hanoi was ready for negotiations. Ho had apparently realized that a stubborn refusal to parley on his part might very likely lead to disaster. The U.S. strength in South Vietnam stood at 565,000 in addition to 753,000 South Vietnamese and 59,000 Allied troops, while the Viet Cong and North Vietnamese forces were estimated at 303,800 including 88,100 who had infiltrated from the

North that year. The presence of large numbers of U.S. forces and aircraft in the South had given Ho deep concern, and prompted him to agree to peace talks. Most importantly, North Vietnam had suffered enormously from the bombing and its endurance was approaching the limit.

A faithful practitioner of the Communist principle of "talk and fight, fight and talk," however, Ho was determined to score a few victories before approaching the conference table. Consequently, during the *Tet* holidays in January, 1968, Viet Cong and North Vietnamese launched massive attacks on Saigon and twenty-eight provincial capitals.

Then on March 31, President Johnson's announcement of his unexpected decision to withdraw from politics and of a limited bombing halt caught the North Vietnamese off guard. Three days later, Hanoi declared its readiness to "talk" with Washington. Ho had changed his position. He had abandoned his previous insistence on a complete cessation of all bombing and other acts of war against North Vietnam as a first step toward negotiations.

After some diplomatic haggling, representatives of the United States, North and South Vietnam, and the NLF finally met in Paris on May 10, 1968.

In order to understand Ho's position on negotiations one should examine his attitude toward Peking and Moscow, from which he received military, economic, and technical assistance to pursue the resistance war against the French and the "liberation" war in South Vietnam.

8 ☆ Comrade Ho Between
Peking and Moscow[1]

PERSONAL AMBITIONS ASIDE, Ho Chi Minh was a realist endowed with a good knowledge of history. Imbued with his country's past experiences, he shared the Vietnamese sinophobia, a deep distrust felt by all Vietnamese for Chinese influence, deriving from nearly ten centuries of Han rule. Yet, as a small country with a giant neighbor which to all intents and purposes remains the "Middle Kingdom," Vietnam, for reasons of survival, could not afford to antagonize China.

By training and inclination, Ho had a warm spot in his heart for the Soviet Union, the leader of the socialist camp, the country of his youth, and the land of Lenin, his idol. "Leninism is not only a miraculous 'book of the wise,' a compass for us Vietnamese revolutionaries and people," wrote the late DRV President, "it is also the radiant sun illuminating our path to final victory, to Socialism and Communism."[2] Ho also witnessed the Soviet Union's metamorphosis from an underdeveloped country into one of the leading industrialized nations of the world. There was much to learn and a great deal to gain from close collaboration with Moscow.

Nevertheless the pragmatic leader of North Vietnam followed a middle-of-the-road policy, uncommitted to either China or the Soviet Union. His neutral position guaranteed Hanoi independence and abundant economic and military aid from both Communist colossi. A close identification with the Soviet view, on the contrary, would make Hanoi a satellite of Moscow and an enemy of China, while an unqualified support for the Chinese stand would transform it into a vassal of Peking.

DRV relations toward China and the Soviet Union may be divided into four phases beginning with the proclamation of the People's Republic in Peking on October 1, 1949, after which Vietnam was no longer "in the grip of the enemy encirclement and was henceforth geographically linked to the Soviet bloc:"[3]

1. 1949–1956, Chinese influence
2. 1957–mid-1962, Soviet influence
3. Mid-1962–1964, Chinese influence
4. 1965–1969, Soviet influence.

1949–1956, Period of Chinese Influence

After the establishment of the Communist regime in China, one of Mao Tse-tung's first diplomatic acts was his recognition of the DRV as an independent sovereign state. The new ruler of China answered Ho's appeal for help by dispatching one of his ablest commanders, General Lo Kwei-po, to Vietnam to serve as military adviser to the Vietnamese Liberation Army, as well as a large number of Chinese experts and technicians to work in various administrative capacities. While Chinese officers taught guerilla tactics to the Viet Minh troops in Ho-controlled areas, numerous Viet Minh officers went to China for military training. Besides furnishing cadres, Peking also supplied Ho with foodstuffs, arms, and ammunition, which arrived in large quantities at the conclusion of the Korean armistice. Chinese assistance thus enabled the Viet Minh to launch a general offensive against the French, which led to their victory at Dienbienphu.

China's prestige was riding high in North Vietnam when a conference on Indochina was convened in Geneva in 1954. Even at Geneva, besides political guidance, the Vietnamese had to rely on their Chinese colleagues to make arrangements for hotel and food services. It was Chou En-lai who prevailed upon Pham Van Dong, the head of the DRV delegation, to abandon his stubborn demand that the Khmer and Lao "resistance governments" be given recognition, and thus prevented a deadlock at the conference. After the settlement of the Indochina war, Hanoi continued to follow Peking's advice and receive Chinese assistance for the reconstruction of war-torn North Vietnam. Chinese advisers and technicians enjoyed great influence in the DRV, and the ambassador from Peking appeared to be the most popular diplomat in Hanoi.

The 1953–56 period was one of land reform, a process that had been carried out in China and slavishly imitated in the DRV. Chinese patterns, such as the anti-landlord campaigns, people's court, and public executions, were copied without any modification. Fanatic Viet Minh cadres, under the supervision of Chinese advisers, shoved the Maoist reforms down the people's throats, victimized landlords and poor peasants alike, and pitilessly eliminated hundreds of thousands of persons, including party members. Instead of abundance and prosperity, it was terror and confusion, poverty and hunger. The campaign was disastrous in its effect, adversely affecting farming and all other programs of rehabilitation and industrial reconstruction. In September, 1956, the Lao Dong Party Central Committee admitted that grave errors had been committed during the execution of the agrarian reforms, and promised to correct them. The 10th Plenum of the Central Committee also issued a communiqué announcing that the party would extend and safeguard democratic liberties and work toward improving the living conditions of the workers, soldiers, cadres, and officials. It was not by sheer coincidence that the rectification campaign occurred at the same time as the "destalinization" process in the Soviet Union. The Lao Dong Party's prestige had dipped to an extremely low ebb and, more importantly, significant changes had taken place in the Kremlin. Thus, it was Khrushchev, not Ho Chi Minh, who should have received credit for this temporary relaxation.

The brutal land reform campaign affected people in every position. Among the famous victims figured Truong Chinh, the Lao Dong Party's Secretary General who had closely identified himself with the program, and Ho Viet Thang, the Deputy Minister of Agriculture in charge of the campaign. While Thang was dismissed from his post, Truong Chinh, at a session of the Central Committee held late in October, was forced to make a public confession admitting major errors and to resign from his office. With a view to salvaging the party, Ho himself assumed the post of Secretary General. The correction campaign and the dismissal of Truong Chinh, who served as a scapegoat for Ho Chi Minh, did not appease the people whose furor had reached the boiling point.[4] Outraged peasants revolted in many parts of the country. On November 4, 1956, for instance, at the very moment when Russian troops and tanks moved into Budapest to suppress the Hungarian Revolution, 20,000 peasants in five villages in the Quynh Luu District, Nghe An Province, Ho Chi Minh's birthplace, armed with sticks and knives, marched against the battle-tested 325th Division of the Vietnam People's Army sent in by the DRV President to discipline them.

Meanwhile, following the lead of Mao Tse-tung who had opened the "One Hundred Flowers" campaign,[5] in May, Ho allowed the Vietnamese people to discuss their different tendencies for a limited period of time. Permission was issued to *Nhan Van* (Humanism), a journal published under the editorship of Phan Khoi, the grand old man of Vietnamese journalism, who had spent five decades of his life denouncing the French rule and spreading patriotic feelings among his countrymen. To Ho's surprise, *Nhan Van* carried articles contributed by the most distinguished journalists in the capital, all levelling devastating charges against the regime. Phan Khoi was especially direct and eloquent in his criticism of the Lao Dong Party's leadership in arts and letters. The other opposition papers, *Tram Hoa* (Hundred Flowers), *Giai Pham* (Literary Pieces), *Dat Moi* (New Soil), etc., also published equally damaging articles. The party suddenly found itself attacked from all political and nonpolitical quarters by prominent people in various fields, including those who had unswervingly believed in Marxism.[6]

Greatly alarmed, Ho, three months after he had allowed the different "flowers to blossom" and the different tendencies to contend, decided to suppress the intellectual rebellion in December, 1956, by closing down the opposition papers, which had argued too freely. Again, Mao's ways prevailed. The four principles put forth by the Chinese Communists to reform intellectuals were adopted by the Lao Dong Party in their entirety. These rules required intellectuals, artists, and writers to (a) change their old outlook of life and develop a revolutionary view, (b) adopt the proletarian view, (c) study Marxism-Leninism and Mao Tse-tung's thoughts, and (d) harden themselves through manual labor.[7]

If the failure of the agrarian reform and the "Hundred Flowers"

campaigns rested squarely on Ho Chi Minh's shoulders, it was also
attributed to Mao Tse-tung who had devised them. This disappointing experience with some of the Chinese policies caused the Lao
Dong Party to reassess its position. The Maoist system of people's
communes, which the Russians disapproved, was not adopted in
North Vietnam, and Ho also refused to imitate Mao's "leap forward."

In view of its traditional deficiency in foodstuffs, North Vietnam
had always depended on South Vietnam for agricultural products,
especially rice. Since the partition of the country along the 17th
parallel in 1954, the North has been cut off from the rich rice-
growing South, known as the ricebowl of Southeast Asia. In spite of
its emphasis on industrialization, the DRV is essentially an agrarian
country, in which industry heavily depends upon the returns of
agriculture and an overwhelming majority of its population rely on
the soil for their livelihood. While the land in the South yields
excellent crops, the soil in the North, with the exception of the
narrow Red River delta, is notoriously poor. In the Nghe An, Ha
Tinh, and Quang Binh provinces, for instance, the hard-working
peasants could not even eke out a meager living—meager on the
Vietnamese standard—out of the unproductive soil. Added to the
low yield of the land are the natural calamities such as floods and
typhoons, which frequently visit upon the country.

The experiments with the Chinese methods in the first few years
following the partition, instead of taking care of the food shortage,
aggravated it. By the end of 1956, Ho Chi Minh realized that this
problem could be solved only through large-scale industrialization,
which would permit the DRV to export its manufactured goods and
obtain foreign currency with which to buy rice and other foodstuffs.
And large-scale industrialization required modern machines to
equip new factories and technicians to train people to run them.
China, who had helped North Vietnam with elementary restoration
work, was not able to meet the new Vietnamese need. The Soviet
Union and the Eastern European countries, on the other hand, were
in a good position to supply the DRV with machinery, technical
knowledge, and trained specialists. A move toward Moscow was
thus discussed in Hanoi. In the Lao Dong Party, however, there
have been factional divisions between pro-Soviet and pro-Chinese
groups. The latter wing, which had been in the ascendency until the

failure of the land reform and "Hundred Flowers" campaigns, did not idly watch their influence being eroded by such a switch. Thus, a very serious intraparty struggle followed. The Politburo, the powerful body that ruled over North Vietnam, had been far from unanimous in its attitude toward China and the Soviet Union.

Who were these men?

How much power did they wield?

Of the thirteen men who composed that supreme organ, eleven were full members and the remaining two alternate members. With the exception of Ho Chi Minh, President of the DRV, Chairman of the Lao Dong Party, the source of all power, who, in the past, had expressed the Vietnamese wariness toward China[8] but remained outwardly "neutral," the Politburo men were almost evenly divided in their orientation.

Heading the pro-Chinese group was Truong Chinh, Secretary General of the Lao Dong Party from 1941 to 1956, the Party's leading theoretician, and author of two of the most important works on the Vietnamese Communist movement, *The August Revolution* (1946) and *The Resistance Will Win* (1947). The second book is considered as the best exposé of the Vietnamese Communist revolution. An ardent advocate of the Maoist line, Truong Chinh was the guiding force behind the land reform campaign, transplanting without modification into Vietnam the barbarous Chinese system of trials and summary executions of landlords. The brutal campaign backfired, and Truong Chinh was forced to make a public self-criticism and relinquish his office in October, 1956, while retaining his membership in the Politburo. Apparently, he was too powerful and too important a person to be brushed aside in spite of his widespread unpopularity. Less than two years later, however, he fought his way back to power, was named a Deputy Premier and, in July, 1960, appointed Chairman of the Standing Committee of the National Assembly, one of the most influential positions in the DRV. During his fifteen-year tenure as Secretary General of the Communist party, he had undoubtedly built up a strong following that made him indispensable.

A close ally of Truong Chinh was Nguyen Duy Trinh, a tough Viet Minh guerilla leader south of the 17th parallel for nine years, and Foreign Minister since 1966. Trinh has often expressed, in unequivocal terms, his admiration for China, most notably in his speech delivered at the Albanian Party Congress in 1961, when the DRV still leaned toward the Soviet Union.

Le Duc Tho, a theoretician in his own right, was the DRV official delegate and head of the resistance in the South from 1951, when Le Duan was called to the North after a serious quarrel between the two men regarding the conduct of the war. In view of his experience, Tho was appointed to the Lao Dong Party's Special Committee responsible for the overall direction of the Viet Cong movement in South Vietnam. Tho's Maoist inclination has been reflected in his articles condemning "subjectivism and pacifism," especially "revisionism, the principal danger"[9] in the socialist camp, at a time when North Vietnam badly needed Soviet antiaircraft missiles and MIG planes to defend itself against American aerial attacks.

Nguyen Chi Thanh, the one-time rival of Vo Nguyen Giap, was a protégé of Truong Chinh. As the top Political Commissar in the Vietnam People's Army, Thanh was promoted to the rank of general equal to Giap in September, 1959, thanks to Truong Chinh's machinations. In March, 1961, however, as General Giap reasserted his influence, Thanh was stripped of his military rank and transferred to the Ministry of Agricultural Cooperatives.

Of the protagonists of the Soviet Union, General Vo Nguyen Giap appeared to be the most articulate. A Deputy Premier, Minister of Defense, and Commander-in-Chief of the People's Army, Giap had been a leader of the Communist party since the pre-World War II days. As the Victor of Dienbienphu, the general was one of the most popular figures in the DRV, second only to Ho Chi Minh himself. Endowed with inexhaustible energy but subject to emotional outbursts, Giap very seldom concealed his distrust for the Chinese. His celebrated quarrel with Truong Chinh began in the resistance days when the Commander of the Viet Minh forces stubbornly resisted the Party Secretary General's pressure to use Chinese troops against the French. It was Giap who presided over the rectification campaign following Truong Chinh's discomfiture over the land reform fiasco in 1956. The general is now commanding the second most powerful army in Asia.

In the pro-Moscow wing one may notice Deputy Premier Pham Hung, a top guerilla leader in Cochinchina until 1954, an intimate friend and protégé of Pham Van Dong, whom the Prime Minister had admitted to Politburo membership to counterbalance Truong Chinh's ascending influence.

Premier Pham Van Dong, a close associate and confidant of Ho Chi Minh since 1925, was a cautious man who, perhaps because of his official position, and his loyalty to the President, very seldom expressed his personal preference regarding the DRV alignment within the Communist bloc. As one of Ho's faithful followers, the Prime Minister tended to favor a moderately pro-Soviet line, but had publicly endorsed the middle-of-the-road policy. An able and experienced administrator, Pham Van Dong was the perfect bureaucrat, fully devoted to the task of running the government. He had not built up any important following and had made no enemies among the Lao Dong leaders who appreciated his devotion and contributions to the Party.

If Truong Chinh and Vo Nguyen Giap had a long-standing quarrel, Le Duan and Le Duc Tho also had disagreements, especially, as previously discussed, in regard to the conduct of the war in Cochinchina before 1954. Although he was not officially appointed First Secretary[10] until September, 1960, Le Duan had in fact run the Party on Ho's behalf since the ouster of Truong Chinh. The fact that he assumed such an important position after the disastrous failure of the Chinese methods should indicate that Le Duan's sympathy did not lean toward Peking. As First Secretary, the official number two man in North Vietnam who outranked the Premier and the Minister of Defense, both long associates of Ho Chi Minh, any ambitious man would put his followers in key positions and build up a solid following within the party to protect himself. And the Lao Dong Party's First Secretary seemed to be that kind of man. It should not have been by sheer coincidence that the official appointment of Le Duan, who had long years of experience with guerrilla warfare in South Vietnam, took place at the same time as the decision regarding the formation of the National Liberation Front.

While the alternate members enjoyed a less exalted status, the remaining two Politburo full members, economist Le Thanh Nghi and international relations expert Hoang Van Hoan, favored the pro-Soviet faction and the Truong Chinh group, respectively.

Thus, under a façade of unity, the men who held in their hands the destiny of the DRV were sharply divided in their orientation, struggling among themselves for power and Ho Chi Minh's favor, each trying to consolidate his position and increase his influence.

Soviet Influence, 1957–mid-1962

The amount of aid given by one country to another usually reflects the degree of influence the giving state enjoys in the receiving state. It is, therefore, useful to compare the Soviet with the Chinese aid to the DRV in any given period. During the 1955–57 period, China's aid to North Vietnam amounted to U.S. $200 million, most of which was spent on the reconstruction of run-down industrial installations, railways, bridges, and roads that had been destroyed during the Indochina war. At the same time, the Soviet Union offered U.S. $100 million to be used in the building of enterprises in industry and public services. Thus, up to 1957 the DRV had received much more help from China than from the Soviet Union and, consequently, had been in closer collaboration with Peking. In the next three years, however, the trend reversed itself. While China's aid slipped down to U.S. $100 million, that of the Soviet Union went up to U.S. $133 million, in addition to U.S. $26 million worth of assistance from the countries of Eastern Europe.[11] Beginning in 1957, therefore, Hanoi relied more heavily on Moscow than on Peking for the solution of its economic problems. Externally, such a shift passed almost unnoticed, but internally it caused a serious conflict within the Lao Dong Party.

After the visit of Soviet President Voroshilov to Hanoi in May, 1957, Chairman Ho embarked on a long tour of North Korea, the Soviet Union, and Eastern Europe, including Yugoslavia, in July and August of that year. The trip was obviously undertaken to strengthen North Vietnam's ties with the Soviet Union and her satellites. Upon his return on August 30, however, the DRV President found his party deeply divided. According to a French observer who lived in Hanoi at that time,[12] peculiar developments took place in the North Vietnamese capital. The intraparty feud had gotten out of hand. The pro-Chinese faction had refused to yield. Ho Chi Minh, failing to win over the intransigent Politburo members to his view, that is, a slightly pro-Soviet "neutral" policy, secretly left for Moscow to participate in the celebration of the fortieth anniversary of the October Revolution, and stayed out of the country for roughly two months. During his absence, Ho's name, strangely, was not mentioned by the DRV press and radio, and rumors were circulated that he was dead. Neither was General Vo Nguyen Giap, leader of the pro-Moscow wing, seen in public nor his name mentioned by the mass media. Meanwhile, a hectic exchange of letters took place in which Ho laid down his conditions. The founder of the DRV did not return until December 24, after he had received full satisfaction from all those who had disagreed with him. Thus, the first move toward the Soviet Union, which was necessitated by the DRV economic conditions, was strongly resisted by the pro-Chinese group in the Politburo. Peace and equilibrium were restored only after Ho Chi Minh himself had resorted to a self-imposed exile for two months, and threatened to prolong it indefiniately.

Very seldom did Ho speak out on controversial ideological issues. Statements made by his associates, however, reflected his position. During the periods when Hanoi leaned toward Peking or Moscow, Ho still tried to maintain his neutrality by making statements favorable to the side with which North Vietnam was not closely identified. On the occasion of the thirteenth anniversary of the founding of the DRV, for instance, when pro-Moscow views prevailed in Hanoi, Politburo member Le Duan still approvingly quoted Chairman Mao:

About the Chinese peasantry Mao Tse-tung has said: "Our country has over 500 million peasants, how their situation is is very important in relation to the economic development and the strengthening of power in our country." This applies to our country: in the socialist revolution in North Vietnam every work must proceed from the interests of over 13 million people, including 12 million peasants.[13]

In reference to the Chinese achievements, he continued:

The extremely rich experience of China in Socialist construction has given us a very new conception about the path to build Socialism in the countryside. Without machines, the Chinese peasants could proceed to Socialism through co-operativization. Recently after a political remoulding drive, their mind being set free, they have progressed by leaps and bounds. . . . In the leap-and-bound upsurge they have impelled culture rapidly to develop; they have not only wiped out illiteracy, vulgarized elementary education, but they have also opened high-education schools and vocational schools. In the Chinese countryside at present there is an intense movement to set up people's communes.

Flattering as this statement might sound, the Vietnamese refused to imitate the Chinese commune system.

The Sino-Soviet ideological discord, which had erupted to the surface in 1958, became critical in 1960, when the Kremlin recalled its technicians from China. With the failure to reach an agreement at the Moscow talks in July, 1963, the dispute grew in intensity and bitterness. Until the Lao Dong Party Third Congress in September, 1960, Ho Chi Minh had remained strictly neutral in the Sino-Soviet feud. Early in August, 1960, the North Vietnamese leader reportedly made a secret visit to Moscow where he "bargained with Khrushchev, offering Vietnamese support for the Soviet line and closer links with Russia in the future in exchange for greatly increased economic aid from Russia in the industrial sphere."[14] In view of the ambitious five-year plan announced at the Third National Congress of the Lao Dong Party Khrushchev was assumed to have compiled with Ho's request. In his opening speech at the Congress which lasted from September 5 to 10, the DRV President made clear his support for the Soviet line:

We avail ourselves of this opportunity to express our warm feelings of gratitude toward the fraternal socialist countries headed by the great Soviet Union. . . . The Democratic Republic of Vietnam is a member of the big socialist family headed by the great Soviet Union.

. . . Our people strongly support the foreign policy of peace and disarmament program advanced by the Soviet Union and other countries of the socialist camp. . . . The peoples of the world, uniting closely with one another and struggling actively, will undoubtedly be able to prevent a world war and establish a lasting peace.[15]

After clarifying his position, Ho ended his speech with a final tribute to Moscow by stressing Communist unity under Soviet leadership, exclaiming: "Long live the solidarity and unity of the fraternal Parties and the big socialist family headed by the Soviet Union!"

Similarly, Pham Van Dong, Ho's faithful Prime Minister, remarked:

Nowadays the Soviet Union and other Socialist countries are successfully building Socialism and Communism and have become an invincible force. Along with peace-loving people all over the world, they are able to prevent war, to check the bloodstained hands of the imperialists, preserve peace, and save mankind from a new World War, a nuclear war.[16]

The report on the revision of the Party's constitution, read by Le Duan, referred to dogmatism, with which the Chinese had been accused, as limiting the creative power of the Party and the masses and hindering the development of the wisdom and experience of the whole organization.[17]

In his address to the Congress, Defense Minister Vo Nguyen Giap emphasized construction instead of military preparedness, a line that echoed the Soviet policy of peaceful coexistence. "At the present time," said the North Vietnamese Commander-in-Chief, "economic construction in the North has become the central task of the Party. That is why our defense budget must be reduced and military effectiveness cut."[18]

Thus, the tone of the whole Congress greatly pleased the Soviet leadership with whom Ho, for the first and only time, identified himself so unequivocally.

At this very moment, however, the DRV President also decided to revive the revolution in South Vietnam, hoping to bring it under Communism through subversion and armed infiltration. Contrary to his expectations, the election scheduled for 1956 had not been held. Such an election would have unified Vietnam under Ho's rule since, regardless of the outcome of the balloting, the North with its larger population and a Communist-supervised election would have carried the day. In view of the distressing political and economic conditions in the North, which undoubtedly needed time to recover from the land reform nightmare, the disappointed Ho could not have resorted to force to bring about reunification. Only in September, 1960, was it decided that the *Mat-tran Dan-toc Giai-phong Mien Nam*, National Front for the Liberation of South Vietnam (NFLSVN), uniting all anti-Diem forces be created to overthrow the Saigon regime, implicitly through armed insurrection. The Party, on September 10, adopted a resolution which read in part:

In the present stage, the Vietnamese revolution has two strategic tasks: first, to carry out the socialist revolution in North Vietnam; second, to liberate South Vietnam from the ruling yoke of the U.S. imperialists and their henchmen in order to achieve national unity and complete inde-

pendence and freedom throughout the country. The two strategic tasks
are closely related to each other and spur each other forward. . . .
Therefore, to carry out the socialist revolution in the North, in the South
we must endeavor to rally all national and democratic forces, expand
and consolidate the national unity bloc; isolate the U.S. imperialists and
their henchmen, and speed up the struggle to strengthen peace and
reunify our fatherland. . . .

In the completion of the national people's democratic revolution
throughout the country and achievement of national reunification, our
compatriots in the South have the task of directly overthrowing the rule
of the U.S. imperialists and their agents.

The two revolutionary tasks of the North and the South belong to two
different strategies, each task being aimed at satisfying the definite re-
quirement of each zone under the specific conditions of our divided
country. . . . The immediate task of the revolution in the South is to
achieve unity of the whole people, to fight resolutely against the aggressive and warmongering U.S. imperialists, to overthrow the dictatorial
Ngo Dinh Diem ruling clique. . . .

To insure the complete success of the revolutionary struggle in South
Vietnam, our people there must strive to establish a united bloc of
workers, peasants, and soldiers to bring into being a broad national
united front directed against the U.S.-Diem clique and based on the
worker-peasant alliance. This front must rally all the patriotic classes and
sections of the people, the majority and minority nationalities, all patriotic parties and religious groupings, together with all individuals inclined
to oppose the U.S.-Diem clique.[19]

Thus, while publicly adhering to the Soviet line of peaceful coexistence, Ho followed an aggressive policy which was in agreement
with the Maoist position. He was not concerned with the ideological
issue under dispute but primarily interested in extending his rule to
South Vietnam. In order to realize his ambition, Ho needed both
Chinese and Soviet assistance and, consequently, was not ready to
identify himself completely with either Communist colossus. Although North Vietnam had favored peaceful coexistence since the
second half of 1959, beginning in 1961 it was the course of the war
in the South and the amount of aid it received from China and the
Soviet Union that determined Hanoi's attitude toward Peking and
Moscow. To the practical leader of the DRV the question of military and economic aid was of paramount importance, and the ideological issue under dispute—revisionism *vs.* dogmatism, peaceful

coexistence *vs.* protracted confrontation—unless it affected the conduct of the war, should be minimized. Besides, peaceful coexistence began to appear unattractive to Ho when he decided to conquer South Vietnam and Laos by force. As the main obstacle to Ho's plan was "American imperialism," any detente between Moscow and Washington was resented by the North Vietnamese. In the 1960–61 winter, the Soviet Union took an active part in the war in Laos. During and after the battle for Vientiane, for instance, Russian aircraft busily parachuted supplies, ammunition, and Vietnamese military personnel to reinforce the Kong Le and Pathet Lao units. Following the second Geneva Accord on Laos concluded in July, 1962, however, Khrushchev discontinued his active policy in Southeast Asia, and refused to increase military and economic aid to Ho Chi Minh. This Soviet decision, in addition to Khrushchev's attempt to mobilize the collective support of the foreign Communist parties for his position against the Chinese, made it increasingly difficult for Ho to endorse the Moscow line. The balance of forces within the Lao Dong Party began to shift in favor of China. It should be recalled that Hanoi's alignment with Moscow during the 1957–mid-1962 was not a total commitment on the North Vietnamese part. At the Twenty Second Congress of the Soviet Communist Party in October, 1961, for example, Ho, while leaning toward Moscow, refused to endorse the general condemnation of Albania, China's Eastern European ally.

Mid-1962–1964, Return of Peking

As the Sino-Soviet discord grew in intensity, Ho continued to maintain his neutrality, making tireless efforts to prevent a split between the two Communist giants that would force him to take sides. In view of his seniority and influence in the international Communist movement, both Peking and Moscow made serious attempts to enlist his support for their cause. This put the Lao Dong Party Chairman in a very unenviable position and left him with no other alternative than nonalignment. With a view to bringing about a rapprochement or at least preventing an irreparable schism, Ho praised both China and the Soviet Union for their achievements and minimized their differences.

During the two-week visit of Soviet General Batov late in December, 1962, General Giap, reflecting Ho's position, lauded the Soviet Union for settling the Cuban missile crisis and, in spite of his lukewarm feeling for the Chinese, equally praised China for solving the Indian border dispute. The DRV Minister of Defense especially emphasized the need for socialist solidarity:

At the present time the Vietnamese people and the Vietnamese People's Army more than ever must hold high the banner of solidarity and unity of mind, the victorious banner of the international Communist movement, that is, the 1957 Declaration of the Conference of Representatives of the Communist and Workers' Parties and the 1960 Moscow Statement of 81 Communist and Workers' Parties, and uphold our solidarity of proletarian internationalism with the peoples and armies of the Soviet Union, China, and other brother countries of the Socialist camp.[20]

Meanwhile, at the East German Party Congress, which opened on January 15, 1963, it became apparent that a rupture between the two Communist colossi was inevitable. Khrushchev defiantly defended his position on peaceful coexistence, and warned that if war broke out it would likely be a nuclear war in which 700 million people (China's population) would be killed in a few hours, called for an end to mutual public recrimination, and demanded that pro-Chinese Albania cooperate more closely with the rest of the Communist parties. The Chinese delegation was not cowed into submission, but opened an attack on Yugoslav—meaning Soviet—revisionism. The speech was met with shouting and desk banging by most of the other delegates. The Vietnamese were obviously shaken by this lack of socialist tolerance and solidarity.

Late in January of that year, Czechoslovakia's President Novotný, a strong supporter of Chairman Khrushchev, visited the DRV. The communiqué issued at the conclusion of the state visit emphasized the need for unity among socialist countries, and supported the Soviet call for a cessation of open polemics in order to create an atmosphere favorable for mutual consultations among brother parties. Although the statement referred to the Soviet Union as the center of the socialist camp and to peaceful coexistence as the most correct policy under then existing conditions, it was not entirely pro-Moscow at the expense of Peking. While the communiqué praised the Soviet Union for the correct handling of the Cuban crisis, it also lauded China for her willingness to settle the Indian border problem. Both Communist leaders, Novotný and Ho Chi Minh, equally declared their full support for Peking's just stand in regard to the liberation of Taiwan.[21]

Since the East German Party Congress, Ho Chi Minh took upon himself the difficult task of keeping the talk going between Peking and Moscow, extolling the great achievements of the socialist bloc, and blaming the United States for scheming "to sabotage the socialist camp and split the international Communist and Workers' movement." In its February 10, 1963, statement broadcast over Radio Hanoi, the Lao Dong Party Central Committee expressed its wish that discords between brother parties should not be permitted to harm the unity of the socialist camp because "Communists have all the necessary conditions to overcome differences of views and firmly to maintain and enhance unity within their ranks."[22] The Central Committee also reiterated its view that the 1957 Moscow Declaration and the 1960 Moscow Statement

have laid down principles on the strategy and tactics of the international Communist and Workers' movement, rules guiding the relations among Communist and Workers' parties, methods to overcome divergences of views which may arise between parties, that is, to meet and consult one another in order to reach unanimous views. All Communist and Workers' parties must most scrupulously respect all stipulations of these declarations and statements which have been recognized by all.

The Lao Dong Party went on to praise the Soviet Union, the cradle of the socialist movement:

The great Communist Party of the Soviet Union, the party of Lenin, is the vanguard of the international Communist movement. The Soviet Union is the first country to have carried out the socialist revolution, the country which has successfully built the first socialist society in the world, and is building communism. The victory of the October Revolution and the building of socialism and communism in the Soviet Union have strongly stimulated the working people and land-oppressed peoples of the world to rise up and struggle for self liberation and to build a new life for themselves. The experiences of the great October Revolution and of socialist construction in the Soviet Union are of tremendous significance for the international Communist movement as a whole.

And in order not to implicate his neutrality, Ho heaped similar praises upon China:

The great Communist Party of China has led the people's democratic revolution to victory and is taking the 650 million Chinese people to socialism. Following the victory of the Soviet October Revolution, the victory of the Chinese Revolution is of tremendous historic significance. The victory of the Chinese Revolution and the achievements recorded by China in the building of socialism have dealt crippling blows to imperialism and helped the balance of world forces tip in favor of the socialist camp and world peace. They are strongly stimulating the national liberation movement and the revolutionary struggle of the world's peoples.

Ho also revealed that for a year he had tried to prevent a showdown between Peking and Moscow and, in January, 1962, the Lao Dong Party had sent letters "to a number of fraternal parties expressing its concern and proposing that a meeting be held between representatives of Communist and Workers' parties to settle the discord together and that, pending such a meeting, the parties cease attacking one another in the press and over the radio."

In spite of the Lao Dong Party's apparently neutral position, Peking remained disturbed about the Czech President's visit to North Vietnam. With a view to placating the Chinese, Ho invited President Liu Shao-chi to make an official visit to the DRV, which was subsequently scheduled for May 10 to 16. To sound out Ho's views and to neutralize the effects of General Batov's and President Novotny's visits, the Chinese Head of State thus made a stopover in Hanoi during his Southeast Asian tour. Liu and his delegation were given an unusually warm and elaborate welcome. At the evening banquet honoring his guests, Ho made a speech supporting China's stand on Taiwan, the Sino-Indian dispute, the United Nations issue, and pleading for solidarity among socialist states. Liu's answer was moderately subdued. On the third day of his visit, however, the Chinese President let loose a barrage of attacks against the Soviet Union in a speech delivered at a mass rally in Ba Dinh, Hanoi's Red Square. In reference to the Soviet position he commented:

Peaceful coexistence refers to relations between socialist countries and capitalist countries. It must not be reinterpreted at will or stretched to apply to relations between the oppressed and oppressor nations or between oppressed and oppressor classes. Peaceful coexistence must not

be used to abolish the socialist countries' duty to support the revolutionary struggle of oppressed nations and people. The foreign policy of
socialist countries, moreover, must not be used to supersede the revolutionary line of the proletariat of various countries and their parties.[23]

The Chinese leader added that if the socialist countries respected
each other's independence and sovereignty, treated each other as
equals, refrained from intervening in each other's domestic affairs,
and cooperated on the basis of mutual benefit, the unity of the
Communist camp could "certainly be strengthened."

In his second major speech, delivered at the Nguyen Ai Quoc
School for cadres, Liu launched a vehement attack against the
modern revisionists that must have greatly embarrassed his hosts,
who had tried to remain neutral in the dispute. In regard to the
Sino-Soviet discord, he noted:

The polemics are centered on whether the people of the world should
carry out revolutions or not, and whether proletarian parties should lead
the world's people in revolutions or not. The course of this struggle has a
bearing on whether the entire cause of the proletariat and working people throughout the world will succeed or fail, and on the destiny of the
whole mankind.[24]

The modern revisionists (Russians), continued Liu, actually distorted Marxism-Leninism, emasculated it of its revolutionary soul,
repudiated the historic need for proletarian revolution and dictatorship during the period of transition from capitalism to Communism,
and replaced Marxist-Leninist concepts with bourgeois viewpoints.
All true Marxist-Leninists, therefore, must face the challenge of
modern revisionism and defeat it completely.

The joint communiqué issued at the end of the visit[25] seemed to
indicate that Ho had gone only half way to please Liu by agreeing
to support Peking on some issues but avoiding statements that
would offend Moscow. Ho endorsed Liu's position that "unanimity"
instead of "single view" should be the principle regulating relations
between socialist states. Both Presidents supported general disarmament, but "In the circumstances in which imperialism rejects
disarmament and continues preparation for a nuclear war, it is
highly necessary to strengthen the national defense might of the
countries in the socialist camp, including the development of nuclear superiority of the socialist countries." While this statement

apparently approved China's effort to develop her own nuclear weapons, it did not conflict with the Soviet view in this regard. Revisionism or right opportunism was also condemned as "the main danger of the international Communist movement." However, the attack was not aimed directly at the Soviet Union, because "Yugoslav revisionism is the concentrated expression of the modern revisionist theories." Significantly, the communiqué was silent on the issue of peaceful coexistence, which the Chinese President had vehemently criticized in his May 12 speech. Thus, in spite of Liu's persuasive effort and warning that it was not possible "to act as onlookers or follow the middle course,"[26] Ho refused to commit himself irrevocably and continued to emphasize the need for unity.

Meanwhile, the DRV, together with North Korea, did not sign the Moscow test ban treaty although its National Assembly, at the sixth session held in the 1956–57 winter, had "approved a declaration welcoming the appeal of the Supreme Soviet of the U.S.S.R. on the banning of atomic weapons and on reduction of armament."[27] Ho's refusal to sign the treaty caused Moscow to cut its aid to Hanoi. Such reduction in Soviet assistance made it difficult for the DRV to support the insurgents in South Vietnam, Laos, and Cambodia and rendered her increasingly dependent on China. Ho's disapproval of this unchivalrous Russian treatment seemed to find expression in *Hoc Tap* (Studies), the Lao Dong Party's official paper, which began to carry a number of articles critical of Tito's revisionism. Was this criticism also intended for Khrushchev? Possibly.

Throughout the year of 1963, both China and the Soviet Union tried to gain support not for reconciliation but for their respective position. By the winter (1963–64), all efforts having proved futile, a Sino-Soviet split became imminent. Mao Tse-tung had gone as far as to demand Khrushchev's ouster as a price for rapprochement. Late in January, 1964, Ho sent a Vietnamese delegation headed by the Lao Dong Party First Secretary Le Duan and including Politburo members Le Duc Tho and Hoang Van Hoan to Peking to talk with Mao, then to Moscow (January 31–February 10) to see the Soviet leaders, and back to Peking in a desperate attempt to prevent a schism. The Vietnamese held long meetings with Chairman Khrushchev and Suslov, the Soviet Communist Party's leading theoretician, and Mao Tse-tung, Chou En-lai, and Liu Shao-chi, the Chinese counterpart of Suslov. The failure of the Le Duan mission was marked by the absence of a communiqué at the end of its visit to Peking and a routine statement at the conclusion of its meetings in Moscow. In reply to a plea for stronger Soviet support for the war, the Soviet Communist party vaguely stated that it resolutely supported the just struggle of the Vietnamese people against U.S. imperialism in South Vietnam.

In spite of their efforts to promote a Sino-Soviet rapprochement, the DRV leaders appeared to have committed themselves to Peking's approach in world affairs, agreeing with the Chinese that the Marxist-Leninist concept favored the use of violence to eliminate reactionary and counterrevolutionary regimes and that popular violence would eventually defeat imperialist aggressors. According to Le Duan, "the Party's line is a revolutionary line which is incompatible with modern revisionism."[28]

In 1964, South Vietnam was in the midst of a grave crisis. The fall of Ngo Dinh Diem in November, 1963, was followed by a series of coups d'état that plunged the country into a nearly chaotic state: generals were fighting generals, civilians denouncing military men, religious groups quarrelling among themselves, and striking students and workers demonstrating on the street. The Viet Cong and North Vietnamese sat and watched, waiting for the Saigon government to crumble. Disregarding the U.S. appeal against the military takeover of power and the dissolution of the civilian Parliament, General Nguyen Khanh declared that the Vietnamese armed forces would not fight to "carry out the policy of any country."

The rapidly deteriorating situation in South Vietnam led many serious observers to believe that the United States, unless it decided to withdraw, had to increase its involvement drastically. Of the two alternatives the second seemed to be the less likely choice as 1964 was a presidential election year. Events seemed to go the Communist way when, suddenly, the Tonkin Gulf incident provoked a sharp reaction from the United States. In retaliation against alleged attacks by North Vietnamese PT boats on American vessels in international waters President Johnson, on August 5, ordered air action against a number of DRV naval bases and oil installations in what was described as a "limited and fitting" response. A joint resolution[29] was subsequently passed by the U.S. Congress permitting the President to take all necessary measures to promote the maintenance of international peace and security in Southeast Asia. The war was finally brought home to Ho Chi Minh, who grew increasingly worried about further bombing. On August 6, following the first air strike against the DRV, Peking warned Washington that the attack meant aggression against China, the United States had gone too far and "the Chinese people will not sit idly by without lending a helping hand." Mao also ridiculed the Soviet proposal to invite representatives of all the parties involved to the United Nations to discuss the incident on the grounds that the world organization had degenerated into a tool of U.S. imperialism and a forum of American-Soviet collaboration, and had nothing to do with the Vietnam problem.

At this juncture, the pro-Chinese wing within the Lao Dong Party seemed to come to the fore again. Khrushchev's announcement on August 10, 1964, that a preparatory meeting of all Communist parties would begin in Moscow on December 15 fell on deaf ears in Hanoi. As expected, the Chinese Communist Party, on August 30, reiterated its decision not to attend the international Communist conference. Along with Albania, North Korea, the Indonesian and Japanese Communist parties, the DRV followed suit by declining the invitation to participate in the meeting.

Meanwhile, in the United States, President Johnson, after a resounding victory at the poll, decided to put the Saigon situation in order, deny the Communists whatever advantages they might have benefited from the political instability in South Vietnam, and strengthen the Allies' bargaining position should negotiation take place. When rumors spread that the United States was considering retaliatory measures against both the DRV and China, Hanoi and Peking reacted frantically. For the first time since the Korean war China felt herself menaced. The arrival of two U.S. nuclear submarines caused great concern in the two Asian Communist capitals. The subdued tone of the Chinese protest seemingly reflected a genuine fear of American attack and an attempt to prevent it. The *People's Daily* editorial, for instance, condemned the sailing of the nuclear submarines into waters off the Asian mainland as

a brazen war provocation by U.S. imperialism against the Chinese and other peoples of the Western Pacific, and a most despicable act of nuclear blackmail and threat by the Johnson administration. . . .

This is additional proof that the tripartite partial nuclear test-ban treaty praised to the skies by Lyndon Johnson and his like is a big fraud and that the U.S. talk about its concern over the "contamination of the atmosphere" is sheer hypocrisy. In sending nuclear submarines to carry out provocations at China's door, is not the Johnson administration aggravating the danger of nuclear war and trying to precipitate the people of Asia into a nuclear holocaust?[30]

The editorial took pains to explain that Peking entertained no aggressive aims in its attempt to become a nuclear power, but wanted only to strengthen its defense and safeguard peace:

Having possessed them [nuclear bombs], the Chinese Government did not take them to the doorsteps of the United States, much less did it use them to threaten any Asian country. On the contrary, the Chinese Government, simultaneously with the explosion of its first atom bomb, proposed to the world governments that a summit conference be convened to discuss the question of the complete prohibition and thorough destruction of nuclear weapons.

With a view to dissipating any doubt regarding the Chinese desire for peace and denying the United States any pretext to attack China, Peking "solemnly declared to the whole world that China would never, at any time, and under any circumstances, be the first to use nuclear weapons," and asked Washington to prove its sincerity for peace by reaching "an agreement with China on not using nuclear weapons."

Similarly, Peking's reply to Hanoi's request for aid and support was unusually mild; it made no mention of Chinese intervention, but merely referred to the Indochinese people's effort to resist any imperialist move:

The Chinese Government severely condemns U.S. imperialism for its playing with fire in Indochina, and firmly supports the people of Vietnam, Laos, and Cambodia in their just and patriotic struggle against U.S. imperialism. . . . There should be no doubt that any U.S. imperialist move to expand the war will be repulsed still more vigorously by the peoples of Indochina (not China!).[31]

Following the February 7, 1965, American aerial attacks directed at barracks and staging areas in the southern area of the DRV, which U.S. intelligence believed had been actively used by Hanoi for training and infiltration of Communist troops into South Vietnam, General Lo Jui-ching, Chief of the General Staff of the Chinese Army, simply warned that Peking would not stand by idly, but would do its utmost to support North Vietnam against U.S. imperialist aggression.[32] As the war escalated, Peking's apprehension that it might spill over into China also grew in intensity. This Chinese frenzy emerged in war preparatory measures and in numerous official statements.[33]

China's unusually moderate pronouncements did little to heighten Ho's morale in the face of such a serious crisis. The vehement DRV condemnation of the intrusion of the American submarines as an act of war provocation against the peace-loving people throughout the world was accompanied by a feeble warning to the United States that China's nuclear capability constituted "an important contribution to the common struggle of the peoples of Asia."[34] In this hour of distress, Ho became painfully aware of the disastrous consequences of repeated U.S. bombings and the inability of China to provide North Vietnam with effective aid against American aerial attacks. Gradually, Hanoi veered toward Moscow. Again, the move toward the Soviet Union was dictated by the DRV need for military and economic aid, not by Ho's desire to get involved in the deepening ideological quarrel in which he had cautiously avoided taking position. While swinging toward the Soviet Union, North Vietnam took laborious steps so as not to antagonize her giant neighbor, seizing every opportunity to extol Sino-Vietnamese solidarity. On January 30, 1965, for instance, Hanoi's papers front-paged the text of the letter addressed to the DRV National Assembly by the Chinese National People's Congress, in which the Chinese people reaffirmed "their determination to side with the brotherly people of Vietnam . . . and struggle to smash the adventurist war plans of the U.S. imperialists," and recalled their government's statement that "any encroachment by the United States on DRV territory would be an encroachment on the Chinese People's Republic and that the Chinese people decidedly will not sit with folded arms in that event."[35]

In the meantime, the Kremlin, while anxious to keep Ho Chi Minh on its side, was not eager to help him continue his protracted "people's war" and risk a military confrontation with the United States in Southeast Asia. In a letter to the DRV Foreign Minister Xuan Thuy on December 30, 1964, Gromyko simply reiterated Soviet support for the national liberation of the Vietnamese people, but made no definite commitments:

The Soviet Government demands [said the note] that the United States discontinue all interference in the affairs of South Vietnam, evacuate troops and armament from there, and allow the Vietnamese people themselves to settle their internal affairs. . . .

The USSR, loyal as it is to the principles of proletarian international-ism, will not remain indifferent to the destinies of a fraternal socialist country and is prepared to give the DRV the necessary assistance should the aggressors dare encroach on its independence and sovereignty.[36]

Moscow also rewarded the new Hanoi shift by extending a warm welcome to the National Liberation Front members in the Soviet Union. In one of its January 1, 1965, broadcasts, Radio Moscow announced:

At a meeting with the delegation of the National Liberation Front of South Vietnam which visited Moscow, Comrade Ponomarev, Secretary of the CPSU Central Committee, affirmed the Soviet stand of continuing to support the South Vietnamese people in their struggle against U.S. imperialism and its lackeys for their rights to freedom and the peaceful reunification of their country.

With the visit of the new Soviet Premier Kosygin scheduled for early February, 1965, another era of close Soviet-Vietnamese col-laboration began.

Return of Moscow, 1965–1969

As *Nhan Dan* is the Lao Dong Party's official paper, a careful reader will detect Ho's position mirrored through its lines. The is-sues preceding and following the Soviet delegation's visit to Hanoi certainly brought great satisfaction to the men in the Kremlin. On January 31, for instance, *Nhan Dan* spoke of Kosygin's pending visit as one of "splendid significance," an event that would strengthen Soviet-Vietnamese friendship and cooperation, and invigorate the solidarity among socialist countries. It expressed the feeling of the Vietnamese people who, "educated by their party, . . . have a warm and profound sentiment toward the Soviet people and the Soviet Communists, the first in the history of mankind to rise up and carry out a socialist revolution and who have built the first socialist country in the world." The paper also paid homage to the Soviet heroes who had selflessly fought for the liberty of the proletariat all over the world, and praised the achievements of the whole socialist camp which, following the examples of the October Revolution, had changed the face of the world. The Lao Dong Party thus extended a specially warm welcome to the delegation that represented the Soviet Communist Party and people, to whom the Vietnamese were bound by a "profound friendship." Ho also pledged his service to retrieve the predicament in the Communist camp, that is, to restore the solidarity and friendship between the Soviet Union, China, and all socialist countries.

Upon their arrival on February 6, Premier Kosygin and his delegation, which included several high ranking military officers, were exuberantly welcomed by some 100,000 Hanoians who turned out at the Gia Lam airport and lined the streets in the capital, dressed in their holiday best. Premier Pham Van Dong and his Russian guests slowly walked past the flag-waving crowd amidst the cheering hurrahs resounding all over the airport. The DRV Prime Minister's welcome speech and the Soviet Premier's reply were consistently interrupted by prolonged applause.[37] Such was Hanoi on the day the Russians arrived.

At the grand reception given in honor of the Soviet guests on the following day, Dong again expressed the Vietnamese admiration for the Soviet Union, the mighty socialist country with "the most advanced science and technology in the world, as shown by the wonderful flights of the spaceships Vostok and Voskhold," and voiced his confidence that the Soviet Communist Party and people would overcome all difficulties and obstacles, achieve still greater successes in building Communism and defending world peace, and make still greater contributions to the revolutionary cause throughout the world. Voicing the DRV support for the Soviet leadership, Premier Dong stated that, in their happy as well as trying days, the Vietnamese had always maintained their unshakable trust in the Soviet Communist party and people.[38]

In contrast to Pham Van Dong's profuse speeches, Kosygin's replies were noticeably restrained, pledging Soviet support and repeating the points contained in the Gromyko note to Xuan Thuy on December 30, 1964.[39] In an address delivered in Ho Chi Minh's presence, Kosygin aired the Soviet wish for fraternal cooperation between members of the socialist family, cordial settlement of discords, and increasing closeness among them. While this process developed in complicated conditions and involved the overcoming of serious difficulties, it would ultimately lead to the victory of the Leninist principle of internationalism.[40] The reasonable tone of the Soviet Premier's speeches greatly encouraged the DRV President whose view was consonant with the Moscow line as expounded by Kosygin. Hanoi's realignment, necessitated by the changing face of the war, was thus made easier by the change of leadership in the Kremlin, where Brezhnev and Kosygin had replaced Khrushchev in October, 1964. Ho, along with many other Communist leaders, hoped that the new Soviet rulers would be more flexible and more successful than Khrushchev in solving the ideological dispute that had so seriously split the Communist world. Brezhnev and Kosygin had in fact made serious efforts to patch up their difference with the Chinese comrades. With a view to reconciliation, the Soviet Premier and his delegation stopped over twice in Peking, en route to and from Hanoi, to extend a personal invitation to the Chinese leaders to attend the meeting of all Communist parties called for March 1. Mao Tse-tung, however, remained adamant. According to reliable Communist sources, Premier Chou En-lai coolly informed Kosygin on February 5 that China would not participate in the preparatory meeting for the international Communist conference, on the grounds that it was based on a unilateral Soviet proposal, and that sufficient preparations were needed for the convening of such a meeting.[41]

While Kosygin was still in Hanoi obviously to win the North Vietnamese to the Soviet side, and presumably to inform Ho of Johnson's desire for a peaceful settlement of the Vietnam problem and to persuade him that a negotiated solution would serve as a smokescreen, enabling conquest through political means, American aircraft, on February 7 and 8, struck a number of bases in the DRV. Ho seized this opportunity to ask for Soviet antiaircraft missiles (SAM) and MIG jets to strengthen North Vietnam's defense. The request was promptly complied with by the Soviet Premier. The Soviet generals accompanying Kosygin also held a series of long talks with the DRV Defense Minister Vo Nguyen Giap and several other high ranking officers of the People's Army. The problem of antiaircraft defense was thoroughly discussed. One of the concrete results of those meetings was the subsequent arrival in Hanoi of Soviet antiaircraft missiles and technicians and the building of missile-launching sites in North Vietnam.

Meanwhile, on March 15, 1965, the seventeen nonaligned nations that had met in Belgrade made an appeal for negotiation without preconditions. Subsequently, in his speech delivered at Johns Hopkins University on April 7, President Johnson proposed a negotiated settlement and offered one-billion dollars in aid to Southeast Asia, including North Vietnam. Hanoi, while under Moscow's mantle, continued to parrot Peking's line, rejecting these proposals as "a deliberate attempt to absolve U.S. imperialism from its crime," a "ludicrous swindle," or a "cheating peaceful negotiation plot."[42]

In the same month, Premier Pham Van Dong stopped over in Kunning twice, before and after participating in the celebration of the tenth anniversary of the first Afro-Asian Conference in Bandung. At the banquet given in his honor in the Chinese city, exactly one week after President Johnson's Baltimore speech, the North Vietnamese Prime Minister said: "In the just struggle against U.S. imperialism, we have an invincible and powerful ideological weapon, that is, the theory of people's war [the Maoist concept of protracted confrontation]."[43]

Equally uncompromising were the remarks made by the DRV National Assembly delegation in Peking in the summer of 1965. In a Chinese-like tone, it emphatically said:

To fight and win is the road that the Vietnamese people have chosen. If the struggle does not end in one year, they will fight for ten years. If the war does not end in one generation, the next generation will continue to fight. . . .

China is our neighbor which shares with us nearly one thousand kilometers of borderline. The relationship between Vietnam and China is like lips and teeth. In our struggle against the United States for national salvation, China considers Vietnam as the front line and China itself as the rear. Our Chinese friends used to say: "Whatever is needed in the front, the rear will supply. If it needs weapons, there are weapons; if it needs food, there is food; if it needs manpower, there is manpower."[44]

Thus, while veering toward Moscow, Ho adopted a nuanced position by appearing to follow the Chinese bellicose line. *Nhan Dan* regularly published large excerpts from the *People's Daily* editorials, such as the December 14, 1965, statement ridiculing Washington peace talk proposals as a "trick of the U.S. imperialists to carry out their aggressive policy and to obtain what they failed to attain on the battlefield," "a trick to cover their criminal acts," and pledging the firm endorsement of the 650 million Chinese "who will support the Vietnamese as much and as long as the Vietnamese people require" and "will spare no effort to support the Vietnamese people in defeating the U.S. aggressors."

On the twenty-first anniversary of the founding of the Vietnam People's Army (December 22, 1965), *Nhan Dan* front-paged an article by pro-Chinese Politburo member Nguyen Chi Thanh, entitled "Greetings to Our Twenty-one Year Old Army." The fact that the article was broadcast in full by VNA denoted its importance. Thanh, reflecting Mao's position, asserted that the Lao Dong Party, on the basis of scientific socialism and of the Marxist-Leninist ideology, had skillfully applied the experiences of revolutionary war in many countries to the practice of the Vietnamese revolution. "The people's war is a great success of our party," said Thanh. "The victory of people's war in our country not only bears an important practical significance, but also an important significance regarding the theory of the people's war and the people's army in a country which has relatively small population and territory and a backward economy but which has opposed and defeated an enemy many times stronger in equipment, technique, as well as economic and national defense potentials." Expressing his confidence in the invincibility of the people's war, Thanh maintained that the sending of nearly 200,000 American troops into South Vietnam was a U.S. admission of failure. Thanh was "firmly convinced" that the problem of massive and direct American participation in the war would be solved by the "heroic South Vietnamese Army" (Viet Cong and North Vietnamese troops), in spite of the enemy's high mobility and better weapons. Why? Because, Thanh added, of the low morale among U.S. forces, the high spirit of attack of the people's war, and battlefield conditions that rendered the enemy's training, equipment, and training methods completely unsuitable. The United States, therefore, had no other alternative than to fight in the way forced upon it by the "South Vietnamese Army." Regardless of the number of troops it would bring in, the United States would be defeated, due to its inability to solve the problems of strategy and tactics.

These statements either were made for propaganda purposes or reflected the Hanoi and Peking view of the war. If the second assumption is correct, one must then conclude that Ho had been misled by favorable reports from his field commanders. This over-optimism or illusion on Hanoi's part, which had been encouraged by Peking, perhaps caused it to read into the U.S. peace talk offers a failure of the American Command to find a suitable strategy to fight a protracted people's war.

In all fairness to the DRV, one would be inclined to believe that these bellicose pronouncements, made during the period of Hanoi's reliance on Moscow, were intended for Chinese consumption. Ho could ill afford antagonizing Mao, as he still needed Chinese small arms and ammunition and the Chinese railways for shipping Soviet aid to North Vietnam, and wanted to exploit the often expressed American fear of possible Chinese troops' entrance into the war. Thus studiously navigating between Peking and Moscow, Ho continued to receive both Chinese and Soviet assistance and support. Two agreements on economic aid were signed between the DRV on the one hand and China and the Soviet Union on the other in the summer of 1965.

With a view to conveying the impression that the North Vietnamese position was also consonant with the Soviet on such delicate issues as national liberation wars and peaceful coexistence, Hanoi's papers eagerly published excerpts from Kosygin's statements in an interview with *The New York Times* columnist James Reston on December 6, 1965:

We [the Soviet Union] hold that the *wars of national liberation* are just ones, and that such wars will take place as long as there still exists oppression of nations by imperialist powers. . . . The war of national liberation is going on in South Vietnam because the people there do not want to be governed by the puppets of the United States. [emphasis supplied]

and

Coexistence between slave holders and slaves is impossible. We have never imagined such kind of peaceful coexistence [emphasis supplied].[45]

Although the Supreme Soviet of the USSR made only a restrained statement saying that it resolutely condemned the armed intervention of the United States in Vietnam and vaguely pledging "all possible assistance and support" to the Vietnamese, *Nhan Dan,* in a front-page editorial (December 11, 1965), spoke of the "stirringly held meetings and demonstrations in many places in Moscow," of the "volunteers to help our people fight against U.S. aggression," and of the "220 million people of the Soviet Union" being closely united behind the "just struggle of our people."

Since 1966, the Soviet Union had been accusing China of hampering the transit of Russian aid and materials to North Vietnam, and complaining that Chinese assistance to Hanoi was "clearly insufficient."[46] Peking, of course, denied such charges and belittled Soviet aid on the grounds that it was too inadequate and too poor in quality and "The heart of the matter is that the Soviet revisionist leadership group has already degenerated into an accomplice of the U.S. imperialism. Its so-called aid to Vietnam is a sham. Its real aim is to oppose China, and all people persevering in revolution. What it hankers after is world domination through U.S.-Soviet collaboration!"[47]

This confused situation, this troubled water benefited no one but the experienced fisherman Ho Chi Minh, who continued to ask for and receive more and more assistance from both brotherly socialist countries. The temporary Chinese refusal to permit the shipping of Soviet materials overland and Peking's attempt to discredit Russian aid brought about what the Chinese dreaded most: closer Vietnamese-Soviet collaborations.

As the war escalated, serious efforts were also made to put an end to it. As the champion of protracted confrontation, Mao consistently rejected all peace overtures made by the United States or third parties, and condemned the American-Soviet "conspiracy of forcing peace through bombing." Peking went so far as to accuse Moscow of helping the United States in its war in Vietnam, calling it "the broker peddling the 'peace talks' scheme of U.S. imperialism, the accomplice helping U.S. imperialism to conduct a war blackmail, and the renegade selling out the cause of the Vietnamese people against U.S. aggression and for national salvation."[48] The Chinese Communist party, instead, has pledged its firm support to the Vietnamese people "in fighting to the end until final victory is achieved,"[49] and stated that "the 700 million people of China will back the Vietnamese people to the hilt."[50]

In contrast to the provocative Chinese tirades, the Russian declarations were reasonably restrained. The Soviet Union showed its support for the DRV in a more subtle way. Radio Moscow, for instance, gave extensive coverage to the deserting American servicemen, broadcasting their open letters to the American people condemning U.S. action in Vietnam. At the same time, the Soviet Government made frequent reference to the willingness of the DRV, as expressed by Ho Chi Minh, to negotiate a settlement of the Vietnam problem once the United States stopped its military provocation.[51]

The Chinese and Soviet charges and countercharges, in addition to their opposite attitudes toward negotiation, made it increasingly difficult for North Vietnam to accept peace overtures extended by the United States. Painfully aware of the consequences of a miscalculation, Ho bided his time. As the bombing continued to take its toll in the North and the ground war in the South became more and more costly, however, Ho was forced to make a difficult choice: either to follow Peking and carry on the people's war, or to lean on Moscow and negotiate a settlement. A shrewd calculator as always, the DVR President decided to please both Communist colossi, that is, to fight (the Chinese way), then talk (the Russian way). This decision, however, made Ho a *persona non grata* to Mao. In the face of this discomfiture, General Vo Nguyen Giap, with Ho's approval, dispatched troops to South Vietnam at an accelerated rate by the end of 1967, stepped up his war efforts, hoping to reverse the situation and wrest back his lost strategic initiative. With the large-scale infiltration of North Vietnamese regulars, General Giap shifted his offensive to a new stage. The main characteristic of this phase was the expansion of the war of destruction mostly by simultaneous assaults on Saigon and the provincial capitals, such as the attacks launched during the *Tet* truce in January-February, 1968. In order to carry out their scheme, the Viet Cong had proposed the cease-fire which they subsequently violated. Thus, deprived of victories on the battlefield, Hanoi sought to prove that there were no safe places in South Vietnam, and that it was capable of attacking and occupying any town it chose. Both Ho and Giap fully realized that there was no defense against death volunteers, no way to protect cities and people from destruction by men who were prepared to pay any price for it. These masters of terror techniques knew exactly what terror was about. Hanoi partially succeeded in its objective. The attacks frightened the people in South Vietnam and intensified the antiwar feeling in the United States. There was, however, one flaw in this tactic of the people's war. By causing death and destruction to the people and their cities and resorting to indiscriminate slaughter of civilians at the sacred family time, Ho's "valiant" soldiers had turned the South Vietnamese against them. There was no general uprising as Ho had expected. The Saigon government did not collapse. And Giap's troops suffered tremendous losses.

Even in these attacks, Ho did not strictly adhere to all the Maoist precepts regarding the people's war. Contrary to what Mao has said—the people are water and guerillas are fish; and fish need water to live—Ho, instead of winning over the people, resorted to systematic and indiscriminate killings of South Vietnamese. Terror replaced persuasion. In this respect, the Vietnamese people's war was markedly different from the Chinese revolutionary war.

Mao maintains that when the enemy commands superior military power and greater abundance in modern weapons, the people's army must fight a protracted war, a war of attrition to wear out the enemy, and avoid the temptation to achieve a quick victory in decisive battles that would determine the outcome of the war. Ho only paid lip service to Mao's teachings. In contradiction to what he had said in an address to the nation over Radio Hanoi on July 17, 1966 that "the war may still last ten, twenty years or longer," the Lao Dong Party Central Committee in April, 1967, adopted Resolution 13, urging their forces to seek "a decisive victory in South Vietnam in the shortest time possible." Thus, instead of the Maoist concept of protracted partisan warfare, the Communists in South Vietnam had attempted to deal decisive blows to their better equipped enemy in conventional attacks: Bau Bang, Dak To, Plei Mei, Saigon, Hue, Khe Sanh, etc.

General Giap went as far as to deny Mao Tse-tung any credit for the people's war. In an interview given to *l'Humanité* correspondent Madeleine Riffaud, the DRV Defense Minister asserted:

But the idea of people's war is not completely new. It has existed since mankind came into being and took shape since man first became aware of his fundamental rights and rose up against the invader. In our most remote history, our ancestors were already saying: "Our entire country is rising up against the invader." In our literary tradition, the poet Nguyen Dinh Chieu, for example, the blind poet of South Vietnam, speaks of the struggle "of the simple inhabitants of the villages who, out of love for the fatherland, have become volunteers," and the weak and fragile women who, because the enemy was in our country, "rode horses, waved flags, rowed boats, loaded guns, destroyed citadels, scaled ramparts. . . ."[52]

The DRV was thus fighting a people's war, not *à la* Mao Tse-tung, but *à la* Ho Chi Minh.

The war was being escalated by both sides when, unexpectedly, on March 31, 1968, President Johnson announced his decision not to seek renomination and reelection for another term, and ordered a bombing pause in North Vietnam as a gesture toward peace talks. After some initial hesitation and apparent suspicion regarding the Johnson move, on April 3

the Government of the Democratic Republic of Vietnam declares its readiness to appoint its representative to contact the U.S. representative with a view to determining with the American side the unconditional cessation of the U.S. bombing raids and all other acts of war against the Democratic Republic of Vietnam so that talks may start.

Peking's reaction was as expected. Government documents and articles published by official Chinese organs remained silent on the DRV statement. The Hong Kong *Ta Kung Pao*, which has taken its editorial policy directly from Peking,[53] said in its April 3 editorial: "A war of aggression can be ended only when the aggressor is totally defeated or is ready to withdraw from the country he tries to conquer."

According to the *Nihon Keizai* correspondent in Peking (April 4), the Chinese government interpreted the DRV statement not to mean that Hanoi had agreed to hold peace talks, but to prevent the United States from trying to "manipulate public opinion on the pretext that Hanoi is obstinately refusing to agree to U.S. peace efforts."

Another dispatch from the Chinese capital, *Sankei Kyodo*, April

4, noted that Peking apparently regarded the Hanoi statement as a "political counterblow" to the American peace offensive, because the North Vietnamese government emphasized that it would continue to fight as long as the United States continued its war of aggression.

In its May 11 issue, the *Hongkong Star* reported that Xuan Thuy, the head of the DRV delegation to the Paris preliminary talks, during his stopover in Peking en route to the French capital, had asked for a meeting with Mao Tse-tung. The Chinese leader, however, declined to see him. Premier Chou En-lai similarly refused to host a dinner party in honor of the Vietnamese delegation, but made a brief appearance at the end of the reception making a cool excuse for his delay. The Chinese Prime Minister reportedly told Xuan Thuy that Hanoi lent a readier ear to the advice of Moscow than that of Peking.[54]

The Delhi General Overseas Service in English broadcast on May 12 that Chou had warned Xuan Thuy that Hanoi's agreement to the talks in Paris was a major tactical and diplomatic mistake and that North Vietnam had fallen into an American trap. Foreign Minister Chen Yi, in a speech at the reception in honor of a Mali delegation in Peking, also maintained that "if the Vietnamese people continue to carry on a strong war of resistance they will win conclusively."[55]

The Chinese government continued to ignore the negotiations which started on May 13 in Paris. NCNA (New China News Agency), however, on June 5, commenting on President Johnson's speech delivered on the previous day at Glassboro, made a direct reference to the Vietnam problem:

In his speech, Johnson asked the Soviet revisionist renegade clique to continue to cooperate with the U.S. on the Vietnam . . . question(s) in order to step up the suppression of the struggle(s) by the Vietnamese . . . people(s). He particularly asked the Soviet revisionist renegade clique to help the United States push the peace fraud which is being stepped up on the Vietnam question.

Mao's displeasure and uneasiness in regard to the negotiations are easy to comprehend. A peaceful settlement of the Vietnam conflict was not to the Chinese Chairman's liking for it would invalidate his theory of protracted confrontation.

Moscow's initial reaction was studiously cautious. Fearing that any public Soviet endorsement of peace talks would be denounced by Peking as evidence of American-Soviet collusion and, consequently, would discourage Hanoi from entering into negotiation, TASS, the Soviet official news agency, limited itself to reporting on the reaction of the world press and, especially, the response of the DRV as expressed in *Quan Doi Nhan Dan* (People's Army) on April 2:

Our people want peace, but real peace must go with genuine independence and freedom. As long as our beloved homeland is overshadowed by American aggression, our country will not have genuine independence.[56]

In a broadcast in Swahili to East Africa, Radio Moscow also quoted, without comment, from the same Vietnamese paper stating that "the U.S. is finding a pretext to stun public opinion. It does not yet want to completely and unconditionally suspend the bombing and other war activities against North Vietnam."[57] The emission also emphasized that "the powerful Soviet Union and other socialist countries as well as all peace-loving mankind are fully behind the fighting Vietnamese people."

Following the Hanoi statement on April 3, the Soviet government acclaimed the Vietnamese stand as an "unquestionable proof of a sensible and realistic approach to the problem of restoring peace in Vietnam," and a concrete proposal that shattered the American claim that North Vietnam did not want to take any positive step toward peace negotiation.[58]

In marked contrast to the Chinese silence, the Soviet communication media gave extensive coverage to the Paris talks. TASS continued to carry *Nhan Dan*'s articles on the negotiation in the French capital, while Radio Moscow filled the air with flattering comments endorsing Ho's position. Similarly, Soviet commentators competed with each other in praising the DRV stand, stressing that the Paris talks "are the result of Hanoi's peaceful initiative," a move supported by people throughout the world, with the exception of certain warhawks in Washington, the bellicose puppets in Saigon, and the Chinese leaders in Peking.[59] While attributing a peaceful intent to Ho Chi Minh who "did not want war, because war meant the death of people and the destruction of natural wealth," Moscow also jabbed at the Maoist leaders who know that both the DRV Government and the NFLSV have a program for a political settlement, but political settlements imply talks. This means that while waging an armed struggle against the aggressor, the Vietnamese never ruled out negotiations. . . . Hanoi is for talks that guarantee an end to the U.S. aggression and freedom and independence for Vietnam. Peking, on the other hand, rules out this possibility. It advocates war at any cost. It is quite apparent that Peking cares least of all for the interests of the Vietnamese. What it wants is to use the sufferings of the people of Vietnam to promote Maoism. Desiring endless bloodshed in Vietnam, the Peking leaders shun the very idea of talks.[60]

By supporting the North Vietnamese and revealing the Chinese position, Moscow seemed to steadily pull Hanoi away from Peking.

While Xuan Thuy negotiated in Paris, Vice-Premier Le Thanh Nghi headed a Vietnamese delegation to the pro-Soviet countries of Eastern Europe. Agreements on economic, technical, and special material aid were signed in Prague on June 17, 1968,[61] and in Berlin six days later[62] to strengthen the DRV national economy and defense potential. The Le Thanh Nghi mission also spent some time in Moscow, where guests and hosts undoubtedly discussed their common strategy.

Thus, confronted with an increasingly devastating war and Soviet pressure, and perhaps a Soviet promise of support for a peaceful absorption of South Vietnam, Ho again leaned toward the Russians. The shrewd DRV President, however, managed to maintain friendly relations with Peking in spite of the Chinese rebuff. His loyal Prime Minister and long-time associate Pham Van Dong, at the Fourth Session of the North Vietnamese National Assembly Third Legislature still emphasized socialist solidarity and expressed firm support for Mao Tse-tung's aim to recover Taiwan. Addressing his fellow deputies, the DRV Premier said:

We have attached paramount importance to the defense of the socialist camp and of each of its members, conscious as we are that the socialist camp is the greatest achievement of the revolutionary struggle of the world's working class and people. We warmly acclaim the brilliant successes recorded by the peoples of the Soviet Union, China, and the other socialist countries in the building of communism and socialism, successes which contribute to increasing the might of the socialist camp and to the defense of world peace.

We firmly support the determination of the Chinese people to recover Taiwan, an inalienable part of the territory of the People's Republic of China.[63]

The Sino-Soviet ideological struggle was matched only by the Vietnam war in intensity. And it was the course of the war that determined Hanoi's orientation. Peking wanted the conflict to end with a complete American defeat to prove the correctness of the protracted confrontation theory, while Moscow hoped that it would result in a negotiated settlement so as not to compromise its peaceful coexistence policy. In his ambition to conquer South Vietnam by force, Ho Chi Minh was in agreement with Mao Tse-tung. Faced with punishing American airpower, however, Ho had to turn toward the land of Lenin for help.

With the exception of the agrarian reform period, during which the pro-Chinese Truong Chinh slavishly applied the Maoist methods, Ho managed to remain uncommitted to either the Peking or the Moscow line. Apparently, the Chinese course followed by Hanoi until the land reform fiasco in 1956 could be attributed to Ho's feeling of indebtedness to Mao for the latter's assistance during and after the Indochina war, to his admiration for the Communist success in China, and to his belief that, in view of the similar conditions prevailing in the two countries, a Chinese solution would work in Vietnam.

From 1957 to 1962, after the failure of the agrarian reform campaign that had aggravated the food shortage problem, Ho turned to Moscow for the kind of aid that developing China was not able to provide, while maintaining cordial relations with Peking. With the cessation of active Soviet participation in Indochinese affairs since the signing of the July, 1962, Agreement on Laos and the subsequent reduction of Soviet aid, Ho collaborated more closely with the Chinese whose revolutionary warfare theory was more compatible with his aggressive designs than the Soviet peaceful coexistence concept. In 1965, however, the American determination to prevent a Communist subjugation of South Vietnam suddenly transformed the course of the war. In addition to the escalation of the conflict and damaging aerial attacks against North Vietnam, the Chinese inability to provide the DRV with effective and sophisticated antiaircraft weapons steadily pushed Ho closer to Moscow.

Faced with an increasing devastation of his country and aware of the Chinese desire to have him fight to the bitter end, the aging Ho became reluctant to see most of his lifework destroyed. This explained Ho's last swing toward Moscow.

In order to realize his ambition, that is, to industrialize the DRV and unify Vietnam under Communism, Ho needed a united socialist camp from which he could obtain all possible assistance. The shrewd revolutionary, therefore, made all desperate attempts to prevent a rupture between China and the Soviet Union, a distasteful circumstance under which he might be forced to take sides. When the split occurred despite his strenuous efforts, Ho cautiously navigated between the two lines, occasionally veering toward one or the other as the need of his country required.

9 ☆ Death of a Revolutionary

~~~~~~~~~~~~~~~~~~~~~~~~~~~~~~~~~~~~~

As Ho HAD INTENDED, the fruitless "peace" talks dragged on in the cheerful French capital while the sad war continued its course in the rice paddies and jungle of South Vietnam. Confident that American and world public opinion would sooner or later pressure the United States to accept his terms, Ho was not anxious to reach an early settlement. He was convinced, as he had told Bernard Fall in 1962, that he could "marshal world public opinion about this unjust war against the South Vietnamese."[1]

Thus, Ho was prepared to wait. The wheel of time, alas, caught the old revolutionary while he was still waiting. The endless talks had entered their sixteenth month in Paris when Ho Chi Minh drew his last breath on September 3, 1969, in Hanoi.

No Longer a Rumor

The news of Ho's death came as a surprise to the outside world. He had occupied the center of the international stage for so long that people were not prepared to think that he would go away at that crucial moment. Even in his Democratic Republic, where he had been rumored dead numerous times but had always reappeared body and soul together, people had begun to entertain the illusion that Ho would continue to live for a long time.

In the capital of North Vietnam, however, the news of Ho's passing did not come as a surprise. In a land where a man of fifty is considered old, Ho's longevity was quite unusual. Hanoians had seen Uncle Ho growing old and his health deteriorating. On November 25, 1967, Istvan Szabo, a Hungarian reporter who had been stationed in Hanoi, disclosed in Vientiane, Laos, that Ho had been very ill and had delegated more and more authority to Pham Van Dong. His frequent absence from public functions since 1967 seemed to confirm the report. When he appeared at a street party with children in Hanoi early in the year (1969), Uncle Ho did not look very well. His cheeks were pale and his eyes not so lively. And his gait was not as fast as it had been in previous years.

Aware of his imminent death, Ho had actually drafted his will on May 10, 1969. In its preface, the old revolutionary, obsessed with the struggle against "U.S. imperialism" and the revolution, talked about his plan following the people's victory. Yet, he admitted that he was very old and might not live that long. Ho wrote:

Our people's struggle against U.S. aggression, for national salvation, may have to undergo even more difficulties and sacrifices, but we are bound to win total victory.

This is a certainty.

When that day comes, I intend to tour the country, both North and South, to congratulate our heroic compatriots, cadres and combatants, and visit our old people and our beloved youth and children.

Then, on behalf of our people, I will go the fraternal countries of the socialist camp and friendly countries in the world to thank them for their sincere support and assistance to our people's patriotic struggle against U.S. aggression.

Tu Fu, the well-known Chinese poet of the T'ang Dynasty, wrote: "Few people in history have lived to the age of 70."

Having reached my 79th birthday this year, I now count among the "few people in history." Though my mind has remained very lucid, my health has somewhat declined in comparison with previous years. This is no wonder, however, for when a person has lived past 70 springs his health deteriorates with his advancing age.

But who can say how much longer I shall be able to serve the revolution, the Fatherland, and the people?

Therefore, I leave these few lines in anticipation of the day when I go and join the venerables Marx and Lenin and other elder revolutionaries.

This way, our compatriots throughout the country, our comrades in the Party, and our friends everywhere will not be taken by surprise.

Thus, less than four months before his death, Ho sensed that his days were numbered. He lingered on, performed some duties, then fell very ill. Ho suffered frequent bouts of malaria, and the tuberculosis he had contracted in 1931 in Hong Kong finally came back to administer a final devastating blow to the chain-smoking Lao Dong Party Chairman. The innumerable hardships he had suffered during his long revolutionary life, too, finally took their toll. Ho died on September 3, 1969, at 9:47 A.M. The old revolutionary had lost his last battle. His associates had hoped in vain that the durable fighter might be able to muster enough strength to escape death as he had many times in the past. It took them two days to mourn his death and to prepare an announcement to the people among whom, they knew, Ho's passing would cause a serious commotion. When the news reached them, millions of people in Vietnam as well as in other lands finally realized that Ho's death was a reality, not just a rumor. It was announced, not by the "French colonialists" nor the "U.S. imperialists and their lackeys," but by a most authoritative source, the Lao Dong Party's official paper. On September 5, 1969, *Nhan Dan* frontpaged the gloomy news:

With deepest sorrow, the Central Executive Committee of the Vietnam Lao Dong Party, the Permanent Committee of the National Assembly, the Council of Ministers of the Democratic Republic of Vietnam, and the Central Committee of the Fatherland Front inform the whole Party and the whole people of Vietnam that Comrade Ho Chi Minh, Chairman of the Central Executive Committee of the Lao Dong Party and President of the Democratic Republic of Vietnam, had passed away on September 3, 1969, at 9:47 A.M., at the age of 79, following a sudden and very serious heart attack.

Throughout the period of Chairman Ho's illness, leaders of the Party and the State were at His bedside day and night, and a team of eminent professors and doctors of medicine tried every possible method to cure Him. In spite of the best effort of everyone involved, Chairman Ho, because of his advanced age and serious illness, has left us for ever.

Ho's Will

Ho's will reveals his lifetime obsessions: the party, the revolution, and a unified Vietnam under Communism. It should be examined within its proper context, Ho's own life:

FIRST, THE PARTY. Thanks to its close unity and total dedication to the working class, the people, and the Fatherland, the Party has been able, since its founding, to unite, organize, and lead our people from victory to victory in a resolute struggle.

Unity is an extremely precious tradition of our Party and people. All comrades from the Central Committee down to the cell must preserve the unity and oneness of mind as the apple of their eye.

Within the Party, to achieve broad democracy and to practice *self-criticism and criticism* regularly and seriously is the best way to consolidate and further solidarity and unity. Comradely affection should prevail among members.

Ours is a Party in power. Each Party member, each cadre must be deeply imbued with *revolutionary morality*, and show industry, thrift, integrity, uprightness, total dedication to public interests and complete selflessness. Our Party must preserve absolute purity and remain worthy of its role as leader and very loyal servant of the people.

THE WORKING YOUTH UNION MEMBERS AND OUR YOUNG PEOPLE. On the whole they are excellent, always ready for vanguard tasks, unafraid of difficulties and eager for progress. The Party must inculcate upon them the *revolutionary virtues* and train them as our successors, both "red" and "expert," in the building of socialism.

Training and educating future revolutionary generations is a task of great importance and necessity.

OUR WORKING PEOPLE. In both the plains and the mountain areas, they have for ages suffered hardships, feudal and colonial oppression and exploitation. Moreover, they have experienced many years of war.

Yet, our people have shown great heroism, courage, enthusiasm, and industriousness. They have always followed the Party since it came into being and have remained loyal to it.

The Party must work out a sound plan for economic and cultural development with a view to constantly *raising the living standard of the people.*

THE RESISTANCE WAR AGAINST U.S. AGGRESSION. It may drag on for a long time. Our compatriots may have to undergo new sacrifices in property and life. Whatever may happen, we must be resolved to fight the U.S. aggressors till total victory.

Our mountains, our rivers, and our people will always be,

The American aggressors defeated, we will build a country ten times more beautiful.

However difficult it may be, our people will certainly win total victory. The U.S. imperialists shall have to withdraw from our country. Our Fatherland shall be reunified. Our compatriots in the North and in the South shall be reunited under the same roof. Our nation will earn the great honor of being a small country which, through a heroic struggle, has defeated two leading imperialist powers—France and the United States—and made a worthy contribution to the national liberation movement.

THE WORLD COMMUNIST MOVEMENT. Having dedicated my whole life to the revolution, the more proud I am to see the growth of the international Communist and workers' movement, the more deeply I am grieved at the dissensions now dividing the fraternal parties!

I hope that our Party will do its best to contribute effectively to the restoration of unity among the fraternal parties on the basis of Marxism-Leninism and proletarian internationalism in a way which conforms to both sentiment and reason.

I am convinced that the fraternal parties and countries will have to unite again.

PERSONAL MATTERS. All my life, I have tried my best to serve the Fatherland, the revolution, and the people. Should I depart from this world now, I would regret nothing, except not being able to serve longer and more.

When I am gone, grand funerals should be avoided in order not to waste the people's time and money.

Finally, to the whole people, the whole Party, the whole army, to my nephews and nieces, the youth and children, I leave my boundless affection.

I also convey my warmest greetings to our comrades and friends, to the youth and children in the world.

My ultimate wish is that our whole Party and people, closely united in the struggle, build a peaceful, unified, independent, democratic, and prosperous Vietnam, and make a worthy contribution to the world revolution![2]

Last Rites

The service for Ho Chi Minh took place on September 9, 1969, at the Ba Dinh Square in Hanoi. Since 6:30 in the morning, the historic place had been crowded with more than 100,000 people. In the front row were 1,000 of "Uncle Ho's good nephews and nieces," the exemplary grammar school age children, who had earned the honor of standing closest to Ho at the important public ceremonies in the past.

At 7:30, Major Dinh Ngoc Lien, the man who had led the Liberation Army band when it played the Viet Minh march song twenty-four years earlier, on September 2, 1945, just before Ho Chi Minh read the proclamation of independence, began to direct the Vietnam People Army band to play the DRV national anthem. A moment of complete silence followed. All traffic stopped in Hanoi. People stood, silent and grave, facing the Ba Dinh Square, under loudspeakers which had been installed throughout the capital.

At 7:40, Le Duan, the Lao Dong Party First Secretary, slowly stepped forward to the microphone on the platform to deliver the eulogy. In a voice filled with emotion, Le Duan enumerated Ho's achievements and contributions to the Vietnamese revolution. Besides the 100,000 in the historic Square, another million Hanoians intently listened to the First Secretary's words. As soon as Le Duan said "Our nation, our people, and our Fatherland have produced Chairman Ho, the Great National Hero, and He has brought glory and honor to our Nation and our Fatherland," reported *Nhan Dan*,[3] everyone began to sob profusely. Then, on behalf of the Lao Dong Party, the people, and the armymen, Le Duan read the oaths pledging to live up to Ho's ideals. "I swear," shouted the crowd as each was pronounced.

Then came the moving moment of reading the departed revolutionary's will. No sooner had Le Duan finished the first sentence than the crowd both in the Ba Dinh Square and throughout the city burst into tears, *Nhan Dan* continued. The sobbing and crying went on as the reading progressed. Everyone, however, tried hard to control his emotion so that his sobbing would not drown out Le Duan's reading of Uncle Ho's last words.

At 8:05, the band played the *Internationale*, then a hymn to Ho. A twenty-one-gun salute broke the grim silence. Then a squadron of MIGs, in formations of four, roared over the Square, tipping their wings, paying their last respect to the revolutionary fighter.

The service had come to an end. No one wanted to leave. Everyone kept looking at Ho's immense portrait on the platform. A number of "Uncle Ho's good nephews and nieces" in the front row threw themselves into the arms of Le Duan, Pham Van Dong, Truong Chinh, Le Duc Tho, and Vo Nguyen Giap, sobbing uncontrollably. "From now on, we won't get to see Uncle Ho any more," they cried. Gently caressing the young people's heads, even the hardened members of the Lao Dong Party suddenly found themselves at a loss for words.

Slowly and reluctantly, the crowd proceeded past the clear glass coffin containing Ho's body. He was there, dressed in his familiar, faded khaki Mao Tse-tung suit, lying on a red velvet bed, with his head on a white pillow. Outside the coffin, at his feet, was a small glass box containing his simple sandals made of discarded automobile tires. The coffin was displayed against the background of two immense flags with black trim, those of the State and of the Party. Two moving slogans, prominently placed next to the flags, read:

Vo Cung Thuong Nho Chu Tich Ho Chi Minh Vi Dai!
(We immensely miss our Great, Beloved Chairman Ho Chi Minh)

and

Doi Doi Nho On Chu Tich Ho Chi Minh Vi Dai!
(We are grateful to our Great, Beloved Chairman Ho Chi Minh for ever).

Thus, Nguyen Tat Thanh, Nguyen Who Will Succeed, alias Nguyen Ai Quoc, Nguyen Who Loves His Country, alias Ho Chi Minh, Ho Who Enlightens, receded into history.

Conclusion

UNDOUBTEDLY, Ho Chi Minh was one of the most cunning, ruthless, and dedicated Communists the world has yet known. He was at the same time a great patriot whose dedication to Communism never obscured his devotion to his fatherland.

At the beginning of his revolutionary career, Ho was interested only in liberating Vietnam from French rule and making it an independent and respectable member of the international community. Throughout the Versailles Conference following the First World War, Ho made painful but vain attempts to call the attention of the powerful statesmen of the Western democracies to the fate of a little colony contemptuously referred to as "Annam." It soon dawned upon the fragile patriot from Asia that President Woodrow Wilson's fourteen-point program and idea of self-rule would not apply to the lowly, nonwhite people in the colonies.

Profoundly disappointed but not discouraged, young Ho joined the French Socialist party simply because its members showed sympathy toward him and toward the struggle of the oppressed people. As Ho was to admit later, he "supported the October Revolution only instinctively, not yet grasping all its historic importance," and "loved and admired Lenin because he was a great patriot who liberated his country." When the French Socialist party split in December, 1920, on the colonial issue, Ho naturally joined the faction that showed greater sympathy for the oppressed people and thus cast his lot with Lenin's Third International. Having been rebuffed by Western "democrats," Ho eagerly grasped Lenin's hands. Once he joined the East, he never returned to the West. The nationalist-turned-Communist was resolved to dedicate all his life to the new ideology he had embraced. Throughout his life, he served his cause with a zeal, dedication, and selflessness that were second to none.

A man of Ho's caliber and achievements does not appear often in the history of any nation. An extraordinarily self-abnegating man, Ho fought hard to expel the French from Indochina, unify Vietnam under Communism, and, most importantly, maintain its independence in the Communist bloc.

Had he been a non-Marxist patriot, Ho would have commanded the support of most, if not all, Vietnamese, easily defeated the French, and built an independent, unified, and prosperous Vietnam. Circumstances, alas, pushed him into the Communist orbit. Ho's life is the history of his nation, a nation that has suffered immeasurably from two "ideologies" that were not its own: colonialism and Communism.

However one may feel about the ideology Ho had advocated, one could not deny that he had served it with unequalled distinction, overcoming great odds, holding at bay two of the mightiest Western powers, and gaining worldwide respect for a heroic, little nation.

Ho's dreams were grandiose, and his achievements spectacular. Although he is gone, Ho's policies will continue to haunt us for many years to come. The dedicated cadres he molded have been trying their best to complete the task he left unfinished. Lacking Ho's immense prestige, charisma, and devotion, however, they should not be expected to duplicate the achievements of the revolutionary master.

APPENDIX A

*Declaration of Independence of the Democratic Republic of Viet-Nam**

All men are created equal; they are endowed by their Creator with certain unalienable Rights; among these are Life, Liberty, and the pursuit of Happiness.

This immortal statement was made in the Declaration of Independence of the United States of America in 1776. In a broader sense, this means: All the peoples on the earth are equal from birth, all the peoples have a right to live, to be happy and free.

The Declaration of the French Revolution made in 1791 on the Rights of Man and the Citizen also states: "All men are born free and with equal rights, and must always remain free and have equal rights."

Those are undeniable truths.

Nevertheless, for more than eighty years, the French imperialists, abusing the standard of Liberty, Equality, and Fraternity, have violated our Fatherland and oppressed our fellow citizens. They have acted contrary to the ideals of humanity and justice.

In the field of politics, they have deprived our people of every democratic liberty.

They have enforced inhuman laws; they have set up three distinct political regimes in the North, the Center, and the South of Viet-Nam in order to wreck our national unity and prevent our people from being united.

They have built more prisons than schools. They have mercilessly slain our patriots; they have drowned our uprisings in rivers of blood.

They have fettered public opinion; they have practiced obscurantism against our people.

To weaken our race they have forced us to use opium and alcohol.

In the field of economics, they have fleeced us to the backbone, impoverished our people, and devastated our land.

They have robbed us of our rice fields, our mines, our forests, and our raw materials. They have monopolized the issuing of bank notes and the export trade.

* Source: Ho Chi Minh, *Selected Works* (Hanoi: Foreign Languages Publishing House, 1961), Vol. III.

They have invented numerous unjustifiable taxes and reduced our people, especially our peasantry, to a state of extreme poverty.

They have hampered the prospering of our national bourgeoisie; they have mercilessly exploited our workers.

In the autumn of 1940, when the Japanese fascists violated Indochina's territory to establish new bases in their fight against the Allies, the French imperialists went down on their bended knees and handed over our country to them.

Thus, from that date, our people were subjected to the double yoke of the French and the Japanese. Their sufferings and miseries increased. The result was that, from the end of the last year to the beginning of this year, from Quang Tri Province to the North of Viet-Nam, more than two million of our fellow citizens died from starvation. On March 9 [1945], the French troops were disarmed by the Japanese. The French colonialists either fled or surrendered, showing that not only were they incapable of "protecting" us, but that, in the span of five years, they have twice sold our country to the Japanese.

On several occasions before March 9, the Viet Minh League urged the French to ally themselves with it against the Japanese. Instead of agreeing to this proposal, the French colonialists so intensified their terrorist activities against the Viet Minh members that before fleeing they massacred a great number of our political prisoners detained at Yen Bay and Cao Bang.

Notwithstanding all this, our fellow citizens have always manifested toward the French a tolerant and humane attitude. Even after the Japanese *Putsch* of March, 1945, the Viet Minh League helped many Frenchmen to cross the frontier, rescued some of them from Japanese jails, and protected French lives and property.

From the autumn of 1940, our country had in fact ceased to be a French colony and had become a Japanese possession.

After the Japanese had surrendered to the Allies, our whole people rose to regain our national sovereignty and to found the Democratic Republic of Viet-Nam.

The truth is that we have wrested our independence from the Japanese and not from the French.

The French have fled, the Japanese have capitulated, Emperor Bao Dai has abdicated. Our people have broken the chains which for nearly a century have fettered and have won independence for the Fatherland. Our people at the same time have overthrown the monarchic regime that has reigned supreme for dozens of centuries. In its place has been established the present Democratic Republic.

For these reasons, we, members of the Provisional Government, representing the whole Vietnamese people, declare that from now on we break off all relations of a colonial character with France; we repeal all the international obligation that France has so far subscribed to on behalf of Viet-Nam, and we abolish all the special rights the French have unlawfully acquired in our Fatherland.

The whole Vietnamese people, animated by a common purpose, are determined to fight to the bitter end against any attempt by the French colonialists to reconquer their country.

We are convinced that the Allied nations, which at Teheran and San Francisco have acknowledged the principles of self-determination and equality of nations, will not refuse to acknowledge the independence of Viet-Nam.

A people who have courageously opposed French domination for more than eighty years, a people who have fought side by side with the Allies against the fascists during these last years, such a people must be free and independent.

For these reasons, we, members of the Provisional Government of the Democratic Republic of Viet-Nam, solemnly declare to the world that Viet-Nam has the right to be a free and independent country—and in fact it is so already. The entire Vietnamese people are determined to mobilize all their physical and mental strength, to sacrifice their lives and property in order to safeguard their independence and liberty.

APPENDIX B

*Geneva Agreements**

A. Agreement on the Cessation of Hostilities in Viet Nam
(July 20, 1954)

CHAPTER I
Provisional Military Demarcation Line and Demilitarized Zone

Article 1

A provisional military demarcation line shall be fixed, on either side of which the forces of the two parties shall be regrouped after their withdrawal, the forces of the People's Army of Viet Nam to the north of the line and the forces of the French Union to the south.

The provisional military demarcation line is fixed as shown on the map attached, see Map No. 1.

It is also agreed that a demilitarised zone shall be established on either side of the demarcation line, to a width of not more than 5 km. from it, to act as a buffer zone and avoid any incidents which might result in the resumption of hostilities.

Article 2

The period within which the movement of all forces of either party into its regrouping zone on either side of the provisional military demarcation line shall be completed shall not exceed three hundred (300) days from the date of the present Agreement's entry into force.

Article 3

When the provisional military demarcation line coincides with a waterway, the waters of such waterway shall be open to civil navigation by both parties wherever one bank is controlled by one party and the other bank by the other party. The Joint Commission shall establish rules of navigation for the stretch of waterway in question. The merchant shipping and other civilian craft of each party shall have unrestricted access to the land under its military control.

Article 4

The provisional military demarcation line between the two final regrouping zones is extended into the territorial waters by a line perpendicular to the general line of the coast.

All coastal islands north of this boundary shall be evacuated by the armed forces of the French Union, and all islands south of it shall be evacuated by the forces of the People's Army of Viet Nam.

Article 5

To avoid any incidents which might result in the resumption of hostilities, all military forces, supplies and equipment shall be withdrawn from the demilitarised zone within twenty-five (25) days of the present Agreement's entry into force.

Article 6

No person, military or civilian, shall be permitted to cross the provisional military demarcation line unless specifically authorised to do so by the Joint Commission.

* Source: *Further Documents Relating to the Discussion of Indochina at the Geneva Conference, June 16–July 21, 1954.* Miscellaneous No. 20 (1954), Cmd. 9239 (London: Her Majesty's Stationery Office, 1954).

Article 7

No person, military or civilian, shall be permitted to enter the de-militarised zone except persons concerned with the conduct of civil administration and relief and persons specifically authorised to enter by the Joint Commission.

Article 8

Civil administration and relief in the demilitarised zone on either side of the provisional military demarcation line shall be the responsibility of the Commanders-in-Chief of the two parties in their respective zones. The number of persons, military or civilian, from each side who are permitted to enter the demilitarised zone for the conduct of civil administration and relief shall be determined by the respective Commanders, but in no case shall the total number authorised by either side exceed at any one time a figure to be determined by the Trung Gia Military Commission or by the Joint Commission. The number of civil police and the arms to be carried by them shall be determined by the Joint Commission. No one else shall carry arms unless specifically authorised to do so by the Joint Commission.

Article 9

Nothing contained in this chapter shall be construed as limiting the complete freedom of movement, into, out of or within the demilitarised zone, of the Joint Commission, its joint groups, the International Commission to be set up as indicated below, its inspection teams and any other persons, supplies or equipment specifically authorised to enter the demilitarised zone by the Joint Commission. Freedom of movement shall be permitted across the territory under the military control of either side over any road or waterway which has to be taken between points within the demilitarised zone when such points are not connected by roads or waterways lying completely within the demilitarised zone.

Chapter II
Principles and Procedure Governing Implementation of the Present Agreement

Article 10

The Commanders of the Forces on each side, on the one side the Commander-in-Chief of the French Union forces in Indo-China and on the other side the Commander-in-Chief of the People's Army of Viet Nam, shall order and enforce the complete cessation of all hostilities in Viet

Nam by all armed forces under their control, including all units and personnel of the ground, naval and air forces.

Article 11

In accordance with the principle of a simultaneous cease-fire throughout Indo-China, the cessation of hostilities shall be simultaneous throughout all parts of Viet Nam, in all areas of hostilities and for all the forces
of the two parties.

Taking into account the time effectively required to transmit the cease-
fire order down to the lowest echelons of the combatant forces on both
sides, the two parties are agreed that the cease-fire shall take effect completely and simultaneously for the different sectors of the country as
follows:—

Northern Viet Nam at 8:00 a.m. (local time) on July 27, 1954.

Central Viet Nam at 8:00 a.m. (local time) on August 1, 1954.

Southern Viet Nam at 8:00 a.m. (local time) on August 11, 1954.

It is agreed that Peking mean time shall be taken as local time.

From such time as the cease-fire becomes effective in Northern Viet
Nam, both parties undertake not to engage in any large-scale offensive
action in any part of the Indo-Chinese theatre of operations and not to
commit the air forces based on Northern Viet Nam outside that sector.
The two parties also undertake to inform each other of their plans for
movement from one regrouping zone to another within twenty-five (25)
days of the present Agreement's entry into force.

Article 12

All the operations and movements entailed in the cessation of hostilities
and regrouping must proceed in a safe and orderly fashion:—

(a) Within a certain number of days after the cease-fire Agreement
shall have become effective, the number to be determined on the
spot by the Trung Gia Military Commission, each party shall
be responsible for removing and neutralising mines (including
river- and sea-mines), booby traps, explosives and any other dangerous substances placed by it. In the event of its being impossible
to complete the work of removal and neutralisation in time, the
party concerned shall mark the spot by placing visible signs there.
All demolitions, mine fields, wire entanglements and other hazards
to the free movement of the personnel of the Joint Commission
and its joint groups, known to be present after the withdrawal of
the military forces, shall be reported to the Joint Commission by
the Commanders of the opposing forces;

(b) From the time of the cease-fire until regrouping is completed on either side of the demarcation line:—

(1) The forces of either party shall be provisionally withdrawn from the provisional assembly areas assigned to the other party.

(2) When one party's forces withdraw by a route (road, rail, waterway, sea route) which passes through the territory of the other party (see Article 24), the latter party's forces must provisionally withdraw three kilometers on each side of such route, but in such a manner as to avoid interfering with the movements of the civil population.

Article 13

From the time of the cease-fire until the completion of the movements from one regrouping zone into the other, civil and military transport aircraft shall follow air corridors between the provisional assembly areas assigned to the French Union forces north of the demarcation line on the one hand and the Laotian frontier and the regrouping zone assigned to the French Union forces on the other hand.

The position of the air corridors, their width, the safety route for single-engined military aircraft transferred to the south and the search and rescue procedure for aircraft in distress shall be determined on the spot by the Trung Gia Military Commission.

Article 14

Political and administrative measures in the two regrouping zones, on either side of the provisional military demarcation line:—

(a) Pending the general elections which will bring about the unification of Viet Nam, the conduct of civil administration in each regrouping zone shall be in the hands of the party whose forces are to be regrouped there in virtue of the present Agreement.

(b) Any territory controlled by one party which is transferred to the other party by the regrouping plan shall continue to be administered by the former party until such date as all the troops who are to be transferred have completely left that territory so as to free the zone assigned to the party in question. From then on, such territory shall be regarded as transferred to the other party, who shall assume responsibility for it.

Steps shall be taken to ensure that there is no break in the transfer of responsibilities. For this purpose, adequate notice shall be given by the withdrawing party to the other party, which shall make the necessary arrangements, in particular by sending administrative and police detachments to prepare for the assumption

of administrative responsibility. The length of such notice shall
be determined by the Trung Gia Military Commission. The transfer shall be effected in successive stages for the various territorial
sectors.

The transfer of the civil administration of Hanoi and Haiphong
to the authorities of the Democratic Republic of Viet Nam shall
be completed within the respective time-limits laid down in
Article 15 for military movements.

(c) Each party undertakes to refrain from any reprisals or discrimination against persons or organisations on account of their activities
during the hostilities and to guarantee their democratic liberties.

(d) From the date of entry into force of the present Agreement until
the movement of troops is completed, any civilians residing in
a district controlled by one party who wish to go and live in the
zone assigned to the other party shall be permitted and helped
to do so by the authorities in that district.

Article 15

The disengagement of the combatants, and the withdrawals and
transfers of military forces, equipment and supplies shall take place in
accordance with the following principles:—

(a) The withdrawals and transfers of the military forces, equipment
and supplies of the two parties shall be completed within three
hundred (300) days, as laid down in Article 2 of the present
Agreement;

(b) Within either territory successive withdrawals shall be made by
sectors, portions of sectors or provinces. Transfers from one regrouping zone to another shall be made in successive monthly
installments proportionate to the number of troops to be transferred;

(c) The two parties shall undertake to carry out all troop withdrawals
and transfers in accordance with the aims of the present Agreement, shall permit no hostile act and shall take no step whatsoever
which might hamper such withdrawals and transfers. They shall
assist one another as far as this is possible;

(d) The two parties shall permit no destruction or sabotage of any
public property and no injury to the life and property of the civil
population. They shall permit no interference in local civil administration;

(e) The Joint Commission and the International Commission shall
ensure that steps are taken to safeguard the forces in the course
of withdrawal and transfer;

(f) The Trung Gia Military Commission, and later the Joint Commission, shall determine by common agreement the exact procedure for the disengagement of the combatants and for troop withdrawals and transfers, on the basis of the principles mentioned above and within the framework laid down below:—

1. The disengagement of the combatants, including the concentration of the armed forces of all kinds and also each party's movements into the provisional assembly areas assigned to it and the other party's provisional withdrawal from it, shall be completed within a period not exceeding fifteen (15) days after the date when the cease-fire becomes effective.

The general delineation of the provisional assembly areas is set out in the maps (2) annexed to the present Agreement.

In order to avoid any incidents, no troops shall be stationed less than 1,500 metres from the lines delimiting the provisional assembly areas.

During the period until the transfers are concluded, all the coastal islands west of the following lines shall be included in the Haiphong perimeter: meridian of the southern point of Kebao Island, northern coast of Ile Rousse (excluding the island), extended as far as the meridian of Campha-Mines,

2. The withdrawals and transfers shall be effected in the following order and within the following periods (from the date of the entry into force of the present Agreement):—

Forces of the French Union

Hanoi perimeter .... 80 days
Haiduong perimeter .... 100 days
Haiphong perimeter .... 300 days

Forces of the People's Army of Viet Nam

Ham Tan and Xuyenmoc provisional
assembly area—first installment .... 80 days
Central Viet Nam provisional
assembly area .... 80 days
Plaine des Joncs provisional
assembly area .... 100 days
Central Viet Nam provisional
assembly area—second installment .... 100 days
Pointe Camau provisional
assembly area .... 200 days
Central Viet Nam provisional
assembly area—last installment .... 300 days

CHAPTER III
Ban on the Introduction of Fresh Troops, Military
Personnel, Arms and Munitions, Military Bases

Article 16

With effect from the date of entry into force of the present Agreement, the introduction into Viet Nam of any troop reinforcements and additional military personnel is prohibited.

It is understood, however, that the rotation of units and groups of personnel, the arrival in Viet Nam of individual personnel on a temporary duty basis and the return to Viet Nam of the individual personnel after short periods of leave or temporary duty outside Viet Nam shall be permitted under the conditions laid down below:—

(a) Rotation of units (defined in paragraph (c) of this Article) and groups of personnel shall not be permitted for French Union troops stationed north of the provisional military demarcation line laid down in Article 1 of the present Agreement during the withdrawal period provided for in Article 2.

However, under the heading of individual personnel not more than fifty (50) men, including officers, shall during any one month be permitted to enter that part of the country north of the provisional military demarcation line on a temporary duty basis or to return there after short periods of leave or temporary duty outside Viet Nam.

(b) "Rotation" is defined as the replacement of units or groups of personnel by other units of the same echelon or by personnel who are arriving in Viet Nam territory to do their overseas service there.

(c) The units rotated shall never be larger than a battalion—or the corresponding echelon for air and naval forces.

(d) Rotation shall be conducted on a man-for-man basis, provided, however, that in any one quarter neither party shall introduce more than fifteen thousand five hundred (15,500) members of its armed forces into Viet Nam under the rotation policy.

(e) Rotation units (defined in paragraph (c) of this Article) and groups of personnel, and the individual personnel mentioned in this Article, shall enter and leave Viet Nam only through the entry points enumerated in Article 20 below.

(f) Each party shall notify the Joint Commission and the International Commission at least two days in advance of any arrivals or departures of units, groups of personnel and individual personnel in or from Viet Nam. Reports on the arrivals or departures of units, groups of personnel and individual personnel in or from

Viet Nam shall be submitted daily to the Joint Commission and the International Commission.

All the above-mentioned notifications and reports shall indicate the places and dates of arrival or departure and the numbers of persons arriving or departing.

(g) The International Commission, through its Inspection Teams, shall supervise and inspect the rotation of units and groups of personnel and the arrival and departure of individual personnel as authorised above, at the points of entry enumerated in Article 20 below.

Article 17

(a) With effect from the date of entry into force of the present Agreement, the introduction into Viet Nam of any reinforcements in the form of all types of arms, munitions and other war material, such as combat aircraft, naval craft, pieces of ordnance, jet engines and jet weapons and armored vehicles, is prohibited.

(b) It is understood, however, that war material, arms and munitions which have been destroyed, damaged, worn out or used up after the cessation of hostilities may be replaced on the basis of piece-for-piece of the same type and with similar characteristics. Such replacements of war material, arms and munitions shall not be permitted for French Union troops stationed north of the provisional military demarcation line laid down in Article 1 of the present Agreement, during the withdrawal period provided for in Article 2.

Naval craft may perform transport operations between the regrouping zones.

(c) The war material, arms and munitions for replacement purposes provided for in paragraph (b) of this Article, shall be introduced into Viet Nam only through the points of entry enumerated in Article 20 below. War material, arms and munitions to be replaced shall be shipped from Viet Nam only through the points of entry enumerated in Article 20 below.

(d) Apart from the replacements permitted within the limits laid down in paragraph (b) of this Article, the introduction of war material, arms and munitions of all types in the form of unassembled parts for subsequent assembly is prohibited.

(e) Each party shall notify the Joint Commission and the International Commission at least two days in advance of any arrivals or departures which may take place of war material, arms and munitions of all types.

In order to justify the requests for the introduction into Viet

Nam of arms, munitions and other war material (as defined in paragraph (a) of this Article) for replacement purposes, a report concerning each incoming shipment shall be submitted to the Joint Commission and the International Commission. Such reports shall indicate the use made of the items so replaced.

(f) The International Commission, through its Inspection Teams, shall supervise and inspect the replacements permitted in the circumstances laid down in this Article, at the points of entry enumerated in Article 20 below.

Article 18

With effect from the date of entry into force of the present Agreement, the establishment of new military bases is prohibited throughout Viet Nam territory.

Article 19

With effect from the date of entry into force of the present Agreement, no military base under the control of a foreign State may be established in the re-grouping zone of either party; the two parties shall ensure that the zones assigned to them do not adhere to any military alliance and are not used for the resumption of hostilities or to further an aggressive policy.

Article 20

The points of entry into Viet Nam for rotation personnel and replacements of material are fixed as follows:

—Zones to the north of the provisional military demarcation line; Laokay, Langson, Tien-Yen, Haiphong, Vinh, Dong-Hoi, Muong-Sen;

—Zone to the south of the provisional military demarcation line: Tourane, Quinhon, Nhatrang, Bangoi, Saigon, Cap St. Jacques, Tanchau.

CHAPTER IV
Prisoners of War and Civilian Internees

Article 21

The liberation and repatriation of all prisoners of war and civilian internees detained by each of the two parties at the coming into force of the present Agreement shall be carried out under the following conditions:—

(a) All prisoners of war and civilian internees of Viet Nam, French and other nationalities captured since the beginning of hostilities in Viet Nam during military operations or in any other circumstances of war and in any part of the territory of Viet Nam shall be liberated within a period of thirty (30) days after the date when the cease-fire becomes effective in each theatre.

(b) The term "civilian internees" is understood to mean all persons who, having in any way contributed to the political and armed struggle between the two parties, have been arrested for that reason and have been kept in detention by either party during the period of hostilities.

(c) All prisoners of war and civilian internees held by either party shall be surrendered to the appropriate authorities of the other party, who shall give them all possible assistance in proceeding to their country of origin, place of habitual residence or the zone of their choice.

Chapter V
Miscellaneous

Article 22

The Commanders of the Forces of the two parties shall ensure that persons under their respective commands who violate any of the provisions of the present Agreement are suitably punished.

Article 23

In cases in which the place of burial is known and the existence of graves has been established, the Commander of the Forces of either party shall, within a specific period after the entry into force of the Armistice Agreement, permit the graves service personnel of the other party to enter the part of Viet Nam territory under their military control for the purpose of finding and removing the bodies of deceased military personnel of that party, including the bodies of deceased prisoners of war. The Joint Commission shall determine the procedures and the time limit for the performance of this task. The Commanders of the Forces of the two parties shall communicate to each other all information in their possession as to the place of burial of military personnel of the other party.

Article 24

The present Agreement shall apply to all the armed forces of either party. The armed forces of each party shall respect the demilitarized zone and the territory under the military control of the other party, and shall commit no act and undertake no operation against the other party and shall not engage in blockade of any kind in Viet Nam.

For the purposes of the present Article, the word "territory" includes territorial waters and air space.

Article 25

The Commanders of the Forces of the two parties shall afford full protection and all possible assistance and cooperation to the Joint Commission and its joint groups and to the International Commission and its inspection teams in the performance of the functions and tasks assigned to them by the present Agreement.

Article 26

The costs involved in the operations of the Joint Commission and joint groups and of the International Commission and its Inspection Teams shall be shared equally between the two parties.

Article 27

The signatories of the present Agreement and their successors in their functions shall be responsible for ensuring the observance and enforcement of the terms and provisions thereof. The Commanders of the Forces of the two parties shall, within their respective commands, take all steps and make all arrangements necessary to ensure full compliance with all the provisions of the present Agreement by all elements and military personnel under their command.

The procedures laid down in the present Agreement shall, whenever necessary, be studied by the Commanders of the two parties and, if necessary, defined more specifically by the Joint Commission.

CHAPTER VI
Joint Commission and International Commission for Supervision and Control in Viet Nam

Article 28

Responsibility for the execution of the agreement on the cessation of hostilities shall rest with the parties.

Article 29

An International Commission shall ensure the control and supervision of this execution.

Article 30

In order to facilitate, under the conditions shown below, the execution of provisions concerning joint actions by the two parties, a Joint Commission shall be set up in Viet Nam.

Article 31

The Joint Commission shall be composed of an equal number of representatives of the Commanders of the two parties.

Article 32

The Presidents of the delegations to the Joint Commission shall hold the rank of General.

The Joint Commission shall set up joint groups, the number of which shall be determined by mutual agreement between the parties. The joint groups shall be composed of an equal number of officers from both parties. Their location on the demarcation line between the re-grouping zones shall be determined by the parties whilst taking into account the powers of the Joint Commission.

Article 33

The Joint Commission shall ensure the execution of the following provision of the Agreement on the cessation of hostilities:—

(a) A simultaneous and general cease-fire in Viet Nam for all regular and irregular armed forces of the two parties.

(b) A re-groupment of the armed forces of the two parties.

(c) Observance of the demarcation lines between the re-grouping zones and of the demilitarised sectors.

Within the limits of its competence it shall help the parties to execute the said provisions, shall ensure liaison between them for the purpose of preparing and carrying out plans for the application of these provisions, and shall endeavour to solve such disputed questions as may arise between the parties in the course of executing these provisions.

Article 34

An International Commission shall be set up for the control and super-vision over the application of the provisions of the agreement on the cessation of hostilities in Viet Nam. It shall be composed of representatives of the following States: Canada, India, and Poland.

It shall be presided over by the Representative of India.

Article 35

The International Commission shall set up fixed and mobile inspection teams, composed of an equal number of officers appointed by each of the above-mentioned States. The mixed teams shall be located at the following points: Laokay, Langson, Tien-Yen, Haiphong, Vinh, Dong-Hoi, Muong-Sen, Tourane, Quinhon, Nhatrang, Bangoi, Saigon, Cap St. Jacques, Tranchau. These points of location may, at a later date, be altered at the request of the Joint Commission, or of one of the parties, or of the International Commission itself, by agreement between the International Commission and the command of the party concerned. The zones of action of the mobile teams shall be the regions bordering the land and sea frontiers of Viet Nam, the demarcation lines between the re-grouping zones and the demilitarised zones. Within the limits of these zones they shall have the right to move freely and shall receive from the local civil and military authorities all facilities they may require for the fulfillment of their tasks (provision of personnel, placing at their disposal documents needed for supervision, summoning witnesses necessary for holding enquiries, ensuring the security and freedom of movement of the inspection teams, &c. . . .). They shall have at their disposal such modern means of transport, observation and communication as they may require. Beyond the zones of action as defined above, the mobile teams may, by agreement with the command of the party concerned, carry out other movements within the limits of the tasks given them by the present agreement.

Article 36

The International Commission shall be responsible for supervising the proper execution by the parties of the provisions of the agreement. For this purpose it shall fulfill the tasks of control, observation, inspection and investigation connnected with the application of the provisions of the agreement on the cessation of hostilities, and it shall in particular:—

(a) Control the movement of the armed forces of the two parties, effected within the framework of the re-groupment plan.

(b) Supervise the demarcation lines between the re-grouping areas, and also the demilitarized zones.

(c) Control the operations of releasing prisoners of war and civilian internees.

(d) Supervise at ports and airfields as well as along all frontiers of Viet Nam the execution of the provisions of the agreement on the cessation of hostilities, regulating the introduction into the country of armed forces, military personnel and of all kinds of arms, munitions and war material.

Article 37

The International Commission shall, through the medium of the inspection teams mentioned above, and as soon as possible either on its own initiative, or at the request of the Joint Commission, or of one of the parties, undertake the necessary investigations both documentary and on the ground.

Article 38

The inspection teams shall submit to the International Commission the results of their supervision, their investigation and their observations, furthermore they shall draw up such special reports as they may consider necessary or as may be requested from them by the Commission. In the case of a disagreement within the teams, the conclusions of each member shall be submitted to the Commission.

Article 39

If any one inspection team is unable to settle an incident or considers that there is a violation or a threat of a serious violation, the International Commission shall be informed; the latter shall study the reports and the conclusions of the inspection teams and shall inform the parties of the measures which should be taken for the settlement of the incident, ending of the violation or removal of the threat of violation.

Article 40

When the Joint Commission is unable to reach an agreement on the interpretation to be given to some provision or on the appraisal of a fact, the International Commission shall be informed of the disputed question. Its recommendations shall be sent directly to the parties and shall be notified to the Joint Commission.

Article 41

The recommendations of the International Commission shall be adopted by majority vote, subject to the provisions contained in Article 42. If the votes are divided, the chairman's vote shall be decisive.

The International Commission may formulate recommendations concerning amendments and additions which should be made to the provisions of the agreement on the cessation of hostilities in Viet Nam, in order to ensure a more effective execution of that agreement. These recommendations shall be adopted unanimously.

Article 42

When dealing with questions concerning violations, or threats of violations, which might lead to a resumption of hostilities, namely:—

  (a) Refusal by the armed forces of one party to effect the movements provided for in the re-groupment plan;
  (b) Violation by the armed forces of one of the parties of the regrouping zones, territorial waters, or air space of the other party;

the decisions of the International Commission must be unanimous.

Article 43

If one of the parties refuses to put into effect a recommendation of the International Commission, the parties concerned or the Commission itself shall inform the members of the Geneva Conference.

If the International Commission does not reach unanimity in the cases provided for in Article 42, it shall submit a majority report and one or more minority reports to the members of the Conference.

The International Commission shall inform the members of the Conference in all cases where its activity is being hindered.

Article 44

The International Commission shall be set up at the time of the cessation of hostilities in Indo-China in order that it should be able to fulfill the tasks provided for in Article 36.

Article 45

The International Commission for Supervision and Control in Viet Nam shall act in close co-operation with the International Commissions for Supervision and Control in Cambodia and Laos.

The Secretaries-General of these three Commissions shall be responsible for co-ordinating their work and for relations between them.

Article 46

The International Commission for Supervision and Control in Viet Nam may, after consultation with the International Commissions for Supervision and Control in Cambodia and Laos, and having regard to the development of the situation in Cambodia and Laos, progressively reduce its activities. Such a decision must be adopted unanimously.

Article 47

All the provisions of the present Agreement, save the second subparagraph of Article 11, shall enter into force at 2400 hours (Geneva time) on July 22, 1954.

Done in Geneva at 2400 hours on the 20th of July, 1954, in French and in Vietnamese, both texts being equally authentic.

> For the Commander-in-Chief of the
> French Union Forces in Indo-China:
> Deltiel,
>   Brigadier-General
> For the Commander-in-Chief of the
> People's Army of Viet Nam:
>   Ta-Quang-Buu, Vice-Minister
>   of National Defence of the
>   Democratic Republic of
>   Viet Nam

B. Final Declaration of the Geneva Conference on the Problem of Restoring Peace in Indo-China, in Which the Representatives of Cambodia, the Democratic Republic of Viet Nam, France, Laos, the People's Republic of China, the State of Viet Nam, the Union of Soviet Socialist Republics, the United Kingdom and the United States of America Took Part

(July 21, 1954)

1. The Conference takes note of the agreements ending hostilities in Cambodia, Laos and Viet Nam and organising international control and the supervision of the execution of the provisions of these agreements.

2. The Conference expresses satisfaction at the ending of hostilities in Cambodia, Laos and Viet Nam; the Conference expresses its conviction that the execution of the provisions set out in the present declaration and in the agreements on the cessation of hostilities will permit Cambodia, Laos and Viet Nam henceforth to play their part, in full independence and sovereignty, in the peaceful community of nations.

3. The Conference takes note of the declarations made by the Governments of Cambodia and of Laos of their intention to adopt measures permitting all citizens to take their place in the national community, in particular by participating in the next general elections, which, in conformity with the constitution of each of these countries shall take place in the course of the year 1955, by secret ballot and in conditions of respect for fundamental freedoms.

4. The Conference takes note of the clauses in the agreement on the cessation of hostilities in Viet Nam prohibiting the introduction into Viet Nam of foreign troops and military personnel as well as of all kinds of arms and munitions. The Conference also takes note of the declarations made by the Governments of Cambodia and Laos of their resolution not to request foreign aid, whether in war material, in personnel or in instructors except for the purpose of the effective defence of their territory and, in the case of Laos, to the extent defined by the agreements on the cessation of hostilities in Laos.

5. The Conference takes note of the clauses in the agreement on the cessation of hostilities in Viet Nam to the effect that no military base under the control of a foreign State may be established in the re-grouping zones of the two parties, the latter having the obligation to see that the zones allotted to them shall not constitute part of any military alliance and shall not be utilised for the resumption of hostilities or in the service of an aggressive policy. The Conference also takes note of the declarations of the Governments of Cambodia and Laos to the effect that they will not join in any agreement with other States if this agreement includes the obligation to participate in a military alliance not in conformity with the principles of the Charter of the United Nations or, in the case of Laos, with the principles of the agreement on the cessation of hostilities in Laos, or, so long as their security is not threatened, the obligation to establish bases on Cambodian or Laotian territory for the military forces of foreign Powers.

6. The Conference recognises that the essential purpose of the agree-

ment relating to Viet Nam is to settle military questions with a view to ending hostilities and that the military demarcation line is provisional and should not in any way be interpreted as constituting a political or territorial boundary. The Conference expresses its conviction that the execution of the provisions set out in the present declaration and in the agreement on the cessation of hostilities creates the necessary basis for the achievement in the near future of a political settlement in Viet Nam.

7. The Conference declares that, so far as Viet Nam is concerned, the settlement of political problems, effected on the basis of respect for the principles of independence, unity and territorial integrity, shall permit the Vietnamese people to enjoy the fundamental freedoms, guaranteed by democratic institutions established as a result of free general elections by secret ballot. In order to ensure that sufficient progress in the restoration of peace has been made, and that all the necessary conditions obtain for free expression of the national will, general elections shall be held in July 1956, under the supervision of an international commission composed of representatives of the Member States of the International Supervisory Commission, referred to in the agreement on the cessation of hostilities. Consultations will be held on this subject between the competent representative authorities of the two zones from July 20, 1955, onwards.

8. The provisions of the agreements on the cessation of hostilities intended to ensure the protection of individuals and of property must be most strictly applied and must, in particular, allow everyone in Viet Nam to decide freely in which zone he wishes to live.

9. The competent representative authorities of the Northern and Southern zones of Viet Nam, as well as the authorities of Laos and Cambodia, must not permit any individual or collective reprisals against persons who have collaborated in any way with one of the parties during the war or against members of such persons' families.

10. The Conference takes note of the declaration of the Government of the French Republic to the effect that it is ready to withdraw its troops from the territory of Cambodia, Laos and Viet Nam, at the request of the Governments concerned and within periods which shall be fixed by agreement between the parties except in the cases where, by agreement between the two parties, a certain number of French troops shall remain at specified points and for a specified time.

11. The Conference takes note of the declaration of the French Government to the effect that for the settlement of all the problems connected with the re-establishment and consolidation of peace in Cambodia, Laos and Viet Nam, the French Government will proceed from the principle

of respect for the independence and sovereignty, unity and territorial integrity of Cambodia, Laos and Viet Nam.

12. In their relations with Cambodia, Laos and Viet Nam, each member of the Geneva Conference undertakes to respect the sovereignty, the independence, the unity and the territorial integrity of the above-mentioned States, and to refrain from any interference in their internal affairs.

13. The members of the Conference agree to consult one another on any question which may be referred to them by the International Supervisory Commission, in order to study such measures as may prove necessary to ensure that the agreements on the cessation of hostilities in Cambodia, Laos and Viet Nam are respected.

APPENDIX C

On the Use of Vietnamese Names

According to Vietnamese usage, a person's family name comes first, followed by his or her middle name, then given names. Since there are extremely few family names in their language, Vietnamese are generally known by their given names. A reference to family names alone would cause utter confusion. It would be equivalent to calling a man Mr. John or Mr. Joseph in English.

Example: Mr. Phan Sung Huy. Since Phan is his family name and Huy his given name, he will be known as Mr. Huy or, more formally, Mr. Phan Sung Huy.

An exceptional leader, however, may sometimes be referred to by his family name alone. Such practice denotes both profound and widespread respect and admiration for the person involved. Ho Chi Minh, for instance, was known not as President Minh, but as President Ho.

No one, at the present time, is accorded such rare honor. Thus North Vietnam's Pham Van Dong and South Vietnam's Nguyen Van Thieu are known not as Prime Minister Pham and President Nguyen, but as Prime Minister Dong and President Thieu.

APPENDIX D

Political Parties—1945–1946

Can Lao Nhan Vi, Personalist Labor Party, founded in 1946 by Ngo
Dinh Nhu, associated with the Catholic Workers' Movement.

Dai Viet, Party of Great Vietnam, founded in 1941 by a group of nationalists whose famous leader was Nguyen Tuong Tam, one-time Minister
of Foreign Affairs in the Ho Chi Minh government.

Dong Duong Cong San Dang, Indochinese Communist Party (ICP),
founded in 1930 by Nguyen Ai Quoc, the future Ho Chi Minh. Though
officially "dissolved" in November, 1945, it continued to function
more or less clandestinely until it reemerged in 1951 under the name
of Dang Lao Dong Viet Nam, or Vietnam Workers' Party.

Dong Minh Hoi (DMH), short for Viet Nam Cach Menh Dong Minh
Hoi, Vietnam Revolutionary League, founded in 1942 in Liuchow,
China, under the sponsorship of the Chinese Nationalists, with a view
to unifying all the Vietnamese parties then active in China. It was
first led by the ineffective sinophile Nguyen Hai Than. Following his
release from Chinese prison in 1943, Ho Chi Minh, whose Viet Minh
was the only effective intelligence-gathering organization in Indochina,
succeeded in having the Chinese appoint him head of the DMH.

International Communist League, a Trotskyist group formed in 1944.

Lien Viet, short for Hoi Lien Hiep Quoc Dan Viet Nam, Popular National Front of Vietnam, created by the Viet Minh in May, 1946, prior
to Ho's departure for the Fontainebleau Conference to forestall all
nationalist maneuvers.

Phuc Quoc, short for Viet Nam Phuc Quoc Dong Minh Hoi, League for
the National Restoration of Vietnam, founded by Prince Cuong De
then in exile in Japan. It was a monarchist party with pro-Japanese
tendencies.

Viet Minh, short for Viet Nam Doc Lap Dong Minh Hoi, League for
the Independence of Vietnam, founded in May, 1941, by Ho Chi
Minh. While allegedly including all anti-French nationalist parties,
it was skillfully led and exploited by the Communists, who never admitted their political affiliations.

Viet Nam Dan Chu Dang, Vietnam Democratic Party, founded by

non-Communist intellectuals in 1944. It rallied to Ho's movement the following year.

Viet Nam Quoc Dan Dang (VNQDD), National Democratic Party of Vietnam, founded in 1927 by Nguyen Thai Hoc, patterned after the Chinese Kuomintang.

Viet Nam Xa Hoi Dang, Vietnam Socialist Party, a front group created by the Viet Minh in July, 1946.

APPENDIX E

Important Dates

1884
France completes conquest of Vietnam
1885
Can Vuong, or anti-French Monarchist Movement
1890
May 19: Birth of Nguyen Sinh Cung, the future Ho Chi Minh
1901
Abortive uprising led by Phan Boi Chau
1905
Dong Du, or Pan-Asian Movement
1907
Private Schools' or Scholars' Movement
1911
Ho, alias Ba, leaves Vietnam as a kitchen helper on board the *Latouche-Tréville*
1914
Ho settles in London; establishes contact with Overseas Workers' Association
1917
Ho arrives in Paris; as Nguyen Ai Quoc, engages in political activities
1919
Presents eight-point program to Versailles Peace Conference
1920
December 20: Delivers speech at Tours Congress of French Socialist

party; becomes founding member of French Communist party
    1921
Organizes Intercolonial Union
    1922
Publishes *Le Paria* and *Soul of Vietnam*
    1923
Leaves for Moscow; is elected to Executive Committee of Peasants'
    International
    1924
Reports to Fifth Congress of Communist International; as Ly Thuy or
    Lee Suei, joins Mikhail Borodin in Canton; serves as translator at
    Soviet consulate.
    1925
Betrays Phan Boi Chau to French police in Shanghai for money
    1926
As Vuong Son Nhi, organizes the Thanh Nien to train young revolu-
    tionists
    1927
Leaves China for Moscow following Kuomintang-Soviet rift
    1928
Assigned for short mission in Germany, Italy, Switzerland; arrives in
    Siam, disguised as Buddhist bonze; organizes Vietnamese in Siam
    to spread revolutionary ideas; French squash uprising led by
    Nguyen Thai Hoc
    1930
February 3: Ho, alias Nguyen Ai Quoc, founds Indochinese Communist
    Party (ICP); French execute Nguyen Thai Hoc and other leaders
    1931
Arrested in Hong Kong, but soon regains freedom; leaves for Shanghai
    and resumes contact with Chinese Communist party
    1933
As Linov, studies at Moscow's Lenin School
    1935
Attends Seventh Congress of the Comintern
    1936
Popular Front Government in France releases political prisoners in
    Indochina, permits ICP to function openly
    1938
ICP organizes strikes in Hanoi, Haiphong, and Saigon; mass rally of
    50,000 to celebrate May Day in Hanoi; Ho, alias Lin, returns to
    China; alias Ho Quang, joins Mao Tse-tung's Eighth Route Army
    1939

French terrorize Vietnamese Communists; ICP shifts underground

1940

Ho, alias Old Tran, alias Old Chen, alias Comrade Vuong, moves to Kwangsi; establishes contact with ICP

1941

Arrives in Cao Bang (Tonkin); launches Viet Minh League at Pac Bo

1942

Adopts the name of Ho Chi Minh; goes back to China; arrested and imprisoned by Chinese

1943

Released from prison

1944

Gives instructions for the founding of the Armed Propaganda Brigade for the Liberation of Vietnam

1945

March 9: Japanese putsch ends French regime in Indochina

August 15: Japan surrenders

August 24: Emperor Bao Dai abdicates

August 28: Chinese armies arrive in North Indochina

September 2: Ho proclaims Vietnam's independence

September 12: British troops arrive in Saigon, restore French control

November 11: ICP "dissolved"

1946

January 6: Ho organizes first national elections

March 6: Signs Accord with Sainteny

May 31: Journeys to France for further negotiations

June 1: French proclaim separatist Republic of Cochinchina

September 10: End of fruitless Fontainebleau Conference

September 14: Ho signs *modus vivendi* with Moutet

November 23: French attack Vietnamese in Haiphong

December 20: French troops occupy Hanoi; Ho escapes into jungle

1948

June 5: Bao Dai and Bollaert sign Ha Long Bay Agreement

1949

March 8: Bao Dai and Auriol sign Élysée Agreement; establishment of State of Vietnam

May 21: French National Assembly recognizes Cochinchina as part of Vietnam

June 14: France recognizes Bao Dai as Chief of State

October 1: Proclamation of People's Republic in Peking

1950

January 16, 31: Peking and Moscow recognize Ho's Republic

February 7: London and Washington recognize State of Vietnam

October: Spectacular Viet Minh victories at Lang Son and Cao Bang

December 23: U.S. pledges indirect military aid to State of Vietnam

1951

January, March, May–June: Viet Minh defeats at Vinh Yen, Mao Khe, and Day River

March 3: Resurgence of ICP under new name, Dang Lao Dong, or Workers' Party

1953

November 26: Ho expresses readiness to negotiate with France

1954

March 13–May 8: Dienbienphu

May 8–July 21: Geneva Conference; temporary partition of Vietnam into two zones pending general elections to be held within two years

1956

Failure to hold elections as provided by Geneva Accord

1958

Communists resume guerilla warfare in South Vietnam

1960

Hanoi sets up National Front for the Liberation of South Vietnam

1962

February 8: Establishment of U.S. Military Assistance Command, Vietnam; direct American military involvement

1963

November 1: Coup against Ngo Dinh Diem and his subsequent assassination

1964

Shaky military governments in Saigon

1965

February 5: U.S. bombers strike targets in DRV; increased American build-up in the South

February 11: U Thant's call for negotiations rejected by both Hanoi and Washington

April 1: The Seventeen-nonaligned nations' appeal for negotiations accepted by Washington but ridiculed by Peking and Hanoi

April 7: Lyndon B. Johnson's Baltimore proposal for unconditional talks denounced by Hanoi

June 28: U.S. troops participate in first major attacks in Vietnam

July 1: Ho rejects request by a four-nation British Commonwealth Mission on Vietnam for talks in Hanoi

November 17: Ho insists on total cessation of American bombing in the North and U.S. recognition of NLF as conditions for talks

December 24: Beginning of thirty-seven–day suspension of air raids on North Vietnam accompanied by U.S. worldwide peace offensive

1966

January 24: Ho ridicules U.S. move

January 30: Resumption of air strikes against DRV

March 7–11, June 14–18: Canadian diplomat Chester Ronning undertakes peace mission to Hanoi

1967

February 8, 15: Exchange of letters between Johnson and Ho

March 28: U Thant's initiatives accepted by Washington, but rejected by Hanoi

September 29: Johnson calls for cessation of all bombardment of North Vietnam and meeting between Washington's and Hanoi's representatives

December 29: Ho announces Hanoi "will hold talks with U.S." following unconditional cessation of all attacks against North Vietnam

1968

January–February: Communists launch massive attacks against Saigon and provincial capitals

March 31: Johnson announces decision not to seek second term, orders bombing halt in North Vietnam

April 3: Ho agrees to send his men to meet with U.S. representatives

May 10: Talks begin in Paris

1969

September 3: Death of Ho Chi Minh

NOTES

Introduction

1. "Truong Chinh: Portrait of a Party Thinker," in Truong Chinh, *Primer for Revolt* (New York: Praeger, 1963), p. xiii.
2. Jean Lacouture, *Cinq hommes et la France* (Paris: Éditions du Seuil, 1961), p. 12.
3. Hoang Van Chi, *From Colonialism to Communism* (London: Pall Mall Press, 1964), p. 32.
4. *Histoire d'une paix manquée* (Paris: Amiot-Dumont, 1953), p. 164.
5. Truong Chinh, *President Ho Chi Minh: Beloved Leader of the Vietnamese People* (Hanoi: Foreign Languages Publishing House, 1966), p. 6.
6. Wilfred G. Burchett, *Vietnam North* (New York: International Publishers, 1966), pp. 148–149.

Chapter 1

1. Vietnam is divided into three parts: Bac Viet (North), Trung Viet (Center), and Nam Viet (South). Under the French these component parts were called Tonkin, Annam, and Cochinchina.
2. Having failed to obtain Plan Dinh Phung's surrender, the French opened the tombs of his ancestors, removed and exhibited their remains. In a country where ancestor worship was the most sacred of all duties and filial piety one of the noblest virtues, the French were confident that Phung would surrender to stop such outrageous profanation of his ancestors' remains.
3. The *nuoc nam* is a condiment made of salted fish allowed to ferment in specially made earthen jars. This national condiment is so essential to the preparation of Vietnamese dishes that the French earnestly believed that without it there would be no meals in Vietnam.
4. The *quoc ngu* is the Vietnamese language that had been Romanized by the Jesuit missionary Alexandre de Rhodes, who replaced the ideographs with the Latin alphabet in 1627.
5. Hoang Van Chi, *From Colonialism to Communism*, p. 37.
6. Certificate conferred upon candidates who had passed the examination at the end the sixth year in a Franco-Vietnamese school. It entitled the holder to teach at the elementary level.
7. Printed in *La Correspondance internationale*, No. 59, 1924. All of Ho's speeches and writings reproduced in this book are, unless otherwise indicated, from the four-volume edition of his *Selected Works* (Hanoi: Foreign Languages Publishing House, 1960, 1961, 1962).
8. Harold R. Isaacs, *No Peace for Asia* (Cambridge, Mass.: MIT Press, 1967), p. 164.
9. *La Correspondance internationale*, German edition, No. 46, 1924.
10. "Speech at the Tours Congress," delivered at the 18th Congress of the French Socialist Party, December 25–30, 1920.

11. Unlike the British who allowed the Indian members of the Labour Party to run for Parliament, the French limited this privilege to French citizens only.

12. "The Path Which Led Me To Leninism," published in the Soviet Review *Problems of the East*, April, 1960.

13. *Ibid.*

14. *Ibid.*

15. "Lenin And The Peoples Of The East," printed in *Le Paria*, July 27, 1924.

Chapter 2

1. "Manifesto Of The 'Intecolonial Union,' An Association Of The Natives In All The Colonies."

2. *L'Humanité*, May 25, 1922.

3. Printed in *Le Paria*, August 1, 1922.

4. *Ibid.*, January 15, 1923.

5. Truong Chinh, *President Ho Chi Minh*, p. 14.

6. "Report On The National And Colonial Questions At The Fifth Congress Of The Communist International," Moscow, June 17–July 8, 1924.

7. *Ibid.*

8. Truong Chinh, *President Ho Chi Minh*, p. 15.

9. *La Correspondance internationale*, German edition, No. 46, 1924.

10. See Lao Trinh Nhat, "A Secret that has not been revealed," *Cai Tao* (Hanoi), October 30, 1948; P. J. Honey (ed.), *North Vietnam Today* (New York: Praeger, 1962), p. 4.

11. In view of its relationship with the Thanh Nien, with which it had discussed merger by the end of 1925, and of its poor organization, the Tan Viet was gradually absorbed by the more dynamic and more revolutionary Thanh Nien.

12. Nguyen Luong Bang, Vo Nguyen Giap, et al., *Souvenirs sur Ho Chi Minh* (Hanoi: Foreign Languages Publishing House, 1962), p. 65.

13. Cited in Pham Van Dong, *President Ho Chi Minh* (Hanoi: Foreign Languages Publishing House, 1961), p. 57.

14. "Report To The Communist International," July, 1939.

15. Le Thanh Khoi, *Le Viet-Nam, Histoire et Civilisation* (Paris: Les Éditions de Minuit, 1955), p. 444.

16. Paul Isoart, *Le phénomène national vietnamien: de l'indépendance unitaire à l'indépendance fractionnée* (Paris: Librairie générale de Droit et de Jurisprudence, 1961), pp. 287–288.

17. See the report by the French journalist Andrée Viollis, *Indochine S.O.S.* (Paris: Gallimard, 1935), p. 88.

18. Joseph Buttinger, *Vietnam: A Dragon Embattled* (New York: Praeger, 1967), p. 219.

19. Truong Chinh, *President Ho Chi Minh*, p. 20.

20. The *Xo-viet Nghe An* were a replica of Mao Tse-tung's campaign in Hunan of which Stalin had strongly disapproved.

21. Truong Chinh, *President Ho Chi Minh*, p. 20.

22. Quoted in Jean-Yves Le Branchu, "The French Colonial Empire and the Popular Front Government," *Pacific Affairs*, June, 1937, pp. 129–130.

23. The Stalinists did in fact cooperate with the Troskyists until the Saigon municipal elections of 1937.
24. "Report To The Communist International," July, 1939.
25. Roger Levy, et al., *French Interests and Policies in the Far East* (New York: Institute of Pacific Relations, 1941), p. 125.
26. Philippe Devillers, *Histoire du Vietnam de 1940 à 1952* (Paris: Éditions du Seuil, 1952), p. 79.
27. Vice Admiral Jean Decoux, the commander of the French Fleet in the Far East, was appointed Governor General of Indochina by the Vichy Government. He assumed his post on July 20, 1940.
28. Truong Chinh, *President Ho Chi Minh*, p. 24.
29. Le Thanh Khoi, *Le Viet-Nam*, p. 452.

Chapter 3

1. It is the custom in Vietnam to call a close and elder friend "uncle." The term denotes both esteem and respect. While a father is generally stern, an uncle is usually benign and kind.
2. According to Jean Chesneaux, Philippe Devillers, Donald Lancaster, and Le Thanh Khoi, the meeting took place in the little Chinese village of Tsingtsi. Communist sources, however, put it at Pac Bo, a remote village in the province of Cao Bang, Tonkin.
3. Truong Chinh, *President Ho Chi Minh*, p. 24.
4. These associations of peasants, workers, women, students, and old people had been founded by the Communist party.
5. Truong Chinh, *President Ho Chi Minh*, p. 25.
6. *Ibid.*, p. 24.
7. It should be noted that the term "Viet Minh" is composed of the first and last words of Viet-Nam Doc Lap Dong Minh (Vietnam Independence League), or the abbreviation of the name of that organization which was a national movement for independence including Communists and non-Communist elements. The term "Viet Minh" does not mean Vietnamese Communists as foreign reporters and authors usually understand.
8. The legendary founder of the Kingdom of Van Lang, the present Vietnam. The country has undergone many changes of names since its founding.
9. "Letter From Abroad," June 6, 1941.
10. Buttinger, *Vietnam*, p. 266.
11. Isaacs, *No Peace for Asia*, p. 164.
12. Ho Chi Minh, *Prison Diary* (Hanoi: Foreign Languages Publishing House, 1966), p. 32.
13. *Ibid.*, p. 74.
14. *Ibid.*, p. 96.
15. *Ibid.*, p. 99.
16. *Ibid.*, p. 26.
17. *Ibid.*, p. 44.
18. Isaacs, *No Peace for Asia*, p. 164.
19. Devillers, *Histoire du Vietnam*, p. 105.
20. *Ibid.*, p. 106.
21. Although the country had been known as Vietnam of which Annam was

only one of the three component parts, the French used the pejorative term "Annamites" to refer to all Vietnamese.

22. Document of June 4, 1944, cited in Devillers, *Histoire du Vietnam*, p. 110.
23. *Témoignages et Documents français relatifs à la Colonisation française au Vietnam*, pp. V3f, cited in Frank N. Trager (ed.), *Marxism in Southeast Asia* (Stanford, Calif.: Stanford University Press, 1959), p. 149.
24. Viet Minh Document of August 6, 1944.
25. Robert Shaplen, *The Lost Revolution* (New York: Harper & Row, Publishers, 1965), p. 33.
26. *Ibid.*, p. 34.
27. Viet Minh Document of August 6, 1944.
28. "Instruction To Establish The Vietnam Propaganda Unit For National Liberation," December, 1944.
29. "Appeal To The Population To Fight The Japanese," March 15, 1945, in Vietnam Cultural Association for National Liberation, *Factual Records of the August Revolution*, p. 20.
30. "Appeal of July 1, 1945," *Ibid.*, pp. 21–23.
31. Reproduced in Sainteny, *Histoire d'une paix manquée*, p. 57.
32. *Ibid.*, p. 59.
33. Truong Chinh, *The August Revolution* (Hanoi: Foreign Languages Publishing House, 1962), p. 12.
34. Shaplen, *The Lost Revolution*, p. 29.
35. *Ibid.*, pp. 29–30.
36. Truong Chinh, *The August Revolution*, p. 13.
37. *Ibid.*
38. *Ibid.*, p. 14.
39. "Appeal For General Insurrection," issued at the close of the National Congress convened by the Viet Minh General Committee on August 16, 1945.
40. Cited in Devillers, *Histoire du Vietnam*, p. 137.
41. *Ibid.*, p. 139.
42. The Cabinet was formed as follows:
    Presidency and Foreign Affairs: Ho Chi Minh
    Interior: Vo Nguyen Giap
    National Defense: Chu Van Tan
    Finance: Pham Van Dong
    Propaganda: Tran Huy Lieu
    Education: Vu Dinh Hoe
    Youth: Duong Duc Hien
    Justice: Vu Trong Kahn
    Labor: Le Van Hien
    Health: Pham Ngoc Thach
    Without portfolio: Cu Huy Can and Nguyen Van Xuan
    National Economy: Nguyen Manh Ha
    Social Welfare: Nguyen Van To
    With the exception of the last three, all were members of the Communist party.
43. "Declaration Of Independence," September 2, 1945.
44. Message of Interior Minister Vo Nguyen Giap to the Vietnamese People on Independence Day, September 2, 1945, Government of the Democratic Republic of Vietnam, Documents, n.p. n.d., reprinted from Allan B. Cole, *Conflict in Indo-China and International Repercussions: A Docu-*

mentary History, 1945–1955. © 1956 by the Fletcher School of Law and Diplomacy, p. 25. Used by permission of Cornell University Press.

45. Quoted in Shaplen, *The Lost Revolution*, p. 29.
46. Cole, *Conflict in Indo-China*, p. 26.

Chapter 4

1. Isaacs, *No Peace for Asia*, p. 141.
2. While promising economic and political reforms under this policy, the de Gaulle government made it clear that the Indochinese states would be given no more than an autonomous status within a large association composed of France and her colonies.
3. *Journal officiel de la République française*, March 25, 1945, pp. 1606–1607.
4. Devillers, *Histoire du Vietnam*, pp. 149–150.
5. Hansard's *Parliamentary Debates*, Vol. 414, cols. 2149–2150.
6. Isaacs, *No Peace for Asia*, p. 152.
7. Viet Minh leaflet, September 7, 1945; Trager, *Marxism in Southeast Asia*, p. 155.
8. *Bulletin d'Information*, Saigon, September 8, 1945; Trager, *Marxism in Southeast Asia*, p. 155.
9. Jean Michel Hertrich, *Doc lap! L'indépendance ou la mort* (Paris: Vigneau, 1946), p. 49.
10. Bernard B. Fall, *The Two Viet-Nams* (New York: Praeger, 1964), pp. 64–65.
11. Hertrich, *Doc lap*, p. 74.
12. Ellen J. Hammer, *The Struggle for Indochina* (Stanford, Calif.: Stanford University Press, 1954), pp. 116.
13. Isaacs, *No Peace for Asia*, p. 153.
14. Hammer, *The Struggle for Indochina*, p. 116.
15. Isaacs, *No Peace for Asia*, pp. 153–154.
16. Cole, *Conflict in Indo-China*, p. 49.
17. Sainteny, *Histoire d'une paix manquée*, pp. 50–51.
18. Isaacs, *No Peace for Asia*, p. 168.
19. Robert Trumbull, *The Scrutable East* (New York: David McKay Co., Inc., 1964), p. 201.
20. The government collected from the people such donations as valuable jewelry and objects made of gold. As Ho proclaimed, the Gold Week would "collect the gold given by the people, and mainly the well-off families, to devote it to our most pressing and important task at present, which is national defense."
21. The agreement between the Viet Minh and the nationalist organizations was concluded at the second Congress of Liuchow sponsored by General Chiang Fa-ku'ei.
22. *La République* (Hanoi), no. 7, November 18, 1945.
23. Truong Chinh, *The Resistance Will Win* (Hanoi: Foreign Languages Publishing House, 1960), p. 97.
24. In the fall of 1942, the Chinese tried to bring all Vietnamese nationalist organizations, notably the Viet Minh, under their control by convoking

a conference of all Vietnamese resistance movements in Liuchow. This Congress led to the formation of the Dong Minh Hoi (DMH).

25. The elections for the National Assembly had been promised by Ho on September 8. They were to be based on universal suffrage open to all citizens from eighteen years of age, including the ethnic minorities.
26. "Declaration Of The Policy Of The Provisional Coalition Government," January 1, 1946.
27. "Appeal To The People To Go To The Polls," January 5, 1946.
28. Bernard B. Fall, *Le Viet Minh* (Paris: Librairie Armand Colin, 1960), p. 47.
29. Hoang Van Chi, *From Colonialism to Communism*, p. 61.
30. This confirmed the Dong Minh Hoi fear that the Viet Minh would not comply with the announced agreements to postpone the elections. In its official paper, *Lien Viet*, December 20, 1945, the DMH had, in fact, warned: "We must, however, watch them (the Viet Minh) for they are quite capable of conducting elections in certain regions under the pretext that the decision to postpone them until January 6, 1946 did not reach these areas in time."
31. *Notes documentaires et Études*, no. 555, pp. 5–6.
32. Sainteny, *Histoire d'une paix manquée*, p. 95.
33. Pierre Maurice Dessinges, *Le Monde*, April 14, 1947; Sainteny, *Histoire d'une paix manquée*; Jean Chesneaux, *Contributions à l'histoire de la nation vietnamienne* (Paris: Éditions sociales, 1955).
34. Chesneaux, *Contributions*, pp. 242–243.
35. See note 33.
36. *Life*, March 22, 1968.
37. *Ibid.*
38. *Ibid.*
39. Isaacs, *No Peace for Asia*, pp. 172–173.
40. *Ibid.*, p. 173.
41. Sainteny, *Histoire d'une paix manquée*, p. 164.
42. Devillers, *Histoire du Vietnam*, p. 212.
43. Adrien Dansette, *Leclerc* (Paris: Flammarion, 1952), p. 199.
44. *Ibid.*, p. 149.
45. Telegram of August 13, 1945; Sainteny, *Histoire d'une paix manquée*, p. 51.
46. Telegrams of August 28 and 29, 1945; Sainteny, *Histoire d'une paix manquée*, pp. 91, 95.
47. The United States was blamed for not providing the French Expeditionary Corps with enough aircraft and other assistance.
48. Isaacs, *No Peace For Asia*, p. 173.
49. *Ibid.*, p. 163.
50. A *ky* was a political subdivision of Vietnam, which included Bac ky (Tonkin), Trung ky (Annam), and Nam ky (Cochinchina).
51. Isaacs, *No Peace for Asia*, p. 175.
52. Hammer, *The Struggle for Indochina*, p. 149.
53. *Ibid.*
54. Devillers, *Histoire du Vietnam*, p. 204.
55. Sainteny, *Histoire d'une paix manquée*, p. 167.
56. *Ibid.*, p. 176.
57. *Ibid.*
58. Ngo Dinh Diem was Premier of South Vietnam from 1954 to 1956, and its President from 1956 to 1963.

59. Hammer, *The Struggle for Indochina*, p. 150.
60. Devillers, *Histoire du Vietnam*, pp. 216–217.
61. Quyet Chien (Viet Minh official paper in Hue), February 27, 1946.
62. This was in fact the Ministry of Defense. Ho also skillfully maneuvered Vu Hong Khanh, the anti-Viet Minh and anti-French leader of the VNQDD, into accepting the vice-chairmanship of the Committee.
63. During the recess of the National Assembly, this Committee enjoyed the legislative powers in the DRV. Since no national legislative sessions were held in North Vietnam during the period between March, 1946, and December, 1953, the Permanent Committee was, for all practical purposes, the National Legislature itself.
64. Sainteny, *Histoire d'une paix manquée*, p. 179.
65. The French desperately tried to keep Vietnam divided. Cochinchina, they argued, had been a French colony, enjoying a special status which had set it apart from the two protectorates of Tonkin and Annam. While conceding that Vietnam could be a free state, the colonists continued to insist that Cochinchina, too, should be treated as a separate political entity, a republic by itself as d'Argenlieu was to claim later.
66. The provision that guaranteed the evacuation of all French troops from Vietnam within five years was very important to Ho, who justified his decision to permit the return of the French troops on the grounds that Leclerc's army should enter Tonkin with or without an agreement. The Accord, which averted an armed conflict, would also lead to a peaceful and gradual exit of French troops from Vietnam.
67. The Paris government finally appointed Sainteny as French Commissioner for Tonkin and North Annam.
68. Sainteny, *Histoire d'une paix manquée*, p. 167.
69. *Ibid.*, p. 187.
70. *Quyet Chien* (Hue), March 8, 1946.
71. *Ibid.*, pp. 230–231.
72. *Le Monde*, December 27, 1945.
73. Devillers, *Histoire du Vietnam*, p. 234.
74. *Ibid.*, p. 235.
75. *Ibid.*, p. 242.
76. *Ibid.*, p. 244.
77. The Vietnamese delegation included Nguyen Tuong Tam, VNQDD leader and Minister of Foreign Affairs; Vo Nguyen Giap, Ho's trusted lieutenant and President of the National Resistance Committee; Hoang Xuan Han, a civil engineer; Vu Van Hien, a lawyer and specialist in financial questions, a former Minister of Bao Dai; Nguyen Manh Tuong, a lawyer and prominent leader; Cu Huy Can, an agronomist; Nguyen Van Huyen, a physician and important Viet Minh leader; Trinh Van Binh, Director of Customs and Excise Taxes; Vu Trong Khanh, Attorney General; and Duong Bach Mai, former Viet Minh Political Commissar for eastern Cochinchina.
78. The French delegation was composed of two groups: (*a*) metropolitan group: Max André, a member of the Mouvement Républicain Populaire and former Director of the Franco-Chinese Bank; Pierre Messmer, an official in the Civil Service, the first man appointed French Commissioner for Tonkin; Bousquet, Chief of the economic services at the Ministry of French Overseas Territories; Bourgoin, a specialist on Indochinese economic questions; d'Arcy, Chief of cabinet of the Minister of the Army; Pierre Gourou, a specialist on Vietnamese questions; (*b*) local group, strongly

anti-Viet Minh: Léon Pignon, Director of Political and Administrative
Affairs; Albert Torel, legal adviser and gray eminence to the High Commissioner; Clarac, diplomatic adviser; Gonon, financial adviser; Ner, adviser on educational matters; Guillanton, economic adviser; and General
Salan, commander of French troops in North Indochina.

79. *Le Monde*, May 21, 1946.

Chapter 5

1. Sainteny, *Histoire d'une paix manquée*, p. 202.
2. *Ibid.*, p. 203.
3. "Reply At The Luncheon Given By Premier Bidault," July 2, 1946.
4. Shaplen, *The Last Revolution*, p. 47.
5. *Ibid.*
6. *Ibid.*, pp. 48–49.
7. Besides Max André, d'Arcy, Bourgoin, Bousquet, Gonon, Messmer, Pignon,
   Torel, and General Salan who had participated in the Dalat Conference,
   the French delegation included three deputies to the National Assembly:
   Juglas (Mouvement Républicain Populaire), Lorency (Communist), and
   Rivet (Socialist), and a few technicians: Admiral Barjat of the General
   Staff for National Defense, Baudet, Director of the Asian Bureau in the
   Ministry of Foreign Affairs, and Gayet, Inspector General for Colonies.
8. In addition to the negotiators at Dalat, Trinh Van Binh, Duong Bach Mai,
   Nguyen Van Huyen, and Vu Trong Khanh, the Vietnamese delegation
   was composed of Hoang Minh Giam, the Socialist Vice-Minister of the
   Interior and Ho's gray eminence, Nguyen Manh Ha, a lawyer and former
   Minister of National Economy, Chu Ba Phuong, a VNQDD leader, Dang
   Phuc Thong, a liberal engineer and Vice-Minister of Communications and
   Public Works, Huynh Thien Loc, one of the richest men in Cochinchina
   and Minister of Agriculture, Phan Anh, a moderate lawyer and Minister of
   Defense, Prince Buu Hoi, a cousin of Bao Dai and a cancer expert, Director of Research at the Radium Institute in Paris, Ta Quang Buu, an
   independent mathematician and Vice-Minister of Defense, and Pham Van
   Dong, former Minister of Finance and one of Ho's most trusted confidants.
9. Paul Rivet, "Le Drame franco-Vietnamien," *Cahiers internationaux*, no.
   6, 1949, p. 49; Hammer, *The Struggle for Indochina*, pp. 167–168.
10. "Reply At The Luncheon Given By Premier Bidault," July 2, 1946.
11. Devillers, *Histoire du Vietnam*, p. 297.
12. *Ibid.*, p. 303.
13. *Ibid.*, p. 301.
14. Philippe Devillers and Jean Lacouture, *La Fin d'une guerre* (Paris:
    Éditions du Seuil, 1960), p. 17.
15. Sainteny, *Histoire d'une paix manquée*, p. 208.
16. *Ibid.*, p. 209.
17. *Ibid.*
18. *Ibid.*, p. 210.
19. *Ibid.*, p. 211.
20. *Ibid.*, pp. 253–255.
21. Devillers, *Histoire du Vietnam*, p. 312.

22. "Proclamation To The People Upon Return From France After Negotiations," October 23, 1946.
23. *Journal officiel*, Assemblée Nationale, March 18, 1947, p. 871.
24. Quoted in Institut franco-suisse d'Études coloniales, *France et Vietnam*, p. 42.
25. Devillers, *Histoire du Vietnam*, p. 337.
26. Chesneaux, *Contributions*, p. 256; Devillers, *Histoire du Vietnam*, pp. 332–340; Isoart, *Le phénomène national vietnamien*, pp. 370–371; Sainteny, *Histoire d'une paix manquée*, p. 216; Paul Mus, *Temoignage chrétien*, no. 292, February 10, 1950.
27. Devillers, *Histoire du Vietnam*, pp. 339–340.
28. Sainteny, *Histoire d'une paix manquée*, p. 217.
29. *Ibid.*, pp. 217–218.
30. Devillers, *Histoire du Vietnam*, p. 351.
31. *Paris-Saigon*, no. 47, December 11, 1946.
32. Devillers, *Histoire du Vietnam*, p. 351.
33. Trumbull, *The Scrutable East*, p. 197.
34. Mus, *Témoignage chrétien*, November 11, 1949.
35. "Appeal To The Entire People To Wage The Resistance War," December 20, 1946.
36. "Message To The Vietnamese People, The French People, And The Peoples Of The Allied Nations," December 21, 1946.
37. Lucien Bodart, *The Quicksand War: Prelude to Vietnam* (Boston: Little, Brown and Company, 1967), p. 13.

Chapter 6

1. *Journal officiel*, Assemblée Nationale, March 18, 1947, p. 875.
2. Devillers, *Histoire du Vietnam*, p. 362.
3. *Le Monde*, January 5, 1947.
4. Quoted in Devillers, *Histoire du Vietnam*, p. 363.
5. *The New York Times*, February 10, 1947.
6. *Esprit*, April, 1947; Devillers, *Histoire du Vietnam*, p. 363.
7. *Journal officiel*, Assemblée Nationale, November 22, 1950. The italics are General Leclerc's.
8. Quoted in Hammer, *The Struggle for Indochina*, p. 195.
9. April 30, 1953.
10. Since 1945, the Greek Communists, aided by infiltrators from Greece's northern Communist neighbors, had threatened to topple the Athens government. And Turkey had been pressured by the Soviet Union to yield control of the Dardanelles and the eastern end of the Black Sea.
11. These were anti-Viet Minh politico-religious sects.
12. *Débats parlementaires*, Assemblée Nationale, 1947, p. 904; Devillers, *Histoire du Vietnam*, p. 378.
13. Devillers, *Histoire du Vietnam*, p. 380.
14. *Ibid.*, p. 387.
15. Mus, *Vietnam, Sociologie d'une guerre* (Paris: Éditions du Seuil, 1952), p. 315.
16. Japanese weapons had been given to the Viet Minh following Japan's sur-

358 *Vision Accomplished?*

render, while American weapons were sold to them by the Kuomintang troops upon their departure from Indochina.

17. *Journal Officiel,* Assemblée Nationale, March 11, 1949, p. 1569.
18. Mus, *Vietnam,* p. 315.
19. *Ibid.,* p. 316.
20. *Ibid.,* p. 372.
21. "Letter To The Vietnamese People After The Meeting With Paul Mus, Representative Of The French High Commissioner Bollaert," May 25, 1947.
22. The five-man Central Executive Committee.
23. *Le Monde,* May 17, 1947.
24. Vinh Thuy was his given name and Bao Dai the one he adopted upon ascending the throne.
25. *Union française.*
26. The Viet Minh political and military headquarters in the mountainous Tonkinese provinces of Bac Can, Ha Giang, Tuyen Quang, and Thai Nguyen.
27. Bao Dai kept referring to the Viet Minh regime as the Resistance government. While refusing to negotiate on Ho's behalf, the ex-Emperor did not close all the doors.
28. Ton Duc Thang was to succeed Ho as DRV President following the latter's death on September 3, 1969.
29. *Le Monde,* July 25, 1947.
30. *Vietnam Information* (Paris), August 1947.
31. *Ibid.*
32. *L'Express,* December 19, 1953.
33. *Journal de Saigon,* August 25, 1947.
34. *Union française.*
35. Cole, *Conflict in Indo-China,* pp. 62–66.
36. *Le Monde,* December 30, 1947.
37. *L'Année politique,* 1947, p. 310.
38. "The Saddest War," *Life,* December 29, 1947.
39. Quoted in Hammer, *The Struggle for Indochina,* p. 220.
40. *Journal officiel,* March 14, 1953, p. 2409.
41. Devillers, *Histoire du Vietnam,* p. 432.
42. Vietnam News Agency (VNA), June 7, 1948.
43. *Journal officiel,* Assemblée nationale, June 8, 1948, p. 3290.
44. *Vietnam Information* (Paris), November 29, 1948.
45. United Nations, Security Council Document S/2780.
46. *Journal officiel,* Assemblée national, March 10, 1949, pp. 1507–1526.
47. Devillers and Lacouture, *La Fin d'une guerre,* p. 20.
48. *Journal officiel,* Conseil de la République, March 9, 1949, p. 613.
49. *Echo du Vietnam* (Saigon), June 16, 1949.
50. *Pakistan Horizon,* Vol. VII, no. 4 (1954), pp. 171–188.
51. The "people's war," as described by Truong Chinh in his book *The Resistance Will Win,* is divided into three stages: contention, equilibrium, and general counteroffensive.
52. Edgar O'Ballance, *The Indochina War, 1945–1954* (London: Faber and Faber, 1964), pp. 117–118.
53. Fall, *The Two Viet-Nams,* p. 115.
54. Donald Lancaster, *The Emancipation of French Indochina* (London: Oxford University Press, 1961), p. 223.

55. Navarre, *Agonie de l'Indochine* (Paris: Librairie Plon 1956), p. 22.
56. *Mekong Upstream* (Berlin: Seven Seas Publisher, 1959), pp. 89–90.
57. Quoted in U.S. Department of State, *The Situation in Laos* (Washington, D.C., September, 1959), pp. 2–3.
58. Fall, *The Two Viet-Nams*, p. 116.
59. Dwight D. Eisenhower, *Mandate for Change* (New York: Doubleday and Company, 1963), p. 338.
60. Buttinger, *Vietnam*, p. 778.
61. Hammer, *The Struggle for Indochina*, p. 300.
62. O'Ballance, *The Indochina War*, p. 198.
63. Truong Chinh, *The Resistance Will Win*, pp. 80–81.
64. *Journal officiel*, Assemblée nationale, October 18, 1950, pp. 7003–7004.
65. Fall, *The Two Viet-Nams*, p. 221.
66. Shaplen, *The Lost Revolution*, p. 93.
67. *Journal officiel*, Assemblée nationale, October 27, 1953, pp. 4602–4603.
68. *Journal officiel*, Conseil de la République, November 12, 1953, p. 1748.
69. "Replies To A Foreign Correspondent," November 26, 1953.
70. Devillers and Lacauture, *La Fin d'une guerre*, p. 47.
71. Navarre, *Agonie de l'Indochine*, p. 191.
72. Vo Nguyen Giap, *People's War, People's Army* (Hanoi: Foreign Languages Publishing House, 1961), pp. 166–169.
73. *Ibid.*
74. The five states—Communist China, the Democratic Republic of Vietnam, the State of Vietnam, Laos, and Cambodia—had been invited by the Big Four to attend the Conference.
75. Devillers and Lacouture, *La Fin d'une guerre*, p. 136.
76. Cmd. 9186. Miscellaneous no. 16. *Documents Relating to the Discussions of Korea and Indochina at the Geneva Conference* (London: HMSO, June 1954), pp. 112–113.
77. *Ibid.*, p. 155.
78. Frederic Dupont, *Mission de la France en Asie* (Paris: Éditions France-Empire, 1956), pp. 160–171.
79. *Ibid.*, 163.
80. New China News Agency (NCNA), July 6, 1954.
81. *The New York Times*, July 25, 1954.
82. *Documents on American Foreign Relations*, 1954 (New York: Harper & Row, Publishers, 1956), pp. 315–316.
83. *Department of State Bulletin* (DSB), August 2, 1954, pp. 162–163.
84. "Appeal Made After The Successful Conclusion Of The Geneva Agreements," July 22, 1954.
85. Wilfred G. Burchett, *Vietnam North* (New York: International Publishers, 1966), p. 159.
86. Shaplen, *The Lost Revolution*, p. 98.

Chapter 7

1. This period was extended, by agreement, to July 25, 1955.
2. Quoted in Devillers and Lacouture, *La Fin d'une guerre*, p. 286.
3. B. S. N. Murti, *Vietnam Divided* (New York: Asia Publishing House, 1964), p. 67.

4. *Ibid.*, pp. 74–80.
5. DSB, August 2, 1954, p. 163. The collective defense agreement referred to was signed on September 8, 1954. It included Australia, France, New Zealand, Pakistan, the Philippines, Thailand, the United Kingdom, and the United States.
6. "Report to the Vietnam Workers' Party Central Committee, 6th Plenum, July 15, 1954," Ho Chi Minh, *Against U.S. Aggression for National Salvation* (Hanoi: Foreign Languages Publishing House, 1967), pp. 26–27.
7. *Ibid.*, pp. 28–29.
8. VNA, March 1, 1949.
9. NCNA, January 18, 1950.
10. *Pravda*, January 31, 1950.
11. DSB, May 22, 1950, p. 821.
12. Voice of South Vietnam, August 16, 1950.
13. "For a Lasting Peace, for a People's Democracy," April 4, 1952, in Ho Chi Minh, *Against U.S. Aggression*, p. 21. The bishop referred to was apparently the late Cardinal Francis Spellman of New York.
14. *Ibid.*, p. 22.
15. Cole, *Conflict in Indochina*, p. 259.
16. VNA, July 6, 1955.
17. Embassy of Vietnam, Washington, D.C., Press and Information Service, July 22, 1955.
18. *Ibid.*, August 19, 1955.
19. *New York Herald Tribune*, August 31, 1955.
20. United Press International dispatch from Saigon, November 22, 1955.
21. DSB, June 11, 1956, p. 973.
22. Ho Chi Minh, *Against U.S. Aggression*. The Front was created on September 10, 1955, at the Third Meeting of the Congress of the Lien Viet as the latter's successor.
23. Eisenhower, *Mandate for Change*, p. 372.
24. Gérard Tongas, *L'enfer communiste au Nord Vietnam* (Paris: Nouvelles Éditions Debress, 1960), p. 222.
25. Hoang Van Chi, *From Colonialism to Communism*, p. 189.
26. *Ibid.*, p. 213.
27. *Ibid.*, p. 189.
28. *Nhan Dan* (Hanoi), October 31, 1956.
29. "Viet Cong" means Vietnamese Communists. There is nothing derogatory about this term as has often been claimed. It is used in this book to designate the Communists who have been operating in South Vietnam since the partition in 1954.
30. Although Ho had assumed that office in 1956 following the ouster of Truong Chinh, it was Le Duan who actually carried out the duties of Secretary General. He was to be officially elected to that post, which was renamed First Secretary, in September, 1960.
31. "Reassessment of the leadership of the Vietnamese proletariat," Le Duan, *On the Socialist Revolution in Vietnam*, Volume I (Hanoi Foreign Languages Publishing House, 1965), pp. 83–84.
32. "Leninism and Vietnam's Revolution," *Ibid.*, p. 48.
33. "Speech Opening The Third National Congress Of The Vietnam Workers' Party," September 5, 1960.
34. Quoted in U.S. Department of State, *A Threat to Peace, North Vietnam's*

Efforts to Conquer South Vietnam (Washington, D.C., 1961), Part II, Appendix A, pp. 4–5.

35. Quoted in Douglas Pike, *The Viet Cong* (Cambridge, Mass.: The M.I.T. Press, 1966), p. 79.
36. *Ibid.*
37. Captured Communist document reproduced in *A Threat to Peace*, Appendix P, pp. 96–97.
38. Radio Hanoi, December 19, 1963.
39. Department of State, *Aggression from the North: The Record of North Vietnam's Campaign to Conquer South Vietnam* (Washington, D.C., 1965), Appendix G, p. 57.
40. *Nhan Dan*, September 7, 1969.
41. Statistics compiled from defense data in U.S. Senate Committee on Foreign Relations, *Background Information Relating to Southeast Asia and Vietnam*, 4th revised edition (Washington, D.C.: Government Printing Office, 1968), p. 297.
42. *Life*, March 22, 1968.
43. Senate Committee on Foreign Relations, *Background Information Relating to Southeast Asia and Vietnam*, p. 297.
44. DSB, April 26, 1965, pp. 606–610.
45. Ho Chi Minh, *Against U.S. Aggression*, p. 70.
46. VNA, April 12, 1965.
47. Cole, *Conflict in Indochina*, p. 66.
48. "Ho's Answers To The British *Daily Worker*," July 1, 1965, Ho Chi Minh, *Against U.S. Aggression*, p. 81.
49. Senate Committee on Foreign Relations, *Background Information Relating to Southeast Asia and Vietnam*, p. 171.
50. *People's Daily*, December 31, 1965.
51. Ho Chi Minh, *Against U.S. Aggression*, pp. 117–122.
52. United Nations Press Release 683, dated March 28, 1967.
53. VNA, March 27, 1967.
54. Department of State Publication, 8305, released October 1967.
55. Radio Hanoi, January 1, 1968.

Chapter 8

1. An abridged version of this chapter appeared in *Orbis*, a Quarterly Journal of World Affairs published by the Foreign Policy Research Institute of the University of Pennsylvania. Winter 1970. Excerpted by permission. © 1970 by the Trustees of the University of Pennsylvania.
2. "The Path Which Led Me To Leninism," April 1960.
3. Vo Nguyen Giap, *People's War, People's Army*, p. 22.
4. See Nguyen Manh Tuong's speech delivered at the National Congress of the Fatherland Front held in Hanoi on October 30, 1956, in Hoang Van Chi (ed.), *The New Class in North Vietnam* (Saigon: Cong Dan Publishing Company, 1958), pp. 134–165.
5. People mistakingly believed that Mao had intended to liberalize his regime when he said that progress in art and science could be achieved only if different ideas were permitted to express themselves, and approved such slogans as "let a hundred flowers bloom," and "let a hundred schools of

thought contend." Very soon, however, Mao made it clear that blooming flowers and contending ideas must be aimed at improving and strengthening socialism, not at undermining it.

6. Nhu Phong, "Intellectuals, Writers and Artists," *China Quarterly*, January-March, 1962, pp. 47–69.
7. *Ibid.*
8. Harold C. Hinton, *China's Relations with Burma and Vietnam* (New York: Institute of Pacific Relations, 1958), p. 13.
9. Le Duc Tho, "Let us change the trend and step up the party building task in order to insure successful carrying out of the anti-U.S. struggle for national liberation," *Nhan Dan*, February 3, 1966; *Hoc Tap*, February, 1966.
10. The office of Secretary General was renamed First Secretary in September, 1960.
11. These figures are taken from William Kaye, "A Bowl of Rice Divided," *China Quarterly*, January-March, 1962, p. 92.
12. Tongas, *J'ai vécu . . .* , passim.
13. Le Duan, *On the Socialist Revolution in Vietnam*, p. 96.
14. P. J. Honey, "North Vietnam's Party Congress," *China Quarterly*, October-December, 1960, p. 73.
15. "Speech Opening The Third National Congress Of The Vietnam Workers' Party," September 5, 1960.
16. Honey, "North Vietnam's Party Congress," p. 66.
17. *Ibid.*, p. 68.
18. *Ibid.*, p. 69.
19. U.S. Department of State, *A Threat to Peace*, pp. 1–3.
20. VNA, December 23, 1962.
21. *Ibid.*, January 29, 1963.
22. *Ibid.*, February 10, 1963.
23. NCNA, May 12, 1963.
24. *Ibid.*, May 15, 1963.
25. *Ibid.*, May 16, 1963.
26. "Speech Delivered At The Nguyen Ai Quoc School for Cadres," *Ibid.*, May 15, 1963.
27. "Report To The Meeting Of Representatives Of The Hanoi People On The Success Of The Sixth Session Of The National Assembly (First Legislature)," February 15, 1957.
28. Le Duan, *Some Questions Concerning The International Tasks Of Our Party* (Peking: Foreign Languages Press, 1964), p. 51.
29. Public Law 88-408/H.J. Res. 1145/78 Stat. 384, approved August 10, 1964.
30. *People's Daily*, December 31, 1964.
31. NCNA, December 31, 1964.
32. *Ibid.*, February 8, 1965.
33. *Red Flag*, April 25, 1965. "Our principle: We will not attack unless we are attacked. If we are attacked, we will certainly counterattack. We shall wipe out anybody who dares to attack us. On whatever scale the United States attacks us, we will reply on the same scale. We always mean what we say. We are fully prepared for war."
34. *Nhan Dan*, January 2, 1965.
35. VNA, January 30, 1965.
36. TASS, January 4, 1965.
37. VNA, February 6, 1965.

38. *Ibid.*, February 7, 1965.
39. TASS, February 7, 1965.
40. *Ibid.*
41. Tokyo Domestic Television Service, February 7, 1965.
42. *Nhan Dan*, September 22, 1965.
43. NCNA, April 24, 1965.
44. *Nhan Dan*, September 22, 1965.
45. VNA, December 12, 1965.
46. *China Quarterly*, January-March 1968, p. 175.
47. *Ibid.*, July-September 1966, pp. 217–218. In regard to Soviet aid, the Chinese Foreign Ministry said: "Both in quantity and quality, the aid the Soviet Union gives Vietnam is far from commensurate with its strength. It should have been easy for a big power like the Soviet Union to provide Vietnam with several hundred thousand tons of military supplies. But it has given only a few tens of thousands of tons, a deplorably meager amount. It must be further pointed out that most of the Soviet supplies consisted of old weapons of its own armed forces which had been replaced and which even included some that were worn out and of no use at all. As for those of truly good quality, the Soviet Union either does not supply them or is unwilling to supply in large quantities."
48. "Chou En-lai's speech delivered in Peking on the anniversary of the founding of the NLF," NCNA, November 9, 1967.
49. Communiqué of the 11th Plenary Session of the 8th Central Committee of the Chinese Communist Party, August 12, 1966.
50. *China Quarterly*, January-March 1968, p. 175.
51. Radio Moscow, December 5, 1967.
52. *L'Humanité*, June 4, 1968.
53. This was the opinion of most Hong Kong analysts of Chinese Communist affairs.
54. Radio Seoul, May 12, 1968.
55. Radio Moscow, May 21, 1968.
56. TASS, April 2, 1968.
57. Radio Moscow, April 2, 1968.
58. *Ibid.*, April 4, 1968.
59. *Ibid.*, May 15, 1968.
60. *Ibid.*
61. *Nhan Dan*, June 19, 1968.
62. *Ibid.*, June 26, 1968.
63. Radio Hanoi, May 24, 1968.

Chapter 9

1. "A Talk with Ho Chi Minh," *The New Republic*, October 12, 1963, p. 21.
2. *Nhan Dan*, September 10, 1969.
3. *Ibid.*

SELECTED BIBLIOGRAPHIES

BOOKS

Bodard, Lucien. *The Quicksand War: Prelude to Vietnam.* Boston: Little, Brown and Co., 1967.

Burchett, Wilfred G. *Mekong Upstream.* Berlin: Seven Seas Publishers, 1959.

———. *Vietnam North.* New York: International Publishers Co., Inc., 1966.

Buttinger, Joseph. *Vietnam: A Dragon Embattled.* 2 vols. New York: Praeger Publishers, Inc., 1967.

Celerier, Pierre. *Menaces sur le Vietnam.* Saigon: Imprimerie d'Extrême-Orient, 1950.

Chesneaux, Jean. *Contribution à l'histoire de la nation vietnamienne.* Paris: Éditions sociales, 1955.

Cole, Allan B., ed. *Conflict in Indochina and International Repercussions: A Documentary History, 1945–1955.* Ithaca: Cornell University Press, 1956.

Devillers, Philippe. *Histoire du Viet-Nam de 1940 à 1952.* Paris: Éditions du Seuil, 1952.

———. "Vietnamese Nationalism and French Policies," in William L. Holland, ed. *Asian Nationalism and the West.* New York: The Macmillan Company, 1953.

Devillers, Philippe, and Lacouture, Jean. *Le Fin d'une guerre, Indochina 1954.* Paris: Éditions du Seuil, 1960.

Donnell, John C. "North Vietnam: A Qualified Pro-Chinese Position," in Robert A. Scalapino, ed. *The Communist Revolution in Asia: Tactics, Goals, and Achievements.* Englewood Cliffs, N.J.: Prentice-Hall, Inc., 1965.

Eisenhower, Dwight D. *Mandate for Change.* New York: Doubleday & Company, Inc., 1963.

Fall, Bernard B. *Le Viet Minh.* Paris: Armand Colin, 1960.

———. *Street Without Joy: Insurgency in Indochina.* Harrisburg, Pa.: Stackpole Books, 1961.

———. *The Two Viet-Nams: A Political and Military Analysis.* New York: Praeger Publishers, Inc., 1964.

Fischer, Ruth. *Von Lenin zu Mao* (From Lenin to Mao). Düsseldorf-Köln: Eugen Diederichs Verlag, 1956.

Frédéric-Dupont. *Mission de la France en Asie.* Paris: Éditions France-Empire, 1956.

Hammer, Ellen J. *The Struggle For Indochina.* Stanford: Stanford University Press, 1954.

Hertrich, Jean Michel. *Doc lap! L'indépendance ou la mort.* Paris: Vigneau, 1946.
Hinton, Harold C. *China's Relations with Burma and Vietnam.* New York: Institute of Pacific Relations, 1958.
Ho Chi Minh (alias Nguyen Ai Quoc). *Le procès de la colonisation française.* Paris: Librairie du Travail, 1926.
————. *Selected Works.* 4 vols. Hanoi: Foreign Languages Publishing House, 1960, 1961, 1962.
————. *Prison Diary.* Tr. Aileen Palmer. Hanoi: Foreign Languages Publishing House, 1966.
————. *Against U.S. Aggression For National Salvation.* Hanoi: Foreign Languages Publishing House, 1967.
Hoang Van Chi. *The New Class in North Vietnam.* Saigon: Cong Dan, 1958.
————. *From Colonialism to Communism.* London and Dunmow: Pall Mall Press, 1964.
Honey, P. J. *North Vietnam Today: Profile of a Communist Satellite.* New York: Praeger Publishers, Inc., 1962.
————. *Communism in North Vietnam.* Cambridge: The M.I.T. Press, 1963.
Institut Franco-Suisse d'Études Coloniales. *France and Vietnam, the Franco-Vietnamese Conflict According to Official Documents.* Geneva: Éditions du Milieu du Monde, 1947.
Isaacs, Harold R. *No Peace for Asia.* Cambridge: The M.I.T. Press, 1967.
Isoart, Paul. *Le phénomène national vietnamien: de l'indépendance unitaire à l'indépendance fractionnée.* Paris: Librairie de Droit et de Jurisprudence, 1961.
Lacouture, Jean. *Cinq hommes et la France.* Paris: Éditions du Seuil, 1961.
————. *Ho Chi Minh, A Political Biography.* Tr. Peter Wiles. New York: Random House, Inc., 1968.
Lancaster, Donald. *The Emancipation of French Indochina.* New York: Oxford University Press, 1961.
Laniel, Joseph. *Le drame indochinois: de Dien-Bien-Phu au pari de Genève.* Paris: Plon, 1957.
Laurent, Arthur. *La Banque de l'Indochine et la piastre.* Paris: Éditions des Deux Rives, 1954.
Le Duan. *Some Questions Concerning the International Tasks of Our Party.* Peking: Foreign Languages Press, 1964.
————. *On the Socialist Revolution in Vietnam.* 2 vols. Hanoi: Foreign Languages Publishing House, 1965.
Le Thanh Khoi. *Le Viet-Nam, Histoire et Civilisation,* Paris: Les Éditions de Minuit, 1955.
Levy, Roger, et al. *French Interests and Policies in the Far East.* New York: Institute of Pacific Relations, 1941.

Mohan Das, S. R. *Ho Chi Minh: Nationalist or Soviet Agent?* Bombay: Democratic Research Service, 1951.

Murti, B. S. N. *Vietnam Divided: The Unfinished Struggle.* New York: Asia Publishing House, 1964.

Mus, Paul. *Viet-Nam, Sociologie d'une guerre.* Paris: Éditions du Seuil, 1952.

Navarre, General Henri. *Agonie de l'Indochine (1953–1954).* Paris: Plon, 1958.

Nguyen Luong Bang, Vo Nguyen Giap, et al. *Souvenirs sur Ho Chi Minh.* Hanoi: Foreign Languages Publishing House, 1962.

O'Ballance, Edgar. *The Indo-China War, 1945–1954.* London: Faber & Faber, 1964.

Pham Van Dong and the Committee for the Study of the History of the Vietnamese Workers' Party. *President Ho Chi Minh.* Hanoi: Foreign Languages Publishing House, 1960.

Pike, Douglas. *The Viet Cong: The Organization and Techniques of the National Liberation of South Vietnam.* Cambridge: The M.I.T. Press, 1966.

Sainteny, Jean. *Histoire d'une paix manquée.* Paris: Amiot-Dumont, 1953.

Shaplen, Robert. *The Lost Revolution.* New York: Harper & Row, Publishers, 1965.

Starobin, Joseph R. *Eyewitness in Indo-China.* New York: Cameron & Kahn, 1954.

Tongas, Gérard. *J'ai vécu dans l'enfer communiste au Nord Vietnam et j'ai choisi la liberté.* Paris: Nouvelles Éditions Debresse, 1960.

Trager, Frank N., ed. *Marxism in Southeast Asia: A Study of Four Countries.* Stanford: Stanford University Press, 1959.

Tran Dan Tien. *Hu Chih-ming chuan* (Biography of Ho Chi Minh). Shanghai: August Publishing Co., 1949.

————. *Glimpses of the Life of Ho Chi Minh.* Hanoi: Foreign Languages Publishing House, 1958.

Trumbull, Robert. *The Scrutable East.* New York: David McKay Co., Inc., 1964.

Truong Chinh. *The August Revolution.* Hanoi: Foreign Languages Publishing House, 1958.

————. *The Resistance Will Win.* Hanoi: Foreign Languages Publishing House, 1960.

————. *President Ho Chi Minh, Beloved Leader of the Vietnamese People.* Hanoi: Foreign Language Publishing House, 1966.

Vietnamese Studies, Nos. 7, 8, 9, 10, 11, 12. Hanoi: Vietnamese Studies, 1965–67.

Viollis, Andrée. *Indochine S.O.S.* Paris: Gallimard, 1935.

Vo Nguyen Giap. *Dien Bien Phu.* Hanoi: Foreign Languages Publishing House, 1959.

————. *People's War, People's Army.* Hanoi: Foreign Languages Publishing House, 1961.

Vo Nguyen Giap, Bui Lam, et al. *Récits de la résistance vietnamiene.*
    Paris: Maspero, 1966.
Zagoria, Donald S. *The Sino-Soviet Conflict, 1956–1961.* New York:
    Atheneum Publishers, 1964.
———. *Vietnam Triangle.* New York: Pegasus, 1967.

ARTICLES AND PERIODICALS

"A War that Feels Different when You're There," *The Economist,* June,
    1967.
Benda, Harry J. "Communism in Southeast Asia," *Yale Review,* March,
    1956.
Bullit, William. "The Saddest War," *Life,* December 29, 1947.
Buttinger, Joseph. "France and Frenchmen: Saigon Intrigue," *The New
    Republic,* February 28, 1955.
Buu Loc, "Aspects of the Vietnamese Problem," *Pacific Affairs,* September, 1952.
Carver, George A., Jr. "The Real Revolution in South Vietnam," *Foreign
    Affairs,* April, 1965.
———. "The Faceless Viet Cong," *Foreign Affairs,* April, 1966.
Chaffard, Georges. "Le gouvernement nord-vietnamien doit affronter à
    son tour le mécontentement populaire," *Le Monde* (weekly edition), December 5, 1956.
Chang, Ch'u-kun. "The New Military Victory of the Vietnamese People,"
    World Culture, October 28, 1950.
Chen, King C. "North Vietnam in the Sino-Soviet Dispute, 1962–1964,"
    Asian Survey, September, 1964.
———. "Peking's Strategy in Indochina," *Yale Review,* June, 1965.
Crozier, Brian. "The International Situation in Indochina," *Pacific Affairs,* December, 1955.
Dai, Shen-yu. "Peking and Indochina's Destiny," *Western Political Quarterly,* September 1954.
Du Berrier, Hilaire. "How We Helped Ho Chi Minh," *The Freeman,*
    April 19, 1954.
Durdin, Peggy. "The Shadowy Leader of the Viet Minh," *The New
    York Times Magazine,* May 9, 1954.
———. "Why Ho Chi Minh Can Win," *The Nation,* November 11, 1956.
Fall, Bernard B. "The Cease-fire in Indochina: An Appraisal," *Far Eastern Survey,* September and October, 1954.
———. "Crisis in North Vietnam," *Far Eastern Survey,* January, 1957.
———. "A Talk With Ho Chi Minh," *The New Republic,* October 12,
    1963.
Fischer, Ruth. "Ho Chi Minh: Disciplined Communist," *Foreign Affairs,*
    October, 1954.

Griffin, Allen. "Must Indochina Be Lost?" *The New Republic*, March 31, 1952.

Guillain, Robert. "L'aide chinoise au Viet Minh," *Le Monde*, March 19, 1954.

———. "The Tragedy of Vietnam," *The Manchester Guardian Weekly*, May 26, 1955.

"Ho Chi Minh's Way," *The Economist*, January 5, 1957.

Honey, P. J. "Ho Chi Minh and the Intellectuals," *Soviet Survey*, Congress for Cultural Freedom, Paris, April–June, 1959.

———. "North Vietnam's Party Congress," *China Quarterly*, October–December, 1960.

Jen Hsiao. "The Great Success of the Land Policy of the Democratic Republic of Vietnam," *World Culture*, February 5, 1954.

Jumper, Roy. "The Communist Challenge in South Vietnam," *Far Eastern Survey*, December, 1956.

Katzenbach, Edward L., Jr. "Indochina: A Military-Political Appreciation," *World Politics*, January, 1952.

Kaye, William. "A Bowl of Rice Divided: The Economy of North Vietnam," *China Quarterly*, January–March, 1962.

Lacouture, Jean. "Inside North Vietnam," *The New Republic*, May 21, 1962.

Le Branchu, Jean-Yves. "The French Colonial Empire and the Popular Front Government," *Pacific Affairs*, June, 1937.

Le Thanh Khoi. "The Democratic Republic of Vietnam," *Eastern World* (London), December, 1954.

Lee, Chae Jin. "Some Chinese Communist Attitudes Toward the Vietnam War," *Vietnam Perspectives*, February, 1967.

Levy, Roger. "Indochina: A Keystone in Asia: A French View," *India Quarterly*, January–March, 1952.

Lun, J. "The Popular Movement in Indochina," *Communist International* (Moscow), vol. XIV, no. 3, 1937.

Mansfield, Mike. "Reprieve in Vietnam," *Harper's Magazine*, January, 1956.

McCulloch, Frank. "Peace Feelers: This Frail Dance of the Seven Veils," *Life*, March 22, 1968.

Mitchison, Lois. "Life under Communists in North Vietnam," *The Manchester Guardian Weekly*, August 12, 1954.

Mus, Paul. "Vietnam: A Nation Off Balance," *Yale Review*, June, 1952.

Ner, Marcel. "Le Viet-Nam et la Chine de 1945 à 1953," *Les Temps Modernes* (Paris), vol. 9, nos. 93–94, September–October, 1953.

Mende, Tibor. "Les deux Viet-Nam," *Esprit* (Paris) June, 1957.

Nguyen Dac Khe. "The Essentials of the Vietnamian Problem," *Asia*, March, 1954.

Nguyen Thai. "The Two Vietnams and China," *Harvard Review*, II, no. 1, Fall–Winter, 1963.

Oka, Takashi. "The Other Regime in South Vietnam," *The New York Times Magazine*, July 31, 1966.

Rigg, Robert B. "Red Parallel: the Tactics of Ho and Mao," *Army Combat Forces Journal*, January, 1955.

Rivet, Paul. "Le drame franco-vietnamien," *Cahiers internationaux*, June, 1949.

Roberts, Chalmers M. "The Day We Didn't Go to War," *The Reporter*, September 14, 1954.

Sacks, Milton. "The Strategy of Communism in Southeast Asia," *Pacific Affairs*, September, 1950.

Shabad, Theodore. "Economic Development in North Vietnam," *Pacific Affairs*, March, 1958.

Shaplen, Robert. "The Enigma of Ho Chi Minh," *The Reporter*, January 27, 1955.

Sharp, Lauriston. "Paradoxes in the Indochinese Dilemma," *The Annals of the American Academy of Political and Social Science*, July, 1954.

Steiner, Arthur H. "Vietnam: Civil War Again?" *The New Republic*, July 18, 1955.

Taussing, H. C. "Land Reform Abuses," *South China Morning Post* (Hong Kong), November 28, 1956.

———. "North Vietnam's Headaches," *Eastern World*, March, 1957.

"The Implacable Man Named 'He Who Enlightens,' " *Life*, March 22, 1968.

Ton That Thien. "The Geneva Agreements and Peace Prospects in Vietnam," *India Quarterly*, October–December, 1956.

Zhukov, Ye. "China's Revolutionary Victory and Its Influence on the Liberation Movements of the Various Asian Peoples," *World Culture*, September 27, 1952.

GOVERNMENT PUBLICATIONS

Democratic Republic of Vietnam (North Vietnam):

Association culturelle pour le salut du Vietnam. *Témoignages et documents français relatifs à la colonialisation française au Vietnam.* Hanoi, 1945.

Foreign Languages Publishing House. *Documents of the Third National Congress of the Vietnam Workers' Party.* 4 vols. Hanoi, 1960.

———. *Breaking Our Chains: Documents of the Vietnamese Revolution of August 1945.* Hanoi, 1960.

———. *Statements by President Ho Chi Minh after the Geneva Conference.* Hanoi, 1955.

Ministry of Foreign Affairs. *Documents Relating to the Execution of the Geneva Accords on Vietnam.* Hanoi, 1956.

News Service. *Vietnam Information Bulletin.* Rangoon, 1948–62.

Service d'Information. *Causes of the Conflict between France and Vietnam.* Paris, 1948.

———. *Le Président Ho Chi Minh.* Paris, 1947.

Vietnam Cultural Association for National Liberation. *Factual Records of the Vietnam August Revolution.* Hanoi, 1946.

Vietnam Fatherland Front. *For Peace and Reunification of Vietnam.* Hanoi, 1958.

Republic of Vietnam (South Vietnam):

Embassy in Washington. *News from Vietnam* and *Vietnam Bulletin.* Washington, D.C., 1958–64.

Ministry of Foreign Affairs. *Communist Aggression against the Republic of Vietnam.* Saigon, 1964.

———. *La politique aggressive des Viet Minh communistes et la guerre subversive communiste au Sud Vietnam.* Saigon, 1962.

Ministry of Foreign Affairs. *Violations of the Geneva Agreements by the Viet Minh Communists.* Saigon, 1959, 1960.

United Kingdom:

Foreign Office. *Documents Relating to the Discussion of Korea and Indochina at the Geneva Conference, April 27–June 15, 1954* (Cmd. 9186). London, 1954.

———. *Further Documents Relating to the Discussion of Indochina at the Geneva Conference, June 16–July 21, 1954* (Cmd. 9239). London, 1954.

Parliament, House of Commons. *Parliamentary Debates* (session 1953–54), vol. 529. London, 1954.

United States:

Department of State. *Aggression from the North: Record of North Vietnam's Campaign to Conquer South Vietnam.* Washington, D.C., 1965.

———. *A Threat to Peace: North Vietnam's Efforts to Conquer South Vietnam,* Parts I & II. Washington, D.C., 1961.

———. *Background Indochina: The War in Vietnam, Cambodia and Laos.* Washington, D.C., 1953.

———. *Chinese Communist World Outlook; A Handbook of Chinese Communist Statements: The Public Record of a Militant Ideology.* Washington, D.C., 1962.

————. *Political Alignments of Vietnamese Nationalists.* Publication no. 3708. Washington, D.C., 1949.

————. *The Situation in Laos.* Washington, D.C., 1959.

Foreign Broadcast Information Service. *Daily Report.* Washington, D.C., 1948–69.

Senate Committee on Foreign Relations. *Background Information Relating to Southeast Asia and Vietnam.* 90th Cong., 2d Sess. Washington, D.C., March 1968.

Senate Committee on Foreign Relations. *Report of Senator Mike Mansfield on a Study Mission to the Associated States of Indochina: Vietnam, Cambodia, Laos.* 83d Cong., 1st Sess. Washington, D.C., October 27, 1953.

————. *Report on Indochina: Report of Senator Mike Mansfield on a Study Mission to Vietnam, Cambodia, Laos.* 83d Cong., 2d Sess. Washington, D.C., October 15, 1954.

————. *Vietnam, Cambodia and Laos.* Report by Senator Mike Mansfield. 84th Cong., 1st Sess. Washington, D.C., October 6, 1955.

Index

Abbas, Ferhat, 151
Alessandri, General, 217
André, Max, 121, 150, 153–54
Annam, 32, 36, 40, 41, 42,
Archimbaud, Léon, 21
Aubrac, Raymond, 154
Auriol, President Vincent, 210

Bac Kan, 63, 69, 70, 175
Bao Dai, Emperor, 70, 80–81, 90,
    108, 116, 125–26, 163, 182, 189–
    90, 191, 195–213, 235
Bao Long, Prince, 117
Batov, General, 288
Bazin, René, xvii
Bedell-Smith, Walter, 233
Belgium, 23
Belgrade, 266
Bevin, Ernest, 89, 96
Biarritz, 145–46
Bidault, Georges, 146–47, 229, 234
Binh Khe, 4
Bluecher, General Vassily. See General Gallen
Bollaert, Emile, 183, 184, 185, 188,
    189, 192–93, 194–97, 202–203
Borodin, Michael, 25, 26, 29
Boutbien, Léon, 179
Brévié, Jules, 42
Brezhnev, Leonid Ilyitch, 299
Britain and the British, 9, 86–96
Brussels, 29

Buckley, Major Robert, 112
Bukharin, Nikolai Ivanovich, 22
Bullit, William, 199–200
Burchett, Wilfred, 220–21
Buttinger, Joseph, 37
Buu Hoi, 208, 224–25
Buu Loc, 213

Cachin, Marcel, 10, 14, 18
Cam Ranh Bay, 159
Cambodia, 232
Canada, 246, 270
Canton, 26–29, 62
Cao Bang, 51, 63, 69, 70, 216
Caput, Louis, 202
Carpentier, General Marcel, 216, 217
Cédille, Henri, 88, 90, 91, 94–95,
    135–36
Chauvel, Jean, 236
Chen Yi, 307
Chesneaux, Jean, 113
Chiang Fa-ku'ei, Marshal, 58, 61, 62,
    65, 66
Chiang Kai-shek, 29, 62, 66, 88, 97,
    98
China and the Chinese, 24, 27, 30,
    42, 56, 60, 97–112, 275–82, 287–
    97
Chou En-lai, 233, 275, 307
Chu Van Tan, General, 57, 63, 68
Chungking, 57, 61, 62, 63, 66, 111
Churchill, Winston, 88–89, 233

Cochinchina, 32, 36, 40, 48
Cogny, General, 232
Collins, General Lawton, 254
Coste-Floret, Paul, 186, 200, 205
Cung, Sergeant, 56

Dalat, 139–41, 153
Dang Xuan Khu. *See* Truong Chinh
D'Argenlieu, Admiral Georges Thierry, 116–17, 123, 135, 137–39, 142–43, 153, 158–59, 175, 182
Davies, Harold, 268
De Brebisson, Colonel, 236
De Castries, General, 232
De Gaulle, General Charles, 64–65, 88, 180, 185
De Lattre de Tassigny, General Jean, 217–18, 222
Dèbes, Colonel, 165–66
Decoux, Admiral Jean, 47, 50, 65, 70
Delteil, General, 236, 239, 245
Dessinges, P. M., 122
Devillers, Philippe, 154, 166
Dien Bien Phu, 230
Dinh Ngoc Lien, Major, 317
Dong Khe Fort, 216
Dranber, Bernard, 169
Ducroux, Joseph, 38
Dulles, John Foster, 232, 233, 256
Duong Bach Mai, 45, 46
Durdin, Tillman, 238

Eden, Anthony, 232, 233
Eisenhower, President Dwight D., 223, 232, 250, 258
Ely, General Paul, 233, 254
Escoffier, 9

Fall, Bernard, xiv
Fanfani, Amintore, 269
Fontainebleau, 149–54
France and the French, 6, 8, 23, 30, 42, 46, 86–96, 116–43, 149–58, 164–75, 176–232
Frédéric-Dupont, 236

Gallagher, General, 113

Gallen, General, 25
Godart, Justin, 44
Gordon, Laurie, 73
Gouin, Félix, 123
Gracey, General Douglas, 93, 94, 95

Ha Ba Cang. *See* Hoang Quoc Viet
Ha Dong, 195, 196, 198, 200
Ha Long Bay, 137–38, 201, 204
Ha Tinh Province, 1, 2–3, 249
Hailey, Foster, 170–71
Haiphong, 34
Hanoi, 42, 80, 270, 371
Harriman, W. Averell, 270
Helliwell, Colonel Paul, 67
Heppner, Richard, 67
Ho Tung Mau, 26, 29, 53
Ho Chi Minh, aliases of, xiv, 4, 5, 6, 15, 21, 23, 25, 30, 32, 49, 62; and American intervention, 250–73; and Chinese occupation, 97–106, 110–12; arrest and imprisonment in China, 58–62; background of, 1–5; Bao Dai and, 125–26, 195–213; Chinese episode of, 25–29; Communism of, xiii, 13–15, 16–48; daughter of, 8; death of, 314; death rumors of, 38, 58; founder of ICP, 31–48; French episode of, 16–22; last rites of, 317–18; London episode of, 9; negotiations with France, 118–43, 144–58, 232–40; negotiations with the U.S.A., 265–73; Russian episode of, 23–24, 39; Siamese episode of, 29–31; wife of, 8–9; will of, 315–16; writings of, 6–7, 12–13, 17–18, 19–21, 23–24, 43–44, 54, 59–60, 68, 69, 78–79, 81–82, 106, 147–48, 161–62, 173–75, 187, 227, 240–41, 251, 270–71, 315–17
Ho Viet Thang, 276
Ho Ying-chin, General, 100
Hoang Quang Binh, 49, 50
Hoang Minh Giam, 119, 130, 183, 191, 197–98
Hoang Van Hoan, 281

Hoang Huu Nam, 168
Hoang Quoc Viet, 42, 53
Hong Kong, 29, 31, 32, 35, 37, 38
Hong Son, 26, 29
Hue, 42, 44
Huynh Thuc Khang, 127, 129
Huynh Tan Phat, 263

India, 246, 270
Indochina, 30, 33, 35, 46, 61, 65, 67, 71
Isaacs Harold, 9, 98
Isoart, Paul, 34, 35
Italy, 29

Japan, 41, 46, 75
Joffe, Alexander, 25
John, Lieutenant John, 75–76
Johnson, Lyndon B., 266, 267, 269, 270, 272, 273, 294, 300, 306

Khai Dinh, Emperor, 18
Khiem (Ho's brother), 4
Khrushchev, Nikita, 276, 287, 288
Kim Lien Village, 3, 4
Komatsu, Kyo, 22
Kosygin, Aleksei, 297, 298–300
Kunming, 47, 50, 65
Kwangsi Province, 46, 57, 61

La Pira, Giorgio, 269
Lang Son, 69, 70
Laniel, Joseph, 225, 226, 229
Laos, 232
LaPorte, Roger Allen, 269
Le Duan, 260–61, 262, 281, 283, 292–93
Le Loi, 1
Le Thanh Nghi, 281, 309
Le Hong Phong, 26, 43, 46
Le Duc Tho, 280
Leclerc, General Jean, 88, 117, 123, 128, 135, 137, 180
Lenin, Nikolai, 11, 16, 19, 21, 22, 23, 24, 27
Letourneau, Jean, 222
Liuchow, 61, 66, 103

Liu Shao-chi, 290–91
Lo Jui-ching, General, 296
Lo Kwei-po, General, 275
Löfgren, Sven, 227
London, 9, 38
Longuet, Jean, 10
Loseby, Frank, 38
Lu Han, General, 97–102, 104
Lung Yun, 98
Ly Thuy. *See* Ho Chi Minh

Ma Ing, General, 130
Macao, 39
Mai Hac De, Emperor, 1
Mao Tse-tung, 50, 52, 223, 305, 307
Marie, André, 206
Marseilles, 158
Marx, Karl, 10, 17, 18, 59
Mayer, René, 225
Mendès-France, Pierre, 236–37, 239, 247
Merlin, Governor General, 25
Messmer, Pierre, 88
Mitterand, François, 225
Mollet, Guy, 208
Molotov, V. M., 232, 233, 236, 238
Monmousseau, Gaston, 15
Morlière, General, 164–65, 171–72
Morrison, Norman R., 269
Moscow, 21, 22, 23, 25, 29, 33, 39, 43, 282
Mountbatten, Admiral Lord Louis, 88
Moutet, Marius, 10, 45, 46, 123, 136, 177–79, 200
Murti, B. S. N., 248
Mus, Paul, 173, 184, 185–87

Nam Dan District, 3
Nam Dinh, 36
Nam Phuong, Empress, 117
Navarre, General Henri, 218, 229
Nehru, Pandit, 237
Nghe, An Province, 1, 2, 3–5, 15, 36, 37, 249, 277
Ngo Dinh Diem, 124–25, 188, 212, 245, 253–57, 258

Ngo Dinh Khoi, 125
Ngo Dinh Nhu, 225
Nguyen Luong Bang, 32, 33
Nguyen Quoc Dinh, 235–36
Nguyen Manh Ha, 188
Nguyen Van Hieu, 263
Nguyen Van Hinh, General, 254
Nguyen Thai Hoc, xvii, xviii
Nguyen Phan Long, 198, 212
Nguyen An Ninh, 32
Nguyen Ai Quoc. *See* Ho Chi Minh
Nguyen Sinh Sac (Ho's father), 3, 4, 6
Nguyen Van Sam, 182, 192, 195, 198
Nguyen Tuong Tam, 129, 140, 192, 198
Nguyen Van Tam, 213
Nguyen Van Tao, 46, 90
Nguyen Hai Than, 61, 62, 63, 66, 98, 101, 102, 116, 127, 198
Nguyen Chi Thanh, 280, 301
Nguyen Tat Thanh. *See* Ho Chi Minh
Nguyen Van Thinh, 136, 139, 143
Nguyen Huu Tho, 263
Nguyen Duy Trinh, 271, 272, 279
Nguyen The Truyen, 11, 16, 18
Nguyen Van Xuan, General, 143, 203, 205, 207
Noulens, Hilaire, 38
Novotný, Antonín, 288, 289

Pac Bo, 51, 52, 55, 68
Paris, 8, 10, 22, 87, 144, 146–58
Pathet Lao, 220, 221, 234, 235, 239
Patti, Major Archimedes, 112, 119
Paul VI, Pope, 269
Pearson, Lester, 271
Peking, 233, 238, 267, 294, 306
Pham Van Bach, 90, 93
Pham Van Dong, 27, 36, 37, 42, 46, 50, 51, 53, 109, 152–53, 191, 232, 234, 267, 280, 283–84, 300, 309–10
Pham Van Hum, 46
Pham Hung, 280
Pham Ngoc Thach, 197
Pham Hong Thai, 25
Phan Anh, 127, 129

Phan Boi Chau, xvi, xvii, 2, 4, 5, 25, 27, 28, 35, 38
Phan Khoi, 277
Phan Dinh Phung, 2, 54
Phan Ke Toai, 79, 191
Phan Chau Trinh, 8
Phu Ninh Village, 108–109
Pignon, Léon, 119, 129, 184, 210, 213
Pinay, Antoine, 225
Pléven, René, 229
Poland, 246

Quang Trung, Emperor, 1
Quynh Luu District, 277

Radford, Admiral Arthur, 233
Ramadier, Paul, 183, 200, 210
Raphael-Leygues, Jacques, 225
Reston, James, 302
Riffaud, Madeleine, 305
Rivet, Paul, 150
Robertson, Walter, 256
Robin, René, 42
Ronning, Chester, 271
Roosevelt, Franklin D., 88
Roy, M. N., xiv, 28
Russia and the Russians, 21, 22, 39, 282–86, 297–311

Saigon, 34, 40, 56, 90–97, 137–38
Sainteny, Jean, xiv, 73, 74, 97, 99, 112, 116, 118–20, 122, 124, 129, 167–69
Salan, General Raoul, xiv, 144, 222
Samneua, 221, 244
Sanakikone, 234
Sarrault, Albert, 19
Sary, Sam, 234
Savary, Alain, 229
Schuman, Robert, 200, 205
Shanghai, 28, 32–33, 35, 39
Shaplen, Robert, 75
Siam (Thailand), 29–30, 31, 32, 35
Siao Wan, General, 98, 99–100, 103, 126
Sieu Heng, 222

Singapore, 38
Son Ngoc Minh, 222
Souphanouvong, Prince, 220
Souvanna Phouma, Prince, 220
Stalin, Joseph, 22, 23, 41
Sun Yat-sen, xvii, 25
Switzerland, 29
Szabo, Istvan, 313

Ta Quang Buu, 191, 236, 239, 245
Ta Thu Tau, 40, 45, 46, 93
Tan Trao, 74, 77, 78
T'ang Dynasty, 313
Thai Nguyen Province, 63, 68, 70
Thailand. *See* Siam
Thanh (Ho's sister), 4–5
Thant, U, 266, 271
Thorez, Maurice, 41
Tito, Marshal Josip, 266
Ton Duc Tang, 191
Tonkin, 31, 33, 40, 42, 61, 65, 71
Torel, Albert, 184
Tours, 12, 146
Tran Ngoc Danh, 184, 207
Tran Hung Dao, 53
Tran Van Do, 239
Tran Van Giau, 40, 45, 90–93, 104,
     194
Tran Van Huu, 213
Tran Trong Kim, 70, 71, 72
Tran Huy Lieu, 104, 105, 119, 127
Tran Van Ly, 198
Tran Phu, 35, 37
Tran Van Thach, 46
Tran Van Tuyen, 196
Trostky, Leon, 22, 23
Truman, Harry, 88

Trumbull, Robert, 170–71
Truong Chinh, 26, 37, 42, 46, 47, 53,
     77, 78, 103, 224, 276, 279
Truong Boi Cong, 66
Truong Dinh Tri, 200
Tu Fu, 313
Tuyen Quang Province, 70, 74

Ung Uy, 208

Vaillant-Couturier, Paul, 14
Valluy, General, 164, 165, 171, 195
Vietnam, Democratic Republic of, 22,
     31, 77, 232
Vietnam, South, 232, 256
Vinh, 36, 38
Vinh Thuy. *See* Bao Dai
Vo Nguyen Giap, General, 37, 46, 50,
     51, 53, 57, 63, 68, 69, 83–84, 85,
     104, 105, 109, 113, 119, 127, 132–
     33, 140–41, 191, 213–20, 230, 259–
     60, 280, 283, 288, 308
Vu Hong Khanh, 98
Vuong Son Nhi. *See* Ho Chi Minh

Walker, Patrick Gordon, 268
Wang Ch'ing-wei, 29
Washington, 266, 269–70
White, Frank, 113–15
Wilson, Harold, 268
Wilson, Woodrow, 10

Xuan Thuy, 296, 309

Yenan, 50
Yunnan, 49, 57, 61, 66